The Religious
Imagination
in New Guinea

The Religious Imagination in New Guinea

Edited by

Gilbert Herdt and

Michele Stephen

Rutgers University Press
New Brunswick and London

Library of Congress Cataloging-in-Publication Data

The religious imagination in New Guinea / edited by
    Gilbert Herdt and Michele Stephen.
        p.   cm.
    Bibliography: p.
    Includes index.
    ISBN 0-8135-1457-6 (cloth)   ISBN 0-8135-1458-4 (pbk.)
    1. New Guinea—Religion.   2. Imagination—Religious aspects.
I. Herdt, Gilbert H., 1949–   II. Stephen, Michele.
BL.2620.N45V37   1989
229'92—dc19   89-30376
                                                        CIP

British Cataloging-in-Publication information available

Contents

The Religious
Imagination
in New Guinea

Introduction

Michele Stephen
and Gilbert Herdt

RELIGION is among the most durable and powerful of forces in human society. It provides not only for ultimate beliefs about the nature of human existence and for social practices that assist in its own reproduction and legitimation as an institution, but also for the vitality of a culture. What part of this vitality and durability derives from collective needs, and what part from personal intents, is arguable. But that most humans embrace a sacred ethos—a sense of a cosmic order and the emotions that it sustains—which is known through inner worlds as well as through cultural objects, seems beyond doubt. Religion contributes to the definition and organization of social experience, and thereby shapes culture. Yet for an individual, in his or her attempt to live in a particular place and time, there is the tenuous and uncertain effort of trying to match the feelings of one's inner world with the categories of thought, feeling, and spiritual entities as provided by culture. The "booming buzzing" confusion of time and space, William James (1958) said, must somehow be ordered and contained; religion answers this need. The varieties of religious imagination, spun out across cultures old and new, are testimony to human creativity and ingenuity in weaving together these two faces of human existence: the world of individual subjectivity and the collective symbols of culturally shared "realities."

Such, in brief, are the concerns of this volume, which explores certain forms of religious imagination found on the island of New Guinea.

The book began as a dialogue between the editors on the need for an alternative theoretical perspective to draw together a set of symbolic interests that we shared, ranging from states of consciousness, such as dreaming and trance, the subjectivity of ritual and myth, to the interaction between self and culture, and representations of selfhood outside conscious awareness. These topical interests emerged from our respective field researches in two very different New Guinea peoples, one a Highlands, the other a coastal, culture. We were impressed by the durability of phenomena such as dreams, trance, spirit mediumship, and possession in the transformation of Melanesian cultures. Yet we felt that not only had Melanesianists (though with some notable exceptions) given such phenomena inadequate attention, but that the available theoretical and ethnographic modes for understanding them seemed to distance us from, rather than bring us closer to, the issues with which we were concerned. Recent psychological approaches to subjectivity and alternate states of consciousness, new psychoanalytic work on the self, and anthropological approaches to cultural systems of shamanism and spirit possession, are all relevant to our effort. What emerged in our dialogue was a growing recognition that we were dealing with a special kind of imaginative capacity, a creative ability of the individual that is separate from the conscious sense of self but available to it in certain circumstances, an imagination somehow autonomous of the person. What is the nature of this imaginative capacity? How is it related to personhood and self? and to culture? Our explorations of these questions have led to the conceptions of selfhood and autonomous imagination presented herein.

The book is divided into two parts. The first, "Theoretical Orientations," opens up a range of conceptual problems that takes us far from Melanesia, sometimes even far from religion. The interdisciplinary nature of our approach requires laying bare our assumptions in some detail. We explore here a diversity of disciplinary approaches, including psychoanalytic theories and evidence drawn from experimental psychology. Our conclusions are relevant to current debates on culture theory (Schweder and LeVine 1984). Having focused upon conceptions of a special kind of imagination, our interests diverged in two different, but complementary, chapters (2 and 3). These chapters stand as theoretical contributions in their own right, but each enriches and greatly expands the scope of the other. Gilbert Herdt discusses conceptions and contexts of the self and personhood cross-culturally; he seeks a middle ground between those theories that define the self as culturally determined, and those that represent self as the product of panhuman psychological forces. He also points to the processes of imaginative participation whereby each individual creates his or her own cultural world in relation to self. Michele Stephen focuses on the self in relation to inner experience and consciousness, introducing the concept of autonomous imagination. Given the broad sweep of these theoretical issues, it is impossible through ethnographic case studies to illustrate every aspect of our arguments. Our key concepts—the self's imaginative engagement with an Other through cultural objects and autonomous imagination—have theoretical implications for anthropological study in all culture areas, and for substantive topics beyond religion.

In Part Two, "Ethnographic Explorations," we turn to New Guinea and the ethnographic soil that gave rise to our ideas. The previously unpublished case studies provided herein give richly detailed descriptions that pinpoint the subtle processes of self-construction and imagination we identify in general terms in Part One. Though such processes are not confined to religion, we have found that they emerge with particular clarity in relation to the realm of the sacred. Thus, these investigations of self and imagination have led us to reconsider problems of religious experience.

We limit our volume to five in-depth ethnographies illustrating key phenomena. These do not, of course, represent the full range of experience that we might identify as creations of religious imagination. Besides the inevitable limitations on space, our selection was guided by a search for a particular sensitivity to the subtleties of inner experience seldom encountered in the ethnographic literature. Each study is concerned with the experience of some supranatural (in Western terms) or sacred (in Western terms) realm, inhabited by spirit beings and imbued with extraordinary powers. The first essay, by Bruce Knauft, deals with spirit mediumship among the Gebusi. This is followed by Gilbert Herdt's analysis of the Sambia shaman's relationship with his spirit familiars. Witchcraft and subjective experience among the Nalumin is the subject of Eytan Bercovitch's contribution. Michele Stephen's chapter describes Mekeo concepts of the soul as particularly shaped in the individual's experience of dreaming. Donald Tuzin examines the life course and religious imagination of an Arapesh prophet, the leader of a new Christian cult.

Many other topics might have been included and are referred to only in passing: innovation and creativity in traditional ritual cults, cargo cults, magic, visual art, theater and performance in ceremony, wild-man behavior and similar aspects of possession, to mention only a few. Yet we have been fortunate to be able to assemble a group of studies that touches upon seminal aspects of autonomous imagining in New Guinea cultures. Precisely how these studies indicate key dimensions of religious imagination will be taken up in the concluding chapter.

This volume is not the usual collection of essays by several authors, with a summary introduction and conclusion by the editors. Though it represents the work of five authors, who do not necessarily share all the views and support all the conclusions the editors present here, we believe that we have provided a new and integrated theoretical approach focused on a specific topic. The book thus presents a perspective that is informed, broadened, and balanced by the insights not of one but of several minds.

Conventionally, anthropologists are used to dealing with witchcraft, possession, religious innovation, shamanism, and dreaming as separate topics, unrelated except to the extent that they are connected in some way to concepts of a spirit world (though see Lewis 1986). Furthermore, such experience-near topics have often been regarded as being of only peripheral importance to more central anthropological concerns, such as group ritual and publicly shared religious symbols. This book identifies themes linking such seemingly diverse domains in the analytic relationship between self, culture, and the creative role of autonomous imagination. The centrality of subjective experience is also revealed. Just as William James saw, in his classic study *The Varieties of Religious Experience* (1958), that underlying the diversities of the great religious traditions of the world there was a common foundation of subjective experience, so the contributors to this book point to the formative role of the inner world, but with the difference that we do not see religion as determined solely by subconscious factors. Rather, we see this inner world of religious experience as emerging from an interaction between individual experience and culture, mediated by autonomous imagination.

We see this interaction operating through the following three distinct psychosocial processes that connect personal desires and social needs:

1. Social participation. A person's participation (e.g., involvement, interests, social role enactment) in sociocultural life, and his or her subjective experience of such, provides the foundation of religious experience. Of course, participation changes across the course of life, with the involvements of children being different from those of adults, a developmental transformation with strong consequences for the person's subjective experience. For example, age-graded roles in socioreligious activities place children in different positions of access to sacred power, and developmental differences in such roles, and idiosyncratic experiences related to them, affect participation and perspective in adult life.

2. Autonomous imagination. Autonomous imagination continually reworks and reshapes all experience, indeed can simultaneously filter and alter social participation, introducing new and unique meanings and images outside of consciousness into a person's cultural repertoire. Autonomous imagination responds to the person's need to match internal desires with social necessity. In the case of religious experience, this process reshapes, and thereby creates harmony and balance between, needs and desires in the ordinary person as well as the religious specialist.

3. Social action. In future sociocultural action, these reshaped religious images influence the lives of others, even the group. Whereas the innovative effects of autonomous imagination on ordinary folk are largely personal in nature, certain religious specialists have the ability to create new meanings and symbols, which transcend the limitations of the purely personal, and to engage audiences in the acceptance of such innovations, ultimately seeing them become part of the social fabric. The effects of this process may range from slight variations on established cultural themes, infusing them with new vitality, to a radical reformulation of culture such as that which occurs in millenarian movements.

These three processes—which are analytically distinct though pragmatically inseparable—create a finely textured interaction between the subjective realm and the world of social action.

In studying religious experience in tribal cultures a methodological problem confronts us: how to be near enough to these inner states to understand them in anthropological terms. Are imaginative states of religious fervor capable of objective description? How can we be certain that we have not distorted them, misinterpreted their meanings, or substituted our sense of the religious for theirs? Through what kinds of approaches can we get close enough to provide vivid accounts of these subjective/social states? Some anthropologists, such as Geertz (1968), have questioned the possibility of doing so; others, such as Turner (1967a), have felt that we must try. Others have agreed with Lévi-Strauss (1962) that "experience" per se is irrelevant, since the fundamental categories of culture are determined by unconscious structures of the mind. Often, then, anthropologists have had to content themselves with a description of religious observance or, at best, a description of the expressive and evocative texture of these observances, rather than with their interior, as implied by the notion religious imagination. How to move closer to these states without merging into them is the challenge taken up in the following pages.

Such religious phenomena beg the old problems of definition: "What is religion?" "How is it imagined and experienced by the self across cultures?" "What is witchcraft?" And so forth. The terms available to us carry a heavy load of cultural associations and assumptions in the history of anthropology and comparative religion. A long line of distinguished anthropologists have debated these definitional concerns (see Banton 1966; Evans-Pritchard 1937, 1965; Geertz 1966a; Gluckman 1965; Lessa and Vogt 1972a; Spiro 1964, 1965; Turner 1967a, 1978; and cf. also Crapanzano 1977; Obeyesekere 1981; Shweder 1984).

But whether one defines "religious" as a matter of gods, ghosts, and spirit beings, as did Tylor (1871), or of collective reflections of societal categories, as did Durkheim (1915), as an epiphenomenon of individual unconscious needs for authority and protection, as did Freud (1927), or, in more contemporary terms, as a search for ultimate concerns in a pluralistic society, in the sense of Bellah et al. (1985), religious imagination is part of these phenomena, though not reducible to them. Beyond these weighty issues there remains the matter of individual necessity and desires. How do sociocultural systems enable the evocation and representation of the self's interior and passionate states? One thinks here of the images of Nalumin witches and Sambia shamans in the following chapters, beings of power who are felt to hold in their hands the fate of a society—for evil on the one hand and good on the other. The reality of such beings is not open to question in these traditions: they are fixtures on the social landscape, and of necessity the self must participate in them. And in this participation there always will be desire: the self's own strivings and goals to align with these powers or to avoid them in the business of getting on with life. The religious imagination of Nalumin and Sambia must contemplate and respond through the modalities of such sacred power. We ethnographers are witness to the effects of these symbolic figures in our particular field sites as the products of specific cultural traditions. From the perspective of comparative religion, however, we cannot help but be struck by the presence of such figures—

witches and shamans—across cultures; in doing so we wonder if the same durable necessity and desires are always present too.

The durability of religion is a theme relevant to both Western and non-Western traditions. Surely Durkheim and Freud, not to mention Marx, would have been impressed to see the persistence of religion in the late twentieth century. Freud's dour outlook in *The Future of an Illusion* (1927) expressed not only a lingering Victorian sense of decadence in the face of modern society's loss of a religious foundation of morals, but a deep cynicism at the failure of religion to do better than it had in ameliorating the human condition. Freud's view mirrored that of Durkheim in this respect, but it went further, in part because he lived to the advent of World War II, to see the crisis in Europe under the sign of the Nazis, which religion had not prevented. Freud's endeavor to make psychoanalysis a science was tinged with his hope that science—of which, he felt, analysis was the most advanced form—would help turn human desire away from the irrationality of totalitarian charisma. Freud might have been amazed to see how well religion has survived amid the materialism and mass technology of our society, where fundamentalist preachers in cowboy boots host marathon television crusades for the Innocent. One suspects that Weber (1904) would have been a more sanguine witness, however, for he recognized that in periods of change and transition, religious values are transformed and outlive the institutions that support them, surviving to direct the interests of personal desire in confronting new social necessities.

The American experience is telling in this regard. Robert Bellah and his colleagues (1985) have shown both the surprising tenacity of religion in our cultural tradition and its ability, as Weber had forseen, to absorb and imbue with transcendent significance the myriad and disparate social traditions of our way of life. The religious life has become a major metaphor for self-individuation, healing, and communal affiliation in the United States. How notions of healing in psychotherapy have been infused with ineffable spiritual connotations for Americans may seem surprising. Perhaps Freud's substitution of the cult of psychoanalysis for religious worship has here succeeded in part; though of course Freud sought to establish reason in the stead of faith and belief. Yet, as is discussed in the chapters on autonomous imagination, the association of healing with the sacred has a long and ancient lineage. Bellah's informants imply that for Americans today—caught in this postmodern but still Atomic Age of anxiety—personal needs for expression overshadow collective commitments. The individualism of their responses within established religious traditions is impressive and is associated with a loss of collective commitment to the state and the nation as a whole. Here one finds an element of cynicism and frustration in the conclusions drawn by Bellah and his colleagues as well, much as was true of the commentaries of Durkheim and Freud decades ago.

The persistence of religion, in particular the remarkable thirst of modern

Western society for the arcane and exotic in Eastern and other religions, was no surprise to Jung, a younger contemporary of Freud, whose long life extended into the second half of the twentieth century. For Jung (1978), man's images of the sacred arose out of the very nature of the structure of the human psyche, images later appropriated and transformed by culture. When cultural elaborations and institutional demands come to dominate religion to the extent that personal necessities and desires are totally submerged, then, he believed, the individual psyche will seek new images of the sacred through which its passions and struggles can be expressed. Unlike Freud, Jung did not think that reason could replace religion, because he believed religion grew from the self's need to incorporate aspects of experience beyond "rationality." To ignore this need, he warned, was to drive it underground, leading to the search for exotic symbols and gods, or worse, the credulous acceptance of would-be prophets of a new age, whether their insignia be the swastika or cowboy boots.

The concerns of New Guineans living in rural villages, where the affairs of daily life are still patterned by a subsistence gift-exchange economy, are far from these American and European thematics of religious change. Yet New Guinea is no island out of time and space. A century of colonialism, of post-World War II development, modernization, and incorporation into the wider world, is the background against which anthropological discussions of religion must now take place. The inevitable "them" and "us" dichotomies of postmodern anthropology emerge here, raising a warning sign to naive interlopers of the subjectivities of religion (Crapanzano 1986). The problem remains to identify what is essential and intrinsic to these religious traditions, and to understand how their representations of the sacred express and serve personal desires. Only then will we be able to discern, in the contemporary national political debates in Papua New Guinea on change and continuity, what represents only passing change or radical reformulation in the religious ethos of its cultures.

New Guinea is the second largest island in the world, an area approximately the size of France. It has a population of some four million, distributed across a vast range of linguistic and cultural groups now contained within two political states, Papua New Guinea and Indonesia. A recent history of European exploration and of German, Dutch, British, and Australian colonial regimes overlies a much more complex and ancient prehistory of human occupation extending back more than forty millennia. Physical and cultural factors, including the rugged landscape with its natural barriers of mountain ranges and great rivers, and endemic warfare, have interacted over long periods of time to produce extremely diverse local adaptations. A variety of cultural and linguistic settlements and sociolinguistic recombinations forms the bedrock of religious variations across New Guinea.

Today we have many more pieces of this ethnographic jigsaw puzzle than did the early scholars—Haddon, Rivers, Seligman and others—who undertook their "riverboat" surveys of seaboard societies, around the turn of the century. No doubt Malinowski would be surprised at how much better the anthropological topography of New Guinea cultures are charted today. Still, our knowledge remains incomplete.

The cultures of New Guinea have been the subject of many classic studies of tribal religion. Signposts of the extensive literature refer to such classics as Malinowski's *Coral Gardens and Their Magic* (1935), Fortune's *Sorcerers of Dobu* (1932), and *Manus Religion* (1935), Williams's *Drama of Orokolo* (1940), Bateson's *Naven* (1936); not to mention the disparate works of Ian Hogbin, Margaret Mead, Paul Wirtz, and others. These studies were conducted prior to World War II and were confined to seaboard societies or to those few areas of the hinterland under direct colonial control.

The two decades following World War II saw a new wave of anthropological work with the opening to European settlement of the previously uncontrolled and largely unknown Highlands regions, and to ethnographers eager to observe at first hand cultures virtually untouched by the outside world. The immediate job at hand was to capture as much of these cultures as possible while indigenous institutions remained intact. Religion was but one of many aspects, though the most difficult to penetrate, and the majority of studies during these years concerned social rather than cultural organization. Thus, for a time religion seemed submerged by these other concerns. An enormous amount of information was collected, nevertheless, and many of the significant ethnographies of this period contained important statements about the religious. One thinks, for example, of Reay's *The Kuma* (1959), Read's *The High Valley* (1965), Newman's *Knowing the Gururumba* (1965), among others too numerous to list. These years also saw the publication of several ground-breaking studies of messianic movements, whose purpose was to alert scholars to the extraordinary flexibility of New Guinean religious traditions: the late Peter Lawrence's *Road Belong Cargo* (1964) is outstanding here, as is the work of Burridge (1970) and Schwartz (1962). Until the mid-1960s, however, this mounting corpus was scattered throughout the literature, and there was no real sense of its comparative significance or how it might relate to the earlier studies. Lawrence and Meggitt's collection *Gods, Ghosts, and Men in Melanesia* (1965) quickly became a classic in its own right, for it met the need for a comparative statement that drew together the results of two decades of intensive new fieldwork.

Indeed, Lawrence and Meggitt's book seemed to mark the end of one era and the begining of another. It might have appeared by the mid-1960s that the great age of ethnographic discovery was over, both on the coast and in the hinterland, and that traditional cultures, particularly in their religious manifestations, were fast disintegrating in the face of the cash economy and modernization. Highlanders, only so recently brought under European influence, were revealing themselves to be avid entrepreneurs, as calculating and materialistic as any Western capitalist, astonishing anthropologists and government officials alike by their enthusiasm to embrace anything new. Many seaboard societies, as well, were demonstrating their thirst for modernization and development. Yet despite this ferment, the durability of religious traditions has been such that another generation of fieldworkers has been able to explore and ask new questions of the human face of religion late in the twentieth century.

The last twenty years has produced an important new body of sophisticated ethnographies on religion and symbolic practices. One thinks of major ethnographic statements on New Guinean religious traditions by Allen (1967, 1984), Barth (1975), Gell (1975), Godelier (1986), Hauser-Schaeublin (1977), Herdt (1981, 1982a, 1984b), Keesing (1982a, 1982b), Langness (1974), Lewis (1980), Meigs (1984), Poole (1981a, 1986, 1987a), Rubel and Rosman (1978), Schieffelin (1976, 1982), Schwimmer (1980, 1983), Stephen (1979, 1987a), A. Strathern (1979), M. Strathern (1988), Tuzin (1980, 1982), Wagner (1972, 1978), Weiner (1976), Van Baal (1981), and Young (1983). There have also been new publications stemming from fieldwork begun decades ago, such as Hogbin's *The Island of Menstruating Men* (1970) and Lawrence's *The Garia* (1984). Of major collections, that of Lawrence and Meggitt (1965) remains the classic; newer ones by Herdt (1982a, 1984b) emphasize themes in male initiation and ritual homosexuality. Stephen's *Sorcerer and Witch in Melanesia* (1987a) is, in its thematics, the collection most centrally concerned with religion since *Gods, Ghosts and Men* (1965), and is relevant for understanding contemporary issues of religious experience and self. A notable recent contribution is Kenneth Read's *Return to the High Valley* (1986), a personal record of continuity and change among the Gahuku-Gama of the Eastern Highlands and a rare gift to the student of New Guinean religions.

Though imagination and subjective experience are themes rarely considered in the Melanesian literature, they have not been totally absent. Individual differences in experience and belief have been significant concerns, for example, in the work of Newman (1965), Keesing (1982), and Young (1983). And we acknowledge the pioneering lead of Burridge (1960, 1969) and Wagner (1972, 1978) into the deep waters of the imagination; their insights remain important guides to others. We also pay tribute to the often neglected but remarkable work of Layard (1942), whose investigations on Malekula in Vanuatu were strongly influenced by Jungian theories of imagination.

We are indeed fortunate to have such a rich collection of literature, old and new, on Melanesian religions; but still there are gaps, which suggest the need for further exploration. We search especially for accounts of necessity and personal desire in the self's participation in the sacred. With the few exceptions just noted, we look largely in vain, even in the highly sophisticated and detailed cultural analyses of recent years. These ethnographies are—rightly—concerned foremost with the elucidation of shared ritual and symbol. They are less focused on the individual person or self—the personalization of necessity and desire—as such. Experience and subjectivity, their forms, meanings, and directive force in the transformation of institutions and practices, are often hinted at but rarely developed. It is understandable that such concerns have generally been passed over, even in the recent literature; the aims of cultural anthropology are nomothetic and only indirectly concerned with the person and the intimate communications of such (Herdt and Stoller 1989). There is, furthermore, a reluctance on the part of many anthropologists to generalize beyond the findings of their own study. These trappings of anthropological science are, in part, responsible for the reluctance to examine the deeper experience or flights of fancy embedded in the use of the term *religious imagination.*

Our aim here is not to review the varieties of religious forms in New Guinea cultures nor to replace Lawrence and Meggitt (1965). We are concerned only with a particular aspect of what might be termed the "religious" in New Guinea cultures. The territory we cover is a still largely uncharted region: it is located neither in the external time and space world of physical objects and persons nor in the interior of one's conscious thoughts and desires, but lies somewhere between self and Other, neither entirely outside culture nor entirely within it. For in the private thrall of trance, dream, ecstasy, and possession, the person may see revealed things unknown to, forbidden by, or even unthinkable in, culture. He or she may find there the "wilderness" outside culture, as Hans Duerr (1985) puts it; yet it is culture that provides the means to interpret and put to use these revelations in the wilderness.

In a review of the literature a few years ago, Michele Stephen (1979) showed that social expressions of dreams, trance, and possession states, along with other subtle varieties of imaginative experience, play an important, perhaps decisive, role in Melanesian religion. These provide not only validation of new constructs and knowledge but the actual source of cultural innovation, so that "what men see in trances and dreams might in fact become social reality" (1979:15). Change and continuity are possible, but so too are modification, transformation, and even rebellion, in the form of so-called cargo cults. Change is easily accommodated, Stephen suggested, because "if a tradition becomes hopelessly corrupt, or is forgotten, or fails to meet new circumstances," guidance may be sought in direct communication with sacred powers. Dreams and other nonordinary states of consciousness provide the means for a continuing dialogue with the ancestors.

Cultures cannot always attend to all stimuli or events; there is slippage, breakage, corruption in cultural tradition. As we need constantly to remind ourselves, moreover, the categories of a culture do not provide all the necessary vehicles for understanding and representing one's inner world. The cultural actor is in a constant struggle to communicate because of this: our experiences are in many ways opaque even to us. How then are we to relate them to others? It is in this gap between cultural representation, and subjective necessity and desire, that we find the impetus for creativity and innovation. Where culture fails to provide the categories for the communication of subjective experience and fails to satisfy deeply felt personal desires, then new categories and new avenues for expression will be sought, eventually to be found in the dreams and visions of prophets, old and new.

The ancestors cannot truly speak for themselves, and we cannot truly speak back to them, except, that is, through the imaginative dialogue between self and Other (see Tedlock 1987a). Such a dialogue is neither objective nor subjective—a dichotomy we sense as increasingly tiresome. It is a dialogue not contained purely within culture, or within the individual's skin. It is inbetween these, a realm of personal perceptions and representations of cultural objects, the inbetweenness of imaginative/symbolic reality. This is the realm of religious imagination, and it is precisely this subtle and elusive inbetweenness—a wilderness indeed—that we traverse in the following pages.

Our themes of imagination, the boundedness of self, the nature of subjective experience, and problems of cross-cultural interpretation open up far-ranging issues. We cannot explore them all, nor can we expect that everyone will approve of the route we have chosen. Much more could be said about the problems we raise; others have had to be put aside; still other questions have yet to engage our attention. This book, then, should be regarded as an introductory statement of ideas we are continuing to develop in a precipitous and slippery intellectual terrain. For us the journey has been an exciting one; we hope it will be for others. We hope too that this work will lead other ethnographers into an exploration of that territory in between.

THEORETICAL
ORIENTATIONS

PART ONE

Self and Culture: Contexts of Religious Experience in Melanesia

Gilbert Herdt

ANTHROPOLOGY'S renewed concern with self and personhood in cultural context signifies an important paradigmatic shift in theory and method over the past twenty years or so, a period that began with intense interest in alternate states of consciousness, which subsequently evolved to general concerns with the self-concept in self-psychology, "desire" and "narrative" in psychoanalysis, and to symbolic analysis and hermeneutics in anthropology. This shift may suggest a transformation in the design of our epistemology, as some would argue; it certainly involves as well a renewed appreciation of meaning systems and "thick description" (in Geertz's [1973] sense) for anthropology. This chapter surveys these issues, with particular attention to Melanesia, by exploring the interface between imagination and selfhood; yet it also opens a comparative vantage point on problems in the construction of self and person, as these conceptions are located in time, ethos, knowledge, and worldview across cultures. The advances in studies of self in context over the past two decades in Melanesian studies are illuminating, and recent collections edited by White and Kirkpatrick (1985) and O'Brien and Tiffany (1984) provide critical reformulations of earlier work (see also Crapanzano 1980; Keesing 1982a; Langness and Gladwin 1972; Strathern 1988; Whiting 1961). My aim here is to build upon this prior work, especially by studying how conceptions of self and person are related to varieties of religious experience.

The general configuration of Western notions of self, as they relate to religion and thought, has a deep history in our cultural tradition, tracing back to the beginnings of Western civilization. The Ancient Greeks forged our vehicles of thought and perception (Dodds 1951; Rohde 1925; Simon 1978). Judaic-Christian influences, in syncretic and often contradictory ways, created multiple paths to religious imagination—of which the Apollonian and Dionysian prototypes, as Benedict (1934) once compared these metaphoric models—are important ones. Our concept of the individual as a unit of ontology and epistemology is so central and fundamental to these discussions that we must examine this issue as well. Among those who have similarly commented upon self and religious imagination, one thinks especially of Durkheim (1915), Weber (1904), Marx (1977), and Freud (1927) and his students. It is not my intention to survey all this social theory (for which see Geertz 1973; for the Melanesian context, see Herdt 1981 and Strathern 1988). The anthropological and psychoanalytical positions are important for our own rethinking, however, for Melanesia as a culture area figures prominently in the theory of these two fields (Herdt and Stoller 1989; Keesing 1982a; Spiro 1982). Such contributions have shaped ethnographies, and our ethnographic accounts have, in turn, reflected back upon culture theory, thus contributing to a refiguration of psychoanalytic thought.

Though culture and imagination have been seen as dichotomous categories by anthropology and psychoanalysis in previous studies, the very opposite must be true from our vantage point today. The same holds for "self" and "culture." Culture, seen as shared meaning systems in contemporary anthropology, relies heavily upon conventionalized signs of meaning (Geertz 1983b). Imagination, by contrast, is often seen as spontaneous, eccentric, and external, the signs of which are hidden from their context of indexicality (Pierce 1931). I will argue that for both it is the self-concept that functions as the mediator of meaning and creativity (see also Herdt 1987b; LeVine 1982). Culture is not a static extrinsic system any more than imagination is a spontaneous intrinsic system. Human minds are dynamic and operate most lucidly and creatively in optimal social environments. Culture, as a dynamic process, must therefore be seen as an externally and internally motivated, emergent system of and for meaningful communication with the Other, upon which the human organism depends literally for life and soul. This bifocal view, to take Sapir's conception (Singer 1961:63), provides heuristics for understanding imagination in social action.

In the following sections we shall explore relationships between constructs of self and religious forms and experience in Melanesia. If, as I argue, the self provides psychosocial and symbolic boundaries for framing social action and subjectivity in culture, then charting the self-concept is one of the critical tasks of religious anthropology. This is problematic because, as Hallowell (1967) once suggested, the self seems amorphous, leading everywhere and nowhere. Yet, as Hallowell and now LeVine (1982) have shown, we can agree upon certain meaningful domains of self-boundedness across cultures. To locate these in Melanesia I will cull the papers in this volume and the ethnographic literature at large. I will also draw upon examples from Western history and culture, particularly from the Ancient Greeks, in attempting to provide conceptual links between traditional Melanesian and contemporary Western societies.

Some Melanesian Concepts

Melanesia has long been noted for its cultural and linguistic diversity, and considering the pivotal structural integration of religion and social organization in Melanesian cultures, it is no wonder that so many papers and dissertations have emphasized religion (reviewed in Poole 1986; Stephen 1979, 1987; M. Strathern 1988). At the same time, however, Melanesianists have often empha- sized ritual action over belief, consistent with the prior perspectives of Rad- cliffe-Brown and Durkheim in social anthropology (Herdt 1981). Only later, in research begun in the 1960s and 1970s, did notions of religious culture, ideol- ogy, symbols, phenomenology, and identity in ritual experience become more salient. Aside from reflecting the more general paradigm changes in anthropol- ogy, the shift signalled the concerns of a more mature field of study that can benefit from many excellent functional-structural ethnographies on which to build a more semiotic/hermeneutic discipline (Schwimmer 1983).

This conceptual shift manifests itself clearly in the problematics of religion raised within Lawrence and Meggitt's (1965) influential *Gods, Ghosts, and Men in Melanesia*. In seeking to understand and sort the heterogeneity of reli- gious belief, ritual, and spiritual concepts in Melanesia, Lawrence and Meg- gitt's Introduction pursued a path that was clearly social structural, rather than cultural, and was more concerned with objective and verifiable propositions of a formal nature than with the richness of meaning systems and mythopoetic narra- tives. They noted what they called "two broad areas of similarity" in Melane- sian religion (Lawrence and Meggitt 1965:9). The first concerned the close association of the "non-empirical" to the "ordinary world," with gods and spirits usually believed to be living near or in the midst of humans. Second, they found many Melanesian peoples that "share in the same types of spirit beings." Let us examine these two important assertions, taking the latter first.

Every form of research can be seen as "lumping" or "splitting" with regard to its nomothetic or idiographic goals. And every cross-cultural investigation must perforce stress either homogeneity or heterogeneity, the "organization of diversity" or "replication of uniformity," in Wallace's (1969) framework. Such heuristic frameworks are somewhat open but not entirely uncontaminated from our preconceptions (Gadamer 1965). Now in the heuristic of Lawrence and Meggitt (1965) it seems obvious that they are lumpers: they reduced great varia- tion into types. They saw their classifications as derivative of ecology and social structure, emphasizing "Highlands" versus "Lowlands," or seaboard, differ- ences. Their Lowland/Highland typology today has some utility (see Herdt 1984b), but less than before. Nonetheless, the effort to find significant cultural and structural themes across Melanesia is laudable, for they help us to under- stand myriad cultural variants, so that we can see which are of a piece, a culture area (Bateson 1978). Nonetheless, we are left wondering how much such ty- pologies obscure phenomenological and symbolic differences between groups.

One of the points I will illustrate—siding here with the splitters— con- cerns how the seeming homogeneity of Melanesian religious systems decreases when cultural narratives are analyzed. These narratives and their concepts

18 *Gilbert Herdt*

relativize our search; it becomes harder to lump and sort via broad institutional emphases, such as ancestor worship or initiation rites. What is needed, and what Lawrence and Meggitt missed, is the perspective of selfhood to compare Highlands and Lowlands or related typologies.

As lumpers, Lawrence and Meggitt (1965) tended to see *all* kinds of spirits as either ancestral or natural. The soul was for them a rather self-evident and simple variant—albeit an impoverished one—of our Judaio-Christian ethic. The soul's content and functions were "similar" everywhere. Whether there were differences (consciously or unconsciously) between cultures was not a matter of great concern. The lack of detailed narratives created a seamless quality to this nomothetic tapestry, because problems in exegesis, and disagreement between categories of persons (religious specialists versus lay persons, women versus men), were largely ignored in structural functional ethnographies. The seamlessness was an illusion on the level of the outsider, a point to which we shall return directly.

The Melanesian world, with its very rich cultural systems and spiritual concepts is, however, fertile and original; and we must look for its elementary forms in animistic notions of belief, thought, and imagination as they inform action in both secular and sacred contexts. Roger Keesing (1982a:27) has thus remarked on the symbolic richness of religion among even tiny Melanesian societies—sometimes numbering only a few hundred persons. It is easy to lump such concepts as spirits, soul, self, and mystical, and here Lawrence and Meggitt (1965) found relatively similar notions in form and content. Lumping here entails what is consciously (and even unconsciously, Bateson 1973) self-evident: not in need of exegesis by natives or reinterpretation by their ethnographers. Today this view seems too simple (Crapanzano 1986). (See, in this context, Turner 1978 and Geertz 1983a; the critiques of Spiro 1986 and Shweder 1984, on rationalism in magical and scientific "world" views of meaning systems.) Yet the pervasiveness of soul concepts is very impressive and widespread here.

Regarding the other of Lawrence and Meggitt's theses, we are inclined to agree with their revision of our ideas on the supernatural. Anthropology has argued increasingly for a close nexus of the empirical and spiritual in other systems around the world, including—if we are to see this idea in its furthest reaches—in our own culture (Shweder 1977). The natural and supernatural are a false dichotomy, many argue (Geertz 1966a, 1983b; Shweder 1984). Yet there is a sense in which we have not escaped the limitations of our own cultural lens here: To agree that empirical agents and spirits are close, ever-present, is to agree with Durkheim and Freud that these conceptions are fundamentally a part of psychological or social reality. The Melanesian view is somewhat different.

A look at the spiritual and empirical conceptions of our own cultural ancestors, the ancient Greeks, may be instructive here. As Vernant (1983) has argued, the Greeks personalized their gods; a modality similar to numerous New Guinea conceptions. A doctrine of *psyche* developed, embodying self, body, and soul; and this facilitated a sense of idols, of gods, as without body (1983: 330–331), as being a network of relationships mostly invisible, but entirely credible, to personal identity, especially to the Hero: a "special individual." Heroes in Greek and New Guinea thought mediate spiritual and earthly worlds, separate from normative social rules, cults, and official power (Wagner 1972, on New Guinea). Psyche as soul qua person "was both an objective reality and a subjective inner experience" (Vernant 1983:334), providing a framework for understanding the world and the "mysterious power of life which animates nature as a whole and sets it in motion" (see Read 1952). Here are distant echoes of our Western religious experience and a touchstone for anthropological accounts of the Melanesian one.

The Greeks' rationalism never obviated supernaturalism in daily life. Nor did classical Attic culture dichotomize natural/supernatural cosmologically as do we (Dodds 1951). Indeed, in Bennett Simon's (1978) analysis of the concept "psyche" in Greek culture, for instance, natural and metaphysical elements were both integral and necessary in the Greeks' understanding of the full range of states of awareness they recognized and which we see referred to in their texts (cf. Rohde 1925). Later we shall examine the problem of the ambiguity of Greek oracles' pronouncements in this context (Flaceliere 1965) and see certain parallels to the Gebusi medium's narratives, as Knauft (this volume) relates these. Here, though, we can do no better than to recall the great classicist Lloyd's (1979:51) remarks on the Greek perspective:

> The explicit expression of a universalized concept of nature involves a corresponding development or clarification in the notion of marvels or miracles: The category of the 'supernatural' develops, in fact, *pari passu* with that of the 'natural'. Even in the philosophers . . . as we noted when discussing Empedocles, quite intensive investigations of nature may be combined with a belief in the possibility of wonder-working—although the exact status of the marvelous effects that Empedocles claimed could be produced is not clear.

"Wonder-working" as a concept combines pragmatism with the spiritualism of certain tenets of Melanesian shamanism, witchcraft, and sorcery, as Stephen (1987) and her colleagues have shown. The notion of divine revelations and inspiration, planted directly into the minds and hearts of cultural actors, is one the Melanesian would recognize in Homer's account of Heracles (Simon 1978), for example. The texts of Sambia and Mekeo, Nalumin, Gebusi, and Ilahita recognize the integral character of spirit and human existence, so much interwoven in Greek culture. Would not these Melanesians recognize the Homeric poems which lament that "the Gods have allotted a life of pain and misery to men, while they themselves remain free to care" (Rohde 1925:3)?

The Greeks embodied (such a wonderful word) a notion of psyche, mind, spirit, and body that was dynamic and holistic—very different from the dualisms of our own tradition. In a fascinating and controversial reinterpretation of Freud's adoption of "psyche" from the Greeks, Bettelheim (1984) suggests that medical and philosophical views in our culture—especially in American culture—corrupted Freud's poetic narratives and emphasis upon an integral psyche akin to that of the Greeks (see also Simon 1978). Freud's translators, in particular, robbed the concept of psyche of its mythopoetic and evocative richness, substituting for it the tawdry and deodorized jargon "id," "ego," and "superego," concepts no one in the world would invent outside of the medical arena. (Bettelheim [1984] suggests instead "it" [id], "self" [ego], and "above-it" [superego].)

But to return to Lawrence and Meggitt's (1965) point: we must question the extent to which certain local concepts, such as soul, mediate and index the natural and supernatural signs of Melanesian thought. The answer rests in how cultural foundations of selfhood are constituted.

Personhood and Self

Anthropologists have returned to old-fashioned concerns with cultural conceptions of personhood in Melanesia, as was best illustrated at one time in K. E. Read's classic piece, "Morality and the Concept of the Person among Gahuka-Gama" (1955). These Highlanders did not define moral conventions as did we in the West: They were splitters, not lumpers; they tended not to generalize moral implications of persons and acts from one situation to another. Traditional morality was more context- and situation-specific, less abstract and universal, less rule-bound. A generation later Read (1986) was to find them altered in these ways, sped along an acculturated track of cash economy and urbanized living. It is interesting that Read's discussion of personhood hinged so much on moral convention. For Gahuka-Gama a person is accountable to culture and restricted in terms of absolute freedom; but he or she is neither a clone of customary roles nor a slave to custom (in Malinowski's 1926 sense). Innovation and symbolic mediation are clearly components of person-definition, of self-constitution, Read (1955) suggested (see Langness and Hayes [1987] on Read's contribution).

To what extent are our Western natural and supernatural relevant attributes of Melanesian person-concepts? How are the latter related to folk notions of human nature? Self and person concepts in folk psychology and local knowledge take variable shape around the world (Geertz 1966b; Shweder and Bourne 1984). Are these concepts similar enough to our own to gloss the comparative symbolic domains as "self" and not "person"? Is the self inside the person and therefore more psychological, or is selfhood also objectified in the Other? In a recent collection on Pacific societies, White and Kirkpatrick (1985) explore this problem, and they offer a relativist approach that is more splitting than lumping.

> We do not deny the existence of psychological universals. We stress, how-
> ever, the point that ethnopsychological judgments are made in terms of
> specific cultural theories and metaphors. It may well be the case that
> Marquesans all see *vivi' is* where Americans all see loneliness—but they
> both actively construct an interpretation, rather than simply record a psy-
> chological reality independent of cultural coding. (White and Kirkpatrick
> 1985:15)

Of course we must see self-experience as relative to specific contexts. One thinks of Geertz's (1973) famous onion-skin analogy: We may think that by peeling away the layers of culture we reach a core, a basic human nature, or the true self, only to discover that the essence we have stripped away—culture and self-experience—is in the whole of what we sought. Having suggested this im-age, however, the problem is always Where do we go from there? White and Kirkpatrick leave us grasping for linking concepts, by the terms embedded in their statements; terms such as *psychological universals, ethno-psychological judgments,* and such feeling states as loneliness. Their language is seductive but too facile. When, for instance, is a judgment not psychological but rather cul-tural in its antecedents or outcomes?

Obeyesekere's (1981) brilliant *Medusa's Hair* argues for origins of sym-bols and categories as their distinctive dimension; for the locus of a judgment as being, first, in personal or psychogenic symbols, and then in public culture; for a fluid shifting of the actors' awareness from objectification of personal mean-ings to subjectification of public ones. Here the universalist problem is circum-vented in part by Obeyesekere's psychoanalytic language, which tends to assume the universality of unconscious processes, across all societies. These conceptions challenge Geertz's (1966b) ideas on person and self, seeing them as richly textured, at different levels of awareness. In short, the self as cultural rep-resentation is too facile for psychoanalytic analysis; contextualized and made relevant to the self in symbolic action—consistent with Geertz's (1973) atten-tion to Weberian and Parsonian social action theory—it ignores, for instance, the internal representation of one's self to one's self, especially in personal nar-rative (LeVine 1982; Kracke and Herdt 1987). Likewise, we look in vain for the nuances, defensive and creative imaginings of the self, in the Freudian and Jungian emphases (LeVine 1982). Perhaps, with regard to these various para-digms of culture, society, and personality, we should speak of those that are "person-centered" (LeVine 1982) or semiotic (D'Andrade 1986), and those that are not.

The need for a person-centered view in the old literature on consciousness is very clear when we notice the strong tendency to anchor "reality" in the lone individual, apart from culture (Peters and Price-Williams 1983). Hartmann's (1975:71–75) well-known reformulation of "Why do we hallucinate?" into "Why don't we hallucinate all the time?" is a good example of this. We humans imagine ourselves in social groups. Small, face-to-face societies create the conditions of ego's reality testing in a way that is inescapable; and yet the phenomenology of the world involved here is not natural but symbolic reality. For this, the notion of the lone individual is inadequate: the mythopoetics of imagery in cultural context are essential foundations (Price-Williams [1987]). The infusion of collective imagination—of Durkheim's (1965) collective consciousness as well—may go beyond the practical scientists's empirical reality schema, suggesting states of being that are Other-centered, sociocentric. Rather than functions, traits, processes, and complexes, we need to see whole persons in real-life situations, talking and interacting, to critically explore our Western culture-bound discussions of awareness and their consequences for the religious imagination (Crapanzano 1980).

When we come to the structuring of concepts of "self" and "person" in narrative discourse, moreover, and particularly their grounding in religious narrative and ritual events, the implications of these differences seem dramatic (LeVine 1982). The Delhi psychoanalyst, Sudhir Kakar, in *Shamans, Mystics and Doctors* (1983:272), provides an insight on the contrast between India and the West that aptly demonstrates the Third-World critique on the problem: "The Indian emphasis has been on the pursuit of an inner differentiation while keeping the outer world constant." The implications of this value for the construction of selfhood are subtle and profound. "In contrast, the notion of freedom in the West is related to an increase in the outer world and enlarging the sphere of choices, while keeping the inner state constant to that of a rational, waking consciousness from which other modes of inner experience have been excluded as deviations. Each culture, though, has consistently underestimated the strength and attraction of the other's freedom idea." (Kakar 1983:272) Here we have a passage that throws into relief the symbolic contrasts of inner/outer, change/constancy, activity/passivity, choice/restraint.

Locating Experience in the Relational Self

Our problem is to clarify the boundaries of the experiencing subject in a world of diffuse cultural discourse and symbolic objects. Lichtenberg's nihilism comes to mind: "As we do not exactly know the location of our thought, we can place it where we want." Many Melanesian peoples place thought on the skin or in the soul or dreams. That such a subject cannot be limited to or defined by our historical individual, as a monad of analysis, was argued by Mauss (1938) and is generally agreed to by many analysts in cultural and psychological anthropology at large (reviewed in Crapanzano 1986; Doi 1986; Herdt 1987e; Kakar 1986; Kracke 1987; Levy 1973; Poole 1987a; Shweder 1984, 1986; and cf. Kakar 1983, Spiro 1986), and in Melanesian studies in particular (Poole 1986; Schieffelin 1985; M. Strathern 1979, 1988). To take the prevailing point of view: The person as a category is culturally constructed in context, as earlier suggested in the work of Maurice Leenhardt (Clifford 1982). The self-concept, the I/me-ness of personhood, is not defined merely by one's skin, by the boundaries of the anatomical individual or the mind as a unit, or even by the unconscious (Stoller 1979). But if our bodies do not define our boundaries of selfhood—of me-ness—then what does?

Hallowell's (1967:89) classic analysis—functional and cultural—was to argue for "certain basic orientations" of "self-awareness" across cultures, including spatiotemporal, object, motivational, normative, and self "orientations"—"necessary conditions," and denominators of ontology. They also interact with cultural factors, such as developmental timing effects, modes of bonding, attitudes toward body, and notions of awareness, to influence the personal narrative in the time and space world (reviewed in Cohler 1982). Self is thus a universal foundation, an inner reality (Moerman 1979), but one whose shape is constrained always by cultural representation.

The Japanese concept of *amae* offers another perspective on our American ideas of selfhood (Doi 1973). Amae connotes passive dependence, a psychology of love and attachment in which I, as a knowing subject, take for granted that you, as my knowing object, are expected and permitted to depend upon me as a foundation for your dependence in our relationship. "Japanese see human relations completely as a function of *amae*," Doi (1986:153) says; the nature of selfhood extends this me-ness to include this Other via amae relations. In Japan of course this modality of selfhood is embedded in a hierarchical social system, where reflexive merging is structurally limited by one's social status. Thus, the self-concept is, in the new popular idiom, relational, where the emic sense of selfhood is understood, in the context of obligations, as a set of vertical relationships to self, parents, community, and emperor (Benedict 1946).

The subtlety of Japanese selfhood as an object of social relations arises further from the contrast *omote/ura*, which translates roughly to surface/public versus deeper-than-surface/private (Doi 1986). The same contrast gives rise to the sense of staging so pregnant in Japanese presentations of self, as well as to the self-consciousness of mask and self so manifest in the fiction of novelists like Natsume Soseki and Mishima. Indeed, this is an old cultural self-consciousness that can be seen even in the seventeenth-century literature of Ihara's *Comrade Loves of The Samarai* (1972). The main contrast between Japanese and Western self concepts, Doi argues, originates in Christianity,[1] which fragments the nature of awareness and religious imagination differently than the *omote/ura* dichotomy.

> The Japanese never experience the splitting of the body and soul that occurs in the consciousness of the Western people. And they are not afflicted by the Christian conflict between soul and flesh, nor burdened by the severe dichotomy of subject and object that is inherent in the Western philosophical tradition. This may be true. But the Japanese are afflicted, nevertheless, with the splitting of the consciousness into *omote* and *ura,* and we seek to become one with nature precisely because of this affliction. (Doi 1986:155–156)

Interestingly enough, a bit later Doi (1986:157) links William James (1958) to Japanese social psychology: "A man has as many social selves as there are individuals who recognize him and carry an image of him in their mind" (see also Bateson 1973:285 ff). We can see in this image of James an uncanny resemblance to the Greek notion of psyche, the Japanese omote, and the Sambia concept of *koogu* (soul) in waking and dreaming states (Herdt 1987d).

Discussions of this type raise questions about models and languages used in conceptualizing selfhood and awareness across cultures. They also raise questions about what Hallowell (1967:94) referred to as "self-continuity" through time within a culture. How is self-experience represented to others? Bateson (1973) suggested that self and Other were merged in deeper Western experiences of healing (see his thoughtful and neglected essay, "The Cybernetices of Self"). What part of this discourse is metaphoric and what part is discursive language? Michele Stephen raises this point lucidly in Chapter 6. Of Mekeo, she says, "The actions of the soul in dreams cannot be interpreted in any literal manner. They obey a logic quite different from that of conscious awareness." But what is the nature of this logic?

The theoretical answers are several. On the one hand we have the social constructionists, such as Geertz (1983b), who suggest that our experience, indeed our sensory impressions, reflect upon social ideas and images, rather than their expressing the inner world—subjective processes and creativity as such. On the other hand we have the psychological reductionists, including (though not always stridently, according to his text) Freud, who tended to see these experiences as reflections of deeper mentalistic elements, especially unconscious drives. Now let us explore the latter further.

In Search of Self-Interpretation

The problem in deconstructing our Western ideas of selfhood as they bear upon religious imagination and culture is to understand the reductionism inherent in psychoanalytic models without dismissing their concerns with deeper meaning and imagination. Recent critiques of the issues recognize this dilemma (Shweder 1984, 1986). The new narrative approaches in psychoanalytic self-inquiry show a path of discovery (Cohler 1982, Schafer 1980). The extreme relativism of those such as Lutz (1985) and Rosaldo (1980) is problematic (Spiro 1986), among other reasons, because it belies cross-cultural comparison of self-interpretation. We need a middle ground; an intermediate conceptual level through which to circumvent the absolutisms of universal psychological reductionism, on the one hand, and descriptive relativism and particularistic textual narration on the other (Spiro 1986; Kakar 1986; Kracke and Herdt 1987).

A comparison of Freud and Jung is illuminating here. In spite of their differences, Freud in his concern with the metapsychology of the Oedipal complex and sexuality, and Jung with his interest in unconscious archetypes, expressed little concern for the conscious experience of selfhood. To have done so would have raised new questions: recognition of the individuals' identity and its sociolinguistic constituents in real-life contexts, and ways of according value to how the self as a sentient being coordinates conscious and unconscious representations (Kohut 1971; Ricoeur 1970). Though Freud and Jung argued on many things, including the role of sexuality and drives in intrapsychic life, and the extent to which metaphysical or nonrational factors affect human subjectivity, this much they agreed upon as a structural formulation: that Unconscious was primary and this Unconscious transcended, in certain ways, the particular culture in which one observed its manifestations (Ellenberger 1970). In Jung, however, there was great interest in symbols and far greater emphasis upon religiosity, which explains one of Jung's favorite assertions: "Man is naturally religious" (Ellenberger 1970:724).

Freud's use of fantasy/reality as indexes of self-interpretation depends upon the authority of the writer and the text: his hermeneutic position was, at bottom, that only the psychoanalyst can judge latent from manifest, real from unreal—reality from fantasy (Rycroft 1977). So often self and its environs are absent from Freud's commentaries. (I have critiqued this reductionist view in cross-cultural dream interpretation [Herdt 1987d].) Such an observer-centered view, the perspective that interprets things neither in terms of our anthropological emic/etic contrast nor with regard to the local definition of the situation—even the definition of intersubjective communication—is one the anthropologist finds difficult to accept (see Herdt and Stoller 1989). And yet, the retreat into an observer-centered view is easy for ethnographers to understand. The ethnographer who, struggling to maintain his or her own grip on reality in the face of many skeptics at home and among his village friends, feels compelled to assert silent chauvinism of "true" knowledge for self-protection (cf. Crapanzano 1980). Take, for example, the Sambian concept *numelyu*, which I have glossed "spirit familiar" (Herdt 1977, 1981, 1987d) and which is explored further in

Part Two. Sambia assume a set of meanings of prior events and consequences, in which it is difficult, regarding how they signify numelyu, to explicate what is "conscious" from what is "unconscious." Is the unconscious the index of their communications? Notice that in this last sentence it is unclear whether I index numelyu as a collective representation or as subjective entity, or both (Pierce 1931). For Geertz (1966a), what matters is that religion establishes "models" of and for understanding and representing reality. Yet, Geertz's formulation now seems unsatisfactory too. The nature of self-evident propositions, as Bateson (1973) once said, is that if they are not unconscious, they are at least unself-conscious—tacit knowledge (Polanyi 1966). Now what is the difference between these two views? Sambia understand ("it is self-evident") that when someone refers to numelyu they index an entity in their time and space world; and yet they also know that the personal observation of these events is usually confirmed only in trance or dreams. I say "usually" because rare incidents in village life suggest that through extraordinary events—encounters with spirit beings reported on occasion—"direct observation" is possible. But then we must interpret such persons' experiences, too, because there are few Sambia who claim to directly see spirits. Their discourse on the subject obscures this distinction, however. One can see a black palm tree that "is" a numelyu of oneself, Sambia say; but in what sense is the self, the me-ness of one's inner feeling, a part of this tree? In dreams, the identification is revealed, Sambia say. But the ethnographer must add that the identification is possible by virtue of the symbolic discourse Sambia share, that permits one speaker to extend his image of self, beyond the boundaries of his skin, into objects that others know of by virtue of their intersubjective life in the village environs, culture, and language. These are transcendent representations and even universal events to Sambia: In their religious imagination—where the numelyu (the thing or the concept?) has existed always in past and always will present itself in future—there is transcendence of the life of the body and self. Body and self will not outlive the soul (or koogu), however, because it continues across time and space (see Herdt 1984b) to the indefinite future.

If such notions are indeed understood and shared in, albeit implicitly, by a people, they must be a part of culture. Do they, we may ask, share in a discourse of explicit knowledge about this, and for the entire society? One's perspective depends, in part, upon semantics: how are we to define the meaning of knowledge? What ontology is implied in the nature of this knowing that is special to a people? Is this knowing "motivated" in the sense of Durkheim's famous idea of collective consciousness? Critiques of Freud's constructions of the problem by Ricoeur (1970), Rycroft (1977), and O'Flaherty (1984) suggest that his metapsychology was deprived of a concept of culture. Yet selfhood cannot be understood as a knowing subject, except and only through the phenomenological field of cultural objects and discourses that it participates in, and then only with other knowing subjects (cultural actors or like-minded others such as spirits) with whom one communicates.

The self invests in these particular concepts and narratives. The I/me extends out beyond the boundaries of one's skin through imagination into a world of symbolic objects indexed in the discourse with others. In Mekeo sorcerers, for example, Stephen (1987:57) tells us their constant fasting, celibacy, and advanced age makes them "*lolova*—dry, light, pure." Indeed, the self in this image "becomes more spirit than man, though he still exists on the human plane." Here, as in other examples that follow, we begin to see self and Other merged through a process of representation and action, which exploits the verity of symbolic texts—art, literature, ritual, dance, myth—in culture.

Selfhood and Transitional Objects

A newer conceptual model for this intersubjective communication qua symbolic mediation is provided by object relations theory and self-psychology in psychoanalysis (Winnicott 1973; Kohut 1971). This culturally-sensitive, language-discursive line of recent psychoanalytic thought (see Grolnick 1987) is highlighted by Winnicott's (1969) well-known idea of transitional objects, which provides a fertile ground for exploring Self and Other mergings. Indeed, I have recently argued for greater attention to the intersubjective field of transitional objects in culture (Herdt 1987e). Ritual flutes and impersonated spirit beings are presented to Sambia initiates as halfway between their maternal caretakers and spiritual beings. These are transitional objects that help boys adjust to the trials of initiation and the problems of subsequent development. It is the cultural imagination of Sambia, however, that provides the evocative foundation of these transitional objects that merge Self and sacred Other (see Stephen, following chapter).

The work of Winnicott (1973) poses a question of seminal interest to psychological anthropologists: Where in the mind can we locate cultural experience? Winnicott argues that developmental experience occurs neither in the intrapsychic nor the social (objectively apprehendable) worlds, but rather in a "third area," which is the interpersonal field of "potential space" between self and Other. Culture as a collective and symbolic design enables persons to draw on experiences from their caretakers and beyond to fashion an inner world (cf. Schwartz 1978). Winnicott was most interested in the ontology of the individual's capacity to experience and cultivate this potential arena outside of self that becomes selfhood. The origins of cultural experience lay always in infancy, when the baby learns to tolerate temporary separation from mother, or caretakers who provide great meaning in the infant's small world (Winnicott 1973). Separation from mother causes anxiety, because of frustration and insecurity, for anxiety is the loss of what is vital and familiar. Infantile tolerance is eventually enhanced because of the infant's creation of a "transitional object" —anything that can serve to bridge her caretaker and herself, whether a doll or a pacifier, and later internal representations of these objects. Anthropologically, we see in this conception the elements of an autonomous imagination already at work; and these come to symbolize for the child her union of herself and her mother. This relational emphasis upon very early symbols and objects thus distinguishes Winnicott from Freud and Jung: with this "not-me possession," the infant's growing self achieves clearer boundaries and yet maintains continuity with the earlier period of subjective merging ("me-possession") with mother. Symbolization is here preverbal and less cognitive, more a feeling state than we usually think; it pertains more to the sensual than that which is coded in formal language (Langer 1967). The infant must trust in the caretaker's "holding world" for this capacity to develop of merging with Other, which hinges in large measure on the empathy and dependability of the mother and other significant caretakers, who must not leave the infant alone longer than the fragile self's symbolic participation into the environs can endure. A "lone child" model will not do here. For even the alternate caretakers of tribal villages must attend to this aspect of the infant's needs. As the child's capacity for symbolic activity develops, he is able to endure longer separations from his mother, through language and play, and symbolic forays in social relationships: spaces seen in culture as "play" and "task." Thus, development of transitional objects constitutes the genesis of language, play, work, and ultimately, of cultural action itself.

The transitional object is the result of a process whereby the self feels a necessity, pertaining to the Other, to maintain blissful union with this Other; the necessity emanates as much from what the other wills, however, for the infant's self has scant control and must accommodate itself. The bridge of the symbolic object is in-between: me/not me, other/not other. Desire in turn emanates from these necessities. The form and content of this symbolic merging and separation is strongly influenced by conceptions of child-rearing in culture. The material means, representations, and linguistic vehicles provided by the community are easily infused into the object constructed by the self, and, perhaps—as with dolls or blankets in our society—offered by the other/caretaker as temporary substitutes for the preferred transitional object. Thus desires, not just instrumental behaviors, are mediated by culture. Winnicott (1973) suggests most fundamentally a *desire to engage the Other,* a formulation similar to that of Crapanzano's (1986) recent writings on the self.

Psychoanalytic theory, as critiqued by such analytic writers as Doi, Kakar, and Waud Kracke (1987b), has ignored the background of the person and self, of which the Freudian drives are merely "part-functions." Selfhood in Winnicott's formulation is the realm of transitional phenomenon: symbols of engagement at a point between not-me and me-extensions. This is vague; but as

William James once said, "The boundary-line of the mental is certainly vague."[2] This idea draws support from two other areas of psychological research. The first comes from developmental psychology: The caregiver is the first attachment figure, and through bonding with this person, including learning to separate, the infant's sense of self develops (Bowlby 1969). If the arena of differentiation of self is also mediated by the nature of shared attachments, then clearly the nature of self will be influenced by culture. The second idea stems from a comparison of Winnicott's transitional objects to Hallowell's self-orientation: culture anticipates through value orientation, but does not fully determine, the boundaries and narratives of self. The symbolic activity of the emerging self within the symbolic space between inner-self and outer-world objects is anticipated by Hallowell's (1967) "cultural orientations" of self, object, motivation, norms, and space and time—precepts and concepts of normative selfhood.

Where Winnicott specifies that play and culture are intensely symbolic interactive experiences, Freud saw ego and id as one-directional and drive-directed. Winnicott's objects are not directly instinctual; they are more synergistic and "alive" than Freud's drives. The imaginative process that has the power, Winnicott suggests, of cathecting (energizing) physical objects is so involved in the creation of self (which is "founded on body experiences") that it cannot be so distinct from the awareness of body and desires and gratifications. The "potential space" of the infant, as Winnicott (1973) suggests, is influenced by bodily urges coming from the "intrapsychic" side of the dyadic interaction. Yet it is critical to our understanding of ontology that the infant's use of symbols is energized by desire for social union with mother, with the Other. Here the theories of Winnicott and Freud (1927) come closer, but Winnicott's idea of desire is dependent upon culture and imagination for its construction, as Freud's was not, at least not directly (see Herdt 1987e).

Winnicott thus provides a very different conception of unconsciousness and culture, one that is intrinsically motivated by the human organism, but is emergent and intersubjective. Though the infant's needs can be met symbolically by the imagination, the optimum for the human infant is the need for another self to be there. So great is this sentient dimension that the human will invent an Other if one is not available. Splitting, multiple personality, and possession states are related to this (Peters 1988; Stoller 1973).

William James, toward the end of his *Varieties of Religious Experience*, debates within himself the old subjective-objective dichotomy as it pertains to constructions of religious experience. His conclusion (1958: 382) is instructive:

"The truth of the matter can be put," says Leuba, "in this way: *God is not known, he is not understood; he is used*"—sometimes as meat-purveyor, sometimes as moral support, sometimes as friend, sometimes as an object of love. If he proves himself useful, the religious consciousness asks for no more than that. Does God really exist? What is he? are so many irrelevant questions. Not God, but life, more life, a larger, richer, more satisfying life, is, in the last analysis, the end of religion.

Eventually, James suggests that the fact that an element of the self identifies— to use our modern term—with a similar reality that is more than the self, but continuous with it, is a basic motive that compels religious action. (Freud [1927] touched upon this in his writings on "oceanic" feelings.) Issues of self and religious experience have been omnipresent but marginal to the Western scientific tradition for a very long time. James's ideas, however, provide a useful transition to substantive cultural themes in Melanesia whereby God or gods are understood and sought, used and depended upon as transitional objects: part of the larger texture of the self's symbolic world.

The Self in Culture

To push further our exploration of selfhood and religious imagination means thinking in broader terms about the interrelation of self to mind, body, and soul. We must resist the compartmentalization and pathologizing of an earlier period that made non-Western cultures appear neurotic and their soul-doctors—shamans—psychotic (Kakar 1985:441). In Melanesia studies we need alternative models for reconceptualizing the self, and for heuristic purposes I refer again to the conception of psyche among the Ancient Greeks. The long and well-documented historical/cultural evolution of this concept and its echoes in contemporary society help to symbolically link Melanesian and postmodern Western cultures.

Originally, Homeric Greece drew no clear distinction between the organs of thought and feeling (Simon 1978:59). Abstract concepts or functions were scant. The origins of mental life and the sources of intentionality were generally ascribed to agencies outside the person (1978: 62). Intense mental states, such as courage on the battlefield, were infusions from the gods, and they could drive you crazy. "Psyche" was akin to our present notions of spirit or soul at this time.

While in Homer the psyche usually first appears after death, it may also, curiously, leave a person when he loses consciousness and, presumably, return as he awakens. Psyche is sufficiently concrete to leave the body through a spear wound and also carries a connotation of "breath" . . . Other uses of the term in Homer indicate that the psyche is sacred. One can swear by one's psyche, as by the head or knees. It is ascribed only to human beings, not to animals . . . We can gain some further appreciation of the Homeric notion by considering what psyche is *not*. It is never portrayed as a thinking, feeling, reflecting, and deciding part of the living person. Thus it is not a psychic agency in our sense of the term. It seems to carry some of these functions after death, but as a continuation of the whole person, not as an agency of faculty (1978:56). [But later] Psyche for Plato, is capable of functioning as one's ethical and cognitive core, and as such is frequently equated with the self. For Plato, psyche makes decisions and can make responsible choices; it certainly can be held responsible for its choices. (1978:59)

Homer merged ideas and feelings in psyche; they were split apart and became separate in the conceptions of Plato. Abstract concepts were likewise dependent upon the late philosophical traditions, especially Aristotle (Vernant 1983). Where Homer has no term for self and "does not even have a generic term for man or woman, male or female" (Simon 1978: 61), Plato again supplies these, and references to "itself" and "himself" too, but not to the "self" as such (1978:161). It is only after the advent of the great philosophical tradition of Attic culture, and of Plato in particular, that "intellect is split off from appetite, reason from passion," following which Greek culture "wrestled with the problem of how to put them back together again" (1978:165).

Here we see a cultural evolution in which a single unifying concept (psyche) that once grouped such profound categories of experiences as mind, body, gender, self, and soul gradually became differentiated and relative to certain situations and aspects of persons in Western culture. Freud's effort to make psychoanalysis a holistic science of psyche, in its sense of self-and-soul, was, unfortunately, doomed to failure by the powerful dichotomies of mind, body, and soul still present by inheritance from historical conventions, especially in American medical discourse and popular ideology (Bettelheim 1984; Kleinman 1988).

Developmental differences across the life span may influence conceptions of self and soul through such factors as timing, sequence, and function of cognition, emotion, and their related maturational processes. The earlier achievement of certain aspects of physical growth and puberty by females over males has been interpreted as cultural solutions to the understanding and ritualization of gender and personhood, for example, in Melanesia (Herdt 1987a; La Fontaine 1985; F. Young 1965). But life-crisis rites and accompanying life-span normative changes are not the only developmental processes that differentiate societies.

Let me utilize developmental gender differences in the onset and performance of the shaman's role among the Sambia to illustrate this point. Normative cultural signs and psychological indicators of the shaman's calling are sex-linked (Herdt 1977, 1987a). Structurally, the shamanic role is integrated into all major male institutions, such as warfare and the clubhouse, and male shamans are recruited via male initiation rites. Traditionally, male shamans outnumbered female shamans by a ratio of 4:1. The shaman's calling is defined by criteria whereby dreams, trance experiences, and spirit visitations point toward certain children having been selected by spirits. Both male and female children—usually the offspring of shamans of the same sex—are thus identified (cf. Spiro 1968). However, the intrusion of the male initiation in late childhood introduces a sex difference into the cultural context of the boy's early identification with the shaman's role. First-stage initiation (ages 7–10) among boys culminates in a forest ceremony during which boys are placed into an alternate state of consciousness. Senior shamans go into a trance and predict which boys will become shamans. No comparable experience exists for females. And again, during third-stage initiation (ages 13–16) additional training, ingestion of hallucinogenic agents, and shamanic instruction further socialize the nominated youth along the developmental line of the shaman (see Herdt and Stoller 1985). No structural equivalent of this event exists for females, either. It is only in late adolescence, through unusual, often mystical experiences, that prospective female shamans are confirmed in their roles. This is years later than their male counterparts. Obviously this cultural timing introduces a developmental difference in the age, social effects, and symbolic elaboration of shamanic socialization along sex lines, though the consequences of this difference are at present unknown (see Herdt, this volume).

Another example, taken from adolescent development that figures widely into Melanesian selfhood and religion, is initiation rites. Initiation obeys the law of Van Gennep's (1960) rites-of-passage stage model, whereby separation, liminality, and aggregation back into society, albeit with a new role or status, is widespread but not universal in Melanesia (Allen 1967; Herdt 1982a). Such transitions suggest profound changes in the selfhood and gender identity of the novitiate (reviewed in Herdt 1987a). Particularly in male rites, sexual orientation and object relations, including the elaboration of ritual symbols as transitional objects, are mediated by collective initiation. Some developmental differences arising from initiation are related to the age of first initiation; the harshness of initiation for males versus females, with male initiation often being harsher than the female counterpart; the forms of pseudo-procreative symbolism in male initiation compared to female forms (Hiatt 1971); ritualized homosexual activity shown in strongly marked patterns for males in certain societies, but not for females (Herdt 1984b); and forms of body symbolism being contrasted between prepubertal and postpubertal male development accentuated in initiation. For male initiation, Turner's (1967a) emphasis upon the liminal period seems significant, alongside a generalized tendency in Melanesia, Australia (Hart 1963), and East African Ndembu (Turner 1968) to view male initiates as normless, unruly, and in need of initiation to ensure support of village male hegemony and the cultural order it indexes in normative selfhood. Indeed, Hart (1963:424), speaking of the Tiwi of Australia, went so far as to characterize childhood experience as "part of the secular world [whereas] postpuberty experience [is] part of the sacred world."

This leads us to a set of integrated problems—and we must always be clear for whom such problems are problems, Melanesians or their interpreters—concerning the representation and intrusion of one person into another's thoughts and meanings. I will suggest that although in traditional New Guinea societies persons make attributions about others' subjective states, they are generally reticent to interpret the other's motives. Hence, the understanding and explanation of cultural expressions of selfhood are difficult because of the absence of native exegesis and narrative in certain societies (Barth 1975). Though these latter points are not problems for New Guinea society (cf. Herdt and Poole 1982; Lewis 1980), they raise analytic and interpretive problems associated with divided consciousness as this is manifested in cultural forms, including those such as temporary madness, possession, and witchcraft, that have local meanings of a negative kind for New Guineans.

It has been suggested that the Kaluli of the Great Papuan Plateau, for instance, are loathe to interpret others' behaviors. They say that "one cannot know what another thinks or feels" (Ochs and Schieffelin 1984: 290). For children this attitude has consequences for language acquisition and social affiliation; and for adults, moreover, it must have demonstrable effects upon the boundaries of self and discourse in interpersonal interaction.

> Although Kaluli obviously interpret and assess another's available behaviors and internal states, these interpretations are not culturally acceptable as topics of talk. Individuals often talk about their own feelings ('I'm afraid, I'm happy', etc). However, there is a cultural dispreference for talking or making claims about what another might think, what another might feel, or what another is about to do, especially if there is no external evidence. (1984:290)

Such a view of self and Other is consistent with a long tradition in New Guinea studies, beginning with Read's (1955) work on Gahuku-Gama. (On intentionality and dream sharing, and personal accountability for ritual, see Herdt 1987a, 1987d.)

If one self is reticent to ask another self for an account of behavior and intentions, how smooth and seamless will interaction be? One social function of this dispreference is the avoidance of conflict. Harming others is especially negatively perceived if they are members of one's group, that is, if moral norms apply to them because they are persons (Read 1955). The study of secrecy and social control enters here as well (Tuzin 1982; and see Herdt 1987d). Another means of reading intention is for the self to use cultural symbols to directly or unconsciously represent intents. Here the interpretation and exegesis of symbol, role, or cultural event may be used to elicit and/or convey to audiences (Barth

1975) significant moods and motives of actors (reviewed in LeVine 1982, chap. 19). Bruce Knauft's Gebusi case (this volume) addresses this issue. Whether oral traditions are present within a society, and whether such stories are identified with or a substitute for personal choices and products of imagination (M. Young [1983:17] refers to this as the "brainwashing view of myth"), is an important feature of self-perception and representation, especially in discourse, and we shall consider this shortly.

The use of dreams in Melanesian social life provides a powerful example of a culturally patterned context in which the self's reluctance to directly interpret others is overcome. Though dreams are widely reported to be shared across Melanesia (but not in all cases: reviewed in Herdt 1987d), even in pro-active dream cultures, not all dreams are reported; the Sambia situation will again illustrate. According to canonical dream theory, remembered dream events occur not to self but to soul (koogu), thus protecting the self from remembered dreams of an immoral or rule-violating nature if reported to others. The self is not, in short, accountable for the dreams it experiences. There are three situations for dream narration: public, private, and secret contexts. Dreams of secret ritual symbols must only be told in secret, for example. This implies a screening by self, an implicit (unconscious?) decision regarding which situation the self will report as a dream. In a study of a Sambian man, Nilutwo, I have shown that he revealed his dreams only selectively, and, in the case of highly sensitive manifest content (on incestuous and on adulterous dreams) he told no one else except me. This is tacit awareness of some accountability for the dream content (Herdt 1987d) and anticipatory awareness that the consequences of sharing such dreams would be injurious to self. (See Crapanzano's *Tuhami* [1980] for comparison.)

Tuzin (1975) has made a kindred point on dream experience in Melanesia. He suggests that the Ilahita Arapesh engage in dream sharing such that no simple distinction between individual and culture pattern dreams (Lincoln 1935) can be maintained. Instead, the interpretive system of Ilahita canonical theory plays a "large part in constructing the dream's manifest content" (Tuzin 1975:561). The local theory shields painful, conflictual feelings—via repression—by deflecting attention of self and others away from their "immediate experience" (1975:564). Thus, the dream, the folk ideas of dreaming, and the folk interpretation system must all be seen as products of cultural imagination. How different such a view is from that of Freud's (1933), who remarked that dreams are not "social utterances."[3] (See also Kracke's [1987b] important Amazonia work here.)

The dream narrative illuminates further a problem in self-representation previously alluded to: the function of the concept of soul or spirit to index selfhood in interpersonal relationships. It is difficult to make nomothetic statements about this nexus because comparative ethnographic data are weak (cf. Shweder and Bourne 1984). Is the skin a metaphor for self, as M. Strathern (1979) suggests for discursive language of Melpa? We cannot easily read off of such metaphors self-intentionality, nor do we possess the richly textured historical materials of the classicists who have shown cultural changes in the concept of psyche noted above. Michele Stephen's (1987b; this volume) work addresses this issue directly: The Mekeo soul, through dream narrative, exploits a language of the visible versus unseen power dichotomy, which provides a concept for discussing the antisocial (unconscious?) feelings of self or the Other.

Soul and self are, thus, divisible or "dividual," in Marriot's sense (cited in Kakar 1985:445). Ultimately, these divisions of awareness in selfhood, with regard to dream sharing, may arise from structural contradictions—social and intrapsychic—between what the Greeks would have called psyche in its organic appetites on the one hand, and its higher, abstract functions, which eventually became social selfhood (Simon 1978:160–164) on the other.

The Divided Self and Religious Traditions

These perspectives on self-representation and dream narratives raise a broader question of how the self handles the conflicting demands of roles or contradictory values across social domains. Changes in cultural symbols, personal visions, and metaphors of madness (Herdt 1986) provide examples of divided consciousness and selfhood in Melanesia. Where contradictions occur in social relationships—contradictions between rights and duties for instance—the self or soul is placed in a situation of painful compromise. Here again we are reminded of the division in Greek thought between psyche and selfhood (Simon 1978): Two New Guinea examples of divided consciousness—possession and spirit mediumship —will sharpen our discussion.

Ritual homicide *(laf)* was established as an institution of considerable importance in traditional Ilahita Arapesh society (Tuzin 1980). Tambaran spirits would invade, and seize the bodies of certain advanced male cult members. Men would don full body masks and go in search of victims for the glory of Tambaran. Such crimes were anonymous; the perpetrators were disguised and their victims ideally were to be enemies (1980:229– 230). In fact, some were fellow villagers; and in a pinch, the victims could "perhaps even [be] a member of their own family." Such an idea is shocking and seemingly unacceptable to Ilahita men, not only by their normative moral code, but also by the ethos of their affectionate familial relations. And yet we are not dealing here with the normative code of selfhood, but rather with possession, ritual secrecy, and the divided consciousness of accountability to the men's cult, which takes precedence over obligations to nuclear family (Tuzin 1982). The bifurcation is mirrored in other gender attitudes: for example, women may be suspected of sorcery (1980:287), whereas one's fellow cult members presumably would not be. The Ilahita's distinction supports a radical divisiveness of the social person into a public self versus a Tambaran acting through being in the self's body. This is Durkheim's collective consciousness embodying the self!

Mediums provide an example of a less radical division of awareness in the sense that their identities were known and less submerged by their audience. Kaluli (Schieffelin 1977) and Gebusi (Knauft, this volume) mediums seem to retain some awareness of their actions. They also identify with certain cult spirits, whose voices they may at least share in, if not in fact impersonate (Knauft 1985a). One sees here a division of consciousness on several fronts: of a male self identified with a female spirit; of an adult participant who visualizes himself as an infant in the arms of the spirit (Knauft 1987b). These rich narratives illustrate well the subtlety of divided consciousness in the selfhood of the medium and his audience.

The most extreme form of divided awareness, manifested in a sex-linked way, is the so-called "wild-man madness" syndrome of New Guinea (Herdt 1986). A variety of such disturbances of self have been reported, primarily in males who are in transition to adulthood. Aggressive behavior is their chief symptom. Yet the syndrome also takes a specifically female form. Where exaggerated aggressiveness is manifested in males, exaggerated sexuality occurs in females. These are cultural expressions not only of madness but of perceived essences of selfhood in males versus females (Reay 1977). Most episodes of the madness are temporary, and afterward the person professes amnesia. No loss of status for the afflicted is reported in most societies; indeed, they receive more attention and care (in the "sick role") than before (Freudians refer to this as secondary gains of an illness). Interestingly enough, the idiom of madness here is not one of possession, but of a blockage of the ears: the cultural preconception is that the selfhood and sociality of an actor depend upon his or her being accessible and responsive to others' social demands. One suspects that these are forms of "symbolic protest" in the sense Lewis (1971) argued cross-culturally for peripheral possession cults. What matters is that the self is situated in an idiom of temporary acting out, but acting that provides greater recognition as well as release from burdensome social restrictions.

Thus far our examples of divided self have targeted exegesis as a denominator of symbolic expression for person and sacred Other. What happens when one finds active imaginations embedded in inarticulate cultural traditions? What is the self to do? The example of sacred art among Abelam is illuminating.

In a powerful description of the Abelam of the Middle Sepik River Forge (1966, 1970) has shown a people without verbal exegesis of symbols, mythological or any oral traditions, for that matter. For Forge (1966:24), both the neighboring Iatmül and Abelam emphasize visual art as their primary means of direct communication with the sacred Other. Thus, sacred art is critical in the formation of states of awareness in the self, as "expressions related directly to the culture, not through the intermediate stage of myth" (1966:24). Here is a view virtually at odds with that of Roy Wagner (1972), who has seen in myth and symbolic convention "language" on a higher order. Meaning in Abelam art "does not lie at the level of overt symbolism," but rather at "the level of the relation between symbols, and at this level may not be consciously perceived by either the artist or beholder" (Forge 1966:25). In semiotic terms Forge (1966:30) argues that ceremonial cult houses and carvings among Abelam make "implicit non-verbal statements" about issues such as "the ultimate identity of man, long yam and spirit" (cf. Turner 1967a). Deep-felt meanings are somehow conveyed that yams are phallic symbols, prizes of male ancestors and essences (cf. also Tuzin 1972).

A hint as to how this socialization process works is contained in Forge's essay "Learning to See in New Guinea." Here, Forge (1970:276) tells how the explication of meanings comes about implicitly, through ritual immersion in deep and closed initiation experiences, which assault the self, destroying and rebuilding it, through the aesthetic means of dramatic ritual cult art. "Instruction during seclusion does not include any interpretation of the meaning of the various Tambaran ceremonies or any learning or even telling of myths, of which the Abelam know remarkably few." Furthermore: "The Abelam boy, indulged in secular contexts and violently treated in ritual ones, is proffered no explanation of the ill treatment he receives or of the ceremony of which it is a part" (1970:288). Thus: "The experiences of Abelam boys tend to make them regard paintings as something of great importance [and] intrinsically powerful, but a closed system not referring to other natural or social phenomena and a closed system the meaning of which is not explained beyond the naming of designs" (1970:288). Forge concludes that there is shifting meaning—and therefore shifting states of divided awareness—in and around Abelam art and ritual. There is "no secure iconography" with unambiguous design elements, and hence ambiguous connotations (1970:289), a symbolically dynamic view that boldly contrasts with the structuralism of some (Munn 1973). "The Abelam do not ask what a painting means," Forge (1970: 289) complains.

> Abelam art is about relationships, not about things. One of its functions is to relate and unite disparate things in terms of their place in the ritual and cosmological order. It does this . . . directly and not as an illustration to some text based in another symbolic system such as language [Hence] the initiation system [teaches] the young men to see the art, not so that he [sic] may consciously interpret it. (Forge 1970:290)

This spirited view of meaning systems cautions us against our certain ingrained Western preoccupations with verbal flow. (Cf. Bateson [1973] on primitive art.) Sperber (1975) has well criticized this, and the work of Gell (1975) is an attempt of a Lévi-Straussian structuralist form to address the problem too.

Yet we are still left with the problem of inarticulateness in these symbols, of Geertz's (1968) how-to-find-cultural-meaning-without-meta-commentary position. With regard to the metalanguage aspect of ritual, we would do well to recall one of Victor Turner's (1978:578) last pieces, in which he derides those social realists who "see ritual either as a distorted reflection of 'reality' or as an obsessional defense mechanism of culture against culturally defined illicit impulses." Both positions are inadequate, Turner suggests, because they either exclude or do not take seriously the imaginative and dialogical "reality" of ritual in self construction.

Once again the Greeks provide a useful contrast. A ritual system may embody an individual and societal split in its design, where contradictory structural factors create conflicts within the self, or where individual dissatisfaction is given collective expression. It is difficult to obtain exegesis on this, as the diffuse nature of psyche in the Greek texts attests. However, there is an entirely different interpretation available to us. Where imaginative states emerge from ritual and trance roles, their expressions —cultural performances and narratives of these—may be intentionally ambiguous. They may defy simple exegesis because their ambiguity is useful to the self's side of the hegemonic equation. The following example from the oracular visions of the ever-divided oracle of Delphi is instructive.

> Theoretically, the zygastron at Delphi would have made it possible to test the truth of the oracles, provided of course that it did not contain answers invented by the priests for purposes of propaganda; and there is no evidence that the Delphic priesthood ever committed forgery. But even in the case of an authentic oracle it is not to be supposed that the answer was always clear and precise. It was not for nothing that Apollo was nicknamed Loxias, the Ambiguous One. Often enough the answers were completely enigmatic, and it required all the skill of the official interpreters, the exegetes, to make sense of them; and the same oracle might well be interpreted in different and even contradictory ways. The Greeks always delighted in such mental gymnastics. (Flaceliere 1965:53)

Ambiguity hides intentions from others and conflicts from self. I am reminded here of the heroic complex of Sambia shamanism and the popular devotion of people to oracular sayings of the great shamans, even when these were ambiguous—sometimes purposefully vague—and spoken not by great men but great women (Herdt 1987c)!

The Self, Culture and Religion in Transition

The heritage of Durkheim (1965), which views the structure of society as based in relatively changeless and ahistorical religious institutions, still influences contemporary anthropology. The great symbolic prototypes, such as shamanism, witchcraft, and sorcery purvey this paradigm, in spite of great cross-cultural diversity, no where more so than in New Guinea. Where a long tradition with a rich history has evolved, narrative expectations embed the self in multiple cultural possibilities. Symbolic objects—transitional objects—are ever-present for the mediation of autonomous imagination, transforming thought and feeling, probably even in dreams, as Freud (1965) suggested. The pragmatics and demography of Kuman witchcraft (Reay 1987) and Kalam witchcraft (Riebe 1987), for example, are instructive here. Particularly in the latter case, an ethnohistory of spontaneous experiences of witch accusations gave way to an ideology of advantage and deceit, manipulating both wealth and politics. As Riebe (1987:240) says, "Witchcraft became the idiom of resource conflicts." Witch figures provide a negative model of what not to be for the self (see Bercovitch, this volume).

Once embedded structurally and psychologically, such symbolic forms as witchcraft and shamanism are surprisingly durable in the face of cultural change. For Carlo Ginzburg, the witchcraft of sixteenth-century agrarian Europe was due to the "vitality of [these] beliefs that were impressed upon the minds" of the peasants, first in their infancy, usually by their mothers, "custodians of the inheritance" of traditions, and later, by a culture that regarded them as "an imperishable heritage" (Ginzburg 1985:96–97). The exoticism of witchcraft is not past. Contemporary America and England are not without their cabals of witchcraft covens, devil worship, and revivalist mother-earth cults. But these speak not so much of the historical witchcraft of the Middle Ages as of the self's search for an idiom in which to fashion its imaginings and practices, escapist or not, in a bewildering mass world that lacks Communitas (Bellah et al. 1985).

I mention the latter point merely as a touchstone to reflect upon cargo cults and messianic Christian missionization in New Guinea. The huge and now lifeless cargo-cult literature that once probed similar issues came to naught, its too structural and too little symbolic theory having robbed analyses of vitality (Jarvie 1964). Certainly not all Melanesian peoples have easily succumbed to Christianization, as the Kwaio case shows (Keesing 1982b). Religious syncretism is present in many places (see Boutilier, Hughes, and Tiffany 1978). The regional picture of missionary zeal and change is also uneven in the Highlands (Robin 1982). These, too, must be seen as varieties of the religious imagination in Melanesia, in part, as Margaret Mead (1956) once suggested in *New Lives for Old,* as preparation for new and acculturated roles—not just a changing of the guard. But in another sense, too, because here the self is offered vitalistic symbolic objects and apocryphal discourses for imagining and practicing social life.

We cannot entirely escape the past or the impress of tradition on the present, and many studies of change in religion have been caught between an ahistorical functionalism and a conception of cultural action as such—a higher order of analysis in which the events of innovation and personal mediation are obscured. This is no doubt why Geertz (1973:109) could once say: "If the anthropological study of religious commitment is undeveloped, the anthropological study of religious noncommitment is nonexistent." The work of Donald Tuzin is striking here, for he provides magnificent exceptions to Geertz, in a double sense (1982; this volume).

Which brings me to a final point, consistent with the emphasis upon imagination and cultural creativity in this volume: Let us highlight forms of spontaneity and aesthetics in our ethnographic accounts, rather than merely formalizing structures apart from the selves who embody them. This will require more concern with lives and with the stories of lives, sacred and profane, than hitherto seen. I am reminded again of Victor Turner's (1978:560) last wisdom.

> My formulation, I have come to see, is anything but adequate. It is a flat description of ritual as it appears to an alien observer and says nothing about what ritual means to a native actor. Nor does it capture the transformative capacity of ritual, its competency, from the actor's standpoint, to raise him from a lower to a higher level of knowledge, understanding, or social being. Nor does it correctly characterize the spontaneity present in most ritual, its responsiveness to present circumstance and its competence to interpret the current situation and provide viable ways of coping with contemporary problems.

Here are humble words from a great anthropologist reflecting upon the spirit of the human condition, its psyche, in the Greek sense, and the challenge to us of utilizing ethnographic insights to bring culture and selfhood to life for readers. Let us hope that we and our colleagues can meet the challenge of conveying the traditions, old and new, of religious experience in New Guinea.

NOTES

1. A notion one finds repeatedly in the works of Jung and those influenced by him, such as Mircea Eliade (1964) or Joseph Campbell (1949).
2. James (quoted in Ornstein 1986:8) continues: "It is much better not to be pedantic, but to let the science be as vague as its subject, and

include such phenomena as these if by so doing we can throw any light on the "business at hand."
3. But see O'Nell (1976:49), who notes how contemporary Gestalt therapy in America makes use not only of dream sharing but acting out as a "royal road to (self) integration."

Self,
the Sacred Other,
and Autonomous
Imagination

Michele Stephen

THE difficulties of investigating subjective experience—already a sufficiently vexing problem, for how are we ever really to know what is in another person's mind?—seem almost insurmountable when cross-cultural interpretations are involved. Recent trends in cultural anthropology have created a new awareness of just how difficult, perhaps impossible, the task is. The cultural variability of the very concept of self and the culture-bound nature of Western models of mind make any attempt at cross-cultural interpretation and comparison an extremely hazardous, if not suspect, endeavor. The aim of this chapter is to explore certain subjective experiences that, paradoxically, might be termed self-alien, and to focus attention on a special mode of imaginative thought that plays an important role in the construction of sacred realities in New Guinea and other tribal religions—and in religious experience in general. My subject is only one imaginative mode, but one that clearly underlies much of the New Guinean religious phenomena described in this collection.

Autonomous imagination[1]—a concept representing a synthesis of several existing views—provides new perspectives on many of the theoretical issues raised in this book and on the remarkable ethnographic phenomena depicted here; indeed the case studies provide outstanding examples of its nature and how it operates. The usefulness of the concept, however, lies in its general applicability cross-culturally; and since it represents an essentially new formulation involving concepts from different disciplines, it needs to be outlined independently of the ethnographic phenomena described here. My aim in this chapter is to introduce the concept, with only passing reference to its relevance to the case studies. This will leave readers free to make their own judgments and to examine the case studies on their own merits. In the final chapter of this book, however, I will offer my conclusions as to the relevance of the concept in interpreting religious phenomena in the specific ethnographic context of New Guinea.

Let us begin by reviewing some of the problems inherent in interpreting a range of subjective experience that figures prominently in New Guinea (Stephen 1979) and in the following pages, as it does in religious experience cross-culturally, namely dreams, waking visions, spirit possession, and many other so-called altered states of consciousness.

Self, Not-Self, and the Sacred Other

The human organism must, presumably, come to self-consciousness and awareness by defining itself in relation to two powerful and insistent Others— the outer world of physical objects, forces, and persons and an inner world of thoughts, desires, feelings, and emotions. Recent anthropological discussion of cross-cultural variations in the concepts of self and person have revealed the very different boundaries that cultures may draw across these two frontiers.

This chapter is concerned with the boundaries between self and the inner frontier. A growing appreciation of just how radical may be the differences is beginning to dissolve some of the long debated puzzles of the "primitive mind." What we members of modern Western cultures must accept responsibility for, as the creations of our own minds, members of other cultures may attribute to possession by an external, supernatural entity of irresistible force. The division of inner and outer worlds I have used here represents a culturally determined distinction. What our culture labels inner, mental events are not necessarily so regarded in other cultures, but may be considered events or forces totally exterior to the self —as in spirit possession.

Yet although cultures differ in the boundaries they draw and in their classifications of different kinds of experience and their significance, there are certain inner events (identifiable in both in Western and non-Western cultures) that are experienced as taking place outside the self. Interpretations of their nature and significance vary greatly, nevertheless, certain inner states seem universally marked as alien to the self. I refer to those mental events that have the appearance of being sensory perceptions of an external reality, such as dreams, waking visions, auditory and tactile hallucinations, hypnotic states, and various other unusual mental states.

The definition of the self in relation to inner experience ranges from that which is clearly me (my thoughts, my emotions, my memories), through that which seems alien and foreign to me (desires, thoughts, and emotions that appear to originate from somewhere else), to experiences such as dreams and waking visions, in which purely mental events assume the appearance of a tangible reality existing outside myself. The cultural and analytic distinctions drawn between these various gradations of inner experience may be extremely subtle and shifting, and one may blur into another, but certain states are experientially clearly demarcated as self-alien.

The problem arises, of course, that subjective experience is not independent of culture. The individual can represent his experience, even to himself, only through cultural categories and interpretations. But where the available cultural categories do not fit his private experience or are insufficient to describe new and strange phenomena, there is room, indeed necessity, for the individual to criticize, modify, adjust and innovate on given cultural schemata. My arguments are based upon the assumption that a phenomenological world exists independently of the human mind, and that human cultures represent different ways of describing, interpreting, and ordering its infinite complexity. As human beings, our mental functioning (sensory perception and information processing) is sufficiently similar for us to be able to discern a phenomenological basis to our different cultural orderings. Culture thus undoubtedly shapes individual experience but does not totally determine it.[2]

Indeed, dreams provide an excellent example.[3] When I have had a dream, I tell myself it is a purely mental event having no reality outside my own mind. But the nature of the phenomena is such that it appears to be an external reality I had no part in creating. Only my culture, not my experience, insists that this view is false. When Melanesians describe the reality for them of the dream world, I have no difficulty in recognizing the experiential accuracy of their descriptions. It is precisely this phenomenological self-alien character of the dream and many similar altered states of consciousness that I am trying to identify here.

The West demonstrates much unease, even fear, toward such non-self states. If you or I begin to hear voices, or are confronted by waking visions, our first reaction is likely to be "I am losing my mind"; in other words, my self is not in control of my mental apparatus, and so something is very wrong. Despite the counterculture interest of recent decades in drug-induced out-of-mind and out-of-body experiences, mainstream Western culture continues to regard such non-self experiences as pathological. Even in the case of such commonplace events as dreams, the only serious significance usually attributed to them is as symptoms of psychic disturbance.

Numerous anthropological studies of shamanism, spirit possession, trance, and other alternate states of consciousness have now demonstrated that in a great many cultures (Bourguignon 1972, 1976; Peters and Price-Williams 1980, 1983; Locke and Kelly 1985 for reviews of the literatures), including those of Melanesia (see Stephen 1979), these non-self experiences are interpreted in a very different light. Such events are regarded as exterior to the self, but they are not simply exteriorized in the sense that they are given the same epistemological status as events occurring in the external, physical world. They are seen as external to the self, but also as significantly marked off from the ordinary world of living things—events emanating from or pertaining to a supernatural, or sacred, realm. Inner and outer realities (in our sense) are not confused; instead, particular kinds of inner events (in our terms) are categorized as having a special significance beyond that of the individual self.

Can we identify here a common, possibly universal, area of human mental functioning which, on the level of the individual's most basic perception of sensory data, is experienced as external to his or her own mentation? How this externality is interpreted is a matter of cultural variation. But it is to the area of the sacred—of spirit forces and beings —that these self-alien mental experiences relate most noticeably in non-Western cultures, and, we should not forget, in the religious traditions of the West as well.

William James's classic study (1958) argues that the great religious traditions of the world are grounded in the inner experience of the individual— dreams, visions, and states—that he had to acknowledge were regarded as pathological according to the scientific opinion of the day. His data convinced him that the religious sense of the existence of a powerful, creative, and transformative Other arose from the subconscious mind. Unlike Freud (1927), who was to assert that such conviction was mere illusion, James (1958:189–190) proposed that the subconscious was a source of (psychological) creativity and power that was manifested in religious conversions and revelations, and transformations in individual consciousness. The fact that such automatisms as obsessive ideas or delusions might spring from the same source as religious conversions did not, in James's view, vitiate the positive value of the latter (1958:194):

> [W]hat is attained [in conversion] is often an altogether new level of spiritual vitality, a relatively heroic level, in which impossible things have become possible, and new energies and endurances are shown. The personality is changed, the man *is* born anew, whether or not his psychological idiosyncrasies are what give the particular shape to his metamorphosis.

Though he explicitly excluded tribal religion from his survey, recent anthropological studies of shamanism and possession would indicate that James's conclusions concerning the importance of individual experience in the great religious traditions applies equally, if not more so, to nonliterate societies. (In reading the above passage, one cannot but be struck by its precise relevance to Samuel, the subject of Donald Tuzin's chapter.)

In addition to religious experience, another area of Western culture wherein one finds recognition of a powerful, creative Other is, of course, that of the literary and artistic imagination. The following extract from a letter of George Sand to Gustave Flaubert gives witness to the artist's intimate sense of such an Other:

> I have never ceased to wonder at the way you torment yourself over your writing. Is it just fastidiousness on your part? There is so little to show for it
> . . . As to style, I certainly do not worry myself, as you do, over that. The wind blowest as it listeth through my old harp. *My* style has its ups and its

downs, its sounding harmonies, and its failures. I do not, fundamentally, much mind, so long as the *emotion* comes through. But it is no use my trying to screw it out of myself. It is the *other* who sings through me, well or badly, as the case may be. When I begin to think of all that, I get frightened, and tell myself that I count for nothing, for nothing at all . . . Let the wind blow a little through *your* strings. I think you fret about it all much more than you should, and that you ought to let the *other* have his say more often. Everything would work out all right, and it would be a great deal less exhausting for you. (Maurois 1954:428)[4]

(Shades here of the effortless creativity of Gebusi mediums reported by Bruce Knauft!)

Charles Rycroft (1979:66–67), in drawing attention to the similarities between dreams and the imaginative products of writers and artists, observes that the source of both are felt to be impersonal—both are the creations of some "wider Self." The dream, he points out, is a paradox in that it is both self and not-self; that, of course, is from the viewpoint of our epistemology. Thus, the very experience of the dream involves an awareness of the existence of another self. Since it is not me, my conscious self, that creates the dream, it must be some other part of myself. He further notes (1979:161), "It would be possible to cite innumerable examples of writers who have used their dreams as the initial source of their inspiration."

The association of dreams and other not-self states with a powerful, creative, and sometimes destructive Other—be it the artist's "divine" inspiration or the revelations of the religious truths of prophet or convert, are themes by no means confined to other cultures, though this is often forgotten or overlooked in the prevailing rationalistic view that such states are associated only with pathology.

How to Interpret Self-Alien Experiences

It would be facile to assume that in every culture, or for every individual, these states are interpreted as self-alien; yet there appears, as Rycroft (1979:-66–67) points out, to be an existential self-alien quality to the dream and similar states, which we can reasonably expect may apply universally—an expectation that is supported by the available cross-cultural evidence. If we are dealing with a human universal (and I stress that this remains a proposition to be tested), how are we to interpret such states, what analytic frameworks are available to make cross-cultural comparisons?

Subjective States and Pathology

The problem we immediately encounter is that it is almost impossible to discuss dreams, visions, and similar states without employing terms that imply pathology or a regressed mode of thought: hallucinations, pseudo-hallucinations, dissociated states, unconscious fantasy, symptoms, primary process thinking. The classic Freudian viewpoint maintains that such self-alien states represent the wish fulfillments of the unconscious (Rycroft 1972:36–37, 60), that they are essentially maladaptive or pathological, and are constructed from id desires and superego disguise. Even those who do not accept the Freudian orthodoxy will find available terminology loaded with negative connotations (a circumstance that creates no little difficulty for me throughout this essay); I have already referred to the general unease in Western cultures toward self-alien experiences.

If nothing but the unruly id lies behind experiences that play such important roles in world religions, then anthropologists and other scholars of comparative religion are likely to find themselves backed into a corner where they have little choice but to accept a Freudian interpretation along the lines indicated by La Barre (1972:50) in his powerful anthropological study of the origins of religion: "Sacred culture is in fact a complex of defence mechanisms, usually diffused from an identifiable charismatic individual, and usually a paranoid one."

This dilemma is clearly recognized by the contributors to this volume, but their difficulties in avoiding it are also apparent. Bruce Knauft must insist, for example, that the Gebusi medium's dissociation is "culturally constituted" and not a "symptom"; Donald Tuzin must insist that the prophet, Samuel, is not insane, despite his bizarre visionary experience. I struggle with the seeming fit, yet lack of fit, between Freudian theory and Mekeo dreaming. Eytan Bercovitch shows the inadequacies of theories of unconscious projection to deal with Nalumin witchcraft.

Rycroft (1979:39) observes that Freudian theory creates similar problems for the interpretation of artistic creativity:

> Freud expended much ink and energy trying to prove that artists are neurotics, only reluctantly abandoning the attempt when in 1928 he wrote: 'Before the problem of the creative artist analysis must, alas, lay down its arms.' But, I am suggesting, the creative artist only constituted for him a problem . . . because he had started by assuming that dreams are symptoms and that waking imaginative activity resembles dreaming and must, therefore, also be a symptom. Things would have been much easier for him and his followers if he had made the opposite assumption, viz. that imagination is a normal, universal function or faculty, that dreaming is its sleeping form, and that, if people have neurotic conflicts, these will manifest themselves in their dreams and their waking imaginative products.

I shall later return to Rycroft's intriguing suggestion that dreams are best regarded simply as a special form of imaginative activity.

Altered States of Consciousness

More recently, the concept of altered states of consciousness has provided a different perspective. Its ready acceptance into the anthropological literature is attested to by the ever-mounting number of publications dealing with the topic (for reviews, see Bourguignon 1972, 1976; Peters and Price-Williams 1980, 1983; Noll 1985; Locke and Kelly 1985). Phenomena that had previously been regarded as pathological could be interpreted in more positive terms, in accord with what anthropologists knew to be the emic evaluation. It thus became easier to deal with the widely attested to importance of dreams, trance, possession, waking visions, and other unusual states in tribal religions generally, and in religious innovation and change especially (see Bourguignon 1973; Lewis 1971; La Barre 1972; Stephen 1979 for reviews).

The locus of debate was removed from the Freudian unconscious to the possibility of many different forms of consciousness. Attention focused on the range of different states cross-culturally, and how were they induced and culturally shaped. Such a proliferation of states has emerged from these endeavors that it seems some linking process—psychological, psychodynamic, or psychophysiological—must underlie these apparently discrete phenomena (Peters and Price-Williams 1983; Locke and Kelly 1985).

Altered consciousness has no doubt proven to be a fruitful concept in opening up new lines of debate and inquiry. It is a term used frequently in the following pages, and one I have relied on heavily in previous writing before coming to the conclusion that it obscures two important processes: the imaginative constructions produced by the person experiencing a possession or trance and the self-alien aspect of this experience.

Noll (1985) has recently drawn attention to imaginative constructions, demonstrating that most of the altered states studied by anthropologists involve the generation of complex imagery narratives. Yet the interaction between individual imaginative creativity and cultural instruction has been little investigated. (This, of course, is one of the main themes of this collection and is, in my opinion, one of its most important contributions; see also Tedlock 1987a). Furthermore, though such states are well recognized as validations for innovation, anthropologists rarely seem to have taken very seriously emic representations of them as the locus of a special sort of creativity (Stephen 1979), or if they do (Wagner 1972), it is to reduce it to a cultural level.

A more important criticism of the model itself is that the notion of altered consciousness tends to obscure the experiential quality—the self-alien aspect of the experience. Imaginative narratives of dream, trance, or possession are not constructed in consciousness, even of an altered kind. The origins of the events of the dream, or the imagery of the vision, remain outside one's awareness. As Rycroft (1979:66–67) puts it:

> Since we are unaware, while dreaming, that we are ourselves creating the dream that we are 'having', all psychologies that attribute meaning to dreams have to postulate the existence of two selves . . . The former self is aware of its own identity and refers to itself as 'I' or 'me', the latter self . . . is experienced as impersonal and tends to be referred to as 'it' or 'one'.

The same could be said of other kinds of self-alien experience. Altered consciousness implies, by contrast, a single, continuous self experiencing varying modes of consciousness, and hides the fact that some agency other than the conscious self produces the visionary narrative. If we reject the notion of the unconscious, then we must at least recognize the existence of different selves—one that experiences consciousness of varying kinds, and another, or others, outside conscious awareness.

If the self does not construct the narratives of dreams, waking visions, spirit possession, and mediumship, but merely observes and acts in them as if they were external reality, then who is the hidden dramatist? Who constructs props, scene, and dialogue? If we reject unconscious wish fulfillment as the motivating force, where are we to turn?

We might at this point consider Jung's idea of the unconscious mind as a source of spontaneous and creative imagery, as I attempt to do in my chapter on the Mekeo concept of the soul. But, as I point out there, Jung provides an intuitive interpretive approach—one that defies simple definition—rather than an analytic model. Although I think Jung's insights will become increasing important to anthropologists as they turn their attention to the realm of the "imaginal" (Tedlock 1987a), his viewpoints are yet to be established on independent grounds.

Cognitive and Information-Processing Models

It is not my intention to return the debate to the Freudian unconscious. Instead, perhaps we can look beyond Freud's view of the unconscious as "the cellar . . . to which fearful and painful memories are consigned by a process of repression" (Bateson 1973:108), to a more extensive, information-processing model of it.

Bateson (1973:115–116) explains the logical fallacy of assuming that all thought takes place in consciousness:

> A very brief consideration shows that it is not conceivably possible for any system to be totally conscious. Suppose that on the screen of consciousness there are reports from many parts of the total mind, and consider the addi-

tion to consciousness of those reports necessary to cover what is, at a given stage of evolution, not already covered. This addition will involve a very great increase in the circuit structure of the brain but will still not achieve total coverage. The next step will be to cover the processes and events occurring in the circuit structure which we have just added. And so on . . . *economy* in consciousness will be of the first importance. No organism can afford to be conscious of matters with which it could deal at unconscious levels.

If Bateson's view has had comparatively little influence on the thinking of cultural anthropologists, it is becoming increasingly influential in cognitive psychology, and in many other areas, as the basis of a newly emerging model of mind. It is now well established that a great deal of cognition must take place outside conscious awareness (Bowers and Meichenbaum 1984; Dixon 1981). Information-processing views of an unconscious mind are beginning to offer some new perspectives on self-alien experiences.

In the following discussion, in addition to depth psychology and cross-cultural studies of altered states of consciousness, I will draw upon evidence based on neurophysiological and pharmacological studies of hallucinations, sleep/dream laboratory research, brain laterality studies, psychological studies of daydreaming, experimental research into hypnosis, cognitive approaches to dreams and dissociative phenomena, and studies of imagery techniques in Western psychotherapy. My reason for venturing so far beyond the usual boundaries of anthropological inquiry is that these other disciplines can throw valuable light on the issues considered here. The concept of autonomous imagination could be outlined solely on the basis of anthropological literature, but I wish to show that it can be supported on a far broader basis of evidence. Moreover, the concept can be given much more specific content and a wider applicability in the light of these interdisciplinary findings.

A New View of Hallucinations

Though the term *hallucination* has long implied pathology or a derangement of perceptual or mental processes, research in many fields is now making such a view obsolete. It has been shown that the mind's capacity to produce vivid images with the appearance of external reality —"perceptions which lack appropriate sensory stimuli" (West 1975; cf. Reber 1985:315)—arises from the normal information-processing operations of the brain and is not necessarily associated with pathology or dysfunction. It is precisely this capacity to produce vivid imagery that appears to come not from the conscious self, but from some Other, that concerns me here and characterizes the experiences I have been describing.

Experimental investigation of sensory deprivation, of sleep and dreams, and brain neurophysiology have combined to establish the normality of hallucinatory experience under specific conditions. Normal individuals experience hallucinations during sensory deprivation (Siegel and West 1975; Bowers and Meichenbaum 1984). The regular pattern that dreaming takes in normal individuals (Jones 1976; Kramer 1969) indicates that this pattern is determined by basic physiological and neurophysiological processes, rather than unconscious psychological conflict (Cohen 1979:126–134; Cartwright 1978:74–78, 81; Fishbein 1981).

Hallucinations have been clearly linked to levels of cortical arousal of the brain in relation to sensory input (West 1975; Winters 1975:53; Cartwright 1978), a finding that provides the basis for an information-processing model. West (1975:301), for example, proposes that in ordinary waking consciousness the mind is fully engaged in processing in-coming sensory data; but if sensory input drops below a certain level while cortical arousal is maintained at a high level, then previously recorded percepts stored in memory may "enter awareness and be experienced as fantasies, illusions, visions, dreams or hallucinations." Sleep researcher Cartwright (1969:369–370, 1978:66) suggests much the same model.

From a different perspective, experimental studies of daydreaming and imagination have strongly argued the normality and adaptive value of fantasy (another negatively laden term) in waking thought. Singer (1976, 1977) draws attention to the fact that the ordinary stream of consciousness is interlaced with imagery and fantasy. His information-processing view of imagery thought is similar to the hallucination model (Singer 1974:188–200). External sensory information and internally generated imagery must both occupy the same "channel" within the system, he suggests; when external input is reduced, there is thus more "channel space" for reviewing internally generated material.

Information Processing versus Primary Process

In arguing that hallucinations and imagery thought arise from the normal information-processing procedures of the brain, these various approaches remove the necessity of accepting the Freudian unconscious as the sole instigator. Furthermore, they serve to underline the logical difficulties inherent in Freud's distinction between primary and secondary process thinking.[5] The strict separation implied in such a dichotomy— between conscious and unconscious, adaptive and maladaptive, discursive and symbolic, logical and illogical—is no longer convincing in view of several findings.

Not only have Singer and others (Singer and Pope 1978a, 1978b) demonstrated the ways in which waking thought is interwoven with imagery, and that fantasy has positive, adaptive value; but the experimental sleep/dream research has shown that even during sleep the imagery of dreaming is only one form of mental activity taking place. In non-REM sleep a more logical, sequential mode of thought, closer to that of waking thought, takes place (Foulkes 1966; Cartwright 1978:63–70). Thus, imagery and discursive thought seem to occur in both waking and sleeping.

Brain laterality studies have also drawn attention to the complex admixture of imagery and discursive thought involved in normal mental functioning. The discovery that the two hemispheres of the brain appear to be differentially specialized—the left half dealing with verbal and quantitative information, the right with imagery and spatial data—was initially taken to support the Freudian division of primary and secondary processes (Galin 1974; Fromm 1979a:102). More careful investigation, however, has revealed the extremely complex interaction between the two hemispheres involved in all cognitive tasks (Dimond 1972:193–200; Springer and Deutsch 1981:179–203: Corballis 1983:57–64).

From a different perspective, these findings contribute to the criticisms of Rycroft (1968) and others that symbolic thinking is by no means characteristic only of a regressed mode of thought, but is equally present in abstract mathematical and scientific thought.

Anthropology, too, has made important contributions here. The great opus of Lévi-Strauss and his followers constitutes a powerful testimony to the unconscious logical structures and transformations of myths and cultural symbolism. Psychoanalytically informed anthropologists are revealing that what in Western culture are regarded as the forbidden and disguised wishes of the unconscious, in other cultures may be the subject of explicit acting out in public ritual (Herdt 1981, 1982a; Kracke 1987b). Evidently, then, unconscious thought may be logical, and conscious thought may be wishful. Consciousness and the unconscious provide no stable boundaries across which to map modes of thought; we are in need of more finely drawn distinctions between variations in symbolic and imaginative thought.

The information-processing model variously proposed by West, Cartwright, Singer, and others more satisfactorily accounts for our present data than one tied exclusively to repressed drives, wish fulfillment, and sharp distinctions between primary and secondary processes. Furthermore, we are freed from the imperative of assuming that imagery thought is inferior, or pathological, or exclusively the mode of the unconscious. It can be accepted as an alternative mode of thought, one that has important adaptive and creative aspects.

The Term *Hallucination*

Despite all these developments, the term *hallucination* remains problematic in that many still insist it should only be used when the person is deluded as to the reality of the image he "sees." It has, however, been pointed out by Sheehan

(1979:384–386) that a subject may perceive an image as having the vividness of a sensory perception and yet be still aware that what he perceives does not represent physical reality. I intend to follow Sheehan (1979) and West (1975:288) here and use the term to mean an "apparent perception of external object not actually present" (*Concise Oxford Dictionary*), *without the implication of delusion*. In this sense the phenomena under discussion all represent hallucinatory experience.

Autonomous Imagination

Hallucinations and Imagination

To return to Rycroft's (1979:39) idea, quoted earlier, Freud might have saved himself and his followers much difficulty if he had treated dreams not as symptoms but as products of the imagination, and concluded that pathology, where it exists, will be reflected in both the waking and sleeping thoughts of the disturbed individual. A trend toward regarding dreams and other hallucinatory experience as imaginative productions is now identifiable in several fields.

Though long dominated by Freudian approaches, interest has returned to the manifest, narrative content of dreams (Jones 1976:74). Different theoretical approaches now highlight the importance of dreaming in problem solving and information processing—and creativity, both scientific and artistic (see Jones 1976:164–171; Cartwright 1978; Cohen 1979; Ullman and Zimmerman 1979; French and Fromm 1964; Greenberg 1970; Pearlman 1970; Krippner and Hughes 1970; Hadfield 1974:113–116; Rothenberg 1979:35–40). Much of the stress on dream thought providing answers to practical problems is, perhaps, overstated and reflects our Western cultural values. Although dreams may sometimes provide answers to practical problems, what seems more obvious—and more striking—is the ability demonstrated in dreams to create complex narrative, characters, and plot. It is the dream as a creative production—in other words, the imaginative aspect of the dream—that is emerging.

Experimental studies of hypnosis are now also emphasizing the role of imagination. In contrast to earlier views that the good hypnotic subject is passive and gullible, recent research has revealed the complex cognitive and imaginative skills the subject must bring to the hypnotic task (Hilgard 1977; J. Hilgard 1979; Bowers 1976:115–128; Sheehan 1979; Sheehan and McConkey 1982:106 ff.; Barber 1979; Barber, Spanos and Chaves 1974; Orne 1979; Fromm and Shor 1979a). Many studies indicate that such subjects also demonstrate an ability for vivid imagery and imagination outside the hypnotic context. Bowers and Bowers (1979) have argued strongly for a correlation between hypnotizability and creativity.

Studies of spontaneously occurring dissociative states, such as automatic writing, multiple personalities, and spirit mediumship, further demonstrate a capacity to construct elaborate imaginative narratives outside conscious awareness. Though such states are usually regarded as pathological, eminent hypnosis researcher Hilgard (1977:27, 40) suggests that the emergent personalities may demonstrate greater maturity and be better adapted than the original personality. Also, the pronouncements and revelations of automatic writing and spirit mediumship sometimes may be far superior in intellectual content to the usual achievements of the individual concerned (Jung 1977:89–90; Hilgard 1977:-136; Ellenberger 1970).

A Unique Kind of Imaginative Process

I agree with Rycroft, Barber (1979), and others who, from their various perspectives, argue that hallucinations can be best understood as imaginative products, but the point I wish to stress is that a very distinctive kind of imagination is at work here.

Since imagination is a process that itself is little understood, there are obvious problems in distinguishing between different kinds. One cannot really disagree with Rycroft's (1979:39) observations: "Imaginative activity, waking or sleeping, is independent of the will. . . . Awake we can make ourselves do things or make ourselves think about things, but we can only let ourselves imagine and may be surprised by what we find ourselves imagining."

All imaginative activity seems somehow to originate outside the self. Yet surely there are significant, indeed quite dramatic, differences. It may be that artists and other creative individual experience their imaginings as vividly externalized (cf. Freud 1908), but for most of us, waking imagination has little of the compelling externality of the dream. Price-Williams (1987:247) observes, "In our age and time the term 'imagination' has come to mean a wispy and evanescent process that lacks flesh-and-blood substance."

The *Concise Oxford Dictionary* defines imagination as "a mental faculty forming images of external objects not present to the senses. . . ." It is difficult to see in such a definition what in ordinary thought does not involve imagination. The *Penguin Dictionary of Psychology* (Reber 1985:345) distinguishes between the possible emphasis or orientations of the train of thought: imagination can be purely wishful and fanciful, or it can be directed to concrete, reality-directed tasks. This is often indicated by restricting "imagination" to the latter and "fantasy" to the former (Rycroft 1968:52). But this is not the distinction I have in mind. The Jungian notion of active imagination, Mary Watkins's (1984) concept of waking dream—a state in which the lucidity of consciousness is combined with imagery arising spontaneously from the unconscious—comes much closer. Obeyesekere's (1981:169ff) concept of hyptomantic consciousness, a creative state of dream, vision, or possession wherein subjective, private symbols are transformed into shared cultural truths, approaches the same territory from a different direction. All three, however, describe specific states of awareness in which spontaneous imagery enters consciousness, whereas I am referring to the stream of imagery itself.

Recently, Price-Williams (1987) has identified a unique imaginative mode operating in what he refers to as the waking dream. Drawing on the nineteenth-century idea of the mythopoetic function of the unconscious—a presumed capacity of the unconscious mind to create narratives and myths manifested in dreams and waking reverie—on Jungian concepts of active imagination, and the European therapeutic tradition of guided imagery, he draws attention to the vivid reality given to internal states and imagery in such contexts as hypnosis in Western culture, and trance and possession in non-Western cultures. In these states, he points out (1987:255), "The sense of reality is reinforced by not only participating in the imaginative productions 'in the head' so to speak . . . but by acting out the internal events." Thus, imaginative events become an external, autonomous, and lived reality. He pinpoints precisely the quality of this unique imaginative mode.

But from where do these imaginative events originate? Instead of identifying their source as the mythopoetic function as does Price-Williams (1987: 259–261), or the Freudian unconscious, with the all-theoretical implications that either entails, I wish to take up the information-processing model of imagery thought just outlined.

Autonomous Imagination and Imagining

My proposal is that a unique process of imagination or imagery thought takes place outside conscious awareness. Its products may arise spontaneously into awareness (taking the form of dreams, waking visions, and similar experiences); or they may be brought into conscious awareness deliberately (as in hypnosis, or induced possession and shamanic ecstasy). To indicate its independent, self-alien quality, I refer to autonomous imagination. (Price-Williams also refers to the "autonomous nature of the internal events.")

We need to distinguish the process of constructing the dream or vision, which always remains outside consciousness and hidden from the self, from the imagery produced by it, which may rise into conscious but is experienced as originating outside the self. By autonomous imagination, I refer to the process of construction itself. "Autonomous imagining" will be used to indicate its products—dreams, visions, waking dreams, active imagination, and the like.

Since the process itself always remains outside consciousness, we can only gain knowledge of it from its products as they enter conscious awareness, or influence it. (This, of course, has always been a dilemma of depth psychology in investigating the unconscious).

Three Key Characteristics of Autonomous Imagining

Autonomous imagining is different from imagination operating in ordinary awareness not only in that its images are vividly externalized and have their own momentum—a feature that Price-Williams clearly establishes—but in that it also has a much greater freedom and richness of imaginative inventiveness, and displays a different access to memory. Another highly important feature is its special responsiveness to external, cultural influence and direction. Furthermore, it exerts a special influence over involuntary mental and somatic processes.

These characteristics are richly illustrated in the New Guinean religious phenomena described in the following chapters. But here I wish to show that we are dealing with an intrinsic psychological process identifiable in etic terms, and demonstrable on the basis of data drawn from Western psychology and experience. For the time being, I will make only passing reference to the New Guinean context, but I will return to it in the final chapter.

The distinctiveness of autonomous imagining as a mode of thought

The images of dreams, trance, and hallucination seem to arise of their own accord and are vividly externalized. We are all familiar with the inexorable character of dreams. We cannot alter the script but are compelled to move with the dream action, no matter how terrifying or repellent it may seem to us. This is also true of hypnosis, as Bowers (1976: 108) observes: "Hypnotic subjects are not actively trying, in any ordinary sense, to behave purposefully in accordance with . . . hypnotic suggestion. Instead, suggested events are experienced as happening to them in ways that would require active effort to resist."

Price-Williams (1987) has made much the same points, but I think the argument can be taken even further. Hypnotic imagery can be maintained even despite powerful opposing stimuli; it can, for example, be sustained in the face of—indeed used to block—severe physical pain. Research on subjective experience in hypnosis by Sheehan and McConkey (1982:112–116, 143–144, 147) has shown that in circumstances where subjects reported being frightened by the hypnotic suggestion, or desired not to comply with it, they still felt themselves confronted by the suggested events as an external reality.

In Western religious experience, we find a similar externalizing and vivid reality given to the presence of the sacred Other, even in situations falling short of hallucination. William James (1958:71) wrote: "Such is the human ontological imagination, and such is what it brings to birth. Unpicturable beings are realized, and realized with an intensity almost like that of an hallucination. They determine our vital attitude as decisively as the vital attitude of lovers is determined by the habitual sense, by which each is haunted, of the other being in the world."

Outside the great religious traditions, the spirit medium and the shaman are called upon by their communities to dramatize for the benefit of the group their encounters with the spirit realm, a circumstance that had led some anthropologists to interpret spirit possession and shamanic ecstasy as essentially ritual drama (cf. Price-Williams 1987). But the fact that the mediums are more than acting, that their visions become more real than external reality, is indicated in the imperviousness to fear and pain demonstrated during their performance: fire walking, piercing parts of the body with knives or spikes, and various other ordeals that are commonly part of the shamanic performance (Eliade 1964). We have no examples in the following chapters of such painful ordeals, but the Gebusi medium who is able to perform strenuously throughout a night-long séance and emerge in the morning as fresh as if he had had a full night's sleep comes to mind here.

It is the compelling quality of the imagery of the dream, the hypnotic state, the religious experience, the shamanic vision—imagery so compelling, so powerful it can even override all demands of external reality—that marks off autonomous imagining from imagining in ordinary waking consciousness.

Autonomous imagining is also characterized by a richness and freedom of invention. This is evidenced merely in the dreams of ordinary people. We are inclined to dismiss our dreams because of their nonsensical character, and thus tend to overlook the fact that we regularly invent imaginative tales and fanciful events in dreams that we would be incapable of thinking up during our waking hours. Take, for example, the following dream of a very down-to-earth person. In the dream a friend had recently purchased her first word processor. When she sat down at the keyboard, instead of typing in her commands, the computer flashed up commands to her and she became its puppet, moving and acting as it directed—"Dance!" and she danced, "Smile!" and she smiled, "Weep!" and she wept, a mindless slave to the electronic master. A fine plot for a science fiction story, but the dreamer has never written short stories in his waking hours, and would be quite nonplussed if asked to do so. I recall dream scenes of my own that would make wonderful visual art works, if only I possessed the technical skills with which to translate my dream imagery into some concrete medium! The use many creative artists make of their dreams (Rycroft 1979; Hadfield 1974; Rothenberg 1979:40–52; Ullman and Zimmerman 1979:8–9) has already been noted; my point here is that if dreams are looked at as imaginative products, even those of us who are not artists can be seen to exercise a richer imaginative facility in dreams than is available to us on waking.

An increase in imaginative richness and inventiveness also takes place under hypnosis (Hilgard 1977). This has been observed in age regression, in which a subject is instructed during hypnosis to relive some period in his or her childhood. The highly convincing and detailed acting out of childhood experiences produced by many subjects was at first taken to indicate that accurate memories of childhood events were involved. Further research (Hilgard 1977:46–59; Sheehan and McConkey 1982:150) revealed that although memories of actual events might be incorporated, the age regressions were in fact fabrications—but such ingenious ones that they persuasively portrayed a child of the appropriate age. The subjects were quite unaware of any deception.

The experiences of reincarnation sometimes elicited under hypnosis reveal the same pattern (Hilgard 1977:51 ff). Events the subject had read about, or been told about and long since forgotten, were woven into an elaborate narrative. This then emerged in the subject's consciousness as memories of events that occurred in a previous existence. A similar facility of invention occurs in spontaneous dissociated states (Hilgard 1977; Ellenberger 1970). Presentable novels, travelers' tales, lengthy occult philosophies, even musical symphonies, have originated from the pens of automatic writers, who in ordinary waking consciousness could scarcely compose a line of poetry or sustain an abstract discourse. The songs of the Gebusi spirit medium described in Bruce Knauft's chapter, and the visions of the Ilahita prophet, Samuel, recounted by Donald Tuzin, provide excellent examples of a like mode.

Much of this freer inventiveness seems to arise from a different access to memory. The hypnosis research clearly indicates this. The fact that repressed material might be retrieved under hypnosis led to hopes that hypnosis could provide the means of accurately recalling all past experience (Hilgard 1977:46–48, 51–49; Sheehan and McConkey 1982; 150). Later studies demonstrated, as in the case of age regression and "reincarnation" experiences, the extent to which forgotten memories of real events might be combined with purely fictional ones, indicating clearly the different access to memory prevailing under hypnosis. Even more strikingly, hypnosis has been used therapeutically to alter consciously retained memory (Hilgard 1977:44–46, 58–59). By instructing the hypnotized patient to relive the trauma, the therapist alters the "script" so that the negative emotions attached to the event become inappropriate to the revised memory, and the patient is freed from negative associations formerly attached to the experience.

Further evidence of this differential access to memory is provided by cases of multiple personalities emerging under hypnosis, and spontaneously as well (Hilgard 1977:27, 30–31, 33). These alter egos may have access to the memories of the conscious personality, in addition to memories of their own, whereas the conscious personality has no knowledge of the intruder(s). In shamanism and spirit possession, also, various complex patterns of mutual memories and amnesias are reported (Lewis 1971; Field 1969). Bruce Knauft shows, for example, that the Gebusi spirit medium claims to have no knowledge of the events of the séance.

The responsiveness of autonomous imagining to external influence and direction

Another highly significant characteristic is the responsiveness of autonomous imagining to external direction, whether this comes from another person, arises from the cultural and social context, or comes from the conscious intention of the subject. This can be observed in the suggestibility psychologists identify as an important feature of altered states of consciousness in general (Ludwig 1969; Sheehan and McConkey 1982:7; Peters and Price-Williams 1983), and of hypnosis in particular (Sheehan and McConkey 1982:7; Bowers 1976:85–109; Shor 1965). In such states the subject demonstrates a readiness to invest external suggestions with hallucinatory reality; when, for example, he is told that a long-lost friend is present, he sees the friend actually appear.

Studies of drug-induced hallucinations have established the significance of social context and cultural beliefs in shaping drug experiences (Siegal and West 1975). Furthermore, anthropological studies of shamanism, spirit possession, and trance have emphasized the importance of cultural beliefs and symbols in molding all kinds of visionary experience. Indeed, the great variety found in the cultural patterning of such states demonstrates their malleability and responsiveness to external influence.

Even dreaming, which is usually considered to be totally involuntary, is influenced by external context and suggestion. In many cultures gaining a degree of conscious control over dreaming is the aim of various esoteric disciplines (Evans-Wentz 1967; Watkins 1984:21–24). This is an important aspect of Mekeo magic as I show here and elsewhere (Stephen 1987b); Gilbert Herdt demonstrates a similar importance of dreaming in Sambia shamanism (1977; this volume).

The responsiveness of dreaming to external context is confirmed by experimental investigation in laboratory studies of sleep and dreaming, where it has been found that dreams occurring at home, under usual conditions, vary noticeably from electronically monitored dreams recorded in the sleep laboratory (Cartwright 1978:46–49). Posthypnotic suggestion has been used successfully to influence dreaming (Tart 1969b). It has often been observed in analytic practice (Evans 1979:158) that once the patient begins to pay attention to his dreams, a sort of dialogue with them begins to emerge, and that different analytic techniques tend to elicit different kinds of dreams and dream symbols that vary according to the theoretical bent of the therapist—phallic symbols for the Freudian, shadows and animas for the Jungian!

Suggestibility under hypnosis is often attributed to a breakdown in reality testing, leading to the subjects' inability to distinguish between mental events and physical reality (Shor 1965; Bowers 1976:94; Bowers and Bowers 1979: 366–367). If so, it is remarkable that the only event confused in this way is the hypnotist's suggestion, a circumstance that suggests focused attention rather than generalized confusion. Moreover, recent studies by Sheehan and McConkey (1982) have presented strong evidence to indicate that the hypnotic subject is not confused about the reality status of his imagery. At one level he is aware that these images are not real; nevertheless he experiences them as vividly externalized (1982: 121–128;141–150). This suggests to me that hypnosis involves not a confusion of inner and outer events, but a focusing on an internally generated stream of imagery—a stream of imagery that readily takes up themes presented to it by an external agent, be it the hypnotist or, in the case of auto-hypnosis, the conscious intention of the subject.

Responsiveness to external direction enables the stream of imagery thought emerging in hypnosis, and other altered states of consciousness, to be used to conscious ends. In hypnosis, and various Western psychotherapeutic techniques, the subject is instructed to relax and to visualize certain suggested imagery until it takes on its own momentum and seems to exist independently of the subject's will or intent (Hilgard 1977:163). These images are then directed by the suggestions of the therapist, with the aim of bringing about some somatic, motivational, or behavioral change in the patient.

In other therapies imagery is brought into consciousness and is simply observed, without attempting to guide it (Singer 1974; Singer and Pope 1978a). For example, in Jungian "active imagination" (Greenleaf 1978) or Watkins's (1984) "waking dreams," the intention is to bring random imagery into consciousness to allow communication from this other level of imaginal awareness. Similar patterns can be observed in the various cross-cultural uses of altered states of consciousness. For example, the Amerindian "vision quest" and various meditative practices (Watkins 1984; Taylor 1978) aim at allowing the Other to communicate with consciousness. In contrast, in shamanism and controlled possession, specific hallucinatory experience is sought and guided to culturally determined ends—be these curing, divination, or prophesy (Price-Williams 1975a, 1987; Peters and Price-Williams 1980), as we see here in the case of the Sambia and Nalumin shamans, the Gebusi medium, the Mekeo dream diviner, and the Ilahita prophet.

It should be kept in mind that although the individual (such as the shaman, or the patient using self-hypnosis) may intentionally seek to activate autonomous imagining, once its imagery is brought into consciousness, it is experienced as something quite independent of self: its compliance with external suggestion, expectation, or demand is not mediated by conscious contrivance. In other words, the construction of the imagery responds directly to the external agent, without the intervention of the conscious self. The hypnotic subject, for example, is not aware that he is imagining his arm is getting light, or that the hypnotist is suggesting the arm is becoming light; instead, he actually feels his arm rising of its own accord.

These different uses of autonomous imagining reveal a two-way responsiveness to external and internal events. Via autonomous imagining, ideas and information not available to the conscious self may be expressed and communicated to others, without the intervention of the conscious self. We see this in the case of a possessed spirit medium communicating spirit pronouncements to the group. Reciprocally, the external influence of others (the group, the hypnotist, cultural instructions) is taken up by autonomous imagining and incorporated into the imagery it produces, without the conscious self being aware of this. We see this, for example, in hypnotic suggestion. Thus, autonomous imagining provides a channel of communication whereby inner and outer influences on the conscious self are combined in a stream of imagery, imagery this had no part in creating.

Striking illustrations of this sensitivity of autonomous imaging to external cultural influence on the one hand, and inner emotional states on the other—and its capacity to weave both into a new imaginative creation—are to be found in the following chapters, particularly in Bruce Knauft's description of the Gebusi séance and Donald Tuzin's analysis of the visions of Samuel, a Sepik Christian prophet.

The influence of autonomous imagining on involuntary mental and somatic processes

If autonomous imagining communicates from inner processes taking place outside ordinary awareness, then it is likely that it also communicates back to them. This seems clearly indicated in the context of healing. Spontaneous and induced hallucinations—dreams, waking visions, possession, spirit mediumship, and the like—are closely associated with the health, sickness, and healing of mind and body in modern and traditional cultures. In non-Western cultures, such phenomena are given wide significance as indicators of both physical and psychic disturbance. They are induced by healers in the diagnosis of illness and in the performance of healing rites (Eliade 1964; Kiev 1964; Bourguignon 1973, 1976). Kakar (1983) notes the worldwide association of possession states with healing, and Melanesia is no different in this (Stephen 1979), as we shall see in the performance of the Sambia shaman, the Nalumin healer, the Mekeo sorcerer, and the Gebusi medium.

In Western cultures dreams and other hallucinatory experiences have been given prominence as diagnostic symptoms of psychological disturbance. They are regarded as communicating—in imagery and symbols —information about bodily and intrapsychic processes not available to the patient's consciousness. It is often overlooked, however, that imagery techniques are also commonly used in Western clinical practice for psychotherapy and healing.

Hypnosis has a wide range of practical therapeutic uses (Bowers 1976:21–40;140–152). Behavior modification therapies use it in the treatment of such disorders as stuttering, phobias, and obesity, and such undesirable habits as smoking. It is also used to control pain in surgical procedures, and to treat many physical disorders such as asthma and various skin complaints. In psychotherapy it is used to retrieve repressed material, relive traumatic events, alter memories of traumatic experiences, and treat hysterical symptoms and illnesses (Hilgard 1977:44–46, 58– 59). If the practical results of hypnosis have been exaggerated by unqualified practitioners and popular gullibility, its effectiveness in specific situations and conditions is attested to by a large body of careful scientific investigation (Sarbin and Slagle 1979).

Other studies (Singer 1974; Singer and Pope 1978a, 1978b) have drawn attention to the important role imagery cultivation plays in contemporary psychoanalytic, psychotherapeutic, and behavior modification techniques. Though they offer competing explanatory theories, these studies provide clear evidence of the powerful influence that imagery and imagining is able to exert on inner psychic processes.

The effects achieved by hypnosis and other imagery techniques are yet to be satisfactorily explained, nevertheless extensive experimental and clinical evidence from many sources indicates the reality of such effects. In view of these findings, arguments put forward by such anthropologists as Lévi-Strauss (1972) and Victor Turner (1967a, 1969) that cultural symbols can be used to communicate to levels of the mind outside conscious awareness cannot be regarded as farfetched.

In his chapter on Sambia shamanism, Gilbert Herdt observes that perhaps Eliade and Jung are correct in their conception that shamanism is an archaic mode of awareness in human beings, an imaginative mode that can alleviate suffering, and heal. It is precisely this that I would identify as autonomous imagining. Via autonomous imagining the inner mental and somatic processes of the individual may be influenced without conscious effort, or even rational understanding on the part of the individual concerned.

Finally, it should be noted that gaining voluntary control over autonomous imagining requires special skills and abilities. Only a comparatively few people are, for example, able to develop the skills necessary to perform the more demanding hypnotic tasks (Hilgard 1965; Bowers 1976:79–84). The use of imagery in Western clinical practice and therapy requires special conditions and guidance from a specially trained therapist. In traditional tribal cultures the shaman and the spirit medium are specialists who use their unusual abilities on behalf of their communities.

Conclusion

The evidence discussed in this chapter indicates that a special kind of imaginative capacity operates outside conscious awareness. It is in touch with levels of mind and body outside the reach of conscious control. At the same time, it is in touch with the external, cultural environment, and responsive to it. This distinctive mode of imaginative construction is capable of drawing on information not present in the individual's consciousness—information derived from both internal and external sources —and shaping it into an imaginative product (dream, vision, or automatism), which then emerges into the individual's consciousness in the form of imagery as seemingly external to self as the images of sensory perception.

The reality of its products, we should note, is neither that of the external, cultural world nor the inner world of one's conscious thoughts and feelings, but something else again, something that weaves the two into a third world, a world as imagined. Yet it is not a realm of consciously contrived imagining, but one that is independent of the conscious self.

Nor is this world constructed by autonomous imagination identical, in analytic terms, with the cultural symbolic worldview, though autonomous imagining may be used to vivify this shared symbolic world, as we see in the dramatic performance of the Gebusi medium and his spirit songs. But autonomous imagining may also be used in the visions of Samuel, the Ilahita prophet, for example, to provide the basis of a new symbolic worldview. Autonomous imagining constructs in dream or waking vision another world that is different from the shared symbolic order that a person experiences in waking consciousness and awareness. It may compete with, conflict with, or be seen to be in harmony with that shared symbolic order. Sacred worlds are thus constructed from an interaction between a shared cultural symbolic world view and the products of the individual's autonomous imagining.

Autonomous imagination presumably is a universal human characteristic, since its products in the form of dreams and visions are such. But it is evident that only certain gifted or specially trained individuals are able to intentionally access and use its products to conscious ends. For the artist, the shaman, and the healer autonomous imagining provides the source of symbols that possess the power to move and motivate others. Ordinary people, however, do not control this capacity. If their dreams constantly trouble them, if unsought visions invade their waking hours, they will seek help to dispel them, regardless of whether they are members of a traditional tribal culture or a modern Western one. If these unwelcome visitations can be neither dispelled nor brought under control, the person may become ill. If they are dispelled, the person is cured; if brought under a degree of volitional control, the former sufferer may become a shaman or a prophet. This powerful Other can be both destructive and creative.

For the creative individual, autonomous imagining seems to provide a reconciliation, a harmonizing, of inner and outer worlds in an imaginative form that also stimulates the imagination of others. There are many striking examples of this in the pages that follow, and I shall return to them in the final chapter. Presumably, in the case of the ordinary person —though the process goes on outside conscious awareness and is rarely registered by consciousness (except as fleeting dreams), or shared with others—a similar adjusting of inner and outer experience is mediated through imaginative means. This point will also be developed further in the final chapter.

It is, I suggest, autonomous imagining that reveals the sacred Other. That is to say, the religious and artistic sense of a powerful and creative Other is grounded in the psychological reality of this special imaginative capacity. Dreams, trance, waking visions, and other hallucinatory experience—are valued and sought after as religious experiences because they allow access to its compelling and influential imagery.

In identifying a special mode of imaginative thought with these various distinctive features, I am attempting to trace broad underlying commonalities in a wide range of apparently very diverse phenomena. There are obviously great differences in the extent to which autonomous imagining is responsive to external influence or to inner forces (the dream versus the hypnotic trance), the degree to which it is consciously directed (involuntary possession versus shamanic trance), the richness of its inventiveness (hallucinations of sensory deprivation versus the religious prophet's visions), its relationship to involuntary mental and somatic events (the conversion symptom versus shamanic healing); nevertheless, all these very different phenomena, when compared with the imagination exercised by ordinary waking awareness, share to some extent the features described here. Autonomous imagining is a capacity that takes a multiplicity of forms and is shaped by culture to many varied uses and ends. Indeed, it is this Protean quality that has masked from us its generic similarity. Only when this generic similarity has been recognized will we be in a position to understand the significance of its multiple forms.

It is true that in specific cases and contexts it may be very difficult to decide when autonomous imagining merges with self-aware, self-directed imagining; as for example, in ordinary daydreaming, what may begin as self-gratifying fantasy may sometimes result in a train of imagined events as self-alien as nighttime dreaming. We are dealing with extremely subtle gradations of inner experience here, inner experience to which our culture provides very little in the way of guidelines (as Kakar 1983 and others remind us). In this essay I am attempting to sketch in broad outlines. Undoubtedly, there are many forms of autonomous imagining, and these combine in many possible ways with self (ego)-directed thought. But I cannot take up all these complexities here.

The following chapters provide many outstanding illustrations of the points and arguments I have raised here. Admitting the broad sweep of my gestalt, I will in the final chapter show how the concept of autonomous imagination and imagining may be developed in the specific context of Melanesian religious experience, especially as revealed in the remarkable ethnographic case studies presented in this book.

NOTES

Acknowledgments. I would like to thank for their comments on an earlier statement of the arguments presented here the members of the Faculty Seminar, Department of Anthropology, University of California, San Diego; I am particularly grateful to Roy D'Andrade, Melford Spiro, Fitz Porter Poole, and Donald Tuzin for their detailed comments and for many stimulating discussions on the topic. I am also indebted to Eleanor Wertheim, Department of Psychology, La Trobe University, for guiding me to the hypnosis literature. My greatest debt is to Gilbert Herdt, who has contributed so much to the ideas presented here, and has continually encouraged and challenged me to clarify my arguments and assumptions in the writing of this chapter.

1. The concept of autonomous imagination has grown out of several years of friendship and discussion with Gilbert Herdt. From this continuing dialogue stem the ideas presented here. The specific formulation of the argument represents, however, my individual viewpoint; I, of course, take responsibility for its shortcomings.

2. I do not wish to become enmeshed in all the complex philosophical debates surrounding these weighty issues, but merely to state as simply as possible the assumptions on which I base my arguments. I further assume that all "realities" we can know are constructed; and though I propose that a phenomenal world exists independently of these constructions, I do not consider that we can have knowledge of it that is not shaped and filtered by the very nature of the mind itself.

3. This experiential reality of the dream and the epistemological problem it poses is illustrated in the oft-quoted tale, sometimes charmingly depicted in literati paintings, of the early Chinese philosopher, Chuang tzu. Chuang tzu dreamed that he was a butterfly, and on waking decided he could not be sure whether he was really a man who dreamed he was a butterfly, or a butterfly dreaming he was a man!

4. My thanks to Donald Tuzin for giving me this excellent illustration—and for often reminding me of the connections with the artistic imagination.

5. Rycroft's *A Critical Dictionary of Psychoanalysis* (1972:124–125) defines primary process thinking as a mode characterized by condensation, displacement, and symbolization; lacking reality testing and essentially maladaptive—it is the mode of the unconscious. Secondary process thinking is logical, reality-directed, discursive, and is the mode of consciousness and the ego.

ETHNOGRAPHIC EXPLORATIONS

PART TWO

Imagery, Pronouncement, and the Aesthetics of Reception in Gebusi Spirit Mediumship

Bruce M. Knauft

I N the growing literature on shamanism and spirit mediumship, the performative process whereby images and meaning are formulated has largely been neglected. Typically, linkages are asserted between spiritual experience and symbolism, social action, and/or psychophysiology without considering how meaning is produced in the shamanistic performance itself. In many respects the various concomitants of shamanism and mediumship are themselves generated through the process of symbolic production; spiritual orientations, social desires, and internal states are formulated and elaborated through the creative imagination and practical contingencies of the performative moment. From this viewpoint, shamanism and mediumship are forms of symbolic production that have significant similarities with (and differences from) imaginative experiences such as dreaming and private fantasy.

In this chapter I focus on the performance dynamics of image-making in Gebusi spirit mediumship.[1] After introducing Gebusi spirit mediumship, I present a rather detailed case study of symbolic production in a typical Gebusi sickness-inquest séance. This exposition raises two particularly poignant questions. First, why does Gebusi spirit séance imagery shift so pervasively and discordantly between ribald sexual camaraderie and extremely serious decisions concerning sorcery accusation and potential homicide? Second, why are Gebusi séance audiences so passively disposed to accept the indictment of the medium's spirits as to who the sorcerer is and what action should be taken against him or her? (This question is particularly striking since séances do not simply legitimate decisions reached elsewhere; outcomes are in important ways formulated at the public séance itself.) Consideration of these questions brings into focus the relationship between spirit mediumship and distinctive features of Gebusi sexuality, sociopolitical organization, and psychophysiology. These connections reveal selective ways in which Gebusi spirit mediumship is different from and similar to spirit mediumship and shamanism in other parts of New Guinea and elsewhere. My goal is to move in a gradually widening arc, beginning with the specific images of Gebusi spiritual experience and expanding toward assessments of larger comparative significance—without thereby compromising the particularities of Gebusi spiritual formulations.

Background

Gebusi inhabit a small area (sixty-five square miles) east of the Strickland River at the northern reaches of the vast tropical lowlands of south central New Guinea. In 1980–1982 the Gebusi population of some 450 persons was dispersed among seventeen longhouses and numerous smaller dwellings. Gebusi share broad social and cultural similarities with the dozen or so other groups of the Strickland-Bosavi area (Knauft 1985a, 1985b; cf. Kelly 1976, 1977, 1988; Schieffelin 1976, 1977, 1985; Feld 1982; Sørum 1980, 1984; Ernst 1978, 1984; Beek 1987; Shaw 1975, 1982). As is general in the region, Gebusi subsistence is based on sago production and foraging as well as on rudimentary horticulture and nonintensive pig husbandry. Male coresidence in the communal longhouse is based on a diverse combination of agnatic, affinal, and matrilateral ties. On a daily basis, people move flexibly within the community, sometimes sleeping in small garden dwellings or makeshift forest shelters, frequently visiting neighboring permanent settlements, or retiring to their own longhouse of principal residence. There is a notable absence of big-manship and of competitive exchange, and a strong belief in sorcery. All-night ritual dances between neighboring settlements are common, as are all-night séances led by a spirit medium.

Within the Strickland-Bosavi area, Gebusi are particularly distinctive for (among other things) their hot and flat lowland environment; their extremely decentralized politicoeconomic structure; strong sexual imagery and ribald male camaraderie in rituals, narratives, and spirit séances; and their extremely high rate of homicide—typically against community coresidents suspected of practicing sorcery (see Knauft 1985a, 1985b, 1986, 1987a, 1987b, 1987c). Gebusi are also distinctive in remaining effectively outside the purview of mission and administrative influence; their rituals, séances, sexual practices, and sorcery inquests were practiced avidly and in a surprisingly traditional manner in 1980–1982 (contrast Schieffelin 1981 concerning the Kaluli).

Gebusi Spirit Mediums

Gebusi spirit séances are centered around a spirit medium, that is, a person whose spirit (*fin*) can "go up and talk together with" (*kogwafada*) the beneficent spirit world people (*to di as*). Crucial to this process is that a spirit exchange is made; spirit people come and inhabit the medium's body during the séance while his own spirit is absent. It is these spirit people, particularly the beautiful spirit women (*to di ulia*), who sing the songs that constitute the séance. A clear dissociation is thus marked between the persona of the medium and that of the spirits who enter his body; he may summon them to the séance, but he need not be responsible for their actions, and they are neither fused with nor impersonated by his spirit. The medium's own spirit plays little or no role in the performance. The effectiveness of this culturally constituted dissociation is consistent with the fact that Gebusi mediumship is neither initiated by nor associated with traumatic sickness, hysteria, disruptive or untimely possession, or elaborate personal dreaming (contrast Herdt 1977; Stephen 1979; Wagner 1977).

Gebusi mediums are preeminently men, and only one case of an initiated female spirit medium is known.

As Gebusi say, who will be a spirit medium is not easily recognized a priori on the basis of personal qualities or "symptoms" exhibited by the person himself. (The main exception here is statistical—that close agnates and descendants of existing spirit mediums have a much greater likelihood of becoming mediums than do others). Which young men will become spirit mediums is generally decided by existing middle-aged mediums through their own spirit familiars in séances. The initiating spirit medium sings that a spirit woman is developing a strong and continuing sexual attraction to a Gebusi man. When the spirit woman voices her desire to marry him, the prospective medium undergoes behavioral restrictions that demonstrate his commitment to her. He is then initiated as a spirit medium and holds his own séances several nights in succession to reinforce his relationship with her. (This does not prevent the spirit medium from marrying, or from already having married, a real Gebusi wife. The spirit wife and the Gebusi wife are cowives of one another, polygyny being infrequent but acceptable among real-world Gebusi.) Through his spirit world wife, the new medium gains access to other spirit people, including the spirit children his new wife bears him. It is these spirit persons and their friends who come and reside in the medium's body during séances. This allows the medium's own spirit to depart during the séance and experience firsthand the hedonic life of the spirit world.

Although spirit mediums seldom convey or talk about their own spirit world experiences, those few accounts that could be elicited were ones of great personal pleasure, for example, attending spirit feasts and dances, having sexual affairs with spirit women, or accompanying the spirits on a successful inquest. The opportunity to become a spirit medium is gladly embraced by most young men if it is presented to them.

Spirit mediums exhibit a wide range of temperaments, personalities, and intellectual abilities or limitations, and they constitute approximately 15 percent of the adult male population. The practical sense one gets is not that mediums are chosen primarily for their imaginative abilities, but that of those who are chosen, some develop much greater acumen and creative imagery than do others. It is the former who receive greatest social reinforcement and who are in greatest demand for their services. Correspondingly, it is they who have the greatest opportunity to further develop and elaborate their spirit world renderings through the frequent giving of séances.

Gebusi spirit mediums are not paid or otherwise remunerated for their services (contrast Dwyer and Minnegal 1988); mediums are considered to have a civic responsibility to make spirit world inquiries on behalf of their community at large. Mediums, for their part, are afforded the ability to experience and to create an elaborate spirit world reality, and they are an artistic and entertaining focus of community attention during their séances. Spirit mediums also have a significant degree of de facto authority about this-worldly issues subject to spiritual pronouncement.

In the all-night séance itself, a Gebusi spirit medium becomes entranced and his spirits sing numerous spontaneous songs, these being chorused by the male audience. The trance of Gebusi mediums is voluntarily self-induced; he sits in the longhouse, closes his eyes, and in a few minutes begins mumbling the increasingly audible songs of his spirit familiars. Unlike shamans in many parts of the world, Gebusi mediums do not rely on drugs, sleeplessness, strenuous exertion, percussion, sickness, fasting, or other forms of stress to induce their entrancement, even when this is first experienced (contrast Winkelman 1986; Locke and Kelly 1985; Prince 1982).[2] Nonetheless, Gebusi mediums do appear to experience an altered state of consciousness during their séances. The medium's songs and his occasional comments between them conform consistently with the distinctive persona of spirit world people and with their strange falsetto voices. In their speech, medium's spirits employ highly metaphoric idioms that are multifaceted and often obscure. This is said to reflect the fact that spirit world speech and experience are by nature not totally comprehensible to Gebusi. As discussed below, the medium's song imagery reflects cognitive processes that can perhaps be characterized as free-associative. The spirit medium's own spirit is perceived both by himself and by others to be relaxing elsewhere in the spirit world while the séance is taking place. (The adventures of the medium's own spirit during the séance are generally not related or referred to during the séance itself and are not considered particularly relevant to the proceedings.)

The altered experience of the spirit medium during the séance often affects his activity afterward; spirit mediums typically emerge from the night-long performance refreshed and ready for a day of full activity. This stands in marked contrast to the audience of singers (and the ethnographer), who generally spend much of the following day catching up on their sleep. The feat of the medium in this respect becomes more noteworthy when it is realized that he not only stays awake all night but typically composes and sings a hundred or more songs, often about momentous current social issues. It is perhaps significant that Gebusi spirit mediums do not exhibit the deep muscle tremors or other unusual physical movement commonly reported in entrancement. The psychophysiological state of Gebusi mediums is perhaps more akin to self-hypnosis or to the deep relaxation of trophotropic arousal than to the sympathetic central nervous system activation of ergotropic arousal (see Fischer 1971; cf. Prince 1982; Joralemon 1984).[3]

Spirit People

The Gebusi spirit pantheon is rich and multifarious, containing the spirits of many animals and beings. Within this pantheon it is the true spirit people (*to di as dep*) who are the locus of Gebusi spiritual communication, and of these, it is the spirit women (to di ulia) who conduct the bulk of the spirit séance. Although a few mediums have spirit familiars with recognizably different personalities, preeminent focus is upon spirit women, whose individuality is unimportant relative to their generalized traits of beauty, sexual receptivity, and caprice (Cantrell n.d.).[4]

At spirit séances members of the Gebusi male audience often joke sexually with the spirit women and with each other. This joking has a significant practical effect as well as being extremely entertaining; it is believed that spirit women must be enticed to stay at the séance through the night in order for its instrumental goals to be effectively accomplished, for example, cure the sick person, find the lost pig, or determine the sorcerer's identity. If the enthusiasm and participation of the male audience flag too greatly, the spirit woman also loses interest and flies off, forcing the spirit medium's own spirit to return to his body. This terminates the medium's trance and ends the séance prematurely. Since the divinatory work of the spirits is typically believed to take until almost dawn to be accomplished, the termination of a séance before this time typically means that its instrumental goals are not achieved. The persistence of joking audience camaraderie during the night is thus necessary as well as enjoyable for a successful séance.[5]

Despite the preeminence of spirit women in Gebusi séances, their importance is culturally masked. When asked, Gebusi men generally credit the medium's eldest male spirit child (*wuli as*) with having orchestrated the spirit-world inquest and informing the Gebusi audience of its result. Likewise, they say that the spirit séance begins when the wuli as comes down into the spirit medium—often attracted by the prospect of smoking tobacco pipes proffered during the séance—and allows the medium's own spirit to fly off. These statements belie the fact that the male wuli as very infrequently speak and are very infrequently referred to during the séance. When a wuli as does speak, it is usually as a brief ribald jest with the male audience members during the interlude between songs sung by spirit women. It is thus rare for the wuli as to make a substantive pronouncement, and in these cases his statements tend to reiterate the point of view already developed by the spirit women. As will be shown further below, the attribution of divinatory activity to the male wuli as parallels the symbolic appropriation and spiritual control of femaleness in the séance by Gebusi men. As will further become evident, the substitution of a male for a female sexual object also symbolizes the transference from heterosexual to homosexual eroticism among the male audience during the séance.

The beneficence and attractiveness of true spirit world people such as the wuli as and spirit women are reflected in their lively participatory enjoyment of the feasts and dances that are held nightly in the spirit world. In these and other respects, the true spirit people contrast with the general irritability and malice of the spirits of deceased Gebusi (*as golop e fin*). These latter are thought to be angry over their real-world death, and although they can live in the spirit world, they are carefully distinguished from the true spirit people (to di as dep). Spirits of the dead play a minor role in Gebusi séances and rarely speak to the audience directly. In daily life such spirits can induce minor misfortune and illness, but they seldom cause serious illness and almost never cause death. Life-threatening and fatal illness are attributed instead to the agency of living humans—to sorcery (Knauft 1985a).

The main avenue of communication and influence from Gebusi to the spirit world is thus through the beneficent to di as dep, and this contact occurs almost entirely via the spirit medium. Gebusi cannot effectively contact or influence spirits about important matters except through the spirit medium in a séance.[6] Conducting spirit séances is the main distinctive activity undertaken by Gebusi mediums.

Spirit Séances

As aesthetic and entertaining events, Gebusi spirit séances are all-night songfests. They are held frequently—averaging once every eleven days per major settlement—and may address one or more issues for which the omniscient vision of the spirit people is believed crucial, particularly sickness inquest or hunting guidance.

The occurrence of a séance is usually known hours or sometimes even a day or more in advance; the spirit medium quietly lets it be known that he has agreed to the requests of coresidents or visitors to hold a songfest with the spirits. Séances are held at night, usually in the dark interior of a longhouse, and particularly in the men's sleeping section (*tam*). Women are normally prohibited from participating in séance performances, though they can easily hear the proceedings through the thin sago-leaf wall that separates their sleeping section from the men's area of the longhouse. When there is strong urgency or desire to hold a séance despite an insufficient number of male singers (at least four or five), women may be asked to sit with the men and sing.

During the séance the medium sits still—usually in a cross-legged position—and closes his eyes in a meditative posture until his own spirit departs and a spirit woman takes its place. After a short period she begins to mumble and hum, eventually producing intelligible songs in the high falsetto chant characteristic of spirit-world speech.

Each song line sung by the medium is repeated in a full chorus of song by assembled singers who sit huddled around him. These singers are predominantly adolescent and young married men, while other men, often older, listen and comment or joke from the periphery. Males of all ages are free to occupy either role, however, and there is no rigid division between singers and listening audience. The séance as a whole consists of a night-long progression of séance songs, each of which usually lasts several minutes. During the night the singers and other men periodically get up and stretch and talk between songs, sleep sporadically, and may come and go at will from the longhouse. The medium himself, however, remains almost motionless through the night, the main exception being the brief but dramatic "claiming of the spirit" (*fin hup*).

In the fin hup, the medium's spirits attempt to cure a sick person by throttling maleficent beings who have captured his or her spirit. At the séance itself, this is seen as a tumultuous thrashing: the medium suddenly springs up and smashes firebrands and implements wildly about the house. (He returns shortly thereafter to his sitting position and continues his quiet singing for the rest of the night.) Fin hup is performed for sick persons who, though conscious, are believed to have lost their spirit or social essence (fin) in illness. This condition is believed to persist until the spirit is recovered by the true spirit people (to di as dep) and returned to the sick person's body (Knauft 1985a: 86–93; cf. Sørum 1980 regarding the nearby Bedamini). Fin hup cures take place primarily in the unseen spirit world; indeed, the sick person rarely attends the séance and is often not at the settlement where it is held.

Whereas fin hup is used to cure mild or moderate sickness, spiritual loss that becomes potentially life-threatening is believed caused by sorcery; the sorcerer has effectively taken away or tied up the victim's spirit and may destroy it by burning or eating it. The most frequent form of sorcery is *bogay*, a variant of parcel sorcery in which the victim's excrement is believed collected by the sorcerer and eventually burned by him or her to cause a slow death. Assault sorcery (*ogowili*) is believed to involve the direct killing and eating of the victim's spirit by sorcerers who attack when the person is alone and unsuspecting of their presence; its effects are rapid and believed almost invariably lethal. To investigate either form of sorcery, the medium's spirits attempt to identify the sorcerer and locate and/or destroy the means he or she used to make the person sick. As with "lost spirit" sickness and other issues of spiritual inquest, the curing of sorcery can only be undertaken through the spirit world—it requires the cooperation of the spirits (and the spirit medium) in holding an all-night séance. Such sorcery inquests are critical in ascertaining the identity of the sorcery suspect as well as the action to be taken against him or her. This indictment is of particular practical import since virtually a third of Gebusi adult deaths (32.7 percent) are caused by homicide, and the largest category of homicide is the execution of suspected sorcerers in retribution for one or more preceding sickness deaths in the suspect's residential community (Knauft 1985a:chap.5; 1987c).

In aggregate terms about half (50/101) of Gebusi spirit séances are minor sickness investigations and cures (fin hup); an additional fifth (21/101) have as their main instrumental purpose inquest for sorcery, including postmortem inquiries (death inquests). Other séances may be conducted to inquire about hunting or the finding of lost pigs (8/101), to divine the success of fish poisoning (5/101), or for simple entertainment with no instrumental reason ascribed (13/101). Virtually all spirit séances contain a strong element of entertainment if not exuberant festivity, the serious nature of their more instrumental inquiries notwithstanding.

Within these general outlines, the diversity of Gebusi spirit séances is enormous; the issues of séance pronouncement are diverse and the characteristics of the spirit world are creatively malleable. The present study considers only one séance genre—that in which images of sexual incitement are engaged with those of sickness inquest and sorcery indictment. The presentation is in this respect but a prolegomenon to explicating the fuller range and significance of Gebusi spiritual meanings.[7]

A Sickness-Inquest Seance

The effects of spiritual image-production upon Gebusi perception and action can be illustrated by considering a typical sickness-inquest séance. This séance was held primarily to investigate the temporary illness of a teenage boy, Terkabo. Terkabo's settlement was planning a ritual feast, and it was hoped that he would recover so that the event could take place. Since the boy's sickness was of recent origin and was becoming moderately acute, it was generally believed that the illness was of the easily cured "lost spirit" (fin forgop) variety. There was always a possibility, however, that the sickness was caused by potentially lethal parcel sorcery (bogay). The persons within the community frequently suspected as bogay sorcerers in the recent past were two senior men. One of these was Terkabo's senior clansman from a different settlement; the other was Terkabo's true and coresident mother's brother (MB). Neither man was present at the séance. The following is an account of the séance edited from field notes.

Swiman, a middle-aged spirit medium, left word that he was going on a foraging trip for several days to collect sago fronds. When he returned to the main village, he related, he would give a séance to inquire about the sickness of his noncoresident classificatory "MB," the uninitiated youth, Terkabo. Terkabo's elder brother Hogoswimam, who was himself a young spirit medium, came down to the main village for the event, along with his aged mother. The sick boy, Terkabo, did not attempt to make the trip. However, a number of other men were present in the central village, mostly by chance, including the seven other adult men and five boys who attended the séance. (With the exception of Hogoswimam, none of those in attendance was of the same clan as Terkabo.) It was generally anticipated that Swiman, as both a relatively neutral party and the more experienced of the two spirit mediums, would take the greatest initiative in investigating the sickness.

About 8:00 P.M., Swiman and Hogoswimam both went into trance and the séance began. The two mediums each sang songs as the séance progressed.[8] The songs became increasingly ribald, and the issue of Terkabo's sickness was seemingly neglected. In one of Swiman's songs, for instance, a spirit woman coyly teased a male suitor by manually propping up her breasts and then covering them up. Various audience members responded by saying that they would massage her breasts, joking that, if they couldn't, they would have to rub each other's penises (homosexually) instead.

Swiman then sang a brief song announcing, "We will go look; Her child is sick; She has come down." This indicated that his spirits were hoping to investigate Terkabo's sickness, and they conveyed their sympathy for the boy's aged mother, who had come to the central village to listen to the séance.[9] The male audience, however, continued with their sexual banter after the song. Hogoswimam then sang the following song, which further presaged the sorcery inquest.

(The song, like most, was sung by a young female spirit. Each line was sung in a small spirit voice by the medium and immediately repeated in a loud chorus of song by the singers. This collective voice was then quickly superseded by another line from the medium, maintaining the lively tempo of the song. Men and boys singing remained huddled about the medium, while other males listened and/or made comments from further away).

SONG TEXT I

Elder sister
We'll search here, we'll search there
Here elder sister
Here's the yadu, *here's the* yadu*! [*Yadu *in this context usually means sorcery packet or small object, though it can also mean young spirit world pig.]*
At the degwa *tree I grab it*
Come here, help me get it
Should you sit first? Should I sit first?
Elder sister

To sleep, to get up and to lay down
If I had heat [strength, anger, passion]
To me it's gone, it's lost/finished
Elder sister, Elder sister
Over there, what's happening?
My elder sister sleeps, it's lost/finished
Elder sister
It won't be
Upon waking up, she'll call to me
You stretch apart the wall boards
Ulkip *[forehead, glans penis]! Sticking through the wall boards [to the*
    woman's sleeping section]. Come in!
[Yells and hollers from the audience]
By dawn we'll be friends/lovers [literally, like initiation
    sponsor/sponsee]
Go close up the door [to the woman's sleeping section]
I'm joking/lying to you; its only a dog
Dog, what did you come looking for?/end song
WABOY *[audience member, answering the spirit woman's rhetorical*
    "question"]: He came to dig in a woman's crotch!! Moist vagina!
SOLWOY *[another audience member]: Hey Yaba, you'll have to find a dif-*
    ferent woman [because the dog has already occupied the spirit woman]!
YABA *and* SOLWOY *[leaning heads together]: YEY!*
OMAY: *I'm sad/horny (fafadagim-da)!*
YABA: *I can't wait, I'm too horny right now! I'd take a [real Gebusi]*
    woman and have sex with her. But our women aren't like the spirit
    women; they'd yell, "Way, Way Way!" They wouldn't lie and say, "It's
    only a dog." They'd just [tell the truth and] say it was a man trying to
    get them![10]

This séance song, like most, contains emergent and constantly changing
song images that promote dramatic tension, arousal, and aesthetic creativity—
as well as moving sporadically toward pronouncements concerning the instrumental goals of the séance. The primary referent in each song line is often if not
typically superseded within a few seconds. Such unpredictable changes of context, scene, and object continually recontextualize the meaning of previous song
lines. The latter, in turn, become post facto metaphors for the next image of
spiritual reality that emerges. The song thus contains an internal hermeneutic
that is both very rich and very complex.[11]

Let us trace selected image-transformations as they develop in the song.
Near its beginning, the song depicts a search by a spirit woman and her elder
sister, the search being at one level for a sorcery packet (*yadu*), which is then

found near a large *degwa* tree. (During inquests, sorcery packets are commonly found at the base of large trees.) This is followed by images of asking to sit down, possibly taking turns, sleep, lamenting a loss of energy and strength, and, finally, admitting that the chance is finished. The dominant image evoked here—common in sorcery inquests and attested by informants—is of a spirit woman trying to wrest the sorcery packet from an angry but unidentified sorcerer. The spirit woman tires from the struggle, unsuccessfully solicits help from her elder sister, and finally gives up her attempt, at least for the time being.

Correspondingly, however, a subsidiary theme is simultaneously evoked—superimposed upon the first. In this interpretation the two spirit women are trying to catch a young pig (also a yadu) that they have happened upon. They tire and give up their attempt, due to lack of manly hunting skills. This episodic scenario, like the first one concerning sorcery, is common in spirit séances and is thus easily evoked by cryptic song references.

These two interpretations are mutually informing rather than mutually exclusive; there are important conceptual linkages between the sorcery search and the pig hunt. Accused Gebusi sorcerers are, like pigs, often hunted down, killed, and traditionally, cooked for eating in a feasting oven. Indeed, the spirit of the executed sorcerer is reincarnated as a wild pig that is particularly difficult and dangerous to hunt.

These associations are brought to a yet more complex level by considering a third interpretive frame for the song episode: that of sexual adventure. As suggested to me by one young man during transcription, the same initial search scene suggests a sexual escapade in which the woman invites a young man to sit down, wants to sleep with him, but then laments her waning passion and the lost love chance because her elder sister is sleeping nearby and could easily be awakened by the sound of lovemaking.

This theme of sexual lust, which is submerged and secondary in the first half of the song, comes quickly to the fore in the second half—when the spirit woman invites the "glans penis" to stretch the wall boards apart and squeeze through the hole. This depiction, with its obvious coital imagery, marks a major turning point in the song—away from the sorcery inquest and toward an overt sexual adventure. This plot is drawn out and made tantalizing by the quick remetaphorization of the phallus back into a full man, who, as is commonly narrated in séances, has snuck bodily into the woman's section for a sexual rendezvous. By dawn, the spirit woman tells her companion, he'll be her friend/lover. However, the spirit woman then says that she has been joking and that her lover was in fact just a dog. This is comprehensible since the original intruder, the *ulkip*, means both glans penis and head. As such, she jokes, it was only a dog that squeezed its head through the hole to her quarters; she wanted him merely for canine companionship rather than for sexual satisfaction.

As if to compound the complexity of interpretive possibilities, the joke of the capricious spirit woman—that her apparent lover was in fact only a dog—itself remains ambiguous. Spirit women are often depicted as having sexual trysts in the longhouse while their spirit world cohorts are sleeping. Correspondingly, spirit women are often portrayed as trying to hide these affairs from those spirit people who are disturbed and wake up from the sound of lovemaking, for instance, by protesting that the noise "was only a dog that has come in." Whether the spirit woman's joke is on the Gebusi listeners or on her spirit world cohorts is thus uncertain. This is the background for Yaba's audience comment after the song, that is, that spirit women are apt to hide the presence of their lovers, and that this poses a contrast to real Gebusi women, who cannot be so easily accosted for sex because they resist and advertise men's advances. As aptly evident from the other audience comments, the spirit woman's bold and perhaps capricious seduction is for the Gebusi men a cause for much mirth, fantasy, and exclamation of their own sexual frustration.

It is evident from their various interpretive possibilities that Gebusi songs are what Umberto Eco (1979) terms open texts rather than closed or bounded ones; they contain a myriad of overlapping and nonexclusive meanings. This openness, which at one level stems from the free-association consciousness of the spirit medium, is intrinsic to Gebusi séance songs; because their imagery is cryptic, emergent, and often discordant, séance songs require constant shifting of interpretive possibilities to be made comprehensible.

At the same time, a common repertoire of spirit-world metaphors poses important outer limits upon interpretation; the actions of spirit women tend ultimately to congeal into standard plot lines, and superimposed meanings and recontextualized images are thus often resolved with ultimate clarity. This is apparent in the coordinated and internally consistent comments of Gebusi audience members at the end of the song; the ultimate meanings and sexual innuendos were quite evident to those present. This is true generally of Gebusi séance songs; although the interpretive possibilities are in principle endless, the most important plot lines and spiritual pronouncements are ultimately conspicuous to most or all of those in attendance, especially since the more basic themes are progressively elaborated and reinforced over eight to ten hours of singing. The openness of the song for Gebusi audiences thus facilitates polysemic richness without obscuring its basic scenarios and meanings. The potential in the seance for highly unambiguous communication is especially evident in the spirits' ultimate divinatory pronouncements, which can be both quite clear and quite serious in their social repercussions. This is aptly illustrated in the very next song of the present séance, sung by Swiman, which identifies and indicts a sorcery suspect for Terkabo's sickness.

SONG TEXT 2

Elder sister, it's dawn already [the seance is almost over]
Now you wait for me [while I look for the sorcery packet]
Sitting, sleeping there
Their men [the Gebusi singers] are sitting with us
Small man [the sick boy, Terkabo]
You go out to look and find it [find the sorcery packet that made him sick]
[Then] come back and give it to his mother [to the sick boy's mother] . . .
My friends, stay here now, wait
My skirt string is loose
I'll sit down on top of your fingers there
I'm scared of you my friends/lovers
Mother, father, mother, father
The wali *spirit—[I went] to his house [There is a prominent* wali *spirit*
  house right next to the sick boy's longhouse]
Mother, father, mother, father
There he is, the elder man [the sorcerer] with his child [son or sister's son,
  the sick boy]
The child is there with his mother's brother [i.e., the sorcerer is the sick
  boy's mother's brother]
Upper, lower
Is it "upper" Gigi [sub-clan] to whom he [the sick boy] is sister's son?
[No] It's "lower" [Gigi sub-clan]!
Other men have died, you're the only one. [You, the sorcerer, are the one
  remaining senior man from lower Gigi subclan.]
"Mother's brother" [the sick boy had said] "Let's live together."
What can I say [of the sorcery sickness]?
What can I say?
What can I say?
There, now wait for me [while I look/find something]
A little one? A yadu*?*
You adopted and raised a small yadu *[pig/sorcery packet]*
At your ritual feast [like the one planned for Terkabo's settlement] you'll
  hit/kill this one
Along with the greens, I too will eat this one [i.e., I too will eat it along
  with the greens of the feasting oven]
Mother, father
Your eyes [Terkabo's], I won't poke them [like a sorcerer would]
This seems to be, yes, this is it! [emphasizes the certainty of the
  pronouncement]
The child's sickness, will we see it get better?

Don't lay it [the sorcery packet] down
Mother, father
There wouldn't be any more children living there [if we were to allow sor-
cery like this to continue]
Again, later, we won't need to do this again [won't need to have another
seance for this sickness]
[Because] this that we now see [the sorcery packet] we'll give to
you!/end song

KIPTABULBWI *[a spirit man, speaking from inside the spirit medium*
Swiman, immediately after the song]: The women from Kukudobi [settle-
ment from adjacent society] are saying that you're really good singers;
they want to have sex and marry you! They don't want to stay married to
their husbands; they want to come here and sing and take off their skirts!

OMAY: *Rub a vagina! I'll have to pull on a "noseplug" [penis] [because I*
can't wait for the women]. [General laughter]

GWABI: *Why don't you pull on Mogosoyl's, he's no longer a spirit medium.*

OMAY: *I'll pull on his little nose plug and hide it away.*

GWABI: *We'll all pull on it.*

OMAY: *Yes, we will! [All laugh]*

YUWAY: *I'll also pull yours!*

SOLWOY: *And I'll pull yours!*

SOLWOY *and* YUWAY: *Yey!!*

UBOLE: *The spirit women's vaginas, we'd really like to see them and*
"stick" them, we're so sad/horny! . . .

KIPTABULBWI *[spirit man]: The drum opening is leaning over and a finger*
comes up [inside it].

[Audience erupts in laughter and yelling—at the metaphor of vaginal
penetration]

OMAY: *The "skin" hair [pubic hair], I'll take that, too!*

KIPTABULBWI: *Are you thinking of that also [as I am]?*

YABA: *Mogosoyl's nose plug can't come up.*

KIPTABULBWI: *The drum was wrapped up [out of public view] and the*
finger went up inside it. [pauses] It's getting to be dawn. The
kosaym *[nightly spirit-world dance] is almost over.*

IMBA: *Mother's vagina, that guy [the spirit man, Kiptabulbwi] is really see-*
ing a lot of dances up there!

In stark contrast to the joking that immediately follows it, this song gives
for the first time a specific and unambiguous pronouncement concerning the
bogay sorcery now assessed to have caused Terkabo's sickness: it was sent by
his true mother's brother, Muswayay. This pronouncement is clear from (a) the
designation of the kin relationship (mother's brother) between the sorcerer and

Terkabo, (b) the fact that the sorcerer and Terkabo are depicted as coresident, (c) the specific designation of the sorcerer/victim coresidence site (by reference to the *wali* spirit place), (d) the subclan identification of the sorcerer ("lower" Gigi subclan), and (e) the fact that, as indicated, Muswayay is the only surviving adult male of Gigi-lower subclan. In short, the sorcerer must be Muswayay.

Partway through the song, as in the previous one, the sorcery accusation was mediated through the word *yadu*, which means both sorcery packet and young pig. In the present case, the spirit woman proclaimed that she would like to eat the young pig that Terkabo's kinsmen would slaughter at the upcoming preparatory feast for the male initiation—a feast that was to be held only if Terkabo recovered. The double meaning was that if the sick boy did not recover, the one who "adopted the sorcery packet"—the sorcerer—would be the one eaten instead. [12]

Toward the conclusion of the song, the spirit woman promised that she would give tangible evidence of her sorcery indictment by producing the sorcery packet itself, so that no more séances would be necessary to find the cause of Terkabo's sickness.

Despite the seriousness and specificity of the sorcery indictment— which was first made evident in this song—the focus of the audience was, in seeming paradox, one of sexual joking. As narrated above, one of Swiman's own male spirits, Kiptabulbwi, teased the audience immediately after the song by saying that the women at Kukubodi were sexually attracted to the Gebusi singers. This fostered a round of ribald joking about frustrated sexual desires among the men present. Through this process the sorcery indictment was rather soft-pedaled, though it was no less definitive on that account.

It could be argued in one sense that norms of friendly camaraderie were invoked by the medium at the end of the song to defuse potential disputes between relatives of the sick boy and the closest kinsmen of Muswayay, the indicted mother's brother. (Muswayay was himself not present at the séance, though several of his clansmen were in attendance.) At the same time, this denial or supersession of tension did not preclude a later consensus of judgment against Muswayay. Indeed, it is possible, as discussed further below, that sexually provocative imagery itself predisposes acceptance of negative assessments against the sorcery suspect.

Though there was neither discussion of the sorcery pronouncement nor an aura of particular seriousness among the audience, the indictment of Muswayay by the spirit woman was accepted de facto and acted on convincingly by those present (see further below). This indictment had not been agreed upon or publicly discussed prior to the séance; indeed, it was a surprise that Terkabo's sickness was attributed by the spirits to bogay sorcery at all, as opposed to being a transient illness that could be easily cured by the medium's claiming of the lost spirit (fin hup).

The sorcery indictment and audience banter were followed by a song sung by Hogoswimam. His spirit woman narrated how she was alone and wanted a sexual partner. She joked with several of the Gebusi men present, saying to one of them that he was too young to have sex with her, and complaining to another man that he was married already. When a widower in the audience spoke up and said that he was sexually available, she joked that his "head" was down: that he was too tired/hunched over to be sexually responsive; that his phallus was too limp. The men in the audience, including the targeted individual, joked heartily in response. In short, the sorcery indictment was again left in abeyance.

The next song, sung by Swiman, started with a sexual tease by a spirit woman. She proceeded to describe Terkabo's weathered longhouse, which had been newly enlarged to accommodate extra guests for the coming feast. The spirit woman lamented rhetorically that if Terkabo's true father were alive, he would have helped build an entire new longhouse for the anticipated festivities. She concluded by saying that because the pigs at Terkabo's settlement were becoming a nuisance in their gardens, they should hurry and have the feast, pending the repentance of the sorcerer and the recovery of Terkabo.

Several songs later, Swiman spat out the purported sorcery packet (bogay) that had been ostensibly used by Muswayay to ensorcell Terkabo. The packet, which appeared to be a small, partially decomposed seed assemblage (i.e., a totally natural object), was received matter of factly and without much comment by audience members, and it was given to Hogoswimam and Terkabo's mother following the séance. The rendering of the bogay packet by the spirits during the séance was taken as tangible proof that they had indeed identified the correct sorcery suspect.

(There is neither wonderment by the audience nor flagrant deception by the medium in the production of such a sorcery packet during the séance [contrast Lévi-Strauss 1967:chap. 10]. Spirit women may direct spirit mediums to find such packets in the course of their daily foraging activity as well as during séances. It is but a short metaphoric extension of this capacity for the medium-as-spirit woman to introduce such a sorcery packet at the séance itself. From the medium's point of view, it would appear that the spirit woman is simply retrieving [e.g., from the spirit medium's hair] and then expectorating the same packet she had directed him to obtain previously. There is no objective evidence that any of the ostensible sorcery packets found were actually made by Gebusi.)

During the remainder of the séance, the spirits made only sporadic references to the sorcery inquest; given the certainty of the pronouncement and the concrete "evidence" of the sorcery packet, the séance focused increasingly around spirit women's sexual enticements and ribald audience commentary. There was no discussion of the sorcery indictment during the night; the indictment was accepted de facto as a social and cultural fact (notwithstanding that it was not preagreed upon).

Following the séance, the two spirit mediums left the main village and returned to their respective settlements. Most of the rest of the men went to sleep. Later in the day, several of the séance participants (four men, along with their wives and children) went up to the settlement of Hogoswimam and Terkabo to formally communicate the findings of the séance to Muswayay, the indicted sorcery suspect.[13] Swiman, the medium whose spirits had made the indictment, was not present and played no further role in the emerging accusation.

Muswayay was confronted with the bogay packet and accused of sorcery. Terkabo's aged mother, who had listened carefully to the séance, took the leading role in the accusation despite the fact that she was also Muswayay's true full sister. Hogoswimam took very little role in the proceedings, apparently since, as an entranced spirit medium, his own spirit had not been present; he had not "heard" the séance accusation and thus could say little to substantiate it.

The implications of the accusation were extremely severe; if Terkabo were to die of sickness, Muswayay would run a high risk of being executed as a sorcerer. (Muswayay's father's brother [FB] and father's brother's son [FBS] had both been executed as sorcerers.) Despite this threat—or perhaps all the more because of it—there was an awkward reluctance on both sides to confront the issue of sorcery except through innuendo and deferral to the evidence supplied by the spirits. Thus, accusatory statements were hedged, many conciliatory remarks were made by both Muswayay and his accusers, and there was little if any direct animosity. Although both sides were privately incensed at each other—the accusers at Muswayay for ensorcelling his true sister's son [ZS], and Muswayay and his accusers for believing that he could actually do such a thing—both sides implicitly realized it was too risky to express these sentiments. Muswayay, for his part, risked reinforcing the perception of himself as an irascible man who was unwilling to admit or relent in his practice of sorcery; an expression of anger on his part would risk increasing his chances of being executed were Terkabo to die. The accusers, for their part, risked antagonizing Muswayay to the point that—so they thought—he might make another bogay packet and kill Terkabo or someone else. Given the "evidence" of the "sorcery packet" supplied by the spirits and given the general consensus against him, Muswayay could put up little in the way of effective verbal defense. The meeting ended with a show of conciliation on all sides, though these feelings were somewhat discounted later in private conversations. Fortunately for Muswayay, Terkabo recovered from his sickness, and the feast planned by his settlement was held as originally anticipated.

Discussion

The events recounted above are indicative of numerous Gebusi sorcery inquests observed in the field, several of which were documented through complete transcripts of the spirit séances and public discussions (cf. Knauft

1985a:chap. 2). Many aspects of the séance and its aftermath could be discussed; however, my primary present concern is the aesthetic and pragmatic impact of spiritual imagery in the séance. These images constitute the spirit world as Gebusi know it, and provide their recognized reason for undertaking various forms of this-worldly action, such as accusing or executing a given sorcery suspect.

Sorcery indictments in Gebusi spirit séances appear to have a formal truth value by the simple fact of their legitimate proclamation: they have poignant illocutionary force (Austin 1962). Like a court judgment in our own society, this does not mean that there are never objections, but rather that the verdict itself is a preeminent social fact that puts those who may disagree decidedly on the defensive and makes them very quiet.

Hence, Gebusi sorcery indictments generate a surprising degree of consensus and compliance among the coresidents and close kinsmen of both the person indicted and the sickness-victim—despite the lack of any objective evidence that parcel sorcery has been practiced, and despite the life-threatening results that the attribution of such sorcery entails. In the present case diagnosis of bogay, much less the indictment of Muswayay, was not preexpected, and yet it was not disagreed with in any significant way, even by Muswayay himself! Indeed, it was Muswayay's own true sister who took the role of primary accuser. In several ways, then, the indictment of Muswayay appears as a particularly powerful genre of deviation attribution or scapegoating.

The consensual acceptance of the accusation against Muswayay can be traced back to the way the indictment was originally formulated within the spirit séance itself. In terms of spiritual imagery, this outcome appears curiously linked to the overarching context of ribald sexual banter and entertainment within which the sorcery indictment was couched and by which its poignancy was effectively masked. Indeed, one of the most striking and ultimately revealing aspects of Gebusi inquest séances is their seemingly discordant superimposition of matters of life and death concern—indictment and potential execution of sorcery suspects—with ribald camaraderie. What makes the disjunction between ribaldry and serious pronouncement so pervasive and so aesthetically appealing in Gebusi spirit séances? And why should this disjunction so strongly predispose the audience to accept spiritual pronouncements that have potentially violent this-worldly import? These questions can be approached by considering two key aspects of Gebusi sexual and emotional life: the relationship between sexual arousal and homoerotic transference, and the linkage between sexual frustration and the incitement to anger.

Homosexuality and Erotic Transference

Perhaps the most aesthetically central and emotionally charged theme of Gebusi ritual, spiritual, and mythical practice is the heightening of eroticism through gender transference. A number of South New Guinea cultures, including the Gebusi, have practiced ritualized male homosexuality (Herdt 1984a; Knauft 1986, 1987b). Among Gebusi, male homosexuality has several interlocking dimensions. In one respect it is a significant dimension of masculine growth and development; boys' sexual relationships with initiated men are believed to imbue them with semen as a vital life force, allowing them to reach full male stature and vigor. Oral insemination of adolescent boys by adult men is pronounced prior to the boys' initiation in late adolescence, and it is during the preinitiation period that boys' sexual and physical capacities are believed to burgeon. This celebrated development culminates in the elaborate costumed display of the novices at the male initiation (*wa kawala*), literally, "child become big."

In a second respect, Gebusi homosexuality is part of a more diffuse pattern of homoeroticism among Gebusi men. Although homosexual insemination is most appropriately directed from initiated men to those uninitiated adolescents who are unrelated to them, a strong sense of homoeroticism pervades adult male relationships in general. This is reflected in affectionate sexual joking relationships among male affines and matrikin, and in lewd banter of homosexual attraction among adult men who are unrelated (*awa*). Such homoeroticism is especially evident at those collective events that constitute the primary focus of Gebusi collective interest and symbolic expression: ritual feasts and dances, spirit séances, and the telling of narratives. These events are not necessarily accompanied by homosexual trysts (indeed, sexual trysts among the primary joking participants—adult men—would be anomalous), but they do entail a strong aura of collective camaraderie and diffuse homoeroticism. In their jesting with each other, men loudly lament their pent-up sexuality and joke that they would gladly use each other for purposes of sexual gratification, often feigning to grab another man's genitals as the mock prelude to such an encounter.

In a third respect, Gebusi homosexuality and homoeroticism are regarded as replacements for heterosexuality. This is the dimension of homoeroticism perhaps most highlighted in men's own jokes and teasing. Hence, the preeminent male joking theme: "If there was a woman available I would have sex with her, but I'm so pent-up I can't wait for a woman! I'll have to have sex with *you* (another man)!"[14] The theme of frustrated male heterosexuality—and its transference from fantasized female objects onto men themselves—is pervasive in Gebusi ritual dances as well as spirit séances; it merits further comment.

In Gebusi dance rituals (*gigobra*), the center of attention is an elaborately costumed male dancer (Knauft 1985a:chap. 9; 1985b; 1989). Although the dancer embodies many spiritual images, the preeminent one, both iconically and in Gebusi description, is the red bird of paradise—the primary incarnate form of beautiful young spirit women. During the dance, the assembled men comment lewdly on their arousal in watching the beautiful red bird of paradise, who dances to the accompaniment of Gebusi women's off-stage songs of loneliness and seduction. In reality, of course, the dancer is a man. This sexual replacement finds its culmination in the men's pronounced sexual joking and camaraderie; a man's attraction to the dancer is teasingly redirected in friendly sexual frustration to another man near him. This sexual transfer from hetero- to homoeroticism is paralleled by the inversion of male and female space in the longhouse during the dance. The men watch the male dancer(s) from the communal dirt floor and domestic hearths in the lower part of the longhouse (*ba masam*), while the women are granted ritual license to occupy the men's sleeping platforms for the purpose of singing—they occupy the elevated male part of the house normally off limits to them. The normal positioning of men and women is thus reversed during the ritual while gender separation between them is maintained.

Themes of sexual arousal and erotic transference also infuse Gebusi spirit séances. Here the focus of erotic attention is the spirit woman, who is in one very concrete sense impersonated by the male spirit medium. In addition, the amplified voice of the spirit woman is that of the young men, who chorus the medium's song lines. These singers, predominantly the younger men, are frequently the same males most active as recipients in homosexual relationships.[15] This gender transference is symbolically indicated by the Gebusi designation of the wuli as, the spirit medium's male spirit child, as responsible for the spiritual work of the séance, though it is in fact the spirit women who sing the songs, carry out the inquest, and make the pronouncements.

The transfer of erotic attention from spirit women to Gebusi men is effectively predisposed by the teasing and caprice of the spirit women themselves. During the séance, the spirit women fly capriciously about the forest looking for sexual adventure, hover about or come inside the longhouse where the singing is taking place, and teasingly describe acts of sexual foreplay and coitus. To the male séance audience, these erotic portrayals are both extremely entertaining and excruciating. The spirit woman presents the fulfillment of Gebusi men's heterosexual fantasies: she is beautiful, alluring, openly seductive, and quite available for sex. However, the spirit woman remains on a separate plane of existence; she lives in the spirit world and is hence unavailable to the Gebusi audience regardless of how much she and they both wish to consummate their relationship. (There is apt evidence that Gebusi men's heterosexual desires are quite strong and genuine in their own right [see Knauft 1986]). Men's sexual arousal is thus crosscut by intense sexual frustration—a pronounced sense of longing (fafadagim-da) (Knauft 1986; Cantrell n.d.:chap. 3). This sentiment of passionate longing is the preeminent emotional dynamic of the successful séance, and one that strongly engages erotic transfer under conditions of gender separation.

Most immediately, of course, men at the séance make uproarious comments and displays of their pent-up sexuality, for example, bawdy screams, stomping about, or shaking houseposts. In concrete social terms, these displays of frustrated heterosexuality are directed to the other men present. In this context men's cries of longing for the spirit women easily become lewd jests that a male comrade could substitute as a means of obtaining more immediate sexual release.

In the most boisterous séances, teasing between a man and a coy adolescent can escalate until the pair make a departure from the longhouse for a brief homosexual tryst in which the adolescent manually stimulates the man to the point of orgasm and orally consumes the semen. Although most séances do not entail such homosexual trysting per se, they typically do entail a large measure of homoerotic joking and display during the night. It is this more diffuse aura of homoeroticism as collective camaraderie—rather than completion of the sexual act itself—that is central to the performative dynamic of the séance.

In summary, although spirit séances and ritual dances entrain heterosexual arousal that is quite genuine in its own right (Knauft 1986), they simultaneously escalate homoeroticism through gender switching and erotic transference. First, the ostensible female love-object is in both cases actually a male impersonator. Second, the heterosexual arousal incited by the impersonator's persona is redirected among the men present; it is the male audience members themselves who become the social and sexual targets of each other's eroticism. Significantly, the absence of available women which necessitates this homoerotic transfer is itself mandated by men; Gebusi women are excluded by men from participating in the séance, and the imagery of the spirit woman is, of course, also a product of the men's own creative formulations. In important respects, then, it is men themselves who preclude heterosexual contact; they actively create the gender separation that drives their heterosexual frustration and homoeroticism (Cantrell n.d.). Men thus effectively distance themselves from female sexuality at the same time that they appropriate and redirect its erotic potential among themselves (Knauft 1987b). What results is the symbolic construction of male sexual autonomy, epitomized in the notion that men can "grow" boys into adulthood through homosexual insemination.

Longing and Aggression

Erotic transfer in Gebusi séances is strongly juxtaposed against and complemented by the displacement of aggression directed against the various targets of longing (fafadagim-da). As will be shown, fafadagim-da motivates the linkage in Gebusi spirit séances between sexual arousal and the potential violence associated with serious spiritual pronouncement.

The sentiment of fafadagim-da encompasses for Gebusi both the frustration of sexual separation and the disgruntlement of social loss or grief. Both these dimensions of longing are deemed to motivate aggressive anger (*gof*). Thus, for instance, male cries of sexual frustration are explicitly tied to those of animosity; the exclamations "I'm lonely/longing!" (*ay fafadagim-da*) and "I'm angry" (*ay gof*) are practically synonyms for one another in audience commentary, and they are often shouted together in a single phrase. Such expressions are often accompanied by aggressive or violent display, e.g., stomping about the longhouse, grabbing and thrashing about with sticks, plucking bows, throwing cooking stones, or firing arrows into the longhouse roof, thus feigning in anger to hit or shoot the source of sexual arousal and frustration.

The Gebusi association between sexual arousal and aggression is virtually intrinsic (Cantrell n.d.:chap. 3). The word *gof* means angry, violent, strong, and hard. An erotically aroused man is inherently "hard" (phallically) and is aggressively strong. Likewise, the pursuit of a sexual mate is often portrayed through hunting metaphors, with the sexual act itself often being described as "fighting" (*bwisam*) or "bow-and-arrow shooting" (*geala*), in which the successful arrow is the phallus penetrating its target.

The object of this sexual antagonism, as with sexual arousal, slides easily between the men present and the spirit woman, who may be the subject of misogynistic or sexually aggressive remarks, that is, how the aroused man is going to pierce her with a vengeance. These displays of aggressive virility are common to both Gebusi ritual dances and spirit séances.

In addition to its primary association with sexual longing and frustration, fafadagim-da also evokes separation in the sense of grief or bereavement. Fafadagim-da in this respect conveys the sorrow of loneliness that stems from the loss of deceased relatives as well as the separation from a sexual partner, the former theme being quite pronounced in some other groups of the Strickland-Bosavi area (see Schieffelin 1976 concerning the Kaluli). Although this dimension of longing is not emphasized in most Gebusi séances, it can subtly inform the proceedings at key junctures, particularly during séances for sickness and death inquest. In particular, the mock anger of sexual frustration can subtly inform the more serious anger ultimately targeted against the sorcery suspect believed responsible for the illness or death of the sickness-victim.

The shifting of context from mock to more serious anger is linked in important ways to the transference of erotic arousal between female and male objects of sexual desire described above. Gebusi women, like sorcerers, may be subject to unilateral and unreciprocated violence—from their husbands (Cantrell n.d., chap. 9). The force of this gender animosity in the context of heightened sexual arousal may be playfully dispelled among men themselves during the séance, but it can fuel a sense of righteous indignation and underlying animosity with respect to the sorcery suspect.[16]

The outcomes of this affective transfer are variable, depending on the spirit medium, the audience, and the social context. In some séances the anger of sadness or grief for a sick or deceased community member is largely ameliorated through the longing of exaggerated homoerotic joking and display. Often this articulates as well with the symbolic displacement of aggression into the spirit world through the medium's violent "claiming of the spirit" (fin hup). In other cases, however, sexual frustration and aggressive anger may be displaced onto the sorcery suspect. Gebusi séance songs frequently superimpose images of frustrated sexual opportunity with those of lethal hunting and sorcery inquest. The violent fighting terminology used for sexual adventures facilitates this association on the lexical and conceptual level. This aura of heightened aggressiveness provides the overarching context of the séance, and it is within this context that information concerning the sorcery inquest is so quickly intruded and extruded. In short, the imagery of the sorcery inquest is contextually saturated with the residue of sexual animosity and with the dynamics of aggression-transference. Under these conditions, the maintenance of friendship and cooperation among those in attendance easily finds its complement in the fermentation of anger against the sorcery suspect who is not present. The collective and beneficent setting of the séance itself is thus vouchsafed, while the suspect is scapegoated through the attribution of deviance (see Foucault 1976; Becker 1963; cf. Durkheim 1964 [1895]:66–67).

In facilitating damning assessments, if not lethal violence, the sexually arousing imagery of Gebusi inquest séances appropriates deep-seated psychophysiological potentials. That frustrated sexual arousal facilitates aggression has been frequently documented under laboratory conditions by Western psychologists and physiologists (e.g., Zillmann 1984; Langevan 1985; Baron 1980; Jaffe, Malamuth, Feingold, and Feshbach 1974). Although the mediating cognitive dynamics are certainly culture-specific, the connection between sexual arousal and aggressive incitement is underlain by the fact that the centers of activation for these emotions are only a millimeter apart in the brain (MacLean 1962). As a result, the response of these centers to direct stimulation is rather undifferentiated in terms of nervous system response. The linkage between sexual arousal and aggression is thus inherently potent as a source of cultural elaboration.[17]

It is significant in this regard that Gebusi executions of sorcery suspects were in the past themselves perpetrated through the sexually provocative guidance of spirits in a séance. Informants said that such séances, like those observed in the field, were pervaded by aggressive ribaldry. This ribaldry undoubtedly fuelled damning assessments that the sorcery suspect should be attacked summarily and without mercy. In many such cases, the men attending the séance departed at dawn and went immediately to carry out the killing the spirits had mandated, saying that they were happy (*obeagim-da*) to perform this civic duty.

On other occasions, as is increasingly true today, action against the sorcery suspect is not taken until days or weeks after the final death-inquest séance.

Here, as in the case of Muswayay discussed above, it is the cognitive assessment of the suspect by the community—the extent of the guilt and the magnitude of the alleged crime—that are deeply influenced, if not formulated, during the séance, viz., in the context of sexually arousing and frustrating spiritual imagery. In some cases this connection is quite direct; songs of sexual frustration in the spirit world become thinly veiled allegories for this-worldly discontent over sexual or marital frustrations caused directly or indirectly by the sorcery suspect him- or herself (see further below and séance case example in Knauft 1985a:311–317).

Acceptance of damning sorcery pronouncements is also facilitated by the larger performative structure of Gebusi séances. It has often been remarked that communication frames such as ritual and liturgical orders employ arcane, ineffable, or inchoate imagery, and that this imagery instills special believability because of its nonquotidien nature and extraordinary signification (Rappaport 1971, 1979; Bloch 1973, 1986). Correspondingly, the fantastic spiritual aura of Gebusi song imagery facilitates its ultimate believability. In Gebusi séances the alluring ambiguity of spirit world sexuality forms the ever-present context in which serious pronouncements are briefly intruded. Given fervent participatory embracement by the audience of the larger performative context, these pronouncements are themselves imbued by association with a strong sense of reality and audience concurrence. Particularly for persons neutral to the central issue, it is easy to accept the spirits' instrumental pronouncements almost casually. Hence, audience embracement of spirits' titillating sexual adventures predisposes their acceptance of definitive spiritual pronouncements as well as imbuing this acceptance with particularly deep-seated affective force.

The Sociology of Sexual Asymmetry

The linkage between sexual incitement and this-worldly anger articulates in important ways with the sociology of Gebusi sorcery attributions. Gebusi accused of sorcery following death-inquest séances tend to be persons whose marital interests were actively or tacitly opposed to those of the sickness victim's patriline. For instance, sorcery victims and suspects are frequently affines or matrikin who have been party to an unreciprocated marriage. Such relatives are expected to be—and are overwhelmingly, in fact—indulgent and supportive of one another despite the marital imbalance between them. However, when such persons or their close relatives die from sickness, sorcery attributions across the affinal linkage are made with surprising frequency (Knauft 1985a:chaps. 5–7).

The connection between unreciprocated sexuality and violent sorcery attribution is in important ways backgrounded if not denied by Gebusi themselves (in the same way, perhaps, that the connection between frustrated sexual arousal and sorcery attribution is more experientially real than cognitively realized by séance participants). Even though the accuser and victim have themselves typically long since found wives, and even though their relationship may seem peaceful if not friendly for all intents and purposes, it is easy for latent animosity to be read post facto into an asymmetrical affinal relationship when sickness or death strikes one of the patriline members or their spouses. Marital and sexual asymmetry are in this respect structural fault lines that the perceptive spirit medium can use to locate a "natural" sorcery suspect and generate a convincing sorcery indictment.

This pattern dovetails with the cultural construction of Gebusi emotions. Nonreciprocal marriages are conceptualized by Gebusi as prompted by an inexorable sexual desire that overrides the demands of reciprocity. As such, nonreciprocal marriage almost inherently evokes the notion of self-willed sexuality. In such cases the reduction of fafadagim-da as sexual frustration that the new husband finds in unilaterally claiming a wife finds its natural and ultimate complement in sorcery attribution by his affines—their angry fafadagim-da combining both grief for a deceased relative and the anger of their own lost sexual opportunities. The two notions of aggressive fafadagim-da thus entail each other through cultural and emotional logic.

The sorcery inquest for Terkabo may be reconsidered in this light. As may be recalled, Terkabo was a sister's son to the accused sorcerer Muswayay; Muswayay's sister had been given in marriage to Terkabo's father (now deceased). However, this marriage had been completed without the reciprocity of a young bride for Muswayay himself; he had been forced to marry the widow of his deceased clan brother. That Muswayay and his wife remained childless while his sister had borne her husband two surviving sons and a daughter furthered the potential for the childless couple's disgruntlement and antagonism between the two family groups. Yet Muswayay continued to live in the small hamlet in domestic cooperation with his sister and her grown sons Hogoswimam and Terkabo. Such a situation is easily perceived to engender unacknowledged resentment by the elder man, though the structural origin of the asymmetry was many years in the past, i.e., had no bearing on current marital concerns.

The asymmetric social relationship between Muswayay and Terkabo, like the spirit séance itself, thus combined and yet dissociated friendly camaraderie and potential animosity. Whereas in social life the transition between these states was believed to engender sorcery against the sick boy, this process was reversed in the performance structure of the séance; a juxtaposition between camaraderie and animosity produced an indictment against the sorcery suspect himself.

Good Company and Violence

The striking collapse of friendly camaraderie with ultimate anger, both at the séance and in affinal relations, is informed by larger cultural antinomies as

92   *Bruce M. Knauft*

well by affective and sociological dynamics. Preeminent here is relationship in Gebusi culture between good company (*kogwayay*) and violence (gof) (Knauft 1985a). The Gebusi concept kogwayay is also their word for custom or culture; it is the preeminent concept of their collective identity. The three morphemes of the word—*kog* (togetherness), *wa* (friendly talk), and *yay* (joking yells)— accurately convey the intense sociality of Gebusi men from diverse clans within the residential community (Knauft 1985a:chap. 3). As has been shown, these same dynamics of communal camaraderie and joking banter are strongly characteristic of Gebusi spirit séances. Indeed, the same three concepts that constitute *kog-wa-yay* are present in Gebusi referents for "spirit séance": *kog-wa-fada*, literally, "go up and talk together in friendship (with the spirits)"; and *hi-yay-dogra*, "to cause a joking yell to be 'thrown.'" The séance is thus in several respects an epitome of Gebusi male good company—of togetherness, talking, and joking.

As has been described, the norms of good company so strong and prevalent among Gebusi, particularly between affines, juxtapose against the reality of ultimate violence between these same community members. The most severe context of this violence is, of course, the sorcery attribution and subsequent execution of a suspect within the community following a sickness-death. Yet such sorcery killings are seldom avenged or reciprocated. Neither do they lead to other forms of violence such as feuding or warfare; such collective violence has been statistically rare in Gebusi society.[18] Rather, these killings tend—like scapegoating often does—to intensify the spirit of community solidarity. As Kenelm Burridge (1969) might put it, the tension between good company and violence is the primary dialectic of Gebusi society and culture. This same tension between a predominant spirit of kogwayay and a discordant but intensive thrust of projective aggression is seen in microcosm at the spirit séance, viz., intense male camaraderie crosscut by deeply damning indictments against the sorcery suspect.

Culture and Politics in Spirit Mediumship

Given the complex sociosexual and symbolic dimensions of Gebusi spirit pronouncements, it may be asked what kinds of political ramifications they have. Do spirit pronouncements serve some kind of ideological masking function? Do they legitimate some kind of authority relationship? On one level, Gebusi spirituality enacts the male appropriation and control of female sexuality. This is an important and complex issue that is being considered elsewhere (Cantrell n.d.). For the present, we may consider the political advantages that accrue to the spirit medium.

As has been illustrated, Gebusi spirit mediums have a significant degree of latitude and control in their spiritual pronouncements, including both the naming of the sorcery suspect and the severity of action to be taken against him or her. This influence is highlighted by the fact that the spirit medium's indictment may reflect neither a current dispute nor the prior opinion of the audience. However, the cultural logic of the medium's pronouncements is strongly shaped by the existing norms and constraints of Gebusi sexual, emotional, and cultural life—parameters deeply internalized by the spirit medium himself.

Although a few exceptional Gebusi spirit mediums may be able, if motivated, to use their spiritual pronouncements to enhance their personal interests, the dominant practical sense one gets in the field is that they do not. The pronouncements made by a medium's spirits are expected by other Gebusi to be impartial. Given that séances are public events attended by men of diverse clan affiliations, a spirit medium is unlikely to be successful in generating support for pronouncements that are in the narrow interest of himself or his close kin as opposed to the collective interests of the several clans within the community. Attempting to do otherwise would tarnish a spirit medium's reputation and eventually threaten his status as a conduit to the spirit world. It may be recalled that spirit mediums are not paid or otherwise rewarded for their services; they are supposed to conduct séances as a civic service for their communities. Gebusi also state, however, that a medium's own spirits may become sympathetic or biased to his own point of view in issues about which he has very strong personal feelings, such as the death of his close relative or spouse. For this reason, sorcery and death inquest séances should not be conducted by spirit mediums for those who are of the same patriline or subclan affiliation as the medium himself.

The most important advantage that accrues to Gebusi spirit mediums is that as formulators of sorcery attributions they are themselves relatively immune to sorcery accusation and subsequent homicide. Spirit mediums meet a violent death only about half as frequently as nonmediums—21 percent of all deaths for spirit mediums versus 37 percent for men who are not mediums. This is consistent with the public perception of spirit mediums as the enemies of sorcerers.

The relationship between the collective interests of the community and the self-interest of the spirit medium can be illustrated by a final consideration of the sorcery inquest séance discussed above. It may be noted that the kinship relationship between the spirit medium, Swiman, and the sorcery suspect, Muswayay, was a close one—they were agnatic half-brothers. Such a relationship typically entails close alliance and support in Gebusi society. What, then, motivated Swiman to indict his half-brother? Quite plausibly, several factors were involved, including (a) Swiman's sincere desire to free Terkabo from sorcery, (b) the knowledge that Muswayay had been previously indicted as a sorcerer, and (c) the liberating effects of the dissociated consciousness experienced by Swiman during his séance. A more practical factor, which emerged in discussion following the accusation of Muswayay, was that Terkabo's sickness might retard or even prevent the holding of a feast for the upcoming male initiation. Feasts are a major focus of social attention and cultural value; along with spirit séances, they are the epitome of kogwayay. Yet preparation for and organization of such a festive event are difficult as well as improper when one of the central participants is seriously ill. In his pronouncement, then, Swiman both focused attention on Terkabo's sickness at an early stage in its development and heightened awareness of its larger potential impact on the community. Correspondingly, by identifying and confronting the alleged sorcerer before the sickness became severe, Swiman's indictment was designed to short-circuit both the threat to Terkabo's health and the larger threat this posed for the community.

The question of self- and kin-group interest may also be considered in historical perspective; what patterns of political interest or conflict do spiritual pronouncements reveal over time? Although Swiman and Muswayay were agnatic half-brothers, their patriline had been residentially split since the previous generation, at which time Swiman's patriline segment became allied to a different subclan affinally, through sister exchange (Knauft 1983:571–574; Cantrell n.d.). When two men in this affinal subclan died and two senior men in Muswayay's patriline segment were accused as responsible, the agnates of Swiman's segment had supported the final execution of these sorcery suspects, notwithstanding their own close "brother" relationship to them. Reciprocally (some twenty years ago), Swiman's coresident agnate and matrilateral half-brother was accused of sorcery following the death of Muswayay's father's brother's wife; Muswayay's segment—including Muswayay himself—took the initiative and carried out the execution. In short, a pattern of sorcery accusation and corresponding execution ultimately pitted the halves of the split patriline against each other.

In the present generation, this conflict between the patriline segments appeared to continue; Muswayay had been indicted on five occasions by Swiman's spirits for having sent bogay sickness against members of the community. In four of these cases, the sickness had been diagnosed early by Swiman and the victim had recovered—due, it was believed, to Muswayay's prompt exposure and repentance. In the one remaining case, in which the victim had died, Swiman's spirits had themselves ultimately deflected the indictment away from Muswayay, retargeting it against another person from a different clan (Knauft 1985a:chap. 2). This accusation pattern is thrown into further relief by the fact that a full 80 percent of living Gebusi men in Muswayay's age category have been accused of sorcery (Knauft 1985a:141). That Muswayay's eldership status was cross-cut by sorcery attribution on a continuing basis was thus normative and indeed quite expectable.

Through the pronouncements of Swiman's spirits, the lingering tension between his and Muswayay's patriline segments was both dovetailed with and mediated by collective community orientations and concerns, specifically, the

desire to quickly diagnose and cure sick persons such as Terkabo, the desire to
expose elderly sorcerers, and the desire for the community to cohere through the
holding of feasts and initiations rather than break apart over sorcery deaths and
subsequent accusations. As inheritor of the structural tension between his own
patriline segment and that of Muswayay, Swiman's pronouncements reflected
and reinforced the expectable community sentiment that Muswayay was a sorcerer but also maintained strict propriety; he allowed Muswayay maximal opportunity both to successfully repent and to effectively avoid the most damning
and life-threatening portmortem indictments.

A Comparative Hypothesis

The balance between community interest and the shamans' or spirit medium's self-interest can be highly variable from case to case and with different
personalities—much less in different cultures. In many societies, including a
substantial number in Melanesia, Amazonia, and the circumpolar regions, ambivalent spiritual power and the potential for self-interested or nefarious behavior have been almost intrinsic to the role of shaman or spirit medium, reflected
in his frequently imputed ability to cause as well as cure sickness (e.g., Stephen
1987a, 1987b; Godelier 1986; Descola and Lory 1982; Granero 1986; Brown
1988; Balikci 1963; 1970:chap. 12; cf. Taussig 1987). In a sociopolitical perspective, such self-interested assertion by a shaman or spirit medium comple-
ments or reinforces other aspects of political leadership and status rivalry, for
example, competitive headmanship, kin group leadership, ritual age-grading,
gerontocracy, or opposition to external political hegemony.

Among Gebusi, such forms of adult male status differentiation are relatively undeveloped; Gebusi lie at the highly decentralized end of the Melanesian
political spectrum. Correspondingly, self-interested political competition or
aggrandizement by spirit mediums has been minimal. Conversely, their sensitivity to the collective interests of the various clan segments within the community has been high. It is consistent with this that the potentially threatening and
ambivalent role of the sorcerer- or shaman-as-extortionist is virtually absent
among Gebusi—a trend contrastive with sorcery in many New Guinea societies (see Knauft 1985a: 339–348). Constraints against self-interested and
intimidating shamanistic authority are particularly strong in those societies
where political decentralization is most extreme: societies such as the !Kung
(Lee 1978; Katz 1983) and the Copper Eskimo (Jenness 1922; Rasmussen
1932)—cf. also Turnbull (1961, 1965a, 1965b) concerning African pygmies,
and, comparatively, Woodburn (1982).

It may be hypothesized in general that the actions of shamans and spirit
mediums will be lacking in intimidating and self-interested leadership preroga-
tives to the degree that these features of adult male status differentiation are

otherwise absent in the society in question. In societies where political decentralization is most extreme, the success of the spirit medium or shaman is most closely tied to his or her ability to mediate narrower self and kin-group interests with the collective interests of a much wider community. The consciousness of an entranced shaman or spirit medium in the most highly decentralized societies may thus exhibit a particularly pronounced form of what Michele Stephen (1986; this volume) has called "the autonomous imagination"—a mode of consciousness that can transcend the self-interested motivations of the actor in waking consciousness.

Conclusions

Imagery and pronouncement in Gebusi spirit séances instantiate diverse interconnections among spiritual, sexual, psychophysiological, and sociopolitical factors. The heightened sexual arousal of the Gebusi audience during the séance effects (a) the transfer of erotic attention from the spirit women to the male audience and (b) the mock expression of anger at the séance itself. This anger can be articulated through the Gebusi experience of longing with a parallel opposition and anger among the male audience with respect to the target of séance pronouncement, that is, the sorcery suspect. This process engages the frustration of unsatisfied sexual arousal and gender ambivalence with the more subliminal anger of social loss and separation. This connection appears to be facilitated by the cultural appropriation of underlying psychophysiological propensities as well as by a séance communication structure that predisposes audience acceptance of the spiritually-identified suspect.

On a wider symbolic level, séance performances articulate with the dialectical antinomy in Gebusi culture between good company (kogwayay) and violence (gof), this being reflected in the tension between male camaraderie and the potential for aggression against the targets of séance pronouncement. Similar underlying themes of nonreciprocation and potential anger in the face of stringent norms of good company are evident in marital structure, that is, the schism between Gebusi expectations of affinal forbearance and the violent attribution of sorcery in these same relationships. The symbolic logic of these processes both informs and reflects the highly decentralized and publicly nonconfrontational nature of Gebusi politics, including a mode of spirit mediumship that to a significant degree transcends the individualistic self-interests of the spirit mediums themselves. It is suggested that this pattern has been most highly developed in the shamanism or spirit mediumship of societies exhibiting the most extreme political decentralization. In these and other respects, it would be fruitful to compare Gebusi spiritual practice to shamanism and other forms of elaborate image-making in Melanesia and elsewhere.

NOTES

Acknowledgments: This paper was written as part of a research project funded by the Harry Frank Guggenheim Foundation. Research among the Gebusi between 1980 and 1982 was funded by the National Institutes of Health, the National Science Foundation, and the University of Michigan. Insightful comments on a previous draft of this paper are very gratefully acknowledged from Eileen Cantrell, Gilbert Herdt, Raymond Kelly, Edward Schieffelin, and Michele Stephen; the shortcomings, of course, remain my own.

1. Shamans and spirit mediums are here defined as part-time but all-purpose spiritual practitioners who interpret and define the relationship between people and supernatural forces through encounters with the spirit world. The term *spirit medium* has been prominent in African contexts and in British usage (e.g., Firth 1959:141; Beattie and Middleton 1969), whereas *shaman* has been more commonly used in reference to the New World and Asia, particularly by French and American researchers (e.g., Eliade 1964 [1951]:3ff.; Wallace 1966:86; Reinhard 1976; Lessa and Vogt 1972b:381). In the case of Melanesia, each of these terms has been used, and they will be employed interchangeably in the present context as defined above (see Juillerat [ed.] 1977; Schieffelin 1985; Godelier 1986; Fortune 1935; Layard 1930a, 1930b; Sørum 1980; Van Baal 1966:890ff).

2. The spirits of Gebusi mediums are said to enjoy indigenous tobacco, which is proffered to them in smoke-filled pipes from audience members during the séance (see Knauft 1987a). Such tobacco sharing is also pervasive among the audience, however, and the spirits of mediums do not smoke appreciably more than do other men who are present (contrast Wilbert 1987).

3. As Fischer (1971) has shown, euphoria has a common physiological basis regardless of which channel (intense relaxation versus intense sympathetic arousal) is used to induce it. In this respect the emphasis in much of the current literature on ergotropic concomitants of shamanism and on autonomic nervous system

tuning needs to be complemented by greater consideration of intense trophotropic stimulation (relaxation) in shamanism and spirit mediumship.

4. The pervasive Gebusi focus on the idealized spirit woman contrasts with some other Strickland-Bosavi societies, in which there is great differentiation and dramatic particularity of the medium's spirit familiars (cf. Schieffelin 1977, 1985, concerning the Kaluli).

5. This necessity can be partially abrogated if the spirit woman herself takes a brief nap during the night. This can allow the medium and the singers to doze for a few minutes or perhaps up to an hour in the middle of the night, though they retain their sitting position clustered close together. After such a period, the spirit woman again starts to chant and the singers revive their own song to continue the séance.

6. Gebusi place little emphasis upon magic, spells, sacrifices, or personal dream interpretation. A few forms of minor sickness remedy can be performed by individuals, but these are believed ameliorative rather than curative. One form of cure—infrequently attempted— entails the daytime supplication of spirits by the spirit medium to draw a stone or bone out of the sick victim (*bosa*). However, for any important or persisting divinatory issue, the holding of a full spirit séance is requisite.

7. Other selected symbolic and sociological dynamics of Gebusi séances are discussed in Knauft (1985a:chaps. 2, 4, 12; 1986); some of their psychodynamic features are considered in Knauft (1987b).

8. In my sample of 101 spirit séances, 13 were performed jointly by two spirit mediums. Two of these 13 séances included participation of a third spirit medium as well. In jointly performed séances, the spirits of one of the mediums take primary responsibility investigating the principal issues of social concern, whereas the second medium participates in a demonstration of friendly support and cooperation. In the present case, Swiman was the primary spirit medium and Hogoswimam supported him.

9. Although women rarely participate in séances, they follow with interest topics of special concern to them by listening to the
proceedings through the thin sago-leaf wall
that separates their sleeping quarters from
those of the men (Cantrell n.d.).
10. The séance from which this text was taken
took place on October 13, 1981, in Yibihilu
longhouse. It constitutes part of a large corpus
of séances and song texts recorded, tran-
scribed, and translated in the field between
June 1980 and March 1982. Transcription and
exegesis of tape-recorded events were made
with the help of monolingual informants. (All
fieldwork was carried out in the Gebusi ver-
nacular.) It is unfortunately not possible in the
present context to detail the linguistic and musical features of Gebusi séance songs (cf. Feld
1982).
11. This makes coherent translation into English difficult; as ease of comprehension is increased, the polysemic richness of song
images is reduced. The intricacies of converting spoken (or sung) narration into written
text is an important topic but one beyond the
scope of the present paper (see Tedlock 1983).
In general, I have tried to make the present text
as literal and as open to interpretation as was
the original.
12. Gebusi have until the very recent past can-
nibalized persons executed as sorcerers.
13. Three of the men were true or
classificatory clansmen to Muswayay. One of
these men was also a classificatory sister's
child's husband (ZCH) to Terkabo and sister's
husband (ZH) to Hogoswimam.
14. The most fervent homosexual inseminators

in fact tend to be those adult men without
wives: widowers and unmarried male initiates.
15. A few of these persons actively recapitu-
late spirit woman themes in daily life; they
thrive on relations of coquettish allure with
each other and with the initiated men who joke
with and inseminate them.
16. Though the point cannot be developed further here, Gebusi place greater emphasis on
the metaphoric linkage between women and
sorcerers as common targets of legitimate violence than do societies of the nearby Great
Papuan Plateau. Conversely, the latter societies place more emphasis than do Gebusi on
the metaphoric connection between male de-
pletion and heterosexual contact (Kelly 1976;
compare Cantrell n.d.).
17. Interestingly, an analogous conclusion has
been reached by Stoller (1979) through psychodynamic analysis of erotic fantasies, viz.,
that aggression and sexual excitement are in
significant ways inextricably linked.
18. See Knauft (1985a:chap. 5). Because
sorcery-related violence tends to be directed
surgically against the scapegoated suspect
within the community, the predominant response of community members is to downplay
and minimize the killing's significance. This
orientation reflects a strong desire to return to a
state of collective good company as quickly as
possible. The closest kin of the person executed may privately dispute the killing, but
against the opinion of the other clans in the
community they have little option but to acqui-
esce, accept their kinsman's fate, and gradually reintegrate themselves into the social life
of their community.

Spirit Familiars in the Religious Imagination of Sambia Shamans

Gilbert Herdt

A story about a shaman's *(kwooluku)* dream will serve to introduce the themes of this chapter on spirit familiars *(numelyu)* among the Sambia of Papua New Guinea. If shamans are the central religious authorities of Sambia culture, then their familiars are the key concept for understanding their inner worlds, and a cypher for interpreting how they organize and experience their social roles and cultural identities. Indeed, a central point is that the familiar is neither clearly of spirit, body, or mind, but is a holistic representation of aspects of self and world; and this linkage fundamentally obviates any simple attempt to argue for what is empirical or non-empirical (Lawrence 1973) in New Guinea religious experience and practice. The speaker is Sakulambei, now the greatest practicing Sambia shaman, and a man with whom I have worked for some years (Herdt 1987c; Herdt and Stoller 1989). The story is one of many he narrated to me in 1979.[1]

Saku performed a healing ceremony, a *kwolyi*, on the small, sick child of a classificatory clan brother—Erujundei—one night. He went to bed and dreamt the following:

> I go and fight with a *kumaamdu* [ghost], at Pundei [his natal village]. Erujundei, his father, and my woman [wife] all jump me . . . I'm very strong . . . I really beat up my wife; her eye swells up where I hit her . . . They leave . . . I see my [paternal uncle] Kunouwioko. . . . "I had to fight, I wasn't thinking straight, I hurt them, I think they'll bring a *kot* [native litigation and local council trial] against me," I told him. He asked me, "Why did you fight them?" And I woke up. When I woke I thought, "I've got trouble, I'll be *koted*"; but then I realized I'd dreamt.

> Later that morning a woman came by to say my old stepmother was very sick, "the one you struck." "The village sat in on a healing ceremony and they pointed to [blamed] your *aatmwogwambu* [female hamlet spirit, personal familiar]," she said. And then I thought to myself, "Last night, I hit my wife [dream], but I think it was actually *her*—the old woman. If I hadn't hit my *aatmwogwambu* [in the dream], my old stepmother wouldn't be ill. But at least since I didn't kill her she's not dead."

> So I went to heal her. I "smoked" [shamanic exorcism] her. She was shaking. Meiounjin [powerful, now deceased, male shaman] said my

aatmwogwambu had attacked her. Nothing was removed from her innards.
. . . I only chased her [*aatmwogwambu*] away . . . I took the *narogangu*
[cordyline used in healing], and chased it [spirit] away—saying to it, close
to the old woman's body—"You go away." . . .

But I felt that if I hadn't dreamt she'd not be ill now, and if I had [in the
dream] killed her, they'd have *koted* me. And had I been away [not able to
heal her], she'd really have died. When I tranced I called my Yumalo [de-
ceased maternal uncle, great shaman to whom Saku apprenticed; now a
shamanic familiar] to me . . . I thought of him . . . and of how Papa and
Mama [stepmother] used to hit me [as child] . . . I must *kwolyi* her; need to
exorcise, to get Yumalo to stop hurting her. . . .

But I thought, "It's your [Saku's stepmother's] own fault—you angered me when [as a child] you hurt me. . . ." The old woman says: "I'm
always seeing you [Saku] in my dreams—and sometimes your *dangenj*
[evil lowland spirit], Yumalo." And I retorted, "That's right, my Yumalo
isn't far away, he's always near."

I called his name [last night, in the dream], because a mob jumped
me—He came to fight you all: so it's your own fault!" Then, [step] mother
said: "You're my son, you shouldn't cross me. . . . And I said: "Yes, I
shouldn't cross you. . . . But I'm not afraid now, you used to [childhood]
hit me, and now I get angry. . . ."
GH: "Have you dreamt this before?"
SAKU: "Many times. . . . The familiar of Yumalo wants to kill them all if I
am hurt."

The richness of this text, which is much condensed from an interview ses-
sion that lasted an hour, well illustrates the imaginative life of shamans. Saku is,
in this way, typical, as is this narrative, though it emerged from intensive long-
term interviewing (Herdt and Stoller 1989). Shamans positively revel in the
elaboration of such stories: Their ability to incorporate into a single account the
experiences of night dreams, healing ceremonies, omens and visions, and myriad secular events is remarkable. Ordinary Sambia themselves are sometimes
amazed by the prolixity and verbal ingenuity of their shamans' stories. The
Sambia are, just as well, in awe and somewhat afraid of their shamans. Fortunately, as I have written before (Herdt 1977, 1987c), the shaman is a heroic
figure whose duty to the community is anchored in a moral tradition that village
shamans must do good deeds for their neighbors. Their evil and hostile intents
are to be directed only to enemy villages.[2] This does not settle the matter, of
course, and of their discontent more shall be said. I mention their public response (Peters and Price-Williams 1980) in part to underline the evocative
power of shamanic narratives, which are by no means received as "just so"
stories, though their truths are not at issue (Price-Williams 1987; see also
Kleinman 1988).

The selection of spirit familiars as the orienting concept of this chapter arises from several complementary concerns about the religions of New Guinea. The first of these derives from my general interest: The concept of familiar, so widespread in religious systems, is well represented in New Guinea; and its interpretation helps us to think more generally about problems of meaning that link cultural objects to selfhood and imagination. My second concern derives from the Sambia themselves, for whom familiars are of importance in every person's functioning and development, but most notably and strikingly obvious in shamans. The shaman's inner world draws cognitive focus from familiars as a means of making sense of the "booming, buzzing confusion" (James 1958) of the time/space world. The meaning and motivational power of familiars obviously arises in part from the personal history of shamans, their conflicts and triumphs (Crapanzano 1977, 1980; Herdt 1977; Freeman 1967; Kakar 1983; Peters and Price-Williams 1983; Spiro 1968; and cf. Eliade 1964). The third, and in some ways novel, aspect of my concerns here, is to understand familiars as a linking concept between self subjectivity and cultural representation among shamans. Sambia healers bring special motivations and meanings to their pragmatic and evocative uses of the idea of familiars. Familiars can become, in this sense, personalized cultural images; or, to use Obeyesekere's (1981) concept, psychogenic symbols, which in psychoanalytic terms are pregnant with unconscious and conscious meanings that complement those of their cultural connotations. This last perspective approaches the spirit familiar as providing a rich, evocative language through which inner worlds and symbolic realities are simultaneously encompassed in the narratives of shamans.

Sambia Culture and Shamanism

Sambia are a Highland fringe people who number about twenty-four hundred. Their language and culture belongs to the Anga tradition of societies spread over a large area, from the Papuan Gulf to the southeastern corner of the Eastern Highlands of Papua New Guinea. Social organization is marked by strong patrivirolocal residence and patrilineal descent. Hamlets are small (from 40 to 150 persons) and are built on high mountain ridges for defense. Warfare was endemic in the area until 1964, when the Australian government halted hostilities and began a process of change that has increased in tempo since the introduction of coffee-cropping and a cash economy in the early 1970s. Village organization revolves around localized patricians with in-marrying wives. Leadership is largely achieved, and war leaders, elders, and shamans play key roles in the social regulation of public affairs.

The ethos of Sambia is represented in themes of a rugged warriorhood, sexual antagonism, animism, and heroic shamanism in the self's major conceptions and cultural expressions. Warriorhood is valued as a concomitant of the aggressive training males receive for warfare and hunting. Sexual antagonism is built from gender conceptions of polarity in male and female essences and notions of spirituality (Herdt 1984c). Ritual initiation both cultivates and reinforces gender roles and a hierarchy of status positions between male and female, and younger and older males and females. Because of their view that all things in the cosmos and nature are alive and motivated by vital forces, Sambia religion recognizes many beings and spirits. Most of these are malevolent, which leads to a fatalistic outlook whereby humans are prey and pawns of ghosts and other spirits. The individualism of Sambian religion, however, presents an incomplete fatalism in its folktales and mystic narratives, for it is through the mediation and the correct use of ritual practices, and the heroic efforts of certain persons, especially shamans, that the fates can be mediated. (For details, see Herdt 1977, 1987c.)

Two institutions are central in understanding Sambia religion: ritual initiation cult practices and shamanism. The men's secret cult responsible for initiating boys at ages 7 to 10 and transforming them into aggressive warriors is very important, but it has been studied in previous publications (Herdt 1981, 1982b, 1987c) and shall only be mentioned here. This secret male society bonds males to ritual symbols, the results of which alter their selfhood, sexuality, and spirituality. Because body fluids are perceived as essential to gender and soul, special purificatory and maintenance rites typify male development, and always divide the sexes. Of special significance is the involvement of all males in prolonged oral homosexual contacts believed necessary to masculinize them. Females are also initiated into secret rites by women, but these come later (ages 16 to 20) for girls, and are less elaborate than for boys. Nonetheless, ritual practices figure prominently in the adjustment of both sexes across the life course and the presentation of self in Sambia society (Herdt 1987c:67–99).

Shamanism is the central theme of this chapter; the remainder of my text will be devoted to understanding how Sambia shamans represent, experience, and pragmatically use familiars. For heuristic purposes a description of shamanism can be divided between religious functions of the shaman's role, and the performance and personalities of particular practicing shamans.

A general point: The fatalism and animism of Sambia is pervasive in the symbolic organization of roles and concepts; and whereas the world is filled with entities and beings of power, and all humans are affected by these, only shamans—and then, in certain regards, only great shamans—are able to mediate or partially control them (reviewed in Godelier 1986; Herdt 1977). Shamans are able to interact in both the material and spiritual worlds, a point that Godelier (1972) has also made for the neighboring Baruya. Indeed, it is precisely in the Sambia shamans' capacity to see the unseen, and his or her responsibility to grapple with what is powerful but unmanageable and inarticulable for ordinary folk, that we find a religious figure the likes of which parallels only a few other peoples of New Guinea (Herdt, Part One, this volume; see also Juillerat 1977b; Schieffelin 1977; Stephen 1979, 1987a).

Sambia shamanism is popularly identified with five capacities of the performative role (in approximately this order of importance): (1) soul journeys while in trance—"magical flight", (2) exorcism, (3) healing, (4) divination, and (5) sorcery and countersorcery. All of these capacities inhere in the idealized role; whereas shamans vary in their performative powers. In general, only those labeled as "great" or "strong" shamans *(jerundu),* can manifest all of these capabilities, whereas "weak" or "minor" shamans *(kwooluku wusaatu)* cannot perform (1) magical flight and (2) exorcism. Though we cannot go into all of the reasons for this performative variance or its meaning in folk taxonomy and psychology, inadequate genealogical ancestry—and probably poor shamanic apprenticeship as well—are thought to limit the minor shamans' skills. Moreover, traditional Sambia culture emphasizes male rituals and warfare rites. Female shamans are disadvantaged by an absence of formal initiation mechanisms, as compared with male shamans, and they are structurally prohibited from serving in male ceremonies, which obviously limits their overall status (Herdt 1977, 1987b). Male shamans, conversely, are blocked from performing in female rites, which shifts their roles accordingly. Let us briefly review these five capacities of shamanic performance.

1. The concept of soul journeys suggest that shamans leave their bodies in trance and ascend to the spirits' world. Trance is induced by smoking strong native tobacco; thus, "to smoke" is a metaphor for trancing; and smoking is a sign of shamanic transition from waking consciousness into an alternate state of awareness. We know very little about such trance states among tribal peoples (Peters and Price-Williams 1983);[3] I shall address the phenomenology of such experiences below, albeit to describe communications with spirit familiars. When shamans apprentice, they spend years building their powers, especially to do soul journeys. These are dangerous and taxing. They require relatively deep trance-states, which, in turn, permits one's *koogu*—Sambia would translate this as "soul," as long as one understood that this sense of soul is indelibly connected to one's body and very lifeforce, and that harm to koogu in soul flight can harm one's body, resulting in sickness and even death—to leave the body in search of the souls of sick patients. What guides the koogu is one's familiars; and here, only shamanic familiars, or *kwooluku numelyu,* can serve. Soul journeys thus require long training and experience, discipline and control of trancing, powerful familiars, and the courage to use them. For these reasons only about one half of all Sambia shamans can do soul flight, even though this is critical for successful treatment of the sickest patients (i.e., whose souls have been stolen by ghosts or other spirits).

2. Exorcism also distinguishes strong shamans from weak ones. Only great shamans can perform the ceremony necessary to remove such items as bone,

rocks, teeth, and arrow points from a patient's body. These projectiles shot into the patient's body by a malevolent spirit or enemy shaman are always extracted, and then revealed to the audience and patient. This feat—and the ingenious capacity to reveal such items from thin air—delights and thrills audiences, and surpasses any other kind of individual performance in Sambia culture, because of its exotic and transcendental qualities. The confidence with which the practitioners communicate this act, and the way it confirms the audience's faith in the heroic complex of their shamans, leads me to understand how the psychoanalyst Otto Rank (1971), once looking from afar, could refer to such shamanism as a form of "exquisite narcissism" among tribal peoples.

3. All shamans can heal—at least certain maladies—thus, healing is a general metaphor for shamanism. There are very common, frequent, individual ceremonies, performed ever so casually in the patient's hut, usually at night. These require only one shaman. And there are larger ceremonies, done grandly to heal several patients, or to defensively protect against plagues and ward off spirits. Finally, there are special collective shamanic activities conducted throughout male initiation ceremonies (Herdt 1981, 1987b), which are so characteristic of these great symbolic events, because the shaman's leadership and spiritual entreaties are an essential foundation of collective initiation success.

4. Divination is another function of shamanism, in that trance is required to see deeply inside someone and diagnose a malady. Divining future events for the community is also common: shamans are consulted to produce omens regarding tomorrow's hunt or next week's garden work. No major event, be it warfare or ritual, would be seriously entertained without the oracular visions and dream reports of shamans; and here dreams are central to shamanic practice in all these respects, even in the shamans' calling (Herdt 1977), but especially in omens and soothsaying, as we shall see.

5. Finally there is sorcery, the dark side of Sambia shamanism, propped up and counterbalanced by shamans' abilities to conduct countersorcery against foes, be they spirits, other tribes, or enemy shamans. Sambia can never be sure that their shamans, who after all wield the greatest spiritual power they know, use sorcery only for the general good (Knauft 1985a). By moral convention, shamans must control their familiars. In practice, however, shamans are sometimes accused of conducting sorcery against others, albeit unwittingly.[4] Thus, being a shaman carries a risk of accusation, a possibility that shamans, such as Sakulambei (Herdt and Stoller 1985), experience as a chronic burden.

In practice, of course, not one but all five of these role skills are often used when a shaman takes on a healing case. When the patient turns over his body and soul to a shaman and has his unconscious stroked on the narrative level—to use Lévi-Strauss's (1967) metaphor—the shaman in turn lends his koogu and familiars to the patient's case in the service of the apotheosis of Sambia healing. Given the structural dichotomy in men's and women's roles, we would expect considerable differences between the male shaman and female shaman in the process, and indeed such are present. Yet, one is impressed by the power of strong women shamans, too, in catharsis and healing, as shown by Kaiyunango, the great woman shaman of Nilangu hamlet (Herdt 1987c). Political power and ritual structure mediate shamanic roles and performance in relation to the sex of the shaman, but not so completely that great women practitioners are unable to serve alongside their male peers and, with accelerating social change, in substitution of them.

Spirit Familiars and Shamanic Familiars

Let us return to Sakulambei's text, which opened this chapter. One senses a finely embroidered tapestry of concepts of dreaming, soul, spirit entities, and spirit familiars. Understanding here requires collection and interpretation of narratives in the contexts in which they emerge and via the subjectivities expressed (Herdt 1987d). If spirit familiars are an evocative language through which shamans represent self and awareness, then the meaning of this language is to be found in its phenomenological entities and their syntax (in the Greek sense of joining together).

An aside about my method in interviewing shamans and eliciting their narratives about trancing will help to illuminate my description of images of familiars. During my first two years' fieldwork (1974–76), interviews with shamans were done largely to elicit the sequence of healing events. My concerns with native concepts and the folk psychology related to them was secondary. In subsequent fieldwork, however, beginning in 1979, my focus was more on the subjectivity of these entities and their relationship to core cultural concepts. Fieldwork in later years has added follow-up interviews to further establish what was normative or aberrant in shamanic accounts. My long-term case study of Sakulambei, in particular, was instructive in providing insights on the heterogeneous nature of subjective representations of familiars and koogu. After interviewing Saku over a seven-year period (Herdt and Stoller 1989), I concluded that there were impressive differences in how shamans understand and use their own concepts. To some extent, they are aware of, and refer to, these differences, as for instance in the degree of control over their own familiars that different shamans claim to exert over the course of their careers. More often, however, such role differences are ignored or overlooked in pragmatic healing, and one reason is that the language of spirit familiars provides such a facile heuristic for communicating about interior-to-exterior events with others. My own work has convinced me that the subtle nature of these varieties of religious imagination can be grasped only over a longer period of fieldwork than is usually required in matters of cultural investigation.

Let us begin with the reference point of the person: a social category and a bounded conception in Sambia culture through which time, space, knowledge, and being are shaped. The person in Sambia thought is an adult who has followed a normative life course of achievements and assumed rights and duties. The Sambia person has a koogu, *koontu,* numelyu, and draws upon narrative conceptions of spirits and dreaming in understanding and representing these concepts, to self and to others.

Koogu emerges early in life, in mother's womb—an inheritance of essences from mother and father. Semen and blood, from father and mother, form the body, which indirectly influence koogu (Herdt 1984c). Infants have koogus, but they are tenuous and ill-formed; there is a developmental notion of self-awareness and being through which the maturing child is seen increasingly as an active agent involved in spiritual matters. Self-awareness and agency are not solely tied to humanness, however, since Sambia believe that pigs and dogs have koogus, which must be placated in minor ceremonial ways following the butchery of such animals. There is no ideal of ancestral reincarnation as such (see Herdt 1984c), yet there is the attitude that the koogu of deceased persons as ghosts or spirits inhabit and haunt clan territories and the village environs. Obviously, koogu involves both body and spirit components, so, again, we should gloss this as "soul" only by retaining its holistic indexical elements in Sambia epistemology.

Koogu is, as I said before, associated with remembered experience in night dreams. In canonical Sambia dream theory, dream events occur to koogu, not to the person or self of the dreamer—the I/me—as such (Herdt 1987d). However, one's body and self actions influence koogu; what koogu does in dreams can fatefully affect one's body and personhood. The signs of koogu sometimes refer to residues of body essence: fingernails, hair, spit; even one's breath and shadow. Blood and semen are critical essences here, with implications for preservation or loss of koogu, due for instance, to an implicit sense in which the circulation of semen through sexual intercourse affects koogu. One's shadow *(wakoogu-nambelu)* reveals the koogu to ordinary persons in waking life. Unlike lay persons, however, shamans can also "see" koogu in trance states.

Koontu is closely indexed to the category "thought," where the verb *think (koontutuv)* can become the transitive action *thinking* (or awareness). But *koontu* is also extrapolated to representations of thought; to say, "I think this or that", is to represent one's thought to self and others, so I have concluded that selfhood is mainly indexed by the term *koontu* (Herdt 1987a, 1987d). The linguistic closeness of koontu and koogu permit the speaker to use dreams, ordinary opinions, and even "miraculous" events to objectify or subjectify experience in social interaction as if they were of the same order of reality.

Numelyu is the most subtle and multivalent of such Sambian concepts, for it cannot easily be glossed as "familiar" or "spirit familiar," without doing violence to its native connotations (Herdt 1981). Numelyu, to begin, come in all forms and shapes. They are signified by many species of plants and animals, by cosmic elements (e.g., *kambo,* the north star), and even by spirits. One interpreter for instance, listed forty-one types of numelyu off the top of his head, and this was a very incomplete list! Numelyu, Sambia say, is something inside a man but also outside in the time and space world. Numelyu are inherited, especially from the same-sexed parent, and most germane, from father to son. But not all numelyu are inherited. Some are acquired anew, through familiar-attracting ceremonies in initiations (Herdt 1977, 1981). There is an animism and volition to the numelyu. For if a numelyu does not like a certain man, even though he should be its "father" (because his father has died, releasing his familiars to go to his son), they can resist, going instead to another son. Numelyus therefore link clans and generations, and the song-ropes of Sambia men, sung in their clubhouse songfests, often celebrate these familiars (Herdt 1988).

There are resemblances and similarities between numelyu and the anthropological term *totem,* though numelyu are not merely totems, even while they fulfill some of the conditions Lévi-Strauss (1963, 1966) has identified with the illusion of totemism. It is true that clans have broadly based totems, such as the Harpy eagle, or black palm tree, which are, in certain ritual and social situations, signs of someone's membership in such groups. These species should not be harmed and certainly not killed, and Sambia would gloss them as numelyu, too. However, even in these collective meanings there are inconsistencies of reference and ill-defined pragmatic references to them. For instance, the use of natural species (i.e., red bird-of-paradise) represents one phratry vis-à-vis another (i.e., through black bird-of-paradise), but there are no pragmatic manifestations of this symbolic coding. At any rate, these collective numelyu are distinct and quite different in nature from someone's personal numelyu. These latter are more fluid and their signs are changeable; yet they are also more pragmatic—in that they ensure personal health and well being; they are many and diverse in number; and they are neither exclusive by clan nor inclusive of clan membership per se. To say that these numelyu are totems may be nominally correct but of little help in our effort to understand them. Lévi-Strauss (1963:44) does not help us either in his cursory mention of "dream totemism," which may come closest to the numelyu conceptions of Sambia; and he dichotomizes the individual and collective signifiers of totems in a way that is false to the Sambia meaning system. Schwimmer (1986) has pointed out a similar problem in his work on Orokaiva society plant emblems. These points raise a broader problematic in individual versus collective meanings of religious imagination in New Guinea, to which I return later.

Numelyu are more truly developmental than are the concepts koogu and koontu in the life cycle and ritual formation of full personhood. Children do not have numelyu, for example; only as they enter initiation do boys acquire them. Before this, fathers are at pains to sleep apart from their maturing sons, for fear that their numelyu will be attracted to boys and abandon fathers, bringing illness or even death (Herdt 1981). Furthermore, there are illness numelyu, such as *kaluteku*, identified with respiratory disorders (i.e., tuberculosis) that some fear can be passed from father to son, or patrilaterally through family lines. Here younger males actually avoid older relatives to avoid the kaluteku familiar that would harm them. Other kinds of numelyu may even abandon a man when he becomes ill. At death, his familiars are freed from his body/soul and cling to nearby village flowers and trees, invisible entities that await another related person to attach to, usually through ritual ceremonies or dream journeys that are thought to attract familiars. Indeed, Sambia men widely believe that dreams of certain animals and plants establish claims to these numelyu by virtue of the remembered dream images. Vomiting upon consuming a certain kind of plant (e.g., mushroom) or animal (e.g., pig) dreamed of definitely establishes this numelyu as an active familiar for that person. The familiar protects and provides good health, so it must not be harmed (eaten); to do so harms one's person.

People vary somewhat in their attributions about familiars, though many interpreters agree that numelyu are usually inherited from parents. Some feel that numelyu emerge in the womb. Others suggest that numelyu wait until later (notice here again the volitional animism in the construction) when a male is older before going to him. A father's numelyu may sometimes go to a daughter, if there is no male heir, or they may wait till another patrilateral kinsman claims them, or wait even until the next generation. Only when a person sees them in dreams, or is told by another—a shaman or lay person who provides the necessary personal confirmation—are confirmatory signs of the familiar bond definite. Some feel that numelyu in general rest in the brain, and others in the heart, or both. Numelyu, in this way, strengthen one's thought and vitality.

Coming into manhood is identified with adult manifestations of numelyu. True, children are felt to have familiars attracted to them; but not all children: those who will become shamans, most of all. One minor shaman, Mavelengo, for instance, an older married man with many children, told me that both males and females have numelyu—but not until after their initiations. "At the time of initiation, when a boy has thought, then he can get numelyu," he said to me. Thereafter they remain with the person, unless the soul or familiars are stolen or ensorcelled, as signified by illness. The association of numelyu with mature thought, with accountability to moral norms (Herdt 1987a), seems to argue for a close link between koontu as self and numelyu as its counterpart in soul (or koogu). Again, an inexplicable bond between body, soul, mind, and familiars is communicated.

Among the types of numelyu that can be inherited or attracted are those of spirits that resemble or may assume human form, though they may only be visible in dreams or in shamanic trance. This complicates the definition of numelyu further, since I have suggested that numelyu itself is a kind of spirit being.

Because ghosts (*kumaamdu*, generic for "deceased persons"), forest spirits (*ikeiaaru* and, among the Sambia River Valley Sambia, *dangenj*), and female hamlet spirits (*aatmwogwambu*) are also numelyu for a good many persons—shamans especially—there is a double animation present here: numelyu in the guise of a humanoid spirit. Such numelyu are most often recognized as such and claimed by the self through dream reports made public. A rarer form is the *motaptu,* or witch familiar, that some family lines are thought to inherit; they are reluctant to claim them as numelyu, however, because of their malevolent force (see Bercovitch, this volume).

There is one such humanlike form of numelyu with which we shall be especially concerned: the kwooluku or shamanic spirit, the possession and continued experience of which is the sole claim to authentic shamanism. This being (inherited usually from same-sex parent [Herdt 1977]) is also of human form, though it is invisible to laymen and usually visible to shamen only in trance and dream states. These are more than mere shades. Kwooluku numelyu are named and personified; each one has a sex; they have quirks of personality, such as being adulterous or aggressive; they are possessive and protective of their master (shaman); they are luminous, in the sense that they can pass through walls, through fire, descend into earth or the heavens, and appear, in identical form, in dreams and trances. Of all the familiars of Sambia, then, these kwooluku are closest to being what Rank (1971) would have called a true double, an alter ego separate from one's body, or a shadow self, in Jung's (1966:59f.) sense, seen in visions or dreams.

Because numelyu are intentional agents separate from but linked to self and can also be humanlike spirit entities, the notion of familiar in Sambia culture suggests that it is not just a belief or concept. Familiars are a psychological structure of experiences and relationships that connect awareness with behavior, inside and outside the person. This view raises the strong possibility that shamanic familiars, as a psychological structure, access the autonomous imagination as Stephen (Part One, this volume) defines it. The self invests in and projects feelings and relationship into numelyu, inside and outside of the body. These numelyu are, in turn, indexed to and represented by cultural icons—tokens and signs of nature and humans. Behavior, thought, and emotion are thus linked to these icons in one's internal images of numelyu. Where the icons of numelyu are humanlike images, these suggest an even more powerful autonomous imaginative structure—an inner power expressed as a separate voice within the self, with needs and motivations being expressed through oneself as an Other. One's thoughts and words regarding this Other are, simultaneously, a deeply personal dialogue with unconscious parts of the self, as well as being narrative expressions with the Other as imagined and acted out to family and friends in real-life situations (see Obeyesekere 1981).

Before turning to narratives of shamanic spirit familiars it will be helpful to glimpse accounts of other humanlike numelyu. The kumaamdu or ghost numelyu is a relatively common one, though it is viewed hesitantly, even negatively. Among senior men and women shamans too the forest spirit (male) and hamlet spirit (female) are popular and well represented in folklore. Of interest here is the fact that these forest and hamlet spirits are often known, named, and even personalized beings—similar to the shamanic spirits in this way—and thus different from the faceless and nameless pool of ghosts, the dreaded cannibalistic shades of Sambia. Indeed, so clear are their boundary distinctions that one can posit a conceptual hierarchy of these beings in Sambia imagination:

Higher	*Kwooluku*	*(Shamanic Familiars)*	*Male and Female*
I	Ikeiaaru	(Forest Spirits)	Male
	Aatmwogwambu	(Hamlet Spirits)	Female
I	Kumaamdu	(Ghosts)	Male and Female
Lower	Numelyu	(Personal Familiars)	Androgynous

Some spirits are likened to fictitious kin, as demonstrated in the oft-cited idiom that "aatmwogwambu are the wives of ikeiaaru." And, furthermore, by the saying that this spirit couple produce offspring: cassowaries (only of female gender) *(kaiouwugu)*. This imaginative reproduction is not without interest to us, because cassowaries are the central mythological animal of Sambia (Herdt 1981), and shamans, who often have aatmwogwamu or ikeiraau numelyu, or both, are renowned for their wearing of a ceremonial headdress of cassowary rump feathers to which they, alone, are entitled by status.

One man—Nilutwo—went further in associating cassowaries with shamans by comparing the "X-ray" vision of both. Among Sambia the trance vision of shamans is legend. The ability to see the invisible is requisite of shamans, the key element for divination; it is power at which others marvel and somewhat fear. Nilutwo attributed a similar power to cassowaries. "Kaiouwugu (cassowary) eyes are like kwooluku eyes," he said. The cassowary can approach a thicket of dense vegetation and see all kinds of food for consumption that humans would miss. Further, it can see far, far away, and 360 degrees around itself. He should know—he was the greatest cassowary hunter of the area and his cassowary lore was renowned (Herdt 1981:chap. 5). Interestingly enough, men who have cassowary and kwooluku numelyu are thought to dream more than other men, as if the ability to see in "X-ray" trance vision, or to hunt cassowaries, enabled one to see more in night dreams too. Such a notion is consistent with Sambia dream theory (Herdt 1987d).

Encounters with spirits by ordinary Sambia, but particularly by their shamans, are not miraculous. We should remember that for Sambia, miraculous events exist in the fabric of everyday reality, not set apart from it. And indeed, as Stephen (1979:14–15) has commented, spirit encounters are far more common than one might think in New Guinea, and no wonder—they provide direct communication with spirits.

Here is one such story related by Nilutwo in 1975: Many years ago a great shaman, Meiounjin (who died about 1980), once killed a ghost near the men's house in Nilangu, my field village. Meiounjin was indeed an impressive and daunting figure, aloof and powerful; no one had gained such a reputation until Sakulambei. At this time Meiounjin was still a young shaman. One night he sat with some initiates and saw a kumaamdu (ghost) in the smoke of the clubhouse fire. He sprang up and shouted, grabbed his arrows and rushed outside. As he turned around he shot arrows that went to the wild pandanus tree near the clubhouse, and one of them lodged in the ghost. A pool of blood was found near the arrow. Because of his potency Meiounjin had succeeded in doing this; no one else could. Meiounjin later told the men that the ghost was trying to steal sweet potatoes and sugarcane skins to perform sorcery on them. He had saved their lives.

The ikeiaaru is a highly idealized and clearly etched spirit in folk imagination; it is also the most ferocious. For ghosts are terrifying but vague, and less impinging upon awareness as imagined personae; female spirits tend to stay close to the village and are more benign.[5] Ikeiaaru embody the spirits of great men, the ancestral spirits of powerful and even remembered war leaders and elders. The image of ikeiraaru—as described to me by Weiyu, a key interpreter, in 1975—are of beings large and highly decorated. They have cassowary headdress (identified with male shamans) and pig's teeth necklaces. They are white-haired or even bald: very old in Sambian eyes. Their pig's tusk noseplug (see Herdt 1987d) distinguishes them as being of highest ritual status, and this plug is terrifying, especially to children. They carry spears, bow and arrows, and even the war club. For all of these accoutrements and dignified elements, ikeiaaru are still light and wily and have the power of flight that enables them to hop from one tree to another, or fly from one mountain to the next. Because they are creatures of the high forest, though, and are thought to rest in the tops of great black palm and pandanus nut trees, they seldom are seen. More often the signs of ikeiaaru are recognized in strange noises or happenings in the bush, particularly at night. The great expanses of Sambia alpine forests, so cold and eerily still, indeed lend themselves to flights of imagination of this kind.

In sum, familiars are a core concept in Sambia culture, and the presence of an attachment to familiars is a part of everyone's life. The shamanic familiar-relationship is an expression, in a more personalized way, of this ethos, which involves a special psychological structure. The Sambia make no hard and fast distinction between ordinary and miraculous events; the experience of the miraculous lends itself to a specialized adaptation among shamans to a constant entertainment of other beings in their inner and outer worlds.

The Familiars' Attachment to the Shaman

The shamanic familiars—the kwooluku numelyu of shamans—are usually personified and individualized in the shaman's experience. These beings are named and have their own personalities and power attributes. This fact is consistent with Sambia views on familiars but seems to be a further extension of a trend to personalize the familiars' relationship to the self. This observation is facile, and the associated ethnography should most properly be a "thick description," in Geertz's (1973) sense, though we cannot enter into all of its ramifications here. Rather, I will illustrate with one example.

Inunyuluku is a middle-aged woman shaman of a nearby village. She is married and has several children, now grown. She has practiced shamanism for some years and is generally regarded as a strong shaman, though not as powerful as Kaiyunango or Sakulambei. In 1981 interviews she identified her kwooluku familiars in a succinct manner that exemplified their personalization. She named five familiars as hers: three were male, two were female. Her first and primary familiar she called Meiperako, an adult manlike being, whom she refered to as an *aatmangootu*, a "great man" spirit. This being often aided her in magical flight. Second was another adult manlike spirit, named Lungoreitnum. He was more fickle than the first. Third was Meratmonyeu, an adult womanlike spirit. She and spirit number one (Meiperako) were "married" (in imagination), Inunyuluku said. Fourth was Kooutuvangoogli, who was the youngest and sexiest of her female spirits. Inunyuluku noted, though, that this premenarchal female was a girl *(tai)*, a person who was not yet ready for genital intercourse; she was, however, marked for marriage to spirit number two (Lungoreitnum). These spirit couples assisted one another in trance and magical flight, journeying to ghost places, to retrieve souls of the sick. Last was Bookwolyi, a boylike spirit, not yet a man. Note that although these are reasonable names, they are not held by any Sambia I know, but they might be some day: Shamans are fond of dreaming new names and name songs (Herdt 1977), and they like to name others' children too. Inunyuluku sees her spirits not only in trance but in night dreams. She tells me that Meiperako "bosses" the other spirits, hinting of a closeness between herself and him in her inner world.[6] Closeness, intimacy, even romance, yes; but not marriage as such to her male spirits.

Inunyuluku's report compares with that of other shamans. Her images and names of these beings are not odd or special, and even the number (five) of familiars is about average for shamans, at least for strong shamans. Clearly, the sex and age of kwooluku familiars are key attributes of their salience for the healer, and this is not surprising, since age and sex are major structural dimensions of social classification in Sambia culture writ large. Other attributes are also of importance in understanding the subjectivity of the familiar; many of these are aesthetic in nature.

Shaman's images of their familiars are revealing because although ordinary folk also feel that they have familiars and may even report them from night dreams, shamans can visualize them while awake, albeit usually in a trance. I say usually, since Saku, for one, has told me that he sometimes sees his familiars in a different way when sober (not in trance) as well. Saku's favorite metaphoric image that captures such experiences is that of the butterfly: He calls his familiars while in a trance, and they come, at first looking like butterflies, fluttering in the wind. They are glassy, almost transparent, at least at first; when they come closer and stabilize they are more humanlike. I want to reiterate that Saku sees these butterfly images of kwooluku numelyu while sober, but that his sense of them when sober is as if they were distant, not near, to his experience: as if the vision is less a part of himself than when he is trancing.

Other metaphors express the images of shamanic familiars. At the beginning of trances, when smoking leads into the "whistle" of shamans—the familiar spirits are being called into the setting, to the body of the shaman—practitioners report that they see these invisible beings as humanlike. They may be small, however; Saku speaks of them as being about a foot in height. They may expand and grow, becoming as big (but never bigger than) a normal man in size. Their faces may be distorted or different from ordinary humans', and it is commonplace for shamans to say that the eyes or nose of the familiar are red, as if flushed. Indeed, one cannot help but think here of the state of anger, because Sambia say that the angered person is always red-faced or red-nosed, signs of their rage. (Robert Stoller once pinpointed this image in interviewing Saku, in 1979, by asking him what emotions his familiars' faces revealed; see Herdt and Stoller 1989: chap. 8). These are the images of the onset of trance.

What happens later, in the course of deeper trancing, when magical flight is thought to transpire? Here the familiar may assume a completely different guise, such as that of an animal. In phases of subjective imagery transformation—out of nothing, at the beginning of trance, or into the outer world, in the course of battling ghosts to retrieve souls of the sick, for instance—the familiar reveals touchpoint images of transparence, such as glassy or mirror like surfaces.[7] Again, the image of fluttering objects, particularly fireflies and butterflies, is invoked. But visualized in the nether world, after transmigration of the koogu is completed via the familiar, the familiar appears as another entity altogether, a dog, for example. Indeed, the dog is a favorite familiar-transformation, which is understandable given the Sambia affection for hunting dogs, and the way that individuals bond to these dogs as companions. Saku mentioned them. So did others, including women shamans, and here is a report by Ingotnboru, another middle-aged, senior woman healer.

When I kwolyi [heal], my kwooluku [here: shamanic familiar] does the rounds in ghostly places. I see what looks like a dog, sniffing around and checking out these ghost abodes. I see this and I follow him, since he shows me the places where the koogu [here soul conterpart to someone's body] of the sick are held captive. I look inside and recognize the faces of the ill [patient]; and I retrieve their koogu—what the dog showed me. If I don't see them [faces], if the ghosts have hid the koogu so well, then I say to others that this patient can die.

Perhaps one reason for the familiar's taking an animal guise is that it escapes detection from ghosts or other malevolent beings, with whom shamans must battle to retrieve their patients' koogu.

Why are familiars attracted to the shaman? It often has been argued by scholars such as Eliade (1964) that shamanic familiars are beings driven by sacred power to seek human agents through which to express themselves. Still others, such as Halifax (1979), suggest a special vision or ESP-like channel of communication, available to shamans to "hear" the familiar's voice. Why familiars seek to communicate through particular humans is a seemingly startling and esoteric question. Our Western scientific paradigm has not taken the nature of such psychological posits very seriously; they are too divergent from our own rationality (Shweder 1986). Sambia, however, do pose the question in a certain way by searching to discover who will or will not become shamans. They do this first in childhood, then several years later in the *narangu* ceremony of first-stage initiation and again, years later, at the shamans' initiation and divination "test"—a part of the third-stage initiation proceedings—which I once observed in 1975, the last time it was performed. Understanding this attraction of the familiar to the shaman provides a royal road into the interconnectedness of trance, spirit concepts, and dreams.

To understand these attachments I must mention two developmental phases of their calling, which often arise in the life-history narratives of shamans: Their first experience in childhood of shamanic familiars, and their first trance, years later, following initiation.

I interviewed Aaluvu, a powerful, older shaman, a man related to Saku (they are clan brothers), and I asked him: "Did you know (as a child) that you would be a shaman?" I was astonished by his response. He fluttered his hand, like the wind waving wheat, to indicate how he could see kwooluku numelyu as a child, like "flowers and leaves fluttering in the wind," he says. As a boy of about five or six, he first saw spirits. They looked "just like him." They would come and be with him, and he played with them. These same beings that he saw then he still sees in his night dreams, only now they are his adult age. Saku, too, has noted to me how his initiating familiars, first seen in childhood, physically developed in parallel course to himself. Thus, shamanic familiar attachments begin in childhood.

For the second stage I turn to a fragment of interview from still another shaman: Kamiyungo, a somewhat younger man than Aaluvu, closer in age to Saku, who is about thirty-three). (I think of Kamiyungo with the nickname "Bright Eyes," because he has wonderful smiling eyes, filled with self-assurance and spunk.) He tells me of his initial trance experience, which occurred for him immediately following his first-stage initiation (about 1966–68). He would have been about nine or ten. The day after seclusion from the months'-long forest lodge, which completes first-stage initiation, Kamiyungo returned to his natal village. He was alone, hunting birds near a small waterfall above his village. There he saw a "boy true," a person who was like an *imbutu,* a second-stage initiate, only this boy wore no decorations like his own; instead he wore only an *ipmoogu kanyelu,* a child's grass apron, forbidden for initiates to wear. He had red eyes, like "fire light," but he was pleasant, even happy. He didn't talk. He put his arm around Kamiyungo's shoulder. They stood around, playing, pushing, having fun. Then Kamiyungo felt dizzy; he noticed the trees and ground swirling. His thought—his koontu—grew foggy. He told me that he knew who he was, and that he knew he wasn't crazy, however; he did not lose his grasp on things (cf. Herdt 1977, 1986 on shamans who have). After a short rest he returned to the village and dozed, at which time he had an intense solitary experience: a great light, an orange, seering luminescence, appeared all around him. This wasn't a dream, he says. He feared it would harm him, but it didn't. Later he told his father—Yumalo, the great shaman, and also Saku's uncle— about the light. "You've seen the kwooluku (familiar)," Yumalo interpreted. "Now I have shamanism," Kamiyungo reported concluding to himself.

These initial trance events have a powerful effect upon the shaman's identity. Their recall is also intense; and indeed, I think we are on safe ground in saying they have what Roger Brown (1982) calls "flashbulb memories." This term conveys the surprise, illumination, and brevity of a great subjective experience. Over time its meaning no doubt gets refigured into a personal story, a mythic charter for the healer's trade; and it serves in narrative as microdot for enumerable conscious and unconscious scripts at a deeper level (Stoller 1979). These deeper meanings need not concern us here, however, for my point is that from childhood development onward the shaman first experiences the familiars as imaginary playmates, and then later trances and reexperiences the same entities in another guise, which are then reinterpreted as shamanic familiars. Cultural socializers reinforce these images, as I have described elsewhere, for the shaman-parents of children who frequently dream are told that they will be called to be shamans (Herdt 1977). The child's spirit encounters further confirm this, and his or her development is then inextricably threaded through lightbulb memories of the early events.

These brief vignettes suggest that in circumstances of isolation, aloneness, and probably of personal need, shamans as children experience the presence of an ineffable Other. It is not entirely clear how much this presence is inside or outside of their own making; the Sambia do not make this distinction, however, for in their world such beings are real, and their appearance, while remarkable, is not irrational or magical or miraculous. The child's particular inheritance (genealogical ancestry, parental role models for trancing and healing), special developmental needs, and special desires for this Other to be there are transformed into events whose realness becomes so compelling that they imprint a lifelong avocation: shaman.

With such a wondrous beginning, of familiars as playmates in childhood who forge into consciousness like lightning, it is small wonder that familiars become indelibly felt and seen in all forms of experience, including night dreams. Constant trancing—which is draining; all shamans complain about it—secures a time/space porthole for communication with the familiar in the adult shaman's everyday life. Familiars are a recognized fixture of shamanic character structure and psychological functioning. Accordingly, the desires, hopes, and fears of shamans are attributed to the familiars and expressed through them in body and soul and thought, and in shamanic healing too, in the "health and maturity mortalities"[8] of adult practice. All of this we glimpsed in Saku's dream text at the start of this chapter, but what is true to the Sambian perspective is dense, coded, and too embedded in everyday discourse for easy narrative understanding to an outsider.

Reinterpreting Saku's Dream

Let us return for an exegesis of Sakulambei's story of dreaming and healing to further understand shamanic familiars in imagination. By his own account, Saku's dream is the cause of his stepmother's illness. But this explanation is deceptive. There is only Saku, who tells us that his familiars in the dream struck his stepmother. For Sambia, dreams show another order of reality than that which is present in this one, and they are as real as social events. Saku's willingness to take responsibility for his dream actions in hurting others were reinforced by—indeed necessitated by—another shamans' vision, itself the product of trance, which pointed to Saku as the source of attack on the old woman. And there is more.

We must examine a series of dream events for the transformations of Saku's real-life desire to harm the woman and his final retribution in the real-life healing of the harmed, which laid to rest the related social conflict (Turner 1967b).

1. Saku dreamed of beating his wife. The history of this dream[9] is that Saku's wife was suspected of adultery. Later, this adultery was confirmed

by her pregnancy by another man. (Saku's hermaphroditic condition makes it very unlikely that he could inseminate for conception.) Her unfaithfulness plagued Saku. He desired, let us say, to beat her, but he did not. Instead he dreamed that he did so.

2. He represents to us that his wife in the dream is an aatmwogwambu, a female spirit familiar of his (but not his shamanic familiar). Saku suggests, therefore, that he is married—in the time and space world—to a woman who appears in dreams as a female familiar. The imaginative bond to this female spirit is a far more perfect union than the real-life marriage.

3. Upon awakening from this dread dream he felt that what he experienced via his koogu actually occurred, his desire to beat his wife had been consummated. He feared the confirmation of this act because he dreaded the real-life consequences of such—that he would be koted for the beating.

4. But no sooner was the threat of this consequence removed when Saku realized his dream of beating his wife was a transformation of beating the old woman. The female spirit represented, so another shaman says and Saku himself confirms, that through the action of this koogu in dreaming he had actually harmed his old stepmother. He harmed her koogu, where koogu means more than soul; his soul assault reached beyond the dream to harm the physical person of the dream object (the stepmother).

5. Saku felt old anger toward this stepmother, and even more toward his father for their belittlement of his hermaphroditic body as he was growing up. They never praised him. They never gave him a wife. Only his shaman-uncle, Yumalo, did this. He desired—now we must speak of an old and not a new script—to harm this aged lady. His dream image of beating his wife *qua* her spirit had harmed the stepmother, he feels. Old conflicts, grudges, and revenge lurk here.

6. Yet divination reveals that it was not his own koogu that was at fault: his dream self had beaten a woman, but it was not that entity that harmed the old lady. He finds, via trance, that it was actually one of his own shamanic familiars who was doing so: indeed, Yumalo himself! His old (and now deceased) uncle, to whom he was not only apprenticed, but who was the saving grace of his shattered childhood (Herdt and Stoller 1985). Yumalo, it seems—here the spirit familiar, not the man—has acted on his own, transforming a hidden desire in Saku's thought, Saku's very koontu (self), into a dream assault committed via Saku's soul, his koogu. "Yumalo will protect me," Saku warns. "He will harm those who would harm me." Yumalo cannot do so, however, except through Saku's dreams. Thus, Saku's genius in the dream narrative carries out in another order of reality his hidden desires to harm in a way that Saku in the time and space world cannot. But Saku is still culpable here.

7. The expression of this old desire in dream imagery has material consequences, Sambia believe. The old lady is now ill, and Saku has harmed her

by failing to control his own shamanic familiar (Yumalo). Therefore, Saku has no choice but to admit his culpability and go to her aid. He must heal her. He sends away his female spirit and puts his shamanic spirit, Yumalo, "on leash." (Shamans, as we saw, visualize their familiars as dogs in the nether world, whereas in real life, Sambia leash their hunting dogs in the forest until they loose them for the kill.) Saku's obligation to heal expresses a social norm for shamans that belies their personal desire to harm. Indeed, this culpability always poses a problem for Sambia shamans, who fear being accused of others' misfortunes. Their burden is to use their power to heal illness in order to remove the suspicion that they are its cause.

8. However, Saku gets his cake and he gets to eat it too. Saku makes retribution after the fact of the illness, and he is comforted by a final warning: Whoever harms his person will be struck by Yumalo, his protective shamanic familiar. Saku's language of the familiar's actions here reveals a seamless identification between himself and this being, a true double. He cannot give up his grudge. His feelings of guilt may motivate his ministrations to his old stepmother. But his desire to harm remains, as he reminds us in the end: "The familiar of Yumalo wants to kill them all if I am hurt." This is a powerful insurance policy.

Conclusion

The world of spirit familiars represents a rich and finely textured parallel reality for Sambia. They have brought into being an imaginative language for experiencing and expressing aspects of the self and body normally hidden in Western tradition, and we must avoid labeling as psychopathology that which deviates from our Western norm (Kakar 1985). At the same time, the self among Sambia is not completely aware of its many faces, which occur in thought (koontu), in dreams, via the soul (koogu), in the actions of familiars (numelyu) and, among shamans, in their trancing and the special powers and needs invested in their shamanic doubles. These are the elements of what Lévi-Strauss (1967:173) referred to as the "shamanic complex," and we can agree with him that "they are clustered around two poles, one formed by the intimate experience of the shaman and the other by group consensus."

Eliade (1964) and Jung (1966) have viewed shamanism as a practice arising from an archaic mode of awareness in humans, whereby divergent realities are manifested in religious practices that invoke a sacred Other. The spirit familiars of Sambia express autonomous imagination in a beautiful and transcendant mode that engages self and culture in a powerful way. Healing is an old art, old as suffering; and it is difficult to disengage these shamanic forms from humankind's struggles with death to find immortality (Becker 1973). We fear death;

we cling to life out of habit, as much as for love of it. The shaman brings the toil and trouble of a lifetime of desires, from childhood longings to adult griefs, into this arena of participation in the healing touch. But there is more than the pathos of Asclepius in the archaism of shamanism. [10]

Sambia shamans have tapped a variety of religious imagination that permits them to express through their familiars the desires of the self: the real-life self that thinks and eats, feels abandoned, and holds grudges. Numelyu are signs of that selfhood. These signs are relatively conscious in their pragmatic consequences, though not in their deepest motivations. The self is in control of dream discourse by how and when someone chooses to report a dream (Herdt 1987d). Not reporting a dream is also a choice. The pragmatics of reporting trouble-filled dreams are as heady as Saku's dilemma regarding his dream text above. Here, however, the shaman has other mental tools at his disposal: trancing and shamanic familiars.

Schwimmer (1986) would refer to these familiars as icons of identity, and he has shown in his reformulation of the Orokaiva of New Guinea the critical way in which semiotic domains protect boundaries and connect the "spaces" of a culture. Our Western tendency, however, polarizes collective/individual signs of such phenomena as familiars or totems. Lévi-Strauss (1963) hinted this, though he could not ultimately escape the dualism, any more than Freud's *Totem and Taboo* (Fox 1967). Schwimmer (1986:372n.) suggests that our attempts to link subjective domains are necessarily related to the questions we ask of informants. This was true of working with Saku. My questions probed the psychological sources of these spirits. In the domain of familiars, the self cannot exist without the Other. The familiar must be forever a relational concept—relating self and Other, and autonomous imagination and consciousness—in this sense.

If the koogu is self in dream action, as Sambia say, then the shamanic familiar is the self in trance action. Actors report dreams. Trancing shamans report their familiars' adventures. The former is probably less conscious and filled with more secondary elaboration than the latter, which is more immediate in the shaman's situational healing. Nevertheless, shamanic familiars do not merely do their shamans' bidding; that is far too simple a formulation as we have seen. These familiars' actions manifest the hidden desires and fears of the healer, and without this underlying psychological current his craft is devoid of passion. And he needs passion to put on a good show, which is, after all, a crass way of summarizing what his audience expects of him. I do not mean to imply, however, that Sambia shamanism is a fraud (see also Lévi-Strauss 1967:161–179). It presents to us a special kind of subjective system, within which a certain kind of selfhood is constructed, and this in turn motivates a form of desire and healing that can heal by proxy and alleviate suffering as surely as any psychiatric clinic that would treat human misery (see Kleinman 1988).

Victor Turner (1967b:350) once suggested that the designs of Western and non-Western healing rested upon fundamentally different notions of ontology, image, and efficaciousness: "Knowledge among the Ndembu is far more literally 'power' than it is with us." Such power transforms what is desired, into what is: "To know something, to understand the meaning of a symbol or the use of a 'medicine', for example, is to increase 'power' (1967b:356). The shaman's use of familiars mediates cultural knowledge and trance power among Sambia: the consolidation of self with the world of others who support the healer, because without healing "these experiences remain intellectually diffuse and emotionally intolerable" (Lévi-Strauss 1967:165).

Shamanism is a response to suffering and to the great wonders of human life. The shamanic institution is a heroic path that tries to remedy fatal forces. Shamanic familiars provide a modus operandi in a world of conflict and sadness, and it is primarily through the subjective artistry and shadow plays of this Other—such a Genius—that they heal Sambia society. This achievement of religious imagination is as much a feat of triumph as any our modern healing provides for us.

NOTES

1. Field research among Sambia (1974–76, 1979, 1981, 1983, 1985) has been supported by the Australian American Education Foundation, the Australian National University, UCLA's Neuropsychiatric Institute, the National Institute of Mental Health, the Wenner-Gren Foundation, and the Spencer Foundation, and I thank them all. I am very grateful to Eric Schwimmer for his critique of this chapter.

2. Stephen's (1987b:74) remarks on Mekeo serve equally well for Sambia: "The shaman may be suspected of controlling dangerous powers, but it is his restorative role as healer that is stressed by the community."

3. To say that we know little of trancing and imaging states is very true, as others have observed (see, here, the marvelous contributions in B. Tedlock's 1987 recent collection). But we should also say that we know little of the details of the related native ontologies in general (Shweder 1984) and, closer to my interests, that when it comes to the clinical ethnography of many other forms of indigenous subjectivity, we are woefully lacking (Herdt and Stoller 1989). Here is the next frontier of anthropology.

4. This positive and negative sorcery practice of shamans is obviously a delicate area to investigate, and one that requires a good deal of subtle ethnography, if we are to take the perceived threat (in the minds of the natives) seriously, and thereby reciprocally understand it from the shaman's point of view. Too often, one fears (Eliade 1964 and popular accounts, e.g., Halifax 1979 are guilty of this), either the concerns are ignored or understood only from some idealized view. If, however, the shaman visualizes, as Jung believed, and has a double self, a shadow, as Rank (1971) thought, then it must be a great temptation to violate these moral norms and go off into the abyss of grandiose sorcery attacks on one's own people. Some tales among Sambia tell of this. Stephen (1987b) has written of this best on Mekeo, and in a different sense, the messianic and cargo cult literature in Melanesia speaks to the same issue, as Tuzin's chapter in this volume shows.

5. This is not quite correct, as I have shown (Herdt 1982a and 1987c), because this depends upon the developmental epoch of the person: hamlet spirits are threatening for new initiates and women, but protective for adult men.

6. We search for a better language with which to describe these subtle native emic concepts and should not be surprised that our language of romance and love relationships provides it; so we must be cautious here not to project alien feelings onto the Sambian idea. (See Kennedy 1967 on the Nubian Zar cult.)

7. Saku, who has had coastal plantation experience, has also used two analogies drawn from his acculturated memories to describe his images of familiars to me. One analogy is the balloon. He evoked this image several times and was fond of it; he seemed to emphasize by it the familiar's lightness and capacity to float and rise to the heavens, like a balloon. The other analogy is the plastic ribbon of a tape cassette. One morning some children in the village had found a broken cassette of mine and had strung up the tape between trees. The wind made it flutter and the sun reflected upon it, spots of mirror and brilliance. Saku's analogy here seemed to emphasize the luminescence and semitransparence of the familiar, and its power to connect disparate things

through a ropelike filament. This latter attribute is important in another sense because of how shamans use the idea of magical fences (or ropes) as a boundary to protect patients and whole villages from evil spirits and sickness (Herdt 1977).

8. The phrase is Kohut's (1979) but I owe the healing and culture connotations to Sudhir Kakar (1983:271).

9. These life-history events are recounted in Herdt and Stoller (1985) and in Herdt and Stoller (1989) more fully.

10. One recalls here the myth of Asclepius' sons: "Perhaps we can glimpse the transition in some lines surviving from a lost homeric poem, *The Sack of Troy*, which state that the two sons of Asclepius the healer became 'specialists', one in surgery and the other in diseases hidden within (internal disease). The latter physician 'was the first to understand the flashing eyes of Ajax raging and his mind weighted down.' *Barunomenon*, 'weighted down', is the metaphor that appears in our term 'depressed'" (Simon 1978:231).

Mortal Insights: Victim and Witch in the Nalumin Imagination

Eytan Bercovitch

> So long as we deal only with the cosmic and general, we deal with the symbols of reality, but *as soon as we deal with private and personal phenomena as such, we deal with realities in the completest sense of the term.*
> —William James, *The Varieties of Religious Experience*

IN his classic study, *The Varieties of Religious Experience,* William James argued that religion is an empirically real phenomenon and that the study of religion is a source of insight into human consciousness. James defined religion as "the feelings, acts and experiences of individual men, in their solitude, so far as they apprehend themselves to stand in relation to whatever they consider divine" (1958, p. 42). As his definition indicates, James placed emphasis on two main aspects of religion: the experiential and the relational. The fact that religion involves actual personal experiences was the basis for James's claim that religion is worthy of serious scientific consideration. In turn, the fact that people stand in some kind of relationship with the divine provided James with his method. James explored how people related to and responded to the object of their religious experience. Throughout most of his book, James took a pragmatic view of the relationship people hold to the divine, finding that it could serve many different personal uses, depending on the needs and situation of the particular individual. In his conclusion, however, James offered a stronger position. The invisible realm of religion, he suggested, may represent areas of subliminal consciousness that people are not ordinarily aware of in themselves. Religious experience could serve to relate people to wider aspects of their individual beings and interests.

Although James's work was shaped by his specific time and culture—a turn-of-the-century America that valued individualism and progress—it contains insights useful for understanding a very different case. My subject in this essay is a system of belief in a form of supernatural violence called *biis* among the Nalumin people of Papua New Guinea. Biis, which I will translate as "witchcraft" for reasons that I will explain shortly, is one of the main areas of religion in Nalumin life.[1] My method places emphasis on the relational aspect of Nalumin witchcraft, much as James did in his study of Western religion. Specifically, I explore the relationship that the individual bears to the witch, a figure he imagines far more than he ever actually sees.

The first part of this chapter provides background for the Nalumin case and describes the general characteristics of their theories of witchcraft. The second presents the most obvious aspects of the relationship of an individual to a witch, that of a potential victim who seeks to learn the identity of the agent who wishes to harm him or her. The third explores the internal meaning of the relationship between victim and witch. Somewhat in the manner that James suggested that the divine represents subliminal areas of consciousness, I argue that the witch embodies essential aspects of the self. This leads me, in the fourth part, to suggest that witchcraft serves as a moral system through which the Nalumin self is constructed. Finally, I argue that the case of witchcraft among the Nalumin offers far-reaching implications for better understanding of the individual human subject.

Background

On the night of April 15, 1985, I was sitting on a palmwood floor in the settlement of Bomtem, where I had been living and carrying out anthropological research for over two years. Around me was the familiar sight of the small, dark interior space of the house of Katim and his brother-in-law Wengsep.[2] A wood fire burning in the hearth at the center of the floor cast a red glow on almost twenty people crowded close together, some already sleeping. At my side Katim and Wengsep, two men about thirty years old who had become friends of mine, were describing a recent hunting trip they had taken together. In the middle of their account, Wengsep said he had to relieve himself outside. He removed a stick from the fire to light his way and went out through the doorway of the house.

Katim continued the story alone. He had just recalled his courage in standing up to a charging boar when we were startled by loud cries coming from outside the house. We immediately recognized the voice as Wengsep's. Moments later, Wengsep came running back into the house and we waited anxiously for his explanations. But before he had a chance to speak, Wengsep was interrupted by voices coming through the thin walls of the house from people in neighboring houses only a few yards away. "What was it?" they demanded. "What's going on?" Katim answered: "It's Wengsep. Wait a moment for him to tell us." Then, as we listened intently, Wengsep recounted his experience: "I heard a whistling sound, and something moved towards me. I think there was a biis keeping watch out there!" Wengsep's words were relayed to the other houses and the village exploded in commotion. Katim and several other men took torches and searched for footprints unsuccessfully. The doorways were closed shut. Few people slept well that night.

Victims of *Biis:* Nalumin Theories of Witchcraft

I will return again to Wengsep's nocturnal encounter as I explore its significance at different levels. Scenes like this occurred frequently in the village where I stayed among the Nalumin, a people of approximately three thousand members who live in Papua New Guinea.[3] The Nalumin speak a non-Austronesian language, a member of the Mountain-Ok Family. They occupy an area of about 1,500 square kilometers along the north slope of the Star Mountains, a region of rugged terrain (falling from more than 4,000 meters at the crest of the range to barely 1000 meters at the Sepik River), thick forests, and heavy rainfall (over 5,000 millimeters a year in most locations). The Nalumin live in small, widely separated settlements, mostly located on ridge tops between 800 to 1,500 meters in elevation. Their settlements consist of an average of three to five small houses each, with total settlement membership averaging thirty to forty. The Nalumin practice shifting cultivation, moving on to clear a new area after a single planting and harvesting (the average fallow period is about twenty years). Sweet potato and taro are the main crops. They supplement their diet by hunting wild game and by collecting a wide variety of natural plant foods. Cognatic descent groups, locally known as *tenum miit* ("human source"), are the broadest principle of Nalumin social organization. A single tenum miit ranges in size from 30 to about 300 members (the average is about 100) and claims a large territory for itself. Settlement organization, however, centers around much smaller groups, with most residents sharing a common ancestor no further removed than three generations above themselves. Indeed, the core members of a settlement are usually a group of actual siblings living together with their spouses, children, and sometimes their aged parents.

While I carried out my research, for three years between 1982 and 1985, I lived in Bomtem, the largest settlement of the Kuyakmin tenum miit, a centrally located Nalumin descent group. Wengsep's encounter occurred during a period when the people of Bomtem were especially afraid of biis and when sightings of them were unusually frequent. The high level of fear was inspired by a series of recent deaths in the local region of the Kuyakmin descent group. The first had occurred in Bomtem itself. Akapkon, a child, had died in January. Two weeks later the old widow Dikipkon had died in the settlement of Silendum, only a shouting distance from Bomtem. Most recently and most shockingly, in late March, two prominent older men, Mikim and Wilyap, had died the same week in the settlements of Tilamiyap and Astembil respectively, also close neighbors to Bomtem. These four deaths, like virtually all deaths among the Nalumin, were accounted for by the actions of biis. Four deaths in a little more than two months is a large number, especially in a total local population of less than 300. As the people of Bomtem understood it, the biis were plainly on an offensive. Wengsep's encounter confirmed their fear that their lives were in imminent danger.

As they see it, the Nalumin live under desperate circumstances: they are being killed off by biis. Kupsep, regarded as the wise man and informal leader of Bomtem, drew a bitter lesson from sixty years' experience. "So many of the people I knew are gone, killed by the biis," he told me. "Once there were many of us, now there are few. Soon there may be none of us. The biis will have triumphed." As I came to learn, the term *biis* has three different but related meanings. Biis, in its first, most general, and most common sense, refers to people who kill other people—in a manner unlike ordinary violence—and who then eat their flesh. It is also used in this general sense to refer to whatever supernatural actions they use to accomplish this end. Second, biis is the name for the human flesh that is eaten by such people, a kind of flesh unlike the flesh that can be seen and touched by ordinary people. Finally, biis is the word for the more deadly of the two main techniques used by such people for killing others. It is distinguished from another technique called *yakop*. To avoid confusion, I will refer to this technique as *biis yemin* ("to kill by biis"). When I refer to biis, it will be in the more general sense that encompasses all those who kill others using either technique.

There are both differences and connections between the techniques of *yakop* and biis yemin. In yakop the aggressor obtains a piece of something intimately associated with the intended victim—such as a scrap of food, a piece of fingernail, or body hair.[4] When no one is looking, the aggressor wraps this up in a leaf, takes it away, and puts it some place where it will be gradually destroyed, such as in a termite nest or within the ashes inside the margins of a fireplace. As the bundle is slowly eaten or burned away, the person from whom it has been taken is slowly consumed by sickness. Victims are attacked directly in the second technique of biis yemin. The aggressor fires arrows from a bow or strikes with an ax or piece of wood. The wounds are invisible to the victim and other ordinary people, but if the wounds are mortal the victim will die immediately with the symptoms of a stroke or heart attack, or die in the next few days with the symptoms of a short and sudden severe illness. Yakop is associated primarily with women, though men are often said to practice it, and biis yemin is associated with men, though some women are said to practice it. The two forms are linked together, for yakop is often used as a preparatory means of weakening the intended victim so that he or she will be an easy target for the biis yemin attack that proves fatal. After their victim dies, the killers butcher and cook his or her body. Then they consume the flesh in a feast they share with other biis. But like the two techniques used by biis, their cannibal feast and its effects on their victim's body are not visible by ordinary means of perception.

A major reason why the malevolent action of biis can be effective without being visible is that, using either technique, they cause harm to the victim's invisible *simik* rather than to his or her visible physical body. In the Nalumin language, the term *simik* is used to refer to a shadow or image, whether reflected or drawn. It also refers to the soul of a living being. During sleep, a person's soul, or simik, is active and may travel, causing him or her to experience dreams *(yungti)* that may be remembered upon awakening. While awake, a person's soul stays with him or her, attached to the skin and concentrated at the upper back. By their actions, biis cause harm to another person's soul. Using yakop, they weaken the soul, whereas by using biis yemin they cause fatal wounds to it. A person dies only if his or her soul is killed. Kupsep told me, "When biis kill someone, it is the soul they kill first. When we say biis eat someone, it is really the soul that they eat."[5]

The invisibility of the actions of biis is one of their most distinctive and terrifying qualities. Unlike ordinary people, they have ways of hiding and disguising their actions. They can make themselves invisible. They can travel through the air or under the ground. They can see in the darkness and travel at night. They can also change their shape into other physical forms, including those of birds, snakes, pigs, dogs, and crocodiles. These supernatural powers are held by practitioners of the techniques of both biis yemin and yakop. I was told varying accounts of how biis acquire and exercise their powers, but most accounts emphasized that the powers of biis are partly acquired and partly innate and inherited.[6]

Nalumin theories of biis and their powers creates a problem of translation. For many years anthropologists have made a distinction between witchcraft and sorcery on the basis of whether the power to effect harm is possessed innately (witchcraft) or requires the use of techniques and knowledge that have to be acquired (sorcery). Anthropologists usually trace this distinction to Evans-Pritchard's study of the Azande (1937), an African people who sharply distinguish between two different ways of causing harm along these same lines. In the borderline Nalumin case of biis, however, the anthropological distinction between sorcery and witchcraft proves more troublesome than helpful. It would be preferable to use a word that encompassed both terms, like the Nalumin term *biis* in its more general sense. In the absence of such a term, and because it is awkward to use Nalumin idioms exclusively, I will describe the phenomenon of biis as a case of witchcraft in the rest of this essay. My decision is based on the fact that the Nalumin say that biis possess mysterious powers that are at least partly inherited and that their basic nature is different from ordinary people as a consequence. It also reflects the way the Nalumin view biis in an almost entirely negative light, stressing that their actions are despised by ordinary people and profoundly damaging to society.[7]

Problems of Recognition and Avoidance

The same powers that enable witches—biis—to keep their actions hidden make it difficult for people to perceive witches and take action against them. The most direct evidence is sickness and death itself. To avoid witchcraft, Nalumin individuals try to minimize their exposure to situations that place them in danger, making sure, for example, they do not leave bits of their food on the ground or travel alone and at night. They also rely on indirect evidence about witchcraft. As the example of Wengsep's encounter shows, the Nalumin are on constant watch for any auditory or visual indications of the presence of a witch. The single most distinctive sign is a whistling sound that people say witches make. Other auditory signs are the sound of a body snapping or scraping against twigs and underbrush. The main visual signs are movements or suggestive shadows or shapes, usually at some distance and obstructed by darkness or intervening objects. Other visual signs are unidentifiable footprints or traces of physical passage.

The Nalumin are also on constant watch for certain natural species they associate with witchcraft. When people encounter one of the species of birds and animals whose forms witches may take, they observe it closely. If there is anything unusual in its appearance (size, features, coloring) or behavior (traveling at night, showing a lack of fear of humans, or collecting bits of human food) they suspect it is a witch in disguise *(biis diip)*, and may try to scare it away. Men may even try to shoot it with an arrow. In a different manner, a number of species of frogs are suspected of being "friends" of witches *(biis imi yakon)*. They are said to accompany witches, much as the black cat is said to accompany the witch in our own Western tradition. The sound of one of these frogs croaking nearby is a sign that a witch may be about to strike and a cause for taking special precautions, such as shutting the doorway.

Finally, the Nalumin believe that several species of birds and a species of bat may be human ghosts in disguise *(sakbal diip)*. Ghosts of the dead, they say, often take the forms of these species in order to warn their living kin of an imminent danger of witchcraft to them. Measures are taken soon after someone dies to enlist his or her help in this way (including sacrifices of game and verbal appeals directed to the ghost of the dead person). When people see, or more commonly hear, one of the species associated with ghosts fly past, they try to gauge the direction from which it has come, since that will be the same direction as where the danger lies (a witch waiting or coming down a trail for them). Many mornings in Bomtem begin with people comparing their experience of hearing bats fly by on the previous night.

As the Nalumin themselves admit, the means by which ordinary people come to learn about and try to avoid witchcraft are limited and largely ineffective. Of equal importance, they yield little in the way of clues about the identity of the witch. As soon as I became aware of the importance of witchcraft, I began asking people who precisely were the witches afflicting them. In reply, people told me that witches could be any one, male or female, but that they did not know specifically who they were, since witches could make themselves invisible and carry out their evil actions in secret. The constant precautions people took against witchcraft suggested to me that witches were everywhere.

The Identity of the Witch

My initial attempts to learn about the identity of the witches were thwarted by the difficulty of gaining direct evidence about them. Witchcraft appeared as a kind of puzzle to me, and my task was to try to solve it. My situation both resembled and differed from that of the Nalumin themselves. For the Nalumin, the problem of the identity of the witch is one of life and death: they regard themselves as potential victims of an unseen enemy. They do all they can to gain knowledge about witches as a means of better defending themselves, and they assume that witches, on their part, will do all they can to keep themselves hidden and unknown.

There are several contexts of Nalumin life in which the struggle over knowledge about witchcraft is most dramatically evident. These are shamanic séances, protests over suspected witchcraft, and confidential disclosures. It was by observing what people said and did on these occasions that I gained most of my knowledge about the details of witchcraft. Based on what a number of individuals told me, it seems clear that the Nalumin find these occasions important for the same reasons.

What Spirits Reveal: A Shamanic Seance

When I asked how I could learn more about the identity of witches, the Nalumin suggested that I go to the experts: observe the shamans at work. Among the Nalumin, shamans (*kusong tenum wanang,* "men and women of the placental twin") are people who have a uniquely direct link to ghosts and other supernatural beings. A shaman acquires this ability only by first establishing a special relationship with his or her placental twin (*kusong*), a spirit that all individuals are believed to possess but few are able to call on.[8] A shaman's placental twin acts as an intermediary with the agents of the invisible world, making it possible for the shaman to become the medium for ghosts (and sometimes also for several other kinds of supernatural beings), who enter the shaman's body and communicate directly through his or her voice to the assembled people. Nalumin shamanism often involves serial possession. A typical séance lasts for one to two hours, during which time one to six ghosts, or other super- natural beings, take turns possessing the shaman's body for exclusive periods of between ten minutes and one hour each. During the time it has possession of the shaman's body, each of these entities not only can inform people of the causes of their illness, but can locate, retrieve, and neutralize the bundles used by witches in the practice of yakop. (Shamans can not save the life of someone who has already been dealt a mortal wound by a witch using the practice of biis). Though shamans are often called to treat one particularly ill patient, they also diagnose and treat other people who are present in the audience, many of whom may show no symptoms of any current illness. Shamans expect to be re- paid for their effort, in small gifts at a later date.

On the evening of September 18, 1984, eight months before Wengsep's encounter, I attended a shamanic séance. It was held in the house of Kupsep and Atulim. Hearing that a séance was about to begin, most of the adults in Bomtem, as well as a few visitors from neighboring settlements, came inside their house, crowding its small interior to the limit. People sat pressed together, leaving a margin of open space in a circle around the hearth. They sang one song after another to encourage the spirits to come and take possession of the shaman. Near the doorway, singing with the others, was the shaman, Finan- gim, a thin man in his early thirties. The patient he had come to cure, a man called Damalim, was lying on the floor at the other end of the house, too tired from his sickness to sing himself. As the purpose of the singing was to appeal to the ghosts of the dead, they sang songs associated with death and with deceased people. One song was about a man who had just brought his wife's corpse to a cave to rest:

Kup muk wiwi neno, dakan nelo
I sing of your breasts, ready to be pulled off like ripe fruit
Fom muk wiwi neno, dakan nelo
I sing of rotten breasts, ready to be pulled off like ripe fruit

After about fifteen minutes of singing, in the middle of the fourth song, the shaman suddenly began to tremble His trembling increased until he was bob- bing rapidly up and down on the balls of his feet as he squatted, shaking the floor of the house. Then he leapt to his feet, and at once the singing came to an end. The shaman moved around the room clicking fingers with people in the manner of greeting between a newly arrived visitor and his hosts, for the spirit that now possessed the shaman's body was a ghost who was glad to see his rela- tives again.

When the greetings were finished, a woman called out to the shaman from where she was sitting: "Come here, my stomach has been hurting me, take a look at me first." The shaman went to the woman who had spoken and looked closely at her. Then he walked quickly to the doorway of the house, reached outside with his right hand, and seemed to receive something in his hand from someone standing outside. He came back, holding his right hand clasped tight, and stood in front of the woman. He opened his hand as if to show her something, but his hand appeared empty. "They say this is yours," he told her. "Yes!" she agreed, looking pleased, "that is the bit of sweet potato they got from me, and with which they made me sick." The shaman struck his open hand down and smacked it resoundingly against the floor. "It is all gone," he announced, "you are fine."

Immediately after this, other people called to the shaman, each demanding to be treated. But Tiliyen insisted that her husband Damalim, the gravely sick man for whom the shaman originally had been called, should have priority. The shaman went over to Damalim and squatted down by his side. The patient indicated a spot on his chest where the pain was localized and the shaman placed his hand there. A moment later, the shaman said with conviction, "There is something like an arrow here. They shot him with an arrow." "That is right. He went to Kilsigin, and stayed at Atiimsep's house and they shot him there," said Damalim's wife, referring to a settlement across the Yak River in the territory of another descent group. The shaman agreed with her and elaborated a bit on her statement: "They [the spirits] saw him [the witch, practicing biis method] come out and shoot him." The shaman bent down and brought his lips just above the spot where the pain was localized and made a sucking sound, like someone slurping a liquid. He kept doing this for awhile, stopping regularly to spit out the substance (which appeared to me to be ordinary spittle).

The shaman kept talking as he did the sucking out and spitting, developing a narrative about the sickness of Damalim. He told Damalim the witch had shot him, and that a small piece of the arrow head remained inside. He also found something else:

SHAMAN: A yakop [witchcraft] bundle, they made a little one. The mother and child [Damalim's wife and daughter] are fine. But, there is one for the father, something of a meal of sweet potato with pandanus oil. Did you cook and quickly eat such a meal?

DAMALIM: It was at Balukon settlement. We cooked it and then ate it.

SHAMAN: It was not taro and pandanus oil.

TILIYEN [Damalim's wife]: Sweet potato and pandanus oil.

SHAMAN: Sweet potato by itself.

TILIYEN: That's right.

SHAMAN: They [the spirits] say "a sweet potato bundle."

TILIYEN: At the settlement there they cooked it and then . . .

SHAMAN: . . . they wrapped it up and it lies deep inside [i.e., the practitioners of *yakop* bundle witchcraft hid it somewhere hard to locate].

This discussion took place before the shaman had found the arrow that he had earlier determined was inside Damalim. While searching for the arrow, he also retrieved several witchcraft bundles (which could not be seen). Several minutes later the shaman finally found the arrow, and the conversation returned to the problem of how Damalim had gotten shot:

DAMALIM: It is swollen up [putting his hand on the spot where he felt pain].

SHAMAN: "This is hurting me," you think, and you put your hand down and hold it.

DAMALIM: I put my hand down and hold it but I don't know where it is.

SHAMAN: "They are hurting me," you think. You have been like this for two days.

DAMALIM: I have been like this for a whole *nakal* [a unit of five] of days.

SHAMAN: Here it comes out! It was inside for a long time and there is pus on it. For it has been in there a nakal of [5] days. There is pus and a bad smell, but there is no blood . . . "He'll think it is just the finger nail of a nature demon *(matong),*" they thought [the witches who had shot Damalim with the arrow]. They thought "They will ask him 'What place did it happen. Did you see a nature demon appear in plain sight?' And he will reply, 'It was a nature demon of the pandanus palm'."

DAMALIM: They said, "He will say, 'It was the nature demon of the pandanus palm of Yulkum [the name of the area where Damalim had his meal of sweet potato and pandanus]'."

SHAMAN: Oh that is how he spoke. Or he said, "He will think 'It was the nature demons of the Yak River'."

The shaman spent about ten minutes removing several pieces of arrow from inside Damalim, all the time continuing to develop a narrative of how the shooting had occurred.[9] The shaman, Damalim, and Damalim's wife decided that when Damalim had crossed the Yak River and climbed up to an old garden area one or more witches, hiding behind a tree, had shot him with an arrow. The arrow had gone inside but had missed any vital organ and so it had not caused a mortal wound. Finally, the shaman told Damalim that he had removed the last piece of the arrow from inside his chest. He assured Damalim that he would be feeling well again within a few days.

The completion of the treatment of Damalim brought a look of relief to the faces not only of Damalim and his wife, but also those of other people present at the séance. The completion of Damalim's treatment also brought on an onslaught of new demands by the other people present for the shaman to look at their ills. The shaman went from one person to another, quickly retrieving and disposing of witchcraft bundles that had been made against each of them. This went on for about fifteen minutes. Then, as the shaman was pausing between patients, he sat down abruptly. "They have departed," a man said, meaning that the shaman's ghost helpers had left his body. The person who had been the shaman was once again merely the ordinary man Finangim. Finangim asked for some tobacco to smoke, his voice betraying his exhaustion. The shaman séance had come to an end a little over an hour after it had begun. People not belonging to Kupsep and Atulim's household quietly began to leave. Most, but not all, of the people who had hoped to be treated by the shaman had been satisfied at the séance that night.

Finangim's séance in September 1984 reveals several characteristics of Nalumin shamanism. In the first place, it shows the stress on narrative in shamanism. Beyond merely divining and treating illness, shamans provide their audience with a detailed account of acts of witchcraft that lie behind the illness. This process is evident in the description I provided of Finangim's treatment of Damalim, especially in the two excerpts I took from a tape recording I made of the event. Finangim began with the most superficial of comments: the location of the pain afflicting Damalim, the length of time it had been afflicting him, and its general cause, an arrow embedded through the practice of biis. From that beginning, he proceeded to elaborate an increasingly detailed story about what had happened, including not only the action of biis that caused the localized pain, but also several acts of yakop that had made Damalim weak and vulnerable to the biis. Several times in the process of developing his account, Finangim asked for specific information from his patient and his patient's wife. More commonly he used the unelicited information they provided him. The information led Finangim to change his account several times. The final result is a collaborative narrative that owes as much to Damalim and his wife as to Finangim or the spirits who speak to him and through him.

It is routine for shamans to collaborate with their patients, questioning them and offering details of the origin of their illness that draw on what the patient tell them. This occurs in divining and treating even minor illnesses caused by a single act of yakop. It has been my experience, however, that the most elaborate efforts at collaboration, yielding long narratives, occur only in cases of serious illness where a person's life is thought to be at stake. Collaboration may have much to do with why the accounts of shamans are convincing and perhaps also why their treatment is effective. Such collaboration also has implications for the role of imagination in witchcraft. I will return to this.

In addition to the stress on narrative, Finangim's séance shows the paucity of information about witchcraft provided by shamans. Although they may develop a detailed narrative about how witchcraft occurred, there are important facts that shamans do not reveal either through their narratives or through any other actions or statements. For example, in the séance I describe, Finangim never names the individuals who made the witchcraft bundles or fired the witchcraft arrows. At his most specific, he links several acts of witchcraft against Damalim to people in a settlement belonging to a neighboring descent group in another area, though he does not specify which individuals among them were involved or whether others belonging to Damalim's own descent group were also involved. During approximately thirty shamanic séances that I observed during my fieldwork, I rarely heard the names of individual witches mentioned. In the few cases where names of witches were specified, the individuals belonged to settlements and descent groups located at a considerable distance from the settlement and descent group of the patient.

Shamans told me they generally know more about the specific identity of witches than they publicly reveal. Some shamans said that the ghosts or other spirits that assist them make it possible for them to directly perceive the witches carrying out actions invisible to ordinary people. Other shamans said that they were told the names of the witches by the same sources. However, the shamans said they were reticent about disclosing the full extent of their knowledge for much the same reason that ordinary people are afraid to accuse witches publicly. Shamans who reveal too much are likely to incur the wrath of any witch whom they have named and to face the threat of witchcraft directed against themselves. For shamans are vulnerable to witchcraft, though they claim to have a better chance of defending against it than ordinary people. In addition, shamans face the danger of having their powers of communicating with the world of ghosts diminished or taken away by witches.[10]

What Anger Reveals: A Formal Protest

Observing the séances of shamans, like the one that Finangim performed for Damalim and others in Bomtem, I learned a good deal about how witchcraft was carried out, but I learned little about who way carrying out the witchcraft or why. One event was especially important in suggesting to me who was responsible for witchcraft. What I learned from it was surprising.

At dawn on August 6, 1984, a group of twenty armed and angry men emerged from the surrounding forest and advanced quickly into Bomtem. As I watched, the intruders divided up and went into several of the houses. They attacked the people inside, rubbing them with stinging nettles, tearing their clothes, and flinging their possessions into the surrounding brush. The people inside made only a feeble effort to protect themselves or their belongings. Their children screamed in terror.

A few minutes later, their initial rage apparently satisfied, the intruders came back outside to the clearing at the center of Bomtem and convened a meeting. Bopsim, a tall man of thirty years who had led the intruders, opened the meeting. He spoke furiously, looking at no one in particular:

BOPSIM: What do you think you are doing to Atulim? Women, you are jealous of men, thinking we have money. You make us ill [using the yakop method], and then get the men to come and finish us off with their bows [using the biis method] so you can eat us. But how will you be able to pay compensation when he dies? You won't be able to and you will go to jail! So stop your evil and let him get well again!

Bopsim's words allowed me finally to understand what was happening. Atulim was a prominent older man of Bomtem. That morning, he was lying deeply ill on the floor of his house as he had been for a week. Bopsim and the other intruders led by him were friends and relatives of Atulim from a neighboring settlement. Their assault was a dramatic protest against the witchcraft they believed was responsible for Atulim's illness, a protest they hoped could save his life.

Bopsim's comments led to a debate that lasted over an hour. It began with people of Bomtem responding to Bopsim's words by agreeing with him in a general way about the problem of witchcraft. Nilenim, a Bomtem man, impatient with the lack of specificity in this kind of talk, pointedly reminded everyone that the witchcraft had been started by the people of Bomtem themselves, and others agreed with him:

> NILENIM: It is not those to the sides [i.e., living in neighboring settlements] who did it to us. . . .
> KATIM: They started the witchcraft here in this settlement. They put the witchcraft bundles and made the man sick. . . .
> BOPSIM: Right here in this settlement they made witchcraft bundles [for yakop]. The bats flew here to say that they [practitioners of biis] would get bows and come along the way the bats had come.

To my surprise, instead of remaining on this subject, the meeting returned to the general observations and opinions people had about witchcraft. For a half hour—the greater part of the whole meeting—one person after another spoke about evidence they had observed of witches, evidence that pointed to the recent attempts by witches to strike other members of Bomtem. Finally, Singyonim, another member of the group who had made the attack at dawn, pointed out that witchcraft threatened everyone's survival:

> SINGYONIM: In the time of our ancestors there were many more people and larger settlements. Now, in our time there are only empty sites. The elders are gone, and there are few people who grow up. The witches keep watch at the vaginas of women, and as soon as they give birth, they snatch the children and eat them. Stop what you are doing!

Singyonim's remark made a strong impression. Many people echoed his sentiments. The participants of the meeting had evidently arrived at a common position. "If we stop witchcraft," said Bopsim, "we will bear a great people!" This turned out to be his concluding remark. Moments later, the meeting was over.

Formal protests of the kind that happened over Atulim's illness are rare but revealing events.[11] Formal protests reveal the frustration, anger, and fear that people feel about illness of their friends or relatives. Protests also reveal the limitations of the shamanic séance as a response to witchcraft, for if such séances were effective there would never be a need for protests. In fact, Bopsim led his protest only after several shamanic séances had not stopped his friend Atulim from growing increasingly ill. But, above all, protests reveal that the witches strike people who live in the same settlement as themselves.

The physical attack that began the protest led by Bopsim and others was not directed against the people they suspected of carrying out witchcraft. Quite the contrary, they attacked the people who were closest to Atulim and above suspicion. The point of the attack was to make these people realize that they were responsible for Atulim and that they had better make a stronger effort to prevent his death by witchcraft. They were responsible because the people carrying out the witchcraft were members of the same settlement, who could best be persuaded by their fellow settlement members to put an end to their activity. In the meeting that followed the attack, the original attackers, now joined by the people they had attacked, tried both by entreaty and threat to convince those they believed to be witches to stop their actions.

It is significant that even in the heat of anger during the protest no one specified the identity of the witches suspected in Atulim's illness. During the attack, there was little chance for speech of any kind. Later, during the meeting, the closest that people came to identifying the witches was when they addressed the witches as "you women." Some women in the settlement, the speakers suggested, were envious of Atulim's wealth and had collected bits of his food to work yakop on him and planned to bring in the help of other unspecified practitioners of biis when the time came to finish off Atulim and eat him. But the speakers never identified which women they were addressing. More commonly, the speakers referred to witchcraft in an even more general way, as a common problem to everyone, keeping clear of its individual dimension. In this sense, what seems to be a persuasive conclusion to the meeting—Singyonim's and Bopsim's appeal for an end to witchcraft for the common good—should be understood instead as an acceptance of defeat in addressing and resolving the issue of witchcraft against Atulim at the level of its individual causes. Indeed, this was the view of the meeting that people expressed to me afterwards. "The witches are unyielding *(yung kemin)* and we who are not witches are afraid," Katim told me. But despite pessimistic statements of this kind, Atulim quickly recovered from his illness.

Confidential Sources

At several points it has become evident that people suspect far more about witchcraft than they ordinarily disclose in public. In certain public circumstances, notably when possessed by spirits or driven by passion, people come close to specifying the identity of those they believe to be witches. However, the main context in which the identity of suspected witches is revealed is in confidence rather than in public. A confidential disclosure is one that is made to a limited set of people under a limited set of conditions. Generally, when a person makes a confidential disclosure, he or she makes it to people that he knows well and trusts and in circumstances where the disclosure cannot be overheard, especially in secluded locations away from public places or in public places but in whispered secrecy. The convention of confidential disclosure is central to many areas in the life of the Nalumin people, who refer to it generally as *yawolmin* ("hiding" or "concealing"). It extends, for instance, to the exchange of goods (much is given and received outside of public knowledge) and the men's cult (whose activities are carefully hidden from women and young men). Nowhere, however, is it more important than in witchcraft.

An emphasis on confidential disclosure creates a serious problem for the anthropologist, a person who is almost by definition an outsider rather than a trusted insider. It was only after I had lived for several years at Bomtem and made several close friends that I was permitted to listen in on a few confidential discussions. During the period in August and September 1984, when the protest was made over Atulim's illness and when Finangim performed a shamanic séance for Damalim, I was just beginning to make real progress. A major breakthrough happened several days after the shamanic séance. I asked Damalim's friend Abani some questions hoping to clarify the meaning of what the shaman had revealed. At first Abani was of little help, insisting (as everyone usually did) that he knew little about witchcraft or the meaning of what shamans revealed. But then, unexpectedly, he said that no one was surprised that Damalim had been afflicted by witchcraft. When I asked why, he went on to provide a detailed list of actions that Damalim had done in the past that could have provoked vengeance, counting them off on the fingers of his hand, according to the Nalumin numerical system.

First, said Abani (indicating the little finger of his left hand), Damalim had been having intercourse with an unmarried woman in the settlement Astembil (where Damalim was living), angering her family. Second (ring finger), he had beaten a man in Astembil over another matter, angering the man's family who lived in the settlement of another descent group on the other side of the Yak River. Third (middle finger), he had hunted in the territory of another descent group, though he had later paid wealth to buy rights to hunt there. Fourth (index finger), after a friend of his had died in the settlement of another descent group on the opposite side of the Yak River, Damalim had sent a braid of tobacco to pay for contract witchcraft against those he suspected of causing his friend's death. Fifth (thumb), he had argued with a member of Bomtem over a pig and the two had each killed a pig of the other before the matter was resolved. Sixth, and finally (indicating his wrist), Damalim looked much like a man who had recently died, and the man's relatives possibly felt anger when they saw Damalim and were reminded of the deceased. "Since he had done six different wrongs *(nem)* to people," concluded Abani, "we feared he would not recover from his sickness. We thought, "He will die and we will say of him afterwards, 'He perished from his wrongs *(nem tem unbano).*'"

Abani's disclosure changed my understanding of the shamanic séance I had seen. Knowing who possessed a motive for harming Damalim, I was able to draw more specific meaning from the shaman's narrative. When the shaman spoke of a yakop bundle made by the people of Kilsigin against Damalim, he meant those people angry with him over the hunting dispute and over the tobacco sent for contract witchcraft. When he spoke of a witch waiting along the path who shot Damalim with the biis arrow, he probably meant someone from Astembil, angry over his affair with the unmarried woman.

My new understanding of Damalim's sickness also led me to reexamine what had been said at the meeting over Atulim's illness. In the heat of passion during the meeting itself, Bopsim had disclosed what people regarded as one of the major grudges against Atulim. Atulim is a relatively wealthy man by Nalumin standards, though certainly not the wealthiest man in the area. Jealousy of his wealth was behind the yakop done against him. Asking further information, in confidence, I learned that there were numerous other grudges against Atulim. Perhaps most significantly, Atulim had physically assaulted and killed two people, both suspected witches, one around 1964 and the other around 1968. The surviving relatives of these two, witches themselves, were said to be eager for vengeance. I was told, in confidence, that when several speakers at the meeting mentioned how the "women" of the settlement intended to call for other men "at the sides" to come and finish off Atulim, those other men were in fact the relatives of the men Atulim had helped to kill.

The more access I was allowed to the area of confidential disclosures, the clearer the evidence became that ordinary people possessed an extensive and detailed understanding of witchcraft. For virtually every death and major sickness that had recently occurred, people proved to have specific thoughts about who was responsible for the witchcraft and what their motives had been. The thoughts people disclosed in confidence often differed considerably from what the same people disclosed in public. The people suspected of being responsible for witchcraft cases in the village were often members of the same settlement as their victims, and they were sometimes close relatives.

The best way to convey what confidential disclosures are like is to describe a particular case. Mikim's death, like the death of any person, was the subject of a series of secret explanations. I heard one of the main explanations from Nilenim. On the afternoon of April 8, 1985, Nilenim visited my house and, finding himself alone with Kupsep, Kasakim and myself, revealed to us what he felt to be the true account of the killing of Mikim. Nilenim had been staying with Gamsep, Nilenim's close friend and also the leader of the one-house settlement of Tilamiyap where Mikim had died. "Gamsep told me what happened," Nilenim began in a low, earnest voice. He continued:

> He said it was Mikim's wife [Unipkon] who did it. She sent the word to the biis witches and then went to sleep with him at Tilamiyap. The next day, after she had seen the other men and women of the settlement leave for gardens, she called for them [the biis witches] to approach. . . . They took their bows and arrows and came up onto the veranda and in through the doorway of the house, and they fired arrows down toward the floor [where Mikim lay]. He [Mikim] crawled out and came to rest in the central plaza, perhaps. His wife [Unipkon] got a piece of smoldering wood from the fire and brought it out to the central plaza with her. She thrust the burning wood into his throat, perhaps, and they finished him off. Gamsep said, "I kept talking to her [Unipkon] but she did not reply fully. I kept talking to her, but she just lay there [as if she were asleep]. 'In that case, it is you for certain who killed him,' I told her repeatedly, while she remained silent like that. I kept telling her that, and eventually she fled," Gamsep told me.

During and following the telling of the account of Mikim's death, Kasakim and Kupsep expressed both horror and anger that such a terrible fate had befallen a man who was their friend and relative. Given the grotesque details of the event, such a reaction was predictable. What surprised me, however, was the absence of any debate over the truth of the account. How could Gamsep have found out the details of the killing of Mikim, when neither he nor anyone else had actually witnessed what happened? In the specific case of the account of Mikim's death, the main support for the charge against Unipkon came from the fact that she has long been suspected of being a witch. Her failure to rebut Gamsep's accusation further confirmed a view that was already deeply entrenched. I thought it was just as likely that her response was caused by her fear and grief, and I asked Nilenim if there was any other evidence. He told me that the two shamans who live in the settlement of Tilamiyap—Gamsep's wife Wankon and her brother Finangim—had been given the same information by their spirits.

In fact, there is rarely an emphasis on testing the truth of confidential accounts. Nilenim's description of Mikim's death is like many other confidential accounts I heard. In such accounts, people offer the results of speculation as if this were equivalent to witnessing the events in question. People draw on the disclosures of shamans, which they interpret and elaborate on freely to clarify any implications that may not otherwise be clear enough. They also draw and elaborate on dreams in much the same way as they do on the disclosures of shamans.[12] This is because dreams are understood as a means by which ordinary people can experience (though with less accurate recall) much the same contact with the hidden world of spirits as shamans do in séances. Actions or responses on the part of suspected witches that seemed ambiguous to me are held to be strong proof of the truth of the suspicions. Likewise, sightings of witches or natural signs of witchcraft, especially the animal species associated with witches, are interpreted in a far more specific manner in confidence than in public. Finally, in many cases sick people themselves make confidential disclosures (sometimes in fever-induced delirium) about who is responsible for their condition. After their death, these disclosures are circulated and presumably elaborated upon. When people told me of past cases of disclosures of this kind they would often insist that the victim had actually seen the witch in the act of killing him or her using the method of biis, and then returned to confide the act before dying (though this obviously violates the principle that witches are invisible except in dreams and visions).[13]

A terrifying picture emerges from confidential disclosures. For the Nalumin, there are literally witches everywhere. Every individual is sure there are several among the people who live in his or her settlement, and wonder if there are not others who are unknown. And, of course, even more witches live in other settlements. People have to live with all the people whom they believe are witches without betraying the fact they have such beliefs. They have to meet with suspected witches, speak with them, cooperate with them in routine joint tasks like garden clearing or hunting, exchange wealth and pork with them. Worst of all, they have to eat with them on numerous occasions, allowing the witches an opportunity to take their food and use it to make them sick by the practice of yakop.

Imagine living in close contact with the individual you believe had killed and eaten your mother, aunt, uncle, and several cousins! This is the situation faced by Awonweng, who (he told me in confidence) suspects the person who did it was his uncle Lotim, who lives in the neighboring settlement of Silendum. Likewise, Abutim—a young man who is a member of the same household as Atulim and Kupsep—is sure the man who killed his daughter is Tingdukim, who lives next door. He told me he had seen Tingdukim in the form of a domestic pig, prowling at night in search of new victims.

All the people who shared his or her confidential views with me proved to have a similarly firm conviction that they lived among witches who had killed their friends and relatives and were likely to kill them as well. I collected accounts from all the people who were willing to tell me, about 20 in all. The accounts varied from sketchy outlines to lengthy and detailed lists, depending on how bold the person was from whom I sought the information and, even more importantly, how closely I knew him or her. When I compared the accounts, regularities appeared. Certain people—such as Tingdukim and Lotim—figured on nearly everyone's list of witches. Other people were named by only a small proportion of people. Altogether, 34 people of the Kuyakmin area were named as witches, 16 men and 18 women. Perhaps 20 of these individuals were named particularly regularly. This means that more than one person in every 9 among the Kuyakmin is suspected of being a witch. This figure, however, does not take into account the fact that all but 2 of the named witches were mature adults over the age of twenty-five. If only adults of twenty-five and older are counted, the proportion of suspected witches is more than one in every 4 people. Even if only the most widely suspected individuals are counted, the proportion is still about one in 6 people.[14]

The Witch of the Imagination

Early in my fieldwork, Damalim told me that living with witchcraft is like living in the midst of an unending hidden war. The longer I stayed among the Nalumin, the more accurate this comparison appeared. The Nalumin constantly strive to uncover who their hidden enemies are, drawing on all available sources of evidence. But the more they learn about the details of witchcraft, the greater the threat to them appears to be. There is nothing reassuring in the thought that at least one in every six of the adults around you are homicidal cannibals with secret, superhuman powers.

There are three obvious ways people could solve the problems posed to them by witches: avoid witches, neutralize their powers, or stop them from using their powers. The Nalumin take it for granted that there is no sure way to avoid witches or to neutralize their powers. They also expect only minimal success from trying to persuade witches to stop doing their terrible deeds. The most effective solution to witchcraft, as the Nalumin see it, would be to kill the witches. Carrying out such a direct response to witchcraft, however, is both difficult and dangerous. It is dangerous because witches can fight back, using ordinary weapons or even more deadly supernatural powers. It is difficult because people are reluctant to join together in a group large enough to take on the risk of attacking a suspected individual. One reason is because their understanding of witchcraft is based on evidence of a poor and ambiguous quality. Although people may agree to a large extent about the general set of individuals who are witches, they often disagree about who among these individuals is the culprit behind a specific death. Another reason is that suspected witches are usually members of the victim's settlement. Few individuals are willing to attack a close relative, regardless of the evidence against him or her. Therefore, people rarely take direct action against witchcraft among the Nalumin.[15]

As the Nalumin see it, then, they are at a decided disadvantage in the ongoing war waged against them by the witches. Each sickness is a battle, each death a defeat. Though victories also occur—when someone recovers from a serious sickness—they are only temporary; everyone eventually dies. The connection of witchcraft with issues of life and death means that it is a matter of the highest importance for the Nalumin. The disadvantage people face when combating witchcraft means that the Nalumin response tends to be defensive rather than offensive, passive rather than active. Above all, the response to witchcraft involves a profoundly anxious concern that engages a large part of the imagination at all times.

In the rest of this section, I will examine two main aspects of the Nalumin imagination of witchcraft. The first is the significance that the figure of the witch has for those who regard themselves as a target and ultimate victim. The second is the manner—personal but also interpersonal, consensual but also divisive—in which people arrive at their image of the witch. In either aspect, the figure of the witch plays a vital role in the process by which the Nalumin come to experience and know themselves.

The Witch as a Figure of Imagination

Imagination is commonly defined as the faculty that allows people to think, both visually and conceptually, about things they do not immediately perceive, even if they have never actually seen them before. This definition reflects a long Western philosophical tradition that approaches the faculty of imagination as an attribute of the mind, a creative power of thought that is quite different from merely perceiving external, empirical reality. The Nalumin do not make a distinction between a mental faculty of imagination and a more directly sensual faculty of perception. They do, however, make a distinction that serves much the same purpose between two kinds of perception *(atamyamin)*. On the one hand, they recognize that there are ordinary means of perception, including sight, hearing, smell, touch and taste. On the other hand, they recognize that there are special means of perception, including dreams, visions experienced in a waking state, and revelations that emerge out of divinatory rituals and shamanic séances.

The ordinary means of perception make possible an awareness of those things that are present in an obvious way. This is the aspect of reality that the Nalumin refer to as *fitap* (clear, in plain sight). The special means of perception make possible an awareness of things that are present but ordinarily invisible. This is the aspect of reality that the Nalumin refer to as *uwap* (hidden). Although virtually everyone has the ability to perceive in the ordinary way, few people have a strong ability to use the special means of perception, and nobody has access to special means of perception to an extent comparable with their access to ordinary means of perception.[16]

According to the Nalumin, actions taking place in the hidden world determine much of what happens visibly. For this reason, it is essential for people to try to uncover and understand the hidden world. For us, as Westerners, this means that the Nalumin take their faculty of imagination very seriously. They give the highest importance to the more visual and directly experiential products of imaginary activity, such as vivid dreams and waking visions. They also value the more conceptual (i.e., accounts made in words) products of their attempts to understand witchcraft. There is good reason for us to call this imagination as well. The vivid imagery of dreams and visions needs to be interpreted at least partly in conceptual terms if people are to understand and discuss their meaning. Their conceptual understanding also draws on an ability to speculate about possible realities that we link with the faculty of imagination.

Nowhere is the reality of the hidden world a more serious and urgent matter than in witchcraft. It is not surprising, then, that the Nalumin emphasis on imagination is especially striking in their concerns with witchcraft. As the agent responsible for witchcraft, the witch is the focus of this imaginary involvement. The figure of the witch is the referent of thoughts about witchcraft and the most important object that can be revealed by special means of perception. The witch is a real but hidden danger people must be prepared to encounter at any time with only minimal warning. They prepare themselves for such an encounter by keeping the figure of the witch in mind, and by using their imagination to interpret any sign of witchcraft they may come across.

Wengsep's experience in April 1985 provides a concrete example of the character and variety of people's imagination of the figure of the witch. When Wengsep heard a whistle, saw a shadow, and came running back into the settlement, people began at once to interpret the event differently. They drew not only on their own judgments but also on the judgments disclosed to them by other people in discussions held at varying levels of confidentiality. In Nilenim's house, Wengsep's account was understood as evidence of an attempt to kill Nilenim, due to anger over his pig eating the large sweet potato garden belonging to the household of Nukenip and her family, Katim and his family, and Wengsep and his family. The individuals who lived in Kupsep's house had their own interpretations. The witch could have been waiting for Atulim, or for either of two of Kupsep's sons, Damalim (who was present that evening in Bomtem) or Fasulnuk (who had recently sighted a witch along a trail). The witch could have even been waiting for Kupsep himself. All these men had reason to fear grudges against themselves. In the house where Wengsep was staying, the unmarried woman Dutip suspected that the witch was a man who was angry that she had broken off her covert affair with him and started a covert affair with another man. In the same house, Wengsep feared that the witch had probably been after him. Several months before, Wengsep had been in a serious argument with his elder brother Saangim. Saangim's affines had taken sides with him against Wengsep, and Wengsep had moved away from the area of

Saangim's settlement to Bomtem. Wengsep suspected that some of Saangim's affines were witches.[17]

The varying interpretations made by the residents of Bomtem of Wengsep's nocturnal encounter indicate the extent to which any specific evidence of witchcraft allows for multiple understandings. The experience reported by Wengsep meant something different to different people, each of whom came to his or her own conclusion of the identity of the witch who lay in wait that night and why the witch was there. The high degree of consensus about the general set of people suspected of being witches does not change this fact.

The fact that the identity of the witch varies according to individual and context makes the witch a complex figure. This complexity reflects the close link between the witch and the imagination. The imagination of one person is unlike that of another person. People may disclose aspects of what they imagine to each other, and significantly shape each other's imagination in this way. From all accounts that people hear others tell, they put together a personal interpretation, reflecting their individual fears and interests. Above all, people are likely to show particular concern for threats of witchcraft that endanger themselves and those closest to them.

What Witches Reveal: The Meaning of an Imaginary Figure

The opposition between the hidden and visible world is of key importance in the Nalumin approach to imagination. It also shapes their understanding and experience of the relationship between witch and victim. The Nalumin witch lives both in the hidden world and the visible world: operating in one, he brings about destructive consequences in the other. Imagination is based on another kind of relationship between the visible and the hidden world: a disclosure (of usually limited extent) of one to the other. Unlike the witch, imagination has some benefits, since it gives people a warning of what is acting against them in the hidden world. In either case, however, the Nalumin regard the hidden world itself as predominantly negative, frightening, and unpleasant. But how do the Nalumin come to draw such an opposition between the visible and hidden world? And what implications does this bear for understanding the significance of the figure of the witch, a figure who fully exploits the powers and embodies the dangers of the hidden world?

In the ordinary and visible world that the Nalumin inhabit, there is an emphasis on good will and common interests. As I noted before, the Nalumin live in small settlements where virtually everyone is closely related by cognatic or affinal ties to each other. There is an expectation that closely related people should be on the best terms with each other, sharing food and wealth freely, speaking openly and truthfully, and constantly expressing kindness and friendship to each other. In daily life these normative expectations are followed closely. A Nalumin settlement is a place of appealing communal warmth and good cheer. Rarely is there a sign of conflict, and any conflict that does arise is generally resolved almost immediately with apparent satisfaction to all people concerned.[18]

By contrast, the hidden world of witchcraft is a world in which the same people who appear to be on the best of terms turn out to be secret enemies. In this world conflicts that appeared to have long been settled or were never openly expressed move people to plot and commit desperate acts of vengeance against each other. Lying and deception are taken for granted as strategies practiced by witches and those who seek to evade them.

Nalumin individuals have to negotiate both of these worlds simultaneously. They take actions that fit the image of a largely harmonious visible world while taking actions that help them to learn about and defend themselves against the hidden world of enmity and witchcraft. The separation between these two sides of Nalumin life is a highly complex arrangement. As the Nalumin see it, there simply should not be witchcraft, but witchcraft tragically continues. As the case of the meeting over Atulim's illness showed, they frequently appeal to each other (some of whom are suspected witches) to make a final irrevocable choice between the two dimensions of life. But the problem with such appeals, as the Nalumin themselves recognize, is that people will probably never be as they should according to public ideals. They will fail to avoid conflict, fail to resolve conflicts amicably, fail to renounce and forget causes of slights and anger, and fail to place the common good above personal interests. As long as people fall short of their ideals, and as long as some people are witches, witchcraft will continue. Unrenounced, hidden enmity will not only move those who are witches to practice it, but will also move some of those who are not witches to practice witchcraft indirectly through arranged contracts.

Witchcraft reveals, in this way, the enduring inability of people to be as they should. This may help to explain an otherwise puzzling quality of collective wrong that appears in Nalumin discussion of witchcraft with outsiders. I remember how Saangim (the other outstanding Kuyakim leader besides Kupsep) spoke to an official of the Papua New Guinea government who walked in to census the local population in June 1983. "We are not a good people," he told the patrol officer. "No matter how much we try to stop the witchcraft it keeps on happening. There is nothing we can do by ourselves to end it. You must jail all of us who do witchcraft and terrify the people here. Only then, perhaps, will there be an end to witchcraft for awhile."

Although the Nalumin often talk about witchcraft as a moral problem, it would be highly misleading to leave it at that. The methods and consequences of witchcraft may be unnatural and horrible, but witches do not victimize people without reason. Witches act to take revenge against real or perceived wrongs done to themselves (or sometimes done to other people who have contracted with them to take revenge for them). As a result, as soon as people start thinking about the witchcraft that lies behind a case of sickness or death, they turn (generally privately or confidentially) to the reasons why witchcraft would have been committed against the sick or dead person. In this way, witchcraft makes people look more closely at their relationships with each other. In particular, it forces them to acknowledge the continuing reality of conflict, disappointment, and anger amongst them, a side of Nalumin life that is largely hidden beneath the overshadowing emphasis on good will and friendliness.

Equally important, by reminding people of their accountability to others, witchcraft is implicated in some of the most basic aspects of the people's individual understanding of themselves and others. For example, when Abani, trying to explain why Damalim had been a victim of witchcraft, listed a long set of grudges held against him, he indicated a kind of situation faced by virtually every Nalumin individual. Every Nalumin regularly angers other people. In many cases, the conflict could have been avoided. Damalim, for instance, did not have to beat the man in Astembil. However, sometimes conflict is inevitable. There are circumstances in which people will be angry with someone no matter what he does. A good example is the resentment held against Damalim simply because he lives while another man died. Likewise, there are situations where someone has to make a choice where, no matter what he chooses, or how carefully he chooses, other people will be disappointed. Hence, the consequences of Dutip's decision to break off an affair with one man. If she had continued her affair, the other man would probably have been angry with her.

The relationship between witch and victim discloses two very different aspects of Nalumin life: the failure of the community as a whole to conform to its own ideals, and the failure of people individually to satisfy the demands of specific relationships with each other. It is possible to draw many connections between these two aspects of Nalumin life. Failure to satisfy specific relationships, for instance, is often measured with respect to the public ideals governing these relationships. Failure to satisfy public ideals, in turn, often results from the fact that in order to meet expectations in a specific relationship it is necessary to betray other relationships. Public ideals, in short, are not simply a guide to agreement but also a basis of disagreement between people. Personal relationships appeal to public ideals while also undermining them, since the two both agree with and oppose each other. The result is the kind of conflict neither side can win. Each of the opposed sides depends on the other.

Anthropologists tend to describe social situations of this kind by appealing to a model of social structure based on the conflict or opposition of its elements.[19] The Nalumin view their society in the guise of the public ideals of what it *should* be, while experiencing its contradictions in the form of general and particular problems. The general problem, as the Nalumin see it, is that people who obviously wish to live well together and increase their numbers are instead killing each other and destroying themselves as a group. The particular problems concern all the situations where individuals have to choose among their personal relationships, where any choice is a form of betrayal.

The Nalumin associate witchcraft with both kinds of problems. And more than that—they link both to the facts of sickness and death, thereby amplifying the problems and experiencing them in an entirely different form. This form is the relationship of witch and victim, for the witch that the Nalumin imagine is something more than an individual suspected of witchcraft. The witch also incorporates and personifies all the unwanted, unresolvable problems that witchcraft is associated with. The witch is identified with the general failure of people to prevail as a community and the personal responsibility for wrongdoing. This is not only different from the horrific, supernatural figure of the witch, but directly opposed to it. The witch is not the invisible embodiment of what is alien or other. On the contrary, the witch is everything that people truly *are* as communities and as individuals but would rather not be.

From Identity to Difference

I have suggested that the witch reveals essential but rejected aspects of the community and of individual selves. But equally important is the manner in which people differentiate themselves from the witch, from those things they would rather not be. I never witnessed an individual in the Kuyakmin area admitting to being a witch; on the contrary, even the most widely suspected people vehemently affirmed their innocence (often at the same time demonstrating an accurate knowledge of the extent of suspicions against themselves). It is only natural that people deny being witches, but in doing so they do more than merely declare their innocence. Much of the effort that people put into uncovering the individuals and actions involved in witchcraft can be understood as a means by which people differentiate themselves from witches.

The premise of a shamanic séance is that nobody who is present is a witch; for people who are witches are assumed to keep away from possessed shamans who might be able see their hidden identity. The protest, too, offers an opportunity for people to maintain the appearance of being innocent. Suggestions are made that there are witches acting in the community, but their identities are not revealed. It is easy for people to dramatically demonstrate they are not witches by taking the side of the protesting group. Confidential disclosures serve the same purpose even more effectively. When people disclose information about witchcraft to others, they indicate that someone besides themselves or those to whom they are speaking is a witch. Furthermore, the act of making information about witchcraft available to another person is seen as proof that neither the person who is speaking nor the person who is being trusted with the confidential disclosure is a witch.

The Nalumin are worried about being suspected of witchcraft themselves. Although only a minority of people among the Nalumin are commonly believed to be witches, it is always possible that an individual thought to be innocent is secretly a witch. Adding force to this possibility is the fact that every individual possesses enough grudges against others to provide him or her with a sufficient motive for doing witchcraft. Everyone must struggle against being identified as a witch. Perhaps the strongest way an individual can demonstrate his or her innocence is by demonstrating that the guilt falls on someone else. The inquest into witchcraft that follows every sickness and death serves, in this way, as much to differentiate the innocent from the witches as to identify those witches who were responsible. The fact that an individual's innocence in one case is no guarantee of innocence in another case ensures a high level of involvement of virtually everyone in the community at each inquest.

The problem people face in proving themselves innocent of witchcraft leads directly to a first general point concerning the imagination: the interrelationship between individual and collective imagination. People would not be so concerned about becoming the object of suspicion if there were simple empirical means of proving their innocence. But, as I noted, witchcraft in fact leaves little evidence that is directly available to individuals on their own. They depend largely on indirect evidence provided by other people as well as by the spirits that possess shamans and shape dreams and visions. The result is a high degree of mutual dependency among individuals, and a corresponding emphasis on understandings that emerge gradually as a synthesis of the experiences, disclosures, and conversations of a number of people. It is the way and extent to which people *believe* someone is a witch that the person *is* a witch. There is no basis of truth about witchcraft—at least of a kind accessible to human awareness—that lies outside the complex and interpersonal processes by which witchcraft is disclosed and evaluated.

The collective nature of these processes indicates, as well, an interpersonal dimension of imagination. Much of what seems to us to be the products of personal imagination—dreams, visions, suspicions of other people's evil intentions—Nalumin individuals regard as evidence of important aspects of the world they share with others. People who personally experience this evidence need to disclose it to and discuss it with other people in order to learn what it signifies and what they should do in response. Since people regard the initial judgment of their own experiences as at best partial truths and possibly false, they come to take a different position on their personal experiences according to what other people say or do upon hearing about their experiences. Under such conditions, it is so difficult to separate the imagination of the individual from that of the other people who help to shape it, that there is good reason to question the usefulness of drawing a sharp distinction between individual and collective imagination.

The second general point that emerges from an understanding of the role of imagination in Nalumin witchcraft is the central place of imagination in Nalumin social action. A sickness or death inspires a dramatic increase of interest in witchcraft that engages the imagination of people, individually and collectively. People report more sightings of witches in their waking and dream life, shamans perform more séances, and people make more confidential disclosures to each other about witchcraft. They spontaneously recall and discuss memories of friends and relatives now deceased. They also give much more thought than they ordinarily do to outstanding grievances, both those they hold against others and those held by others against themselves.

At stake in this imaginative engagement is more than the attribution of witchcraft to a few major suspects—it is the understanding that the members of a settlement have of each other as witches, accessories of witches, and victims of witchcraft. This understanding has far-reaching consequences for how people relate to each other, whom they will trust and favor, and whom they will avoid. Individuals hitherto presumed innocent may gain a reputation for witchcraft that they will keep for the rest of their lives. Inquests have, in this way, a significant effect on relationships among people in the same settlement. Individual ties between people are strengthened or weakened, as people choose with whom to identify themselves and from whom to differentiate themselves. The membership of the settlement may change as individuals choose to leave, whether because they are convinced they are endangered by witchcraft or because they are convinced they are suspected as witches. Inquests into witchcraft also have consequences for relationships between the members of different settlements. When someone suffers sickness or death in one settlement, the people who live in the victim's settlement may become convinced (on the basis of their interpretation of the evidence available to them) that people in another settlement were the leaders or accomplices of the witchcraft. Such suspicions discourage people in one settlement from visiting the other settlement, and can contribute to a progressive deterioration of relationships that ultimately results in serious conflicts between the two settlements.

Witchcraft, Morality and the Self

The Nalumin ideology of witchcraft addresses and helps to resolve some of the main moral dilemmas in human life. Chief among these are the existence of evil, the determination of who is responsible for actions and events, and the need to hold people accountable for their actions. But a morality so closely linked with witchcraft creates problems of its own. Where imagination is essential in social action and where individual and collective aspects of imagination are virtually inseparable, it becomes difficult to locate who is responsible. In this section I will examine the consequences of this kind of moral indeterminacy and ambiguity on the lives of the Nalumin and on their construction of self.

The Morality of Indeterminacy

Many major actions taken by the Nalumin are responses to witchcraft. In responding to witchcraft, however, people are acting on the basis of beliefs they acknowledge are often partial and unreliable, a complex synthesis of many indirect sources. One reason people trust and act on these beliefs is that there is no better alternative, but a stronger reason is that they do not arrive at conclusions on their own. They do so with other people and with the help of spirits who reveal themselves through dreams, visions, and the séances of shamans. Under such conditions, it becomes difficult to trace the responsibility for a particular explanation of witchcraft to the judgment of any particular person. It is then difficult to trace responsibility for any action that is taken in response to witchcraft—whether this is merely vilifying an accused witch, making a protest against witchcraft, or even attempting to kill the witch—to a particular person. The responsibility falls instead on many people together as well as on the spirits who have helped them.

Although responsibility for understanding witchcraft is deflected away from individuals, the responsibility for witchcraft itself remains focused on individual people. Every report of witchcraft inspires people to make a quick initial judgment about its significance; and, as might be expected, their initial judgments vary considerably. However, as a result of the interpersonal processes of disclosure and negotiation, they develop a common understanding, one that aims at giving the witch a specific identity. But what prevents everyone from agreeing on the identification of the witch, even in the same settlement, is that people form into several groups. Each group arrives at a somewhat different understanding of witchcraft. The result lies between the individual understandings at the beginning of the process and the collective understanding at the end of the process. Each of these groups are made up of people united by common interests and personal relations. Moreover, due to multiple affiliations of kinship and friendship, the same person may belong to several different groups, each offering a different identification of the witch.

The effects of partisan interests and plural understandings are evident in all the contexts where witchcraft is disclosed and discussed among people. In shamanic séances, like the one that was held for Damalim, the final account of witchcraft emerges only after several initial versions have been offered, and after many of the details contained in the initial version have been changed or discarded. The role that the shaman performs is to bring together a number of differing versions held by people. Significantly, the final account that the shaman produces usually leaves some important questions and discrepancies unresolved, as happened in the séance for Damalim. The lack of resolution of shamanic séances, I would argue, reflects the existence of divisions in interests among the participants at the séance. In particular, the shaman carefully avoids pursuing suggestions of the culpability of people closely related to anyone present at the séance. Likewise, though the people who participate in a formal protest are often bold enough to raise the issue of local involvement in witchcraft, their unwillingness to specify the identity of anyone means that the meeting usually ends with even less of a sense of resolution than a shamanic séance. This was clear, for instance, in the protest over Atulim's illness. Partisan interests are perhaps most evident in what I have called confidential disclosures. The care people take to shape disclosure to fit their audience conceals the existence of alternate understandings held by groups of people possessing different interests while serving to keep the understandings thriving and separate.

The fact that people come to know of witchcraft as a group rather than alone has two major moral consequences. On the one hand, the collective nature of the understanding makes it difficult to hold particular individuals responsible for the response to witchcraft. Responsibility is spread among many people as well as the spirits that help them. On the other hand, the fact that groups of people develop different understandings (according to their divergent interests) places an obstacle to the development of a truly common view about who is responsible for the witchcraft.

The difficulty people face in agreeing about the identity of the witch merits close attention. As I noted before, witchcraft reveals wrongs that people have done: the singular witch as an instrument of vengeance on the wrongs of the individual; the existence of witchcraft as a whole as the means that the community pays for its inability to act according to its own ideals. Processes of disclosure and negotiation among people, however, diffuse much of the moral significance of the witch. Collective understandings tend to center around the evil actions and character of the witch while minimizing reference to the wrong that presumably motivated the witch. They also serve to assuage individual fears of witchcraft by narrowing the identity of the witch and the witch's intended victim for every incident of suspected witchcraft. The vast majority of people who are not named as the witch or the witch's intended victim are relieved to hear that the witch behind some current incident is not *their* witch, that the motive of the witch is not *their* wrong. In a different manner, those few people who are named as victims or intended victims of witchcraft in the collective account find significant relief in the fact that they receive the support of a large group of other people. Even those who have the most to lose from the collective understanding of the group—the people who are named as witches—are offered a way out by the nature of collective understandings. They can ignore those collective under-standings in which they are implicated and turn instead to the collective under-standing of another group who, taking a different position, hold them innocent.

Although collective understandings of witchcraft diminish the moral force that the figure of the witch possesses in the imagination of the individual and community, this force never disappears entirely. Some of the force remains, for instance, in the uncertainty that affects all understanding of witchcraft, whether individual or collective. It is always possible that a mistake has been made about identity of the witch and the witch's victim. No one can be sure that the real victim will not turn out to be himself or herself. All people have done wrongs and everyone expects sometime to be chosen as the target of witchcraft. The plurality of collective understandings protects the moral force of witchcraft in another way. Many individuals know (by means of information they over-hear themselves or are told in confidence by those close to them) that they are named in the accounts of other groups of people as being a witch or a deserving target of witchcraft. Even those who have never heard any suspicions against themselves admit the possibility that such accounts of them exist without their knowledge.

The witch that the Nalumin imagine and speak about, individually and to-gether, is a singularly complex figure—a center of contradictions involving si-multaneous aspects of identity and difference. The witch is both identified and differentiated from the individual. The witch is equally identified and differenti-ated from the group to which he or she belongs. The witch reveals (i.e., identifies) the accountability of the individual while also offering the individual an opportunity for evading (i.e., differentiating himself from) his or her ac-countability. People evade their individual accountability by transforming the wrongs they commit against another person into the other person's motive of re-venge against themselves. People also evade their individual accountability by turning away entirely from the question of their own wrongs and focusing in-stead on collective accounts of witchcraft concerning people other than them-selves. Finally, although people evade accountability in this way, it returns to them again in the form of the uncertainty that attends any understanding that can be gained about witchcraft and the recognition that everyone will many times suffer from witchcraft and (with the exception of those slain in battle) eventually die from it. All processes of differentiation ultimately lead back to identity: the witch who matters most to each individual is the witch who comes to slay him or her, a witch who incarnates the wrongs actually committed by the individual.

Imagining the Witch, Constructing the Self

So we come to the most personal aspect of witchcraft. It is a point com-monly recognized that when we talk about a moral system we are talking about a characteristic way of constructing the self (cf. Geertz 1973, 1983a). If witch-craft plays an important role in the moral imagination of the Nalumin, it plays an equally important role in the construction of the self. The figure of the witch reminds people of the significance of their individual actions and forces them to confront aspects of their individual selves they might rather ignore. For much the same reason, the figure of the witch forces Nalumin individuals to confront essential aspects of other people and of the community that they share with them.

Of course, the witch does not directly represent the self, the other, or the community. The witch's significance depends on the fact that people carry out deeds that put them in conflict with others. In addition, because people's conflicts with others are often at their own expense, the witch reflects these conflicts. The witch embodies, in this way, the aspect of conflict and division in matters concerning self, other, and community. Opposed to the divisive aspect of self, other, and community represented by the witch are the ideals held by the Nalumin of how people should be, individually and together. The Nalumin re-gard these ideals as vitally important, for they establish the conditions of sur-vival of people both as individuals and as a community. These ideals represent identity, whereas the witch represents difference. For the Nalumin, it is neces-sary to consider both the aspect of identity and the aspect of difference to under-stand the significance of an action or statement. The self—as the agency accountable for its own actions—is caught in a dynamic between identity and difference: where identity is the necessity of common interests and difference is the inevitability of conflicting personal interests. The self is represented neither by the witch nor the victim of the witch. It lies instead in the relationship be-tween witch and victim, a relationship that condenses an open-ended dynamic into a simple duality.

Several questions emerge. First, where does the relationship between witch and victim take place? As an action requiring an encounter between witch and victim it takes place above all in the imagination. Witches keep their actions hidden from ordinary perception, and so cannot be seen to meet their victims. Instead, people imagine the event. They imagine it in their waking hours as a constant danger that must be avoided. They imagine it involuntarily in dreams, and understand it later as a sign of what may happen. They imagine it as the cause behind sickness and death, and try to determine how precisely it occurred. The act of imagination that takes place in these contexts involves both the con-struction of images (visual and auditory in particular) and the construction of discursive accounts (with explanatory power).

Second, where does the activity of imagining take place? It occurs not sim-ply in the mind of the individual but in interpersonal processes of disclosure and negotiation. On the one hand, this is because the meaning that individuals find in their own experiences of witchcraft is shaped by how other people respond to the accounts they disclose of their experiences. On the other hand, this is because many of the activities in which there is a stress on imagination are interpersonal from the start, such as in the development of joint accounts that occur during a spirit séance as well as in public meetings and confidential discussions. The Nalumin imagination of witchcraft, for these reasons, is as much a matter of people together as it is a matter of people by themselves.

The close relationship between the individual and interpersonal sides of the imagination has several implications. The Nalumin individual experiences essential aspects of himself or herself through the relationship with the witch, and he or she depends on the help of other people to imagine that connection. This implies a strong link between the subject—the agent responsible for actions—and other people. This also implies a strong link between subjectivity—the processes by which this agent determines and experiences the significance of its own actions—and intersubjective processes.

The word *subject* is often used in a manner synonymous with the word *individual*. The synonymy in common usage of the two words, however, is unlike the much more complex relationship that people bear to their individual selves, interests, and actions. The figure of the witch by itself raises one level of complexity: the splitting of the individual self. People differentiate themselves from aspects of their own actions and interests, with the consequence that these aspects appear to them as the totally alien force incarnated by the witch. The intersubjective processes by which the witch is imagined raise another level of complexity. Those aspects of actions and interests that people differentiate from themselves return to them in a form shaped by the understanding of others. Individuals experience themselves in part through others, and what they experience is no longer just their individual selves. When people imagine witches together, the witch they imagine takes on a form that reflects the conflicts of interests that exist between groups of people. In short, through the figure of the witch, the Nalumin subject relates to himself or herself at least partly through group conflicts.

Conclusion: A Return to the Individual Subject

I began this essay with a reference to William James's *Varieties of Religious Experience*. James found in the study of religious experience a source of insight into ordinarily hidden areas of consciousness. Experiences of witchcraft are a source of insight into aspects of the lives of the Nalumin that they may not speak about or even think about explicitly: the wrongs they have done to others, the suspicions they harbor of one another, and the conflicts that exist among their vital interests, both individually and collectively. For James, the benefit that religion offers individuals is to help them know more about the reality in which they live and to allow them to orient their actions to that total reality rather than the narrower reality of immediate awareness. To the extent that both visible and hidden reality is connected to the self, religion offers individuals a means by which they can address and serve their own best interests. If the Nalumin do not regard witchcraft as possessing benefits of this kind, this is because they do not have an optimistic view of the total reality in which people live. James allows for the possibility of religious reconciliation of the self with its larger reality, but the Nalumin see a larger reality that is marked by unresolvable conflicts and disagreements within and between individuals. The witch who reveals the hidden sides of reality to the self consequently is an instrument of the destruction of the self.

Despite the pessimistic view they take on the nature of reality and the fate of the individual, the Nalumin believe strongly, as did James, in the preeminence of the human subject. The being who acts and experiences is the center of the theory of witchcraft. The witch ensures it is the subject himself—rather than accidental or incomprehensible force outside of his control—that is responsible for sickness and death. From a personal perspective at least, this may indeed be the most important issue in life.

Above all, Nalumin witchcraft indicates the manner in which and the degree to which the subject can be fragmented. Nalumin individuals extend themselves over many different relationships between themselves and other people. A portion of their interests and concerns is attached to each of these personal relationships. The effect of witchcraft is to bring together the different partial versions of self that people adopt. When Nalumin individuals confront the witch they confront the kind of conflict of interests that they would ordinarily avoid referring to in practice. What the witch signifies to the individual is not so much any one of those partial versions of self that he or she offered other people as the difference between the versions. The witch and the difference the witch signifies is at once singular and plural. For though in principle a particular witch (identified with a particular conflict) is responsible for any particular instance of witchcraft, the practical difficulty of determining the precise identity of the witch ensures that there is always a large number of possible identities of the witch. When an individual imagines the witch, his or her imagination focuses on one particular identity but allows for the possibility of many others. In this way the witch signifies all of the different partial versions of self, even though the contrast between two partial versions is always central.

In short, I am offering a model of a two-sided Nalumin subject. The first side is a plurality of partial selves; the second side is the recombining of partial selves that witchcraft imposes. Another way of saying this is that there are two different but related processes of Nalumin subjectivity, and the being who carries out and experiences the consequences of these processes is the individual subject. To the extent that the witch has an important place in these processes, the witch is an aspect of the Nalumin subject. This extends an earlier point that the self is constructed in the relationship between witch and victim.

Let us compare the Nalumin processes of fragmentation and integration with some Western models. The way the witch confronts individuals with the moral significance of their actions is reminiscent of the notion of a conscience. According to this notion, when people carry out actions and thoughts that are wrong, they feel guilt afterwards. The sense of guilt implies that individuals constantly miss doing and being what they should be (and who they really are, at their truest and best). This is not unlike the way the witch reminds people of how they have wronged others. But the witch reminds people that they have done wrong in a manner different from how conscience is said to work: as an external threat of vengeance rather than an internal sense of guilt.

A more recent transformation of the idea of conscience is the psychodynamic model that has been developed in psychoanalysis. Freud—to simplify his position a great deal—said the cause of the sense of guilt associated with conscience actually arises from a part of the mind that he termed the "superego" (cf., Freud, 1961a). The superego is seen as a figure of authority that judges all the individual's thoughts and actions. The superego reminds people of all they have done wrong and insists they conform to an ideal of themselves (in fact, Freud called the superego the "ego ideal" in his earlier writings). The superego is in opposition to many ordinary human wishes and desires. People repress desires in order to satisfy the demands of the superego, but then experience the repressed desires in other forms.

Freud would probably have viewed the witch that existed in the mind of a Nalumin individual as an obvious case of projection, arising from repression. He would have dismissed the Nalumin's grim view of their situation as the unfortunate consequence of endemic paranoid neurosis. But before accepting this position (as some anthropologists have done in other cases of witchcraft), it is important to consider some important differences of the Nalumin case from the Freudian model. The Nalumin witch is a figure of judgment only for the particular external social relationship that concerns him and his victim. Moreover, as the Nalumin see it, what is at issue in witchcraft is a conflict of interest between two people rather the repressed desires of one person. Witchcraft, in short, begins and ends in interpersonal reality, even if it is experienced on a personal level.

Despite such differences, there is one aspect of Freud's account of the mind that is strikingly similar to the case of Nalumin witchcraft: his insistence on dynamics. Freud understood the mind as a dynamic between id, ego, and superego. Ultimately, the opposition of the unconscious and conscious is at the center of Freud's theory. Consciousness is achieved only by the initial suppression of most of the contents of the unconscious, but the unconscious nevertheless reenters the area of consciousness by concealing itself in other forms. In a strikingly similar way, the Nalumin place much emphasis on the existence of forces and facts that are hidden to ordinary perception and consciousness but which reenter the visible world with significant effect. Still, there is a difference between the Nalumin's model and Freud's: the Nalumin view the hidden area of life as an essentially collective concern. Visionary experiences and speculative suspicions that would be treated in psychoanalytical terms as the delusions of individuals or, at most, group illusions are regarded by the Nalumin as vital clues about a reality that everyone shares.

Freud expressed a deep skepticism of cultural institutions that uncritically drew on manifestations of the unconscious. It is likely that he would have dismissed Nalumin witchcraft at least as harshly as he did the Western religious tradition in *The Future of an Illusion* (1961b). But Freud's position does not change the fact that cultural traditions that draw on the unconscious play a vital role for issues affecting both individual psychology and interpersonal social processes. To the extent that anthropologists are more interested in interpretation than therapy, more like James than Freud, they should take advantage of the opportunity to gain new insights into these matters by exploring cases like that of Nalumin witchcraft.

NOTES

Acknowledgments. This essay is based on thirty-six months' fieldwork among the Nalumin of Papua New Guinea between August 1981 and December 1985, funded by the National Science Foundation (Grant Number G00-BNS-8206247), the Fulbright-Hays Program of the U.S. Department of Education (Grant Number 82–00436), and the Stanford Department of Anthropology. The Institute of Papua New Guinea Studies sponsored and aided my work. I would like to thank the editors of this collection, Gilbert Herdt and Michele Stephen, as well as several other people who helped me in the conception and writing of this essay: Bruce Knauft, Fitz Poole, Renato Rosaldo, and Donald Tuzin. A version of this essay was selected for an honorable mention in the 1988 Stirling Award for contributions to psychological anthropology.

1. I use the term *religion* in its widest sense, as referring to human belief in invisible or supernatural entities and powers, whether malevolent or benevolent. The other main area of religious beliefs among the Nalumin besides witchcraft centers around the elaborate rituals and myths of a secret cult from which women are largely excluded. The men's cult is regarded as indispensable for the growth of boys into men; the fertility and health of gardens, pigs, and people; the ability of men to hunt animals and fight against enemies effectively; and the general willingness of people to live together. An account of the complex Nalumin secret cult is not possible here. I will discuss the Nalumin men's cult in separate publications.

2. Names such as Bomtem, Wengsep, and Katim are fictitious. In order to protect the confidentiality of the people concerned, I have made up aliases for all individuals and settlements and for most geographical locations. Most aliases are based on actual Nalumin words and the conventions for forming names with them.

3. The Papua New Guinea administration refer to the Nalumin as "Atbalmin," a name they learned from a neighboring group from whom they have recruited most of their interpreters.

The term *Atbalmin*, however, carries certain negative significance (it literally means "people of the forest").

4. *Yakop* is also known by the alternative name *tamon*. This latter name is found in many neighboring Mountain-Ok–speaking societies for this variety of malevolent magic. For studies of sorcery and witchcraft in some other Mountain-Ok groups, see Barth (1975), Jones (1980), and Poole (1981a).

5. It is worth noting that the soul is subject to other supernatural dangers besides biis. Harm can come, for instance, from demons of nature–called collectively *matong*, that live in the wilderness *(siip)*—as well as from various malevolent spirits that live in human houses and gardens (*am kayak* and *yongbip kayak*, respectively). Harm can can also come from spirits of the dead. However, none of these supernatural dangers are regarded as a mortal peril like witchcraft. Nalumin, laymen and experts alike, pointed out to me that the harm these beings cause is rarely fatal, and that the anger and effects of these beings can be neutralized by routine methods of exorcism and propitiation.

6. The Nalumin told me that the children of biis often become biis themselves since the power is usually inherited. The inherited power of the descendent of a biis remains latent, however, until he or she first consumes the spirit-flesh (also called biis) of a victim killed by those who are already biis. This also provides a way for people not descended from biis to become biis themselves; for anyone who consumes this flesh becomes a different kind of being who possesses supernatural powers. The other biis then must train the new biis—whether descended from a biis or not—about how to use his or her powers to practice the techniques of both yakop and biis. The Nalumin disagreed on whether someone who became a biis could revert to being an ordinary person again. Some said any biis who confessed to holding such powers and renounced them publicly would lose them. Others said that an individual who had become a biis would remain so until death.

7. Members of many other Melanesian societies besides the Nalumin believe that certain people possess supernatural means of causing harm that fall in between the usual distinction between sorcery and witchcraft as it was developed in the ethnography of Africa. Anthropologists who have worked in these societies have often expressed misgivings with the distinction for this reason. In practice, however, they have most commonly chosen to use the term *sorcery* to refer to borderline cases, perhaps because it has seemed to them a less restrictive term (cf., Glick 1973; Patterson 1974; and Zelenietz and Lindenbaum 1981; but see Stephen 1987c for an alternative view). I am currently still formulating my own views on the use of the distinction.

8. According to the Nalumin, everyone is born with an identical but invisible twin. When someone is born, the midwife takes his placenta and throws it in a river. The placenta is carried down the current, only to later emerge downstream as a being on its own right that takes up a life of its own with its own people (the doubles of the kin of the physical person) in a sort of parallel world. (Significantly, in cases of actual twins, one was traditionally exposed to die.) Like the world of ghosts, the world of the placental twins is spatially isomorphic with certain remote and inaccessible areas, but is invisible to ordinary people. Each event a person experiences in his life is mirrored in the life of his placental twin. Finally, when the individual dies, his placental twin dies at the same time in its own world. The shaman initially establishes a close relation to his placental twin either at his own initiative or by the initiative of his placental twin.

9. The pieces of arrows extracted by the shaman were not visible to the audience. In general, none of the objects of witchcraft retrieved by shamans are visible, though people do not doubt that they exist. Only rarely do shamans produce material objects and claim them as the objects of witchcraft. Shamans who do so regularly (and Finangim was not one of them) are regarded as exceptionally powerful shamans.

10. One shaman I interviewed said many of his powers were taken away after he was so bold as to name the people who were witches in a nearby settlement. He lost the ability to directly perceive the spirit world. He added that

originally he had been able to produce the bundles of yakop and the arrows of biis that he retrieved—actual physical objects. But when he produced these objects later, they could no longer be seen by ordinary people. Several witnesses to his earlier séances confirmed that he had once had this power, the mark of the most accomplished shamans.

11. Formal protests occur only once in several years in any given settlement. The protest over Atulim's illness was the only one that occurred at Bomtem in the three years I lived there. Protests are organized in the cases of important and influential people, who have many loyal friends.

12. In fact, a dream was a prominent source of evidence in another account in which Unipkon acted as the chief culprit. In August 1985, Abalkon, the wife of Unipkon's son and the sister of Wengsep, died. Soon afterward, Sitkon, Aboni's wife who lived in a nearby settlement, saw Unipkon creep up and kill Abalkon in a dream. When she reported this, almost everyone immediately accepted that this was what had occurred.

13. The witness experiences the killing of his spirit self (simik) and then returns to die somewhat later in a physically apparent way.

14. Suspicion of witchcraft follows certain patterns. For instance, women were more likely to be suspected than men (19 percent of men but 24 percent of women). Other factors that made it more likely for someone to be suspected of witchcraft were being older (for both sexes), being married and wealthy (for men only), and being a widow (for women only). It would be possible to go into greater detail on these and other statistical patterns. But my purpose here is to explore the significance of the witch in the Nalumin imagination. For this purpose, statistical differences in witchcraft accusations by social categories (like sex, age, and marital status) are too weak to compromise the main point that almost any adult can be a witch. Among those named as witches were men and women of all ranges of age and situations.

15. In the forty years leading up to the government-imposed ban on warfare (around 1970), seven people were killed for suspicion of being witches in the local Kuyakmin area, yielding an annual rate of 87.5 per 100,000. During the same forty-year period, only two people were killed for reasons other than witchcraft. This rate of witch killings may seem high until one recalls that several hundred Kuyakmin people are thought to have been killed by witches in the same period. The Kuyakmin rate is lower than killings of suspected sorcerers and witches among some other New Guinea populations. Bruce Knauft, for example, reports a homicide rate of 568 per 100,000 among the Gebusi, the vast majority killings of suspected sorcerers (Knauft 1985a, p. 2).

16. An individual can have immediate access to these special means only through the aid of spirits. Those spirits who most commonly help people are ghosts of the dead and the spirit of the placental twin (there are several other kinds of spirits that more rarely may help). Most people receive little help from these spirits and have little access to special means of perception. Unassisted people must seek help from one of the few people with closer relations with spirits and access to special means of perception if they are to find out about hidden matters.

17. I learned of these interpretations mostly through confidential disclosures in the days following Wengsep's encounter. The only version that was actually disclosed in my presence on the same night was in Wengsep's house, when Katim said in a low voice that it might be Saangim's affines. Those present murmured agreement.

18. An everyday emphasis on good will has been noted by other ethnographers who have worked in Melanesia; and they also often note like I do that it contrasts with another aspect of life. This opposition has been understood to be between female versus male life (e.g., Bateson 1958; Herdt 1981) and domestic versus ritual life (e.g., Tuzin 1982). Bruce Knauft (1985a) has noted similar dynamics between violence and an ethos of "good company" among the Gebusi. The fact that overt violence is far less frequent in the Nalumin case seems to me a consequence of the fact that the Nalumin are much more secretive about suspicions of

witches than the Gebusi's are about sorcerers.
19. Such a model has been especially associated with students of the Manchester School
(e.g., Turner 1957) and of Structuralism (e.g.,
Lévi-Strauss 1967), but there are many further
examples (e.g., Leach 1954; Kelly 1977). The
contradictions in the Nalumin case could be
analyzed as the product of, on the one hand,
social expectations of relations of equality,
sharing and good will between people and, on
the other hand, conditions (produced in part by
the same social system) of material scarcity,
inequality, and disagreement between the
same people.

Dreaming and the Hidden Self: Mekeo Definitions of Consciousness

Michele Stephen

DURING January 1983 one of my Mekeo informants, a man I had known for many years and one who had been my most important mentor and teacher during fieldwork carried out in 1980 and 1981, visited me in Australia. Aisaga, as I shall call him, is one of the Mekeo region's most renowned magicians and sorcerers, and in his own estimation is "a man of knowledge." An elderly man who speaks no English, he had never before traveled outside Papua New Guinea. His few weeks in Australia passed too quickly for him, and when the time came to return home, he did not want to leave. As we were getting into the car to drive to the airport, he suddenly turned back toward the house and called out quite loudly and urgently, "Hey! You! We're leaving; come on!" There was no one left in the house; it stood closed and empty. I stared at him in amazement. Who could he be calling? When I asked him, he replied, somewhat exasperated by my ignorance, "My *lalauga*."

Observing my look of startled incomprehension, he reminded me of matters he had often told me in the past. If he departed, leaving his lalauga behind, he would later suffer the consequences. All people of knowledge knew this, he said, and therefore took care to summon their lalauga before leaving a place to which they felt attached, for they might become ill if their lalauga refused to follow.

I then recalled my own experience during fieldwork in Aisaga's village the previous year, when I had awakened every morning feeling tired and lethargic—a circumstance I had attributed to the oppressive heat and humidity. Aisaga, however, had diagnosed a different cause. He inquired whether at night I dreamed of the village, or of my home in Australia. When I answered that I seemed to recall only dreams of Australia, he replied that it was quite evident that my lalauga wanted to return home, which it did every night in my dreams, returning reluctantly in the morning and thus causing my lethargy and fatigue. Should it refuse to return, I would become seriously ill. It was in order to avoid such an eventuality that Aisaga had called out to his lalauga as we left for the airport to ensure that it knew he was leaving.

The Mekeo term *lalauga* is conventionally translated into English to mean "soul," but as this brief narrative indicates, "soul" is scarcely adequate, even misleading, as a description of what Aisaga refers to here. It is an invisible entity, yet it affects one's physical and emotional well-being; its desires may conflict with one's conscious intent and these may be revealed in dreams, as in my dreams of home. But at the same time, it is responsive, at least to some degree, to one's conscious control. When Aisaga referred to the actions of his lalauga and of mine, he evidently was not concerned with a purely spiritual entity that survives after death, but with some part of ourselves that has a very pragmatic influence on our everyday existence.

Though it does involve beliefs about the existence of a noncorporeal reality, the notion of lalauga is not based primarily upon metaphysical speculation about, or concern with, life after death. It refers to an intimate aspect of the self—a hidden self that influences one's conscious experience in important ways. Furthermore, through employment of the techniques of magic, certain knowledgeable people, like Aisaga, are able to guide and direct this hidden aspect of themselves to achieve conscious ends.

The lalauga is, for Mekeo, a key concept in defining areas of experience that our own cultural categories divide into self and person, mind and body, natural and supernatural, conscious and unconscious. From our cultural perspective, it is not an easy concept to grasp, in part because it combines the characteristics of both a descriptive, empirical category, and a metaphysical construct. The lalauga, indeed, may be understood as precisely the term that denotes the spontaneous images of what we here call the religious imagination.

In this chapter I have outlined the notion of the soul as it is used in various contexts of subjective experience: (1) the soul and dreaming; (2) the soul, the body, and sickness; (3) the soul and magic; and (4) the soul and the spirit world. The final part of the chapter discusses the importance of "soul" in defining the self in relation to a sacred Other, and compares it with certain Western concepts of the unconscious mind.

Experiences of the Hidden Self

Public and Private, Visible and Hidden

The Mekeo, who speak an Austronesian language, number about seven thousand; they inhabit a fertile, hot, riverine plain of central, coastal Papua within the Central Province, to the west of Port Moresby. The region has been subjected to over ninety years of European contact and external influence (Stephen 1974), but Mekeo culture remains rich and complex, though it has undoubtedly undergone many modifications since the imposition of colonial rule in 1890. It is a society, as Hau'ofa (1981) has shown, characterized by marked social and symbolic inequalities in political power and ritual knowledge. Large villages, consisting of several hundred inhabitants, are composed of localized segments of patrilineal, patrivirilocal descent groups. Each community comprises several descent groups, each of which, ideally, has its own hereditary leader or leaders, whose authority is sanctioned by hereditary sorcerers—powerful and feared magicians who are believed to inflict sickness and death on all who flout the social order (Hau'ofa 1981; Stephen 1987b).

Ritual or esoteric knowledge among the Mekeo is synonymous with magical knowledge; that is, it consists of the knowledge of magical formulae (including myths and spells), and of magical substances and objects, the manipulation of which is directed toward achieving specific ends (see Stephen 1987b for a fuller discussion). The range of magical powers covers all important aspects of human affairs from love magic to war magic and sorcery. Any discussion of Mekeo ritual and religion is complicated by the need to distinguish between the view of the layperson and the adept. The situation is further confused by the range of magical knowledge possessed by various individuals, some of whom have no more than one or two minor powers, whereas others have mastery over many (Stephen 1987b). When I speak of "adepts," I refer to those individuals with a wide range of powers. Both men and women may be considered "people of knowledge" *(ikifa papiau);* but only men are sorcerers *(ugauga).* Aisaga is such a man.

Though one eventually discovers that the lalauga is a crucial concept underlying the whole system of esoteric knowledge, it is not something that immediately attracts the ethnographer's attention; and even when one is alerted to its significance, it is difficult to obtain information by abstract questioning. Indeed, it is one of those notions that is so basic, so intrinsic to a particular world view, that it needs no formal explication—it simply is. The outsider is always in danger of overlooking that which is so self-evident that nobody ever thinks it needs to be spelled out for him. Indeed, it is easy to gain the impression that the soul is a poorly formulated and unimportant concept for the Mekeo.[1] People will tell you that the lalauga is no different from the Christian idea of the soul (the Mekeo have been at least nominal Catholics since the establishment of the Sacred Heart Mission in the region in the 1880s; see Stephen 1974). They say that on death the lalauga leaves the body and goes to Heaven—or Kariko, the traditional abode of the dead. Opinions vary, and no one seems very interested anyway. It is difficult to get much more information on the topic from the ordinary man or woman.

The fieldworker's task is made even more difficult because the soul is an entity bound up with the closely guarded secrets of esoteric magical ritual. The ordinary person feels uncomfortable even discussing such matters, and the adept is determined to preserve the exclusiveness of his knowledge. Yet it is not simply a matter of such information being deliberately hidden from the outsider. The soul relates to areas of experience that are both intensely private and potentially dangerous. One's lalauga is not something one is likely to openly discuss with strangers and mere acquaintances. It relates to one's most intimate and private concerns.

The Mekeo carefully mark off public and private domains. In public the individual intends to present a calm, controlled exterior that masks whatever emotions he or she feels inside (cf. Hau'ofa 1981). What is public, is what is visible *(ofakaega);* but beneath surface appearances lies a hidden *(onevake)* world of private thoughts and emotions. Individuals wonder what really lies in the minds of others, while attempting not to reveal their own true motivations and emotions. In public one behaves in an appropriate manner and expresses the conventional sentiments, all the while disguising one's inner feelings and suspicions about others. Envy, suspicion, spite, and anger do not belong in the public arena and must be kept hidden.

People, of course, share their inner thoughts and emotions with those close to them—their immediate family and intimate friends—but selectively. As an outsider, removed from the web of kin obligations and family and political intrigues, the ethnographer is likely to find him- or herself regarded as a safe confidant on many occasions. Such was often the experience during my first period of fieldwork in the early 1970s; I was frequently amazed by the fears and suspicions harbored by people apparently on good terms with each other, and often very closely related to each other as well. But during this time I learned little about the soul and how it related to this private sphere.

Only years later did I discover (when discussing dreams) that the soul constitutes a yet more private layer of the self—an aspect of one's self that is not merely kept hidden from others, but which is largely hidden from one's own awareness. This hidden self is not the private self that one intentionally keeps from others, but is an aspect of the self screened from the individual's very awareness of himself.

I found that I learned about the lalauga only in relation to actual experiences (of mine or other people) and that such information always involved a disclosure of some sort, an intimate communication between individuals I regarded (or who regarded themselves) as my close friends and associates. My most important source of information was Aisaga, a highly respected and feared man of knowledge. But my description is based upon detailed discussions with several other men and women of knowledge and with many ordinary people concerning their dream experiences, all of whom I had known for several years. I present a summary of my varied data; no Mekeo would describe the lalauga in the abstract, analytical manner I employ here; but I shall try to show how the concept is clearly delineated in different kinds of actual experience.

The Soul and Dreaming

Dreams *(nipi)* constitute one of the most important contexts of everyday experience in which the soul is defined and discussed with others. The actions of the soul, the lalauga, are reflected in the events of the dream. The distinction between waking consciousness and the events of the dream is made very clearly in ordinary speech. Dream accounts usually begin with a statement along the lines of "I dreamed and my 'soul' went and it did such and such" *(Lau la nipi lalauu e pealai e lao. . . .)*. Thus the actions of the soul are related in the third person, at least at the beginning of the dream account, making it clear that the dream is not *my* action, but the action of my soul. Often the first person may be resumed during the dream account, but if the status of the events being recounted is not clear, one needs only to inquire whether they took place in the body *(imaugai)* or through the agency of the soul, to resolve the matter.

Conscious thought is clearly located in the body. People say that thinking *(opolanga)* takes place inside the head *(kania)*, or more specifically, in the brain *(minogai)*.[2] Emotion is also experienced within the body. Different emotions are conveyed by expressions referring to states felt within the trunk of the body; for example, *guau e kupu*, "I am angry" ("my chest/stomach is obstructed"); *alou e kieki*, "I am sad" ("my inside aches").

Ordinary waking consciousness, my sense of myself as a sentient being, is firmly grounded in the body and inseparable from it. When I sleep *(la feu)*, my conscious thought *(opo)* ceases; if I faint or fall into unconsciousness *(mae afu)*, waking thought is also extinguished. In these situations, however, another aspect of myself takes over. Conscious thought (opo) has ceased and the body is immobilized, yet another self, independent of the body and conscious intent, emerges and may engage in travels and adventures in a world very different from that of ordinary waking reality. What I experience in my body is what I think, feel, see, perceive, and understand in ordinary waking reality. What my soul experiences is what this other aspect of my self, unknown to the me of waking awareness, thinks, feels, perceives, and desires in that other realm. Thus, to speak of what "I" think and do is a very different matter from what my "soul" thinks or does.

The actions of the soul are neither controlled by one's waking thought, nor even fully known to it. This independence makes it a potentially embarrassing and dangerous entity. In dreams one's soul may act in ways that conflict with one's conscious attitudes and desires. Furthermore, the actions of one's soul are reflected not only in one's own dreaming but also in the dreams of others. The soul's autonomy was impressed upon me on a number of occasions.

One day, for example, I was discussing with a friend a recent case of snakebite when he confided that he had had a dream only the night before in which the lalauga of a particular sorcerer appeared, aiming a spear at the house of the snakebite victim. The poised spear of the dream represented the snake being sent to attack the victim, and sorcerer thus revealed was none other than Aisaga, my main source of information on esoteric lore. Later in the day I plucked up my courage and recounted this dream to Aisaga himself, being very careful not to reveal its source because I feared an angry reaction. Aisaga was always complaining of being blamed, unjustly, for every misfortune that befell the community.[3] To my surprise, he took the news calmly, sat thoughtfully in silence for a few moments, then nodded his head in affirmation. It was possible, he explained, that the dream was correct in identifying him. Even though he had no conscious intention or desire to harm the man in question, nor had he performed any ritual to this specific end, nevertheless he had recently been feeling angry (with his own relatives) and he had been singing dangerous spells that had the effect of provoking both his own soul and the spirits of his ancestors to attack others. It was possible therefore, that his soul was responsible for the snakebite. In order to be certain, he said, he would later perform a special divination rite.

On another occasion, Aisaga was much perturbed when I reported my dream of the previous night in which he had publicly shouted abuse at me. Although he assured me that he was not at present in any way angry with me, he spent a long time examining reasons why his soul might have been angry with me. The fact that he could find no conscious reason did not vitiate the import of my dream. If his soul was angry and had shouted abuse at my soul, then I would soon get sick, that is, the effects of the dream would be realized in the world of waking thought and the physical body. Likewise, it was useless for me to protest, when he had dreams of my soul acting in a threatening manner, that I harbored no ill will. The intention and attitude of the soul, as revealed in the dream, points to an underlying reality not to be denied.

The significance of the soul's hidden actions was impressed upon me in a different way after I had a series of dreams in which my waking experience seemed to be duplicated in my dreams. For several nights I dreamed that I was sitting together with Aisaga, as I usually did every day, while he told me spells and explained the uses of various magical medicines. I did not imagine that these dreams would be considered significant since people commonly say that if you are preoccupied with something it is only natural that you will dream of it, and there is no significance in this unless such a dream has been ritually induced. When he heard of these dreams, however, Aisaga said that they were of great importance. He explained that they meant that now his soul was instructing my soul, and that without such instruction, the words that he merely spoke "with his mouth" would be of no real use to me. If his soul withheld the knowledge, then I could never learn to do properly what his corporeal self had taught me. He then inquired whether I could remember exactly what his soul had said in the dreams. When, to my discomfort, I had to admit that I could not remember, he replied, "No matter, your *soul* knows."

In case I have given the impression that Mekeo culture encourages a sort of serendipitous dream sharing along the (probably apocryphal) lines of the Senoi (Stewart 1969), I should make it clear that such is far from being the case. People may discuss their dreams with others, but only certain others, and only certain dreams, and this in a guarded manner. Dreams constitute dangerous knowledge; they are not casually told or shared (cf. Herdt 1987d). I found that people were willing to tell me their dreams only when they themselves felt certain of the meaning of the dream. It was never easy to collect dream reports; people were too wary of thus exposing their innermost secrets—things hidden even from themselves. As a man of knowledge, Aisaga knew a great deal about what dreams meant—his dreams and those of others—and he reported many dreams and discussed many dreams with me, but I am certain that he presented me with a carefully chosen selection of his dream experiences. It was impossible to obtain from anyone a complete record of his or her ongoing dream experiences, though many people were happy to recount selected dreams to me (see Stephen 1981 for examples).

Dreams hold dangerous knowledge because though the actions and intent of the soul are hidden from conscious thought, they are true *(ko'a)* in the ultimately binding sense that they prefigure what will happen in ordinary waking reality. Even the adept cannot have complete conscious knowledge of the activities of his soul. Like everyone else, he has only glimpses of them in his remembered dreams, but unlike the ordinary man or woman, he possesses the means to interpret them more accurately, and the ritual means to direct the actions of his dream self.

It is considered no easy matter to trace the link between the dream and the mundane world. It requires the special knowledge, experience, and insight of a man or woman of knowledge. The actions of the soul in dreams cannot be interpreted in any literal manner. They obey an order, a logic quite different from that of waking thought. When I pointed to the absurd or paradoxical features of a dream, people shrugged their shoulders and said, "*Nipi puo*" ("Because it's a dream"). Dream events must often be reversed to reveal their outcome. Thus, to dream of someone being ill may mean that they will prosper, whereas to dream of someone glowing with health and vitality may mean that the subject is about to succumb to some debilitating disease. But by no means can all dreams be made to reveal their kernel of truth by simple reversal. Interpreting the actions of the soul requires esoteric knowledge, and even the expert cannot be absolutely certain of his reading of a particular dream until its message has been realized in the world of waking reality.

Aisaga often remarked to me that I should learn to observe for myself the meaning of my own dream symbols. I should note what I dreamed and then observe what events followed, and in this way I would eventually learn to read my own dreams accurately. Though there are many basic common dream symbols that even ordinary people know how to interpret (Stephen 1981), Aisaga stressed that dreaming was a very personal matter and that the man of knowledge had to learn by experience. The same, he insisted, was true of omens; one had to learn from personal experience how they worked. One day, for example, we were talking while we waited for some visitors to arrive. I sneezed suddenly and Aisaga immediately demanded to know whether the sneeze had come from the left or right side of the nose. Now we could learn how my omens worked, he explained. We would wait and see whether the visitors came. Some people sneezed on the left side as an omen, some on the right; one could learn how one's omens worked only in relation to actual events, just as with dreams.

One's waking self operates in a context of physical bodies and objects, whereas the dream self, or soul, operates in a noncorporeal realm of images. The terminology used in recounting dreams makes it clear that the dream self does not encounter physical entities in dreaming, but other images—it being incorporeal. In dreams one does not encounter other people, but their soul or dream-images. In recounting a dream, for example, one might say, "I saw John's soul" *(John lalauga la isa)*, or, "It was as if I saw John there" *(John ko'a iopoga la isa)*. Nor does one encounter a real pig or bird or tree or truck in a dream, but its image *(oge)*. And the dream itself, as a total entity, constitutes not a physical reality in the way that actions do in the world of waking consciousness, but an image (oge) of that external reality. Thus, someone may refer to a dream in which he spears two people who belong to an enemy group as meaning that he will shoot two pigs if he goes hunting, saying, "That is the image I saw" *(Gaina oge la isa)*. In other words, the dream image of spearing two enemies is a reflection of the outcome in waking reality. Dreams thus consist of images that relate to waking reality but not in any simple or direct way: they prefigure in metaphor events to occur in waking consciousness.

The term *lalauga,* which designates the dream self, or soul, also means "an image without material substance." One's reflection in water or a mirror, a portrait or photograph, and one's shadow, are all lalauga. The shadow is directly equated with the soul. I was often warned when being shown and when handling powerful magical objects that I must take care not to allow my shadow to fall across them for fear of deadly injury to myself. One is always told to turn one's back when the powerful objects were returned to the boxes in which they are stored for fear of having one's soul imprisoned with them. When I asked if the soul existed inside the body, people would point to my shadow saying, "There is your soul." Ghosts are also referred to as lalauga. The term for spirits of the dead is *isage,* but when they appear in visible form to the living they are called lalauga. Thus, both the living and the dead have dream selves (lalauga).

The word *lalauga* indicates a visible but noncorporeal entity, a visual image. But—and this is a most important point—it does not refer to the thought images one holds in one's mind in ordinary waking consciousness. If you had been thinking of a particular person you would say, "I was thinking of Mary" *(Mary la opolania)*. You would not say, "I saw Mary's lalauga"; this would indicate that you had seen an apparition. If you thought you saw Mary standing in front of you and went to greet her only to find to your astonishment that there was really no one there, then you would say, "I saw Mary's lalauga." In our discussion of visual images versus corporeal reality, we must also keep in mind that the Mekeo distinction is not one between body and spirit, as we so easily might assume, but a distinction between the self of ordinary waking thought, located in the body, and another self—a self that is usually hidden from, and may subvert, the waking self. In our terms, it might be seen as a distinction between two different levels of consciousness: that of waking consciousness and that of the dream consciousness.

The Soul, the Body, and Sickness

The lalauga is also defined in the day-to-day experience of the health and sickness of the body. The realm of bodiless imagery inhabited by the soul—despite its incorporeality—has vital links with the body; and the actions of one's soul on that other level of consciousness have important consequences for the body. Nightmares, dreams in which the soul is attacked, beaten, injured, savaged by wild animals, are recognized by everyone as clear signs of impending illness or danger. The adept articulates the matter quite succinctly—"All illness begins in the soul" *(Lalauga isafa gome auga, which means "The soul is the root of sickness")*.

Injury or damage suffered by the dream self later takes root in the body, causing physical sickness. When one stumbles or falls, causing some serious damage, or clumsily cuts oneself deeply with a knife while working in the gardens, this inattention and awkwardness is attributed to the actions of one's dream self. Either it has been weakened or injured somehow during its dream travels, or else has failed to return from them. For example, shortly after I arrived in the field in October 1980, a man fell from a coconut tree, injuring himself quite badly. As his injuries were being attended to, I overheard him telling his relatives that he had had a dream the night before warning him of danger, but he had ignored it; consequently, he had awakened feeling tired and heavy, and when he climbed half-way to the top of the tree he had slipped and fallen. People later pointed out to me that had he heeded the message of the dream he might have avoided the accident. Ordinary people, as well as the adept, stress that dreams provide warnings that should be heeded. The danger indicated in the dream is not inevitable or predetermined, provided one pays heed to it in time.

Even minor indispositions may be attributed to the actions of the dream self. When I felt tired and irritable in the early weeks of fieldwork, Aisaga suspected that my dream self was the cause. In minor indispositions or illnesses, the energy, determination, or coordination lacking to implement one's conscious desires is expressed as the absence of the dream self. Its prolonged absence results in serious illness, with the body becoming progressively incapable of implementing conscious will. Illness is thus experienced as a division, a conflict between conscious desire and thought and the actions of the soul. One may be only dimly aware of the soul's actions, but its absence or presence are experienced quite concretely as physical sensations in the body.

The return of the soul to the body when one wakes from sleep, the sense of waking with a start from the dream to ordinary consciousness, is expressed by the term *kauai;* dream accounts usually end with "Then I awoke with a start" *(Kai la kauai).* The same word is used to describe the sensation experienced when one is severely startled during waking consciousness—even *our* idiom is "jumping out of one's skin." To startle someone in this way is considered to be potentially very dangerous. The soul, in fright, flees from the body and may lose its way and be unable to return. I have rarely seen Aisaga, who usually maintains an inscrutable calm, so openly angry as one night when his son, approaching without warning in the dark, caused him to start violently. He berated his son, demanding to know whether he wanted to kill him by startling him in such a thoughtless manner. The separation of body and soul is always inherently dangerous, and is the aim of sorcery. Though in ordinary circumstances people do not seem concerned about waking a sleeping person, danger is thought to be involved for anyone undertaking ritually induced dreaming, and such a person takes care to sleep alone, away from the children and the rest of the household, so as not to be awakened when the dream self is far away on its travels.

Healing rituals are directed at the dream self of the patient (Stephen 1987b). This is stated with specific clarity by the adept: The dream self must first be healed or returned to the body; only then can the body mend. Healing rituals involve the recitation of spells, the administration of medicinal potions, and the use of various divination techniques to locate the lost dream self and retrieve it. The spell commonly consists of a series of metaphorical assertions directed at removing the symptoms of the complaint. For example, a spell for a broken limb would run along the lines of "I make the leg as firm as . . ." (a particular hardwood tree is named). "I make the bones as firm as. . . ." "I make the blood as firm as. . . ." "I make the flesh as firm as . . . ," and so on. The medicines given to the patient are also in some way symbolically related to the symptoms of the complaint; thus, someone suffering from fever would be given a distillation of the juices of a particular plant considered to have properties of coldness in order to cool the fever.

Both the spell and the medicines are the practitioner's secrets and are not usually revealed to the patient. This emphasizes that it is not the patient's conscious thought that the healer is attempting to influence; the spell and medicines are intended to influence the dream self of the patient. Furthermore, the actions described in the spell—"I make the body firm," or cool, or light, as the case may be—are actions to be performed by the dream self of the healer. That is to say, the cure is thought to be achieved by the action of the healer's dream self upon the dream self of the patient. This is further demonstrated in the circumstance that, having bespelled the patient, the healer awaits a dream that indicates whether the actions of his dream self have been effective.

Serious, prolonged illnesses are usually attributed to the absence of the dream self from the body. In such cases the healer must discover what is preventing the dream self's return. There are three likely causes: the dream self has been captured by water spirits *(faifai),* a human sorcerer has imprisoned it, or inadvertent contact with the powerful and dangerous objects used in magic has affected the dream self, trapping it or causing it to flee to some refuge, such as a tall tree or a cave, from which it is unable to return. The water spirits are often said to fall in love with human beings, luring the dream self of their human lover underwater to live with them. If water spirits are divined as the cause, the healer will wrest the dream self of the patient from their clutches and bring it back, whereupon a quick recovery can be expected. If a sorcerer is responsible, the diviner will not attempt to prevail against him, but will simply suggest to the patient's relatives a number of sorcerers they might approach in the hope of buying them off. Diviners say that they are too frightened for themselves to indicate the sorcerer directly, but merely include him in a list of suspects. The third cause, accidental contact with power objects, is described in detail in the following account of a cure. It seems worth quoting at length as it illustrates the way in which dream divination is seen to relate to the patient's actual experience.

One of my friends—I shall refer to him here as Opu—was a skilled tradesman who had spent many years away from the village in European employment. He was well educated, with a fluent command of English, and much preferred to discuss the latest international political crisis than village gossip. Opu recounted to me his experience of being cured by dream divination. Just after he was married, Opu became very ill and was sent to a hospital in Port Moresby, where he was diagnosed as suffering from tuberculosis. He remembered being very ill and very depressed after learning this, believing that he would die shortly, or remain an invalid for the rest of his life and thus never be capable of supporting a family. While in the hospital he passed some days in a state of delirium in which he recalled lying helplessly in bed, while he could feel underneath him a crowd of people pushing up against him and crying out to let them get out from under him. In his delirium, he thought that these must be the spirits of the people who had died in that bed and that he, himself, was dying. During this time, two old men, whom Opu somehow knew came from the village of Bebeo in his own region, came to his bedside and said that they wanted to make friends with him and that they would look after him if he came with them. But he felt frightened and asked them to go away.

Eventually Opu, very weak and sick, was sent home to his village, he assumed, to die. His relatives decided to call in a dream diviner and healer. The diviner reported the following dream. His dream self had found Opu's dream self locked in a box, being jostled and pushed by all the other souls trapped there. The diviner explained that this dream indicated that Opu must have intentionally, or inadvertently, tampered with some dangerous objects used for sorcery and that his soul, or dream self, had been trapped there. On being told this, Opu recalled that shortly after returning to the village for his marriage, after a long period of working in town, he had noticed an old box in the house with a broken lock. Because he was a mechanic and welder, he decided to try to repair the lock. When he opened the box he was not exactly sure what it contents were but realized that they might be some of the things his dead father had used for magic. Given his education and long absence away in the town, he was little troubled by this, but simply repaired the lock and put the box away again, and thought no more about the matter. The diviner's dream suddenly brought the incident back to him. The diviner also explained that the box he had seen contained the relics of powerful spirits used by sorcerers to capture the souls of their victims, and that Opu's soul was being beaten by the souls of the sorcerer's other victims also trapped in the box. Opu then thought of his delirium in the hospital, when he had felt that the spirits of dead people were trying to push against him and get out from under him as he lay helpless in his hospital bed. Later, he found out that his father, who knew sorcery and whose box Opu had opened, possessed the relics of two powerful sorcerers from the village of Bebeo and that he invoked their souls to help capture the souls of his sorcery victims. Evidently, Opu concluded, these were the two old men from Bebeo whom he had seen by his bedside. Had he given in to their blandishments and promises of friendship, his soul would no doubt have been lost forever and death would have inevitably followed.

In this example, Opu had himself been responsible for endangering his soul by tampering with the powerful magical relics. Following the dream divination and the opening of the box where his dream self had been trapped, Opu immediately began to feel better; he soon made a full recovery and resumed a normal, active life with no recurrence of the disease. What impressed both Opu and myself was the coincidence of the images of (a) the diviner's divination dream, (b) the images of Opu's visionary experience in the hospital, and (c) the actual events, in waking reality, surrounding the offending box and its contents. How and why these coinciding events took place, we cannot enter into here, but it is clear that it provided an effective symbol of release and healing for the sick man.

The Soul and Magic

Our discussion of the dream self and sickness has revealed, among other things, the vulnerability of the dream self: its susceptibility to the influence of entities hidden from waking consciousness. Except in times of sickness and misfortune, laypeople need have little interest in the dream self and its activities. Even to discuss dreaming and the dream self is considered by some to indicate an unhealthy interest in matters that do not concern ordinary, honest folk. Indeed, I found that many people were highly discomforted by my broaching the subject with them, as the mere fact of asking for information could be taken to imply that they possessed esoteric knowledge of some kind. Ordinary people, they would tell me, do not understand or want to bother themselves with matters that are properly the province of the magician and sorcerer.

The layperson's sense of vulnerability to the powers of magic is widely apparent, and not only in relation to sorcery and destructive magic. People often confided in private conversations that certain individuals have "the power to change your mind," and that no matter how strong your intention or desire for something, it can be subverted through magic. Many men, young and middle-aged, confided how their ambitions—to become a teacher, to marry a particular girl, to start a business, to train for the priesthood, to work away from the village (to quote actual examples)—were never realized because of the opposition of senior male relatives. These men explained that though they were not prevented or forbidden by their elders from doing as they wished, after a time their desire simply diminished or was replaced by another. In the end, things turned out as the elders had wanted all along. I have also heard young women express real fear of certain men who are known to possess irresistible love magic. When I flippantly remarked once that one man thus identified seemed an unusually ill-favored specimen not likely to attract any woman, I was warned that this was of no account, and that should he desire her, no woman would be able to resist his advances; she would abandon her husband and even her young children for his sake, for he had the power "to change her mind." Conscious attitudes and desires are seen as no defense against the influences that can act upon the dream self; and what conscious thought and desire rejects, the dream self may welcome.

The rituals of magic, as the layperson at least partly understands, provide the magician with the means of controlling the dream self, converting its vulnerability into a special channel of power to implement his conscious will. All magic rituals, whether for love, war, hunting, gardening, or weather magic, and all forms of destructive magic, depend primarily on the recitation of spells and the use of magical substances or medicines (Stephen 1987b). Both spell and substance, as we saw in the case of healing rituals, consist essentially of a metaphorical statement of the intent of the rite. The practitioner can thus be seen to direct, or attempt to direct, his dream self to implement his conscious desires by communicating a vivid image of this desire to the dream self. In other words, the spell and "medicine" serve as instructions to the dream self; but they are more than this since they are also said to give it force or energy—they "activate the dream self."

The specifically stated purpose of spell and substance is to activate the dream self of the magician and to influence the dream self of the subject (Stephen 1987b). The love magician attempts to send out his dream self causing the woman he desires to dream of him; the hunter sends out his dream self to draw the quarry near. The performance of the ritual should be followed by a dream revealing to the adept the success or failure of his efforts. The rain magician who has bespelled his fishing traps and placed them in the river with the appropriate medicines may dream of crowds of people coming upriver in canoes, representing the fish coming up river to his traps. The garden magician may see in his dreams the "wind people" bringing the light rain needed for the newly planted crops. The sorcerer may dream of catching two small fish in a net, revealing that two children will succumb to his powers (to use examples of dreams actually reported by ritual experts).

The man of knowledge, Aisaga, often remarked to me that his dream self could sometimes be seen in a number of different places while he, in his body, was quietly sitting alone in his house. This could happen when he intended to capture the dream self of a victim and sent an assistant to carry the lethal charm to the victim, while his own dream self, in the company of his ancestors' spirits, followed behind. One afternoon when I returned from another part of the village, I found Aisaga in conference with the village councillors and some other men. Later, when I asked him about it, he told me that one of these men had been threatening to shoot him (Aisaga) with a shotgun because he had been sighted several times walking along the man's garden track (as a renowned sorcerer, Aisaga's unexplained presence in a place he had no business to be in would naturally cause anxiety). The councillors had learned of these threats and had brought the man in question to discuss the situation with Aisaga. Aisaga explained to the group that as he was now old, he rarely left his house these days and that if they had seen a sorcerer walking along their track, it must have been one from another village and not him. This satisfied the councillors, Aisaga told me, but then added with the hint of a smile, "What they saw was not another person but my dream self." He had responded quite truthfully to his interrogators, he rarely traveled far from home anymore; but as for his dream self, that was another matter, and not one he was about to divulge publicly.

Another time, Aisaga confided that the reason he and other sorcerers employed distinctive styles of facial painting when they appeared on public occasions was to make sure their dream selves could be easily identified. When I inquired why he had painted his forhead black to attend an important feast in another village, he had replied that it was in order to frighten people, and indeed he did look awesome. Later he said that the real reason was to make sure that the dream diviners would identify him in their dreams. It was for the same reason, he added, that he had painted his house in a vivid shade of bright blue and had planted his garden with brightly colored flowers. When the diviner's dream self came in search of the dream self of a sick person, it would be immediately apparent in whose house the dream self had been imprisoned. I was flabbergasted by all this, as I had been told for years that the sorcerer did not want to be identified. Not at all, said Aisaga, that is just talk; most sorcery is done to make money, and therefore the sorcerer wants to be identified correctly so he will be paid to cure the victim.

The dream self of the sorcerer is also involved in the curing of his victim. It is said by some people that if the sorcerer wants to release his victim, all he has to do is take the deadly charm off the fire or immerse it in water, but the situation is not quite that simple. The sorcerer's dream self must first be appeased. Aisaga explained that if, for example, he had made one of his own close relatives sick and then relented and wanted to cure him, he would not be able to do so if his dream self were still angry with the victim. This is why the payment made to the sorcerer is so important; if a suitably handsome payment is made, the sorcerer's dream self will be gladdened and the cure will be effective. Reversing the destructive action of the sorcerer's dream self cannot be achieved simply by his conscious intent.

As I have described elsewhere the rituals of magic in some detail (Stephen 1987b), I will only emphasize here that the dream self is the medium through and upon which magic is thought to operate. The magician does not attempt to create changes in the physical world of waking reality, he aims at bringing about a change in the realm of autonomous imagery experienced by the dream self, confident that if he is successful the change will eventually be realized in bodily reality. The layperson is doubly exposed, since not only does he or she lack esoteric knowledge, but magic attacks and acts upon a part of himself that is hidden even from his very awareness and conscious control.

The Soul and the Spirit World

In learning to direct his own dream self, the adept discovers another level of creative, destructive, and transformative power. Through the agency of his dream self he is able to learn the cause of a client's illness and restore his dream self to him, divine the events of the future, bend others to his will, injure and kill his enemies. Though he learns that his own dream self is powerful, he also encounters in the dream realm other even more powerful entities which he is able to summon to assist him. These entities are not normally visible or available to waking consciousness, but the dream self is able to see and communicate with them. They include the spirits of the dead (isage), the water spirits (faifai), and those powerful beings, the people of the myths *(isonioni papiau)*, who are believed to be the originators of the various magical rituals and the present social order.

In most, if not all, the major magical rituals, the magician calls upon the spirits of his forefathers to assist his dream self in its task. Thus, when the dream diviner *(feuapi)* sends out her dream self in search of the sick person's dream self, it is accompanied by the spirits of various dead relatives, which help to combat the water spirits responsible for stealing the lost dream self. When the sorcerer prepares to send out his dream self to attack and capture the dream self of his victim, he calls upon the spirits of his ancestors to go with him; and he waits for a sign or dream indicating their presence before he proceeds with the final part of the ritual. When diviners dream of a particular sorcerer, they see him in the company of the spirits he conjures.

The spirits of the dead, of their own accord, may appear to ordinary men and women in their dreams, giving them warnings or knowledge about the future (See Stephen 1981 for examples); but only the man or woman of knowledge deliberately summons the dead. The dream diviners regularly encounter the water spirits in their dreams, not in the guise of helpers, but rather opponents who must be overcome if the lost dream self of the patient is to be brought back to safety. Sometimes the water spirits appear in dreams in a more positive role, imparting special magical knowledge and power to certain individuals.

The powerful beings referred to in myths *(isonioni papiau)* seem to appear less frequently in dreams than the spirits of the dead and the water spirits, but they are invoked in magic, depending on the type of rite being performed. Major magical rituals involve the use of natural substances or objects believed to be transformed physical relics of the myth people; and the ritual use of such relics is believed to summon their dream selves or images. For example, one man of knowledge related that when he performed a particular kind of gardening magic he would see in his dreams the lalauga of the mythological founder of the rite—a mountainous, pale-skinned woman, her hair bunched in clay-smeared ringlets, who sat quietly humming. She is merely referred to as "an old woman" in the myths, the details of this description having come from the adept's dream encounter with her.

Though the adept commonly invokes the dream images of the spirits, he or she does not claim any comprehensive understanding of the spirit world. The spirits are known from glimpses in dreams, and their power is demonstrated in the effectiveness of the rite; beyond that the adept is not prepared to go. When, for example, I pressed Aisaga for details on such matters as where the spirits are when they are not summoned by him, what do they do, where do they live, and such, he would always reply dismissively, "We don't know; we will only know when we die. Now all we know is that when we call them, they come." Encounters with the spirits in the dream realm give access to their power, but the actual nature of their existence is not revealed; nor is it considered important since it is irrelevant to the magician's task.

Some people claim to have seen the villages or cities of the dead in their dreams, but these appear to be individual experiences not laid down by cultural tradition (see Stephen 1981 for examples). Moreover, all the people who recounted such experiences to me were laypeople, or those with minor magical knowledge. It should be pointed out that there are no rituals for the dead or other spirits, except the rituals of magic. It is only in the contexts of magic and the myths that any specific cultural mapping of the spirit world is provided.

Although dreams are the most important form of contact with spirit beings (for reasons that will be explained shortly), certain types of contact are possible in waking consciousness and need to be discussed as they relate to the whole question of how different levels of consciousness are defined and valued. Signs and omens are considered to be the most useful of those communications that occur in waking consciousness. These include the cries and sightings of various birds, insects, bats, and reptiles; such physical sensations as a ringing in the ears, the throbbing of veins, and sneezing; and various sorts of mechanical divination. The omens are indications of imminent death or serious illness, the arrival of visitors, the presence of poison in the food, and the like. Mechanical divination can be used to secure an answer to any question that can be phrased to require a simple yes or no response. As a means of learning about future events, Aisaga always preferred divination to the more ambiguous messages of dreams, and he regularly checked his dream interpretation against the results of divination. Lesser magicians, however, such as the dream diviner/healer (feuapi), do not possess the knowledge of other forms of divination and must rely solely on dreams.

Much less common, to my knowledge, is the use of waking visions. People described adepts of the past who could ritually induce waking visions wherein they could see the dream selves of the living and spirits. This activity is termed *lalaui isa* ("seeing dream selves"); it is said to have been practiced by war magicians to learn who would die in battle. But I have spoken to no one who claims to use the technique, and can only assume that it is no longer practiced. Involuntary experiences of waking visions—usually of the ghosts of the recently dead—are not uncommon, but neither are they considered very significant. People often suffer some minor illness or indisposition after such an encounter, but no serious harm is thought to result. Sightings of strange sorcerers and other demonic figures occasionally frighten people and are interpreted as glimpses of spirits, but are of no importance. Sometimes laypersons claim to have caught sight of water spirits near lonely swamps and streams; such encounters are said to sometimes result in the acquisition of magical knowledge and power. One man was said to have acquired special powers in this way, but I could never persuade him to discuss his experiences. However, another man who claimed to have magical knowledge revealed to him by the water spirits in dreams was quite willing to discuss the matter with me.

Possession by spirits is never deliberately induced, but epileptic-style seizures and running amok are interpreted as involuntary possession by spirits. A man who was my neighbor during my first extended period of fieldwork, and whom I knew quite well, was subject to attacks of temporary madness during which he ran up and down the village trying to spear anything in sight. He explained to me that at such times his head begins to ache and he can hear the spirits of the dead shouting at him to go out and kill anyone he can see. His outbursts are regarded by himself and the community as an illness and are referred to as *kania e kieki* ("headache"). An elderly woman in the village is known for the many seizures she has had in which she says she communes with the spirits. Most people, however, dismiss her experiences as simply kania e kieki, though she insists that she has had important revelations from God and the spirits in this manner.

Communications with the spirit world in the form of waking visions and possession are evidently not highly valued. Neither constitute a significant part of ritual practice, and when they occur in involuntary, uncontrolled form, they are dismissed either as unimportant or as a regrettable affliction. The reading of omens and divination is considered to be a valuable addition to the hazy messages of dreams in learning the outcome of future events. But even though omens, and divination in particular, provide a channel of communication with the other realm, they are not instrumental; that is to say, they can furnish knowledge of things hidden from waking thought but they cannot bring about changes in the other realm. It is only the dream self that is instrumental in this respect; and it is only through the medium of his dream self, accompanied by the dream images of power (the spirits), that the magician accomplishes his task.

Discussion

Defining Self and the Sacred Other

As revealed in the contexts of experiences just discussed, the soul is evidently a key cosmological concept—it defines the individual self in relation to a sacred Other and establishes the existence of two modes of reality, or being. There is the self of ordinary waking consciousness located in a physical body existing in a physical world; and there is another self, usually hidden from the waking self, existing in another world of incorporeal dream imagery.

The existence of these two modes of being is, however, not a matter of abstract speculation, but rather an observed empirical reality that no one, not even the adept, claims to understand fully. The exact nature of the dream realm, its relationship to the world of spirits and to the world of corporeal reality are not pondered, though certain phenomenological observations are made. It is, for example, considered evident that the dream realm obeys a different order and logic, which often completely reverses the predictable order of waking reality; things impossible in waking reality are commonplace in the dream realm; and the dead and the spirits, beings with suprahuman powers, are to be encountered there. The dream world thus points to unlimited possibilities and power—both destructive and creative—not to be found in the waking world. But as to its exact nature, no one is really sure. The consciously remembered imagery of dreams provides only fitful and hazy glimpses, and is regarded as only a distortion of what is really taking place in the other realm. Beyond the images of the dream world lies the realm of the spirits and the dead; but the relationship between the two is not clear, even to the man of knowledge.

Since the waking self can only have indirect knowledge of the other realm and since the imagery of dreams cannot be taken as a literal revelation of it, the fact that different people have dream experiences that may contradict each other is seen as no argument against the shared reality of the other realm. In any case, it is simply not a matter of abstract speculation. The living person, though he or she participates in both modes of being, is aware primarily of his or her bodily waking existence. On death, the individual ceases to exist in the bodily world, and the spirit (isage) has its total being in the spirit world (the spirit has no body but it does have a lalauga, or dream image self). But, as Aisaga so often insisted, the manner of the spirit's existence is something that we will understand only on death.

Evidently the Mekeo take a very pragmatic view. In the sense that the dream world is conceived of as visual images with no physical substance (precisely the meaning of the term lalauga), it approaches our categorization of dreaming as a realm of purely mental events. The difference remains that we regard these events as the internal products of our own minds, whereas Mekeo regard them as images created by something external to the self. For Mekeo, the real significance of the dream realm is that it is not simply invented by one's thought or fancy but has an autonomous existence. These images appear spontaneously and regardless of the will and intent of the self, confronting it with an Other as undeniable as physical reality—a sacred Other imbued with the power of ancestors and spirits.

Mekeo do not claim to understand the sacred realm from whence these images come, nor to have clearly mapped its territory. They insist on the importance of these autonomous images in influencing waking experience, but this is considered a matter of empirical observation and experience; they do not attempt to explain how or why this influence is exerted, it is simply a fact of human existence. Nor do they attempt to explicate the ways in which the two realms are linked. What they are concerned with are the practical results of this linkage, how it affects their everyday lives and well-being.

What then is the consequence for the individual of this dual, or divided, self? We can see that through the dream self, the individual is intimately linked to the sacred Other. No matter how fearful and essentially unknown the spirit world may be, inevitably each person is in direct contact with it via the medium of his or her dream self. And it must be kept in mind that one's own remembered dreams are not the only evidence of this participation, but so are the dreams of others. Every living person participates in both modes of being—the corporeal, tangible world of waking consciousness and the intangible world of dream imagery. Here the boundaries we like to draw between natural and supernatural have little relevance, and "wonder working," to use Gilbert Herdt's felicitous phrase, is woven through the fabric of everyone's experience. Even Lawrence's (1973) empirical and nonempirical realms will not really do here since the sacred Other is so closely grounded in actual experience!

Yet certainly Mekeo do clearly distinguish two very different realms: one of physical bodies and things perceived in waking consciousness and one of bodiless spontaneous imagery perceived in dreams and visions. But again, the distinction here is not our division of mind and body. As we have seen, body (imauga) and mind/thought (opo) are located in the same realm of physical existence perceived in waking awareness. Opposed to them is the dream image self, the lalauga, that perceives and encounters other incorporeal images like itself. Such images may also be encountered in the ordinary daytime world in the form of shadows, reflections in water or mirrors, and photographs—all visual images lacking physical substance yet having independent existence.

The self, in the sense of my private subjective awareness, is located in conscious thought (opo) which is experienced as taking place inside a physical body. My soul, or dream self, though part of me, is not the locus of my self-awareness. Indeed it is a very problematic entity because its actions—in my own dreams and in the dreams of others—may run contrary to and undermine my conscious desires and interests. It is me and yet not me; its separateness is indicated in the use of the third person to describe its actions. Moreover, I am likely not even to be aware of its actions in the dream realm. But inevitably I will suffer their consequences in waking reality.

The question arises here as to my responsibility for the actions of my soul (cf. Herdt 1987d). The ordinary person is not thought to be in control of the actions of the dream image self. Only the man or woman who possesses knowledge of some major magical rite has the power to influence—for good or evil—their own souls and the souls of others. But this in no way mitigates the consequences in waking reality of the soul's actions nor the social ramifications of it. If my soul gets into trouble of some sort, my body will get sick, regardless of my conscious intent or desire; the results are not changed by my inability to control the action of my soul. But what I can do is seek the assistance of a man or woman of knowledge to help my soul out of its predicament.

Tuzin (1975) has argued that among the Ilahita, cultural beliefs concerning love magic serve to disguise the real nature of unconscious desire revealed in erotic dreams. Thus, an Ilahita woman was able to privately enjoy her dreams of an adulterous liaison, thinking them the product of the dream lover's magic, without having to consciously face her own repressed desires or take responsibility for them. I can hardly imagine a Mekeo woman acting in this way. Unless she consciously desired such an affair, dreams of this nature would probably make her very worried. She would be convinced that her conscious wishes would soon be overpowered by the influence of the love magic and that she would in waking reality find it impossible to reject the dream suitor's advances. Out of fear or shyness, she might do nothing about the situation, but she might also approach an older female relative or friend who could provide or procure for her magical assistance in the form of a protective charm. The situation might indirectly be brought to the husband's attention; the love magician thought responsible for the dreams might also be approached on her behalf and be asked or warned to desist. There are several possibilities, but all of them are likely to lead to the woman concerned becoming more consciously aware of the dangerous consequences of the actions of her soul. If she is spared guilt, she is certainly not spared shame and anxiety; however, by coming to terms with the soul's actions as revealed in the dream, she can avoid the far worse consequences that an adulterous affair would bring in waking reality. In other words, the dreams can serve as a warning to her of a dangerous tension between her conscious desires and those of her soul. Here the dream interpretation provides not a disguise of but insight into hidden conflicts.

We see here another sense of the often repeated Mekeo explanation that dreams are valued as warnings. Ordinary persons cannot control their soul, but they can seek help in interpreting and dealing with its effects on conscious experience. Perhaps it can be said that their responsibility lies in taking this action. So too, the sick individual and concerned relatives are not responsible for the illness, but it is their responsibility to seek help for the endangered soul.

The knowledge of major magical ritual brings not only the power to influence one's hidden self and those of other people, it also brings responsibility for these actions in the dream realm. This is not to say that magicians are fully aware of the actions of their souls, but once these are revealed—especially in the dreams and visions of diviners—they are able, if they choose, to reverse or alter the influence they have exerted. We saw in the case of Aisaga and the snakebite victim that he was prepared to accept the evidence of an ordinary person's dream that he might be responsible, though he had no conscious desire to hurt the person in question. He was highly concerned by my dream indicating that his soul was behaving in a threatening manner to my dream self. As a man of knowledge, Aisaga has special means to perceive the events of the dream realm, but these can also be revealed spontaneously in anyone's dreams. Ultimately, of course, it is the diviners and magicians, like Aisaga, who determine the meaning of these communications.

An important point here is that even for the man of knowledge, dreams—his own and those of others—reveal things about the actions of his soul that are screened from his own awareness. And it is precisely those actions of the soul conflicting with conscious desire and intent that are of the greatest significance. Through the rituals of magic, the man of knowledge attempts either to separate soul from conscious desire or to bring soul back in harmony with conscious desires.

Although the dream realm connects the individual with the sacred Other of ancestors and spirits, our discussion here reveals that the entities encountered by the dream image self, and having an important influence on it, are in fact more likely to be the souls of other living people, in particular those of powerful magicians. The dream world has a great deal to reveal about one's relationships with other people.

In the Mekeo social world of carefully contrived public personas and the disguising of private thoughts and emotions, the "hidden self" poses a constant threat. One can manage one's public actions and deportment, dissemble one's real feelings; but all the while that part of one's self over which one has no direct control may be revealing to others, in their dreams, desires and intentions hidden even from you. Little wonder, then, that the soul is something discussed in private, and only with people one can trust. Or that it is of interest primarily to those who are knowledgeable in magic; or that many ordinary folk, who lack the knowledge to interpret or guide the actions of their soul, would simply prefer to ignore its existence until some unavoidable circumstance such as a serious illness forces it upon their attention.

The Hidden Self and the Unconscious

Although in our terms it is clear that the hidden self is a metaphysical entity, it is constructed not on the basis of abstractly elaborated cultural beliefs, but rather is grounded in observance of quite specific subjective experience. Similarities with Western notions of an "unconscious mind" are readily apparent, indeed are so striking that they seem worthy of closer comment.

The negative aspects of the hidden self find many parallels in the Freudian concept of the unconscious. In the fact that it is known only indirectly to conscious thought, that its desires are reflected in disguised form in dreams, that despite its hidden nature, it has a profound influence on both conscious behavior and the body, the Mekeo soul strikingly resembles the Freudian model (Freud 1971). The subversive and dysfunctional aspect of the soul in deflecting conscious intent, in causing mistakes, lapses, and even physical illness are paralleled by Freudian theories of parapraxes and hysteric illnesses (Freud 1938b), with the difference being that the Mekeo attribute all such occurrences to the soul. (But we should note that in doing so they are positing a psychological rather than a mystical cause of illness and misfortune.)

There is little, however, in Freudian theory to help us understand the positive aspect of the soul as an instrument of creative and transformative power. For Freud, the products of the unconscious were essentially infantile and inferior. The much more positive view taken by Jung and his school, who recognize both destructive and creative elements in the unconscious, in many respects seems to mirror the Mekeo view. Jung (1977) identified the concept of the soul as a level of the unconscious, the level of forgotten and repressed personal memories; and he identified the spirits with the archetypal patterns of the deep unconscious. Jung (1978) and his followers have stressed that the unconscious not only provides clues in dreams as to the nature of psychic disturbance, but that it is capable of spontaneously producing transforming and healing symbols. At the end of his long career, after having examined many thousands of dreams in clinical practice, Jung was convinced of the importance of dreams in the prognostication and curing of illness, of the occurrence of telepathy in dreams, particularly in relation to the death of relatives and loved ones (an aspect of dreaming much emphasized by Mekeo), and of the potency of dream portents. To quote just one brief example, Jung (1978:50) describes a sequence of events in which one of his patients saw himself in a dream step off a cliff into empty space; and despite Jung's warning as to the danger indicated in the dream, the man shortly afterwards fell to his death in a mountaineering accident. This case readily brings to mind the man described earlier who fell from a coconut palm after ignoring his dream premonition. The more daring of Jung's assertions have left his work open to charges of mysticism. Certainly his view of dreaming seems to lie close to that of the Mekeo adept; but Jung himself always insisted that his conclusions were based on empirical observation, not metaphysical theory—as, of course, might the Mekeo adept.

What are we to make of such similarities? It is not my intention to assert that the Mekeo soul is, in fact, the unconscious described by either Freud or Jung, which would be simply to impose our interpretive and analytic categories onto Mekeo thought. (The lalauga is not directly equatable with an "unconscious mind"; the term specifically denotes visual images having no material substance, and these include both what we regard as natural phenomena—shadows and reflections—and mental phenomena—dream images and halluci-nations). Nor do I wish to pretend that the Mekeo concept provides evidence to prove either one of these theories of the unconscious. Yet despite their obvious differences—on the one hand we have Western analytical theories, which at least purport to be established on the basis of scientific evidence and logical rea-soning, whereas on the other we have a descriptive folk category—I am left with a strong impression that all three views represent attempts to identify as-pects of the same phenomenological reality.

What, it seems to me, these three different concepts have in common is a recognition of the powerful effect on conscious experience of fantasy processes operating independently of conscious awareness and intent.

Freud, of course, gives no credence to the positive aspects of unconscious fantasy. Jung has much to say on this score, but his theory of mind is so diffuse—if not mystical, certainly metaphysical—that we look in vain here for any clear analytical model to guide us. And both these surely great thinkers at-tributed little significance to the influence of culture on unconscious fantasy and symbolization, an influence that is most explicitly recognized in Mekeo at-tempts to direct dreaming to conscious ends. Freud and Jung, in their con-trasting ways, have revealed the enormously powerful potential of fantasy processes that, until their findings, had been dismissed by science as trivial and insignificant. Their insights remain compelling, but their models are awkward, and sometimes even misleading, guides in cross-cultural investigation.

My problem here is to find the language to describe the Mekeo soul in etic, analytic terms that do not commit me to a particular theoretical school of psy-chological thought. (This problem seems to stem from the fact that English does not provide ordinary "common sense" discourse in which this entity might be discussed.) The lalauga is a concept based on particular kinds of inner, subjec-tive experience, of which dreams and waking visions are the most significant. In our terms, the soul can be identified as the alter ego that appears and acts in our dreams. As such, it is self-constructed by fantasy processes operating out-side conscious awareness. That is to say, it is not the fantasized self of waking reverie and daydreams, but the self involuntarily recognized in sleep dreams and other hallucinatory experiences.

The assertion that the actions of this hidden self have vital affects on the waking self and the physical body can thus be understood as statements con-cerning the influence of particular kinds of fantasy processes on conscious atti-tudes and physical well-being. Furthermore, the techniques of magic—the way to influence the hidden self—can be understood as culturally devised means to manipulate and use these fantasy processes to particular ends.

This is not to suggest that the soul is simply an illusion created by uncon-scious fantasy, or to argue that it functions as a defense mechanism to disguise unconscious wishes from consciousness. My point is that the soul represents a phenomenologically accurate folk description of particular psychological processes. As such, it does not disguise but rather reveals to the self wider knowledge of those inner mental processes that are usually screened from ordinary awareness.

For the ordinary person, but in particular the man or woman of knowledge, attention to the actions of the soul, as indicated in dreams and other states, provides special insight into their own and others' deeper motivations and desires. Should I stumble and twist my ankle, or clumsily cut myself with a knife, I would think it only common sense to blame the rough track or my fatigue, just as I would be inclined to dismiss an unfortunate slip of the tongue as a meaningless lapse of memory, but a Mekeo adept—along with the depth psychologist —would be alerted to something else. I believed that my extreme fatigue during the early weeks of fieldwork was due to an external, physical cause: the intense heat and humidity. Aisaga showed far greater psychological insight when he suggested a hidden desire, reflected in my dreams, to return home, a desire conflicting with my conscious intent at the time, but one recognizable and admissible in hindsight. In the same way, he recognized a danger to himself in wanting to stay in Australia when the time had come to return home. His sensitivity to this danger allowed him to avoid a split within himself between his soul and his conscious intent, which, in my lack of awareness, I had allowed take place in myself.

Not only does the soul become a source of greater self-knowledge and awareness, but it also provides the key to healing mental and physical illness. By influencing the soul through the rituals of magic, the man or woman of knowledge is able to bring soul, conscious self, and body back into harmony. We saw in the case of the man suffering from tuberculosis that the healer's dream narrative provided an imaginative linking of events associated with the illness that constructed an explanation, and a release and restoration of the soul. Why exactly the dream narrative proved effective, we cannot attempt to explain, but the patient's emotional conviction of restoration to health reflects the powerful positive influence that fantasy processes may exert in such circumstances. The Mekeo insistence that fantasy can be used not only to reveal but also to influence the deepest motivations of one's self and others, is paralleled in many Western psychotherapeutic techniques—a point I shall return to in the final chapter of this book.

In identifying the existence of visual images—both spontaneous and susceptible to human manipulation—that influence ordinary experience, Mekeo describe with some precision the phenomena produced by autonomous imagination. For them, the realm of the sacred is revealed in the transforming power of a special mode of imagination.

Conclusion

The Mekeo soul is a pivotal concept in defining the sacred realm, the self, and the self in relation to Other. It is central to their view of the nature of reality and the potentials of human existence. It is the key to the individual's physical, emotional, and mental well-being. And it is the source of important self-knowledge and insight into the minds of others. It is the basis of the cultural system of esoteric magical knowledge. In life, it links the individual to the sacred realm of the ancestors, spirits, and the dead.

Indeed, it constitutes the means by which Mekeo define and distinguish two modes of being or reality: the mundane world of corporeal reality, and the intangible world of creative and transforming imagery, a dual reality creating a dual existence. Our Western, culturally constructed common sense view recognizes only a single reality—the external, material world. Thus, we would ask someone "Was what you saw real?" Whereas Mekeo would ask whether it was a bodily entity *(imauga)* or a spontaneous image from the dream realm *(lalauga)*—recognizing two separate and real but very different modes of being.

The gap between our respective epistemologies is neatly caught in this aphoristic, if undoubtedly apocryphal, exchange between Castaneda and Don Juan:

"Yes, Carlitos, the double is a dream."
"Do you mean that he's not real?" I asked.
"No. I mean that he is a dream," he retorted. (Castaneda 1974:68)

Gilbert Herdt observes in the opening chapter of this volume that Melanesianists have in general tended to assume that certain religious concepts such as "spirit" and "soul" are self-evident. Even despite the very exhaustive analyses of cultural symbolism to be found in some recent studies—which have largely concerned themselves with the explication of ritual, i.e., publicly enacted, symbolism—general concepts such as "soul" have been taken as roughly equivalent with the English meaning and little investigated. Until recently, anthropology has been dominated by approaches that emphasize public representations, avoiding the whole area of subjective experience as irrelevant to their concerns. Thus, it is understandable that the importance of the "soul" concept has been overlooked. It is only within the context of private, subjective experience that it is possible to gauge its significance—a collective representation revealed only in private; a paradoxical butterfly, the psyche, easily eluding the ethnographer's net!

The renewed interest in subjective experience and in person and self reflected in this book, and other recent works reviewed in the opening chapter, directs our attention back to the soul, a topic of much excited theorizing by the founding fathers of modern anthropology. Our interests in it, of course, are likely to be very different from theirs. Herdt emphasizes the need to present such concepts in the full particularity of their specific cultural context. I agree. Yet at the same time, I cannot escape the sense of a very broad similarity across the cultures of Melanesia, and even much more widely than this.

My argument here has been that the Mekeo notion of soul is not simply a culturally determined construct, but that it also provides an phenomenologically accurate description of an empirical phenomenon—the important influence on conscious experience of fantasy processes operating outside ordinary awareness. If I am correct, then we should, despite cultural variations and idiosyncrasies, find significant parallels in similar concepts cross-culturally. The variations have yet to be charted, however, and future studies will have to decide this.

NOTES

Acknowledgments. Fieldwork carried out in 1980–82 was funded by the Australian Research Grants Council and the School of Humanities, La Trobe University, Melbourne, Australia. My thanks to Gilbert Herdt for comments on the draft of this chapter, and to Fitz Porter Poole, Don Tuzin, and the other members of the Melanesian Seminar, Department of Anthropology, University of California, San Diego, for comments on an earlier version of the arguments presented here.

1. Until I began to investigate dreaming, I had little awareness of the significance of the soul concept for Mekeo. Nor have other ethnographers working in the area given it much prominence. For instance, Hau'ofa's (1981) index lists only two entries under *soul;* whereas Mosko (1985), dealing with the nearby Bush Mekeo, lists only four references; yet both these ethnographies pay detailed attention to cultural beliefs and symbolic expression, though both are concerned primarily with public rather than private representations.

2. It has been pointed out to me that this locating of thought within the brain possibly reflects European influence; this may be so, but even people who know little or no English speak of thought taking place inside the head and brain.

3. Aisaga did not deny his ability to cause harm, nor did he deny that he actually caused harm to certain people, what he objected to was the fact that everything was now blamed on him as there were no longer any other old, powerful men of knowledge alive who might be thought responsible.

Visions, Prophecies, and the Rise of Christian Consciousness

Donald Tuzin

So Eli told Samuel, "Go and lie down, and if he calls you, say, 'Speak, Lord, for your servant is listening.'" So Samuel went and lay down in his place.

The Lord came and stood there, calling, as at the other times, "Samuel! Samuel!"

Then Samuel said, "Speak, for your servant is listening."

—1 Samuel 3:9–10

UNTIL recently, religious imagination among the Ilahita Arapesh operated through ideas and images associated with the secret men's cult—the Tambaran, as it is called throughout the East Sepik region—and with a diversity of notions involving ancestral spirits, ghosts, shape-changing bush demons (*masalai* in Pidgin English), yam spirits, and the alleged machinations of sorcerers and witches. This was the state of affairs at the time of my first fieldwork (1969–72), based in Ilahita village. The small number of villagers who had turned to Christianity were unsophisticated in their beliefs and gave little indication that Christianity was psychologically salient or had become the focus of their imagination in other-worldly matters. Nor, at that time, was there much interest in cargo cults; thus, in 1971 when a major cargo movement centered near Yangaru (Hwekmarin, Jamenan, Ningiga, and Wangu 1971; Roscoe 1987) swept the entire East Sepik region, Ilahita village remained conspicuously aloof and sneeringly skeptical. Memories, it seems, were still too fresh from a time, a decade or so earlier, when a man from the nearby Wosera area had duped many people of the area into decorating their cemeteries and sitting in them all night waiting for something to happen.

Returning to Ilahita for an eleven-month stay during 1985–86, I found that conditions had changed drastically. Much can be said of these changes; but the topic that concerns me in this chapter has to do with the advent of a predominantly Christian construction of religious imagination among the villagers. My approach is to focus on the experiences of one rather extraordinary individual, the reason being three-fold. First, it is an economical way to depict the changes in religious imagination that have overtaken the majority of the members of this society. This is possible because, second, the individual in question is the un-challenged spiritual leader of the Christian community, and thus the products of his imagination are the matériel many others use to furnish their private under-standings of the new religious landscape in which they find themselves. Third, the approach is intended to dramatize a methodological point concerning the lo-cus and operations of religious imagination. Briefly stated, although much that is "religious" is socially and culturally constituted, and is therefore meaningful as precipitates of a Durkheimian "collective consciousness," the idea of "reli-gious *imagination*" implies a psychical activity that is not meaningful apart from the human agent.[1] Both historically and dynamically, religious imagination is the beginning and end of religious culture, for only in the minds of individuals are religious ideas created and tested (cf. Tuzin 1977:220; Obeyesekere 1981; Barth 1987:55). Emphatically, this view does not reduce religious imagination to the level of a narrowly defined psychology. On the contrary, it will be seen that the imagination presented here, though deeply affected by psychodynamic processes, is equally dependent on ambient ideas, events, and social circum-stances. We are dealing, then, with the notion of religious imagination as a crucible—a vessel for the making of alloys, a vessel, moreover, whose con-tents are always bubbling and, therefore, always ready to assimilate new ingredients.

An Unlikely Transformation

My epigraph is a passage from the book of 1 Samuel. This chapter is about a different Samuel. A man in his late forties, he lives in premature retirement in Ilahita, an Arapesh-speaking village situated in the Maprik area of the East Sepik Province (Tuzin 1976). Samuel does not do serious work in the gardens or groves because he is crippled—has been for nearly ten years—and requires a cane in each hand just to move about. Like his biblical namesake, this Samuel is not only rich in religious imagination, he is a prophet and even, in his own way, an anointer. Voices and visions occur to him. Although I would not wish to claim that Samuel is insane, some of the experiences he reports are decidedly bizarre. And yet they are no more bizarre than the cultural and historical circum-stances that surround, encourage, and reward them. "Human imagination," Margaret Mead wrote, "tends to treat any fit between a leader and a situation as a miracle" (1956:189). Like Paliau, of whom Mead was speaking, Samuel is a "man who met the hour." As usually happens in such cases, there were ele-ments in Samuel's character and personal history that predisposed him to meet the hour when it came—beginning, curiously enough, with his name.[2]

Samuel used to be called Falipen. As a young man in the early 1960s he was baptized by European workers of the South Sea Evangelical Mission. As is customary, he adopted a biblical name to mark his membership in the Christian community of Ilahita, which in those days was quite tiny. Literacy was then almost nonexistent in the village, and in any event the Pidgin English version of the New Testament was not published until 1969. Converts either chose their baptismal name from Old and New Testament stories they had heard in church or asked one of the missionaries to pick a name for them. The former Falipen recalls not having had a strong preference at the time; someone suggested "Samuel," and the officiating missionary was pleased enough to baptize him in that name. But because the English vowel combination did not rest easily on an Arapesh tongue, the name became "Samial," and so it remained until the mid-1970s, a period that included the time (1969–72) of my initial association with him. Upon meeting him again in 1985, however, I found that the name had shifted toward its English form, and that despite a slight awkwardness of pronunciation, he and those close to him used the name "Sam-oo-el." At first I assumed that this was simply an attempt to "correct" the name in the light of greater familiarity with English sounds in general.[3] To some extent this may have been true; but I should have remembered the mystical association the Arapesh and other Sepik peoples impute to things and their proper names (Tuzin 1976:135–148; Harrison n.d.), and suspected what soon became evident—namely, that the shift in pronunciation was part of Samuel's increasing emulation of and identification with the Old Testament prophet of the same name. It paralleled other, more dramatic shifts in his comportment and social standing; but before turning to these it is worth dwelling for an additional moment on the matter of the name.

Dr. Onions (1966:602) defines *namesake* as a "person or thing having the same name as another," suggesting it was probably originally "said of persons or things coupled together 'for the *name('s) sake'*." In practice, this coupling usually signifies something about one or the other party, about the relationship between them, or about the linking relationships of a third-party bestower. One might be named after a distinguished ancestor, a beloved relative, an admired member of the bestower's circle, or a public figure—to name only a few of the many possibilities. Sometimes the name is selected purely for its aesthetic appeal, irrespective of any intrinsic or relational standing of the person from whom it is "taken," in which case signification may be absent and the namesake connection spurious. Alternatively, the placing of a name may signify a wishful intention to imbue the person receiving it with some desirable trait belonging to the initial holder, thus indicating the charismatic quality of personal names.

Traditional Arapesh naming practices, however, preclude the possibility of namesakes in the senses just described. Simply stated, names belong either to the men's cult (the Tambaran) or to the patriclan. The former are conferred on members of the novice moiety at each initiation; the latter are given soon after Ego's birth into the descent group. In either case, names may be bestowed only by persons having rights to them—a member of a particular patriclan or Tambaran grade, as the case may be. The association of names with unique persons is such that, within the descent or ritual unit, no two males may use the same name simultaneously.[4] Moreover, names are not directly transferable between individuals, but are returned to the repository of group names before being rebestowed on some eligible individual. This mediating step reconsecrates the name to the sacred core of group identity, resulting in a pattern of spiritual association not between successive users of the name, but between each user and the proprietor group.[5]

For these reasons, Falipen's choice of a baptismal name was indifferent to (and probably ignorant of) the personal attributes of the Old Testament prophet. What mattered at the time, both to him and to the missionaries involved, was that the biblical name established his Christian identity. In later years, however, conditions changed: in the late 1970s, Christianity became the dominant religious orientation of the village, with knowledge of the Bible and its personages increasing dramatically. Samial, whose early conversion was retrospectively viewed as a sign of God's special favor, was given reasons to rise above mere Christian membership and to emulate the person whose name he carried. A namesake relationship was created, and Samial became *Samuel*—a name that in Hebrew means "God speaks to him."

These developments would not have seemed possible at the time I first knew Samial. When I initially arrived in Ilahita, on August 31, 1969, I had no wish to hire a domestic servant. Intent on establishing an egalitarian relationship with the villagers, I regarded the idea as repellent on both moral and methodological grounds. The naiveté of this position was exposed within approximately four hours, when one of the village councillors, upon learning that I planned to stay for a long time, forcefully presented me with the man who would be my house boy. Waving aside my linguistically halting attempts to decline, the councillor instructed me that (1) *all* white men have house boys; (2) as a newcomer to the area, I could not know the first thing about cooking the local foods; (3) the man he had selected was experienced and highly skilled in the work; and (4) this employment would be a way of circulating much-needed cash to the man and his family. The councillor was not only importunate, a good deal of what he said made sense; and I quickly rationalized to myself that a house boy would, come to think of it, be a valuable source of information about village life and could materially assist me in my research. So, I agreed to hire Samial, who, I later learned, was the councillor's classificatory sister's husband and a member of his extended household.

I mention all this in the hope that none will distrust my motives or prejudices when I say that, as an employee, Samial was a disaster. One might charitably infer that he regarded the job as a sinecure—which is true—or that our communication was hindered by the cultural distance separating us—which is also true—or that Samial never understood my point in being there—which none would deny. But the larger truth is that Samial was lazy. In his domestic duties he could not or would not establish a daily routine of simple chores, such as sweeping the floor: each task had to be commissioned anew each day, and, each time, the slightly pained, long-suffering expression in his eyes told me that Samial thought he was being overworked. As a field assistant and informant, Samial was an even greater disappointment. Anything requiring physical exertion, such as map-making and census-taking around the large, sprawling village, was met with sullenness and passive resistence. When it came to answering questions about cultural matters or daily events, Samial was completely hopeless. The youngest of three brothers, he professed total ignorance of family and clan lore; was incurious and poorly informed about his own genealogy, even though his father was still alive and alert;[6] could not be relied upon to give me the correct Arapesh term for everyday objects in the village and its environs; was infuriatingly forgetful of the fact that I wanted to know about events occurring in the village. It is true to say, I believe, that in more than a year's daily intercourse with him, Samial never once told me anything that was useful or relevant to my work. Moreover, my evaluation seemed to be widely shared in the community: the concensus was that Samial was a harmless, indolent, ineffectual man who had no future in traditional politics and whose only use was in being assigned to the service of a resident white man. Content to sit for hours staring vacantly into space, Samial gave every appearance of being a simpleton—a man, I noted in my diary, devoid of imagination.

Besides the fact that it would have been unthinkably offensive to have discharged him, Samial remained with me for two important reasons. First, he was impossible to dislike. He had a sweet, even temperament; was without guile; and had a warm, commiserative manner that was quite soothing at times to a young anthropologist far from home. Second, my association with Samial gave me frequent access to his stunningly talented wife. Ribeka worked as a laundress for the local mission station, and she immediately added me as a customer. She was a striking contrast to Samial: vivacious, jolly, industrious, outspoken, sharp-tongued, and a dedicated gossip. She was also extremely intelligent and, as my chief linguistic informant, had very quickly acquired a facility with difficult grammatical concepts. Ribeka was also childless, which, I suspect, helped to account for her youthful, carefree manner. Although Samial may have been somewhat henpecked, the two were plainly devoted to each other: Ribeka's manner toward him was loyal, protective, nurturant, and forgiving, whereas Samial took obvious pleasure in his wife's *joie de vivre*. The only time I ever saw Samial moved to violence was when someone's cutting remark caused Ribeka to cry.[7]

After thirteen months I took a six-month study break in Australia, and returned to Ilahita with face-saving reasons for not rehiring Samial. We continued on friendly terms for the duration of my fieldwork, and for years thereafter I remembered him, affectionately, as a man whose retiring simplicity would always place him on the outskirts of village affairs.

In 1985 I returned to Ilahita to find that the intervening thirteen years had brought enormous changes to the society, the most dramatic of which had to do with dominant religious orientations. After years of declining importance the men's cult had finally collapsed when, in September 1984, the ritual secrets had been publicly revealed to the women. The village was in the throes of an ec- static Christian movement—a "Revival"—the chief tenets of which were that Christ's return was imminent, and that to share in the material rewards of the Millennium one had to be spiritually cleansed. This requirement applied to the community as a whole, which meant that those few who resisted conversion and held out for traditional values posed, by their presence, a threat to the Re- vivalists' millennarian aspirations. Not content with the destruction of the Tam- baran, Revival zealots were determined to obliterate any and all practices they could identify as traditional—from mortuary exchange feasting, to the wearing of feathers in the hair. Traditionalists, in their turn, produced evidence, such as confiscated "spirit telephones," suggesting that the Revival movement was a thinly disguised cargo cult, and therefore both contemptible and illegal. Ani- mosity prevailed between the two sides, because neither could allow the other simply to go its own way. Altercations were frequent. The traditionalists had their champions, and the Revivalists had Samuel.

Time and the times had changed Samuel. His hair was now speckled with gray, and the inactivity caused by the acquired disability in his legs had given him a fleshiness that is unusual among Arapesh men. Of greater interest, how- ever, were the changes in his bearing. He was still soft-spoken and agreeable, but nothing remained of the simpleton. The waters that had appeared shallow now appeared deep. Where there had been lumpishness, there was now seren- ity; looks that had seemed empty-headed now seemed contemplative; inertia had become gravity. Most striking were the changes in his eyes: where before they had stared vacantly, they were now alert, watchful, missing nothing. Sam- uel had acquired the disconcerting knack of being able, it would appear, to gaze into one's soul. And when he was not studying and weighing the inner thoughts of others, he was deeply absorbed in the contents of his own, now luxuriant, imagination. Amazingly, Samuel had become venerable and wise, and people came from many miles around to partake of his insights and visions, and to be- nefit from his occasional ability to work miracles.

Prophecy under Judgment

Samuel's role as champion of the Revivalist cause rested not on any new- found political activism, but on his unmatched spiritual authority, resulting from a combination of his visionary experiences and his unique position in the gender separation around which the movement was organized. Although men filled po- sitions of formal leadership in the Revival movement, much of the actual power lay in the hands of the women, who, because they were free of past association with Satan (i.e., the Tambaran), were worthy of possession by the Holy Spirit. During the long, twice-daily services, scores of women in the congregation would continually move in and out of putative possession states, uttering, amidst assorted gibberish, prophecies, admonitions, and accusations that fuelled discord among the Revivalists and between this group and both "heathens" and nonmovement Christians, the latter of whom adhered to the conservative tenets of European-dominated Church establishment. When these pronouncements proved wrong, as they often did, none doubted the authenticity of the possession event in question; rather, it was presumed that the possessing agent had been a satanic entity masquerading as the Holy Spirit. Thus arose the need to distinguish between true and false prophecy—a matter that could only be decided from a perspective of categorically higher spirituality. Authorized by God in a vision I shall describe presently, and verified by several correct calls, this degree of blessedness was given to Samuel, and accordingly he became the *man* who prophetically adjudicated the lower-level prophetic claims of *women*. Samuel credited his successes to an abiding "voice," which advised him in each case. Whether or not there was actually a voice, Samuel's success, like that of diviners the world over, is likely to have been a product of luck, common sense, and a shrewd assessment of the relevant personalities and circumstances in the case.

Comparing Samuel with the man he once was, we have an instance of society seeking for its prophets on the margins (Lewis 1971). More precisely, perhaps, the events of the last decade have turned Ilahita society inside-out; center and periphery have reversed places, and those who were last have become first. Without the wave of history to lift and carry him forward, Samuel's obscurity would have continued without interruption. But the same wave also laid bare an entire new field of imaginative possibilities; and it is to Samuel's credit as a creative social and cultural actor that he played a major role in articulating the community's new religious consciousness and parlayed his social gains into a position of preeminence in the newly formed center. Samuel was by no means the only person to experience religious visions; indeed, there was a veritable competition going on among would-be claimants to divine inspiration and favor. But in this context Samuel's humble, marginalized past ironically lent unique force and credibility to his claim. First, having opted out of Tambaran affairs at an early age, he was relatively untainted by past "satanic" associations. Second, his former innocence of political involvements lent an air of personal disinterestedness to his reports of mystical experience and his adjudication of spiritual, but socially consequential, matters. Finally, others besides myself had noticed the seemingly miraculous transformation in Samuel's bearing, and readily attributed it to the touch of divinity.

Thus, in their fevered search for wonders and portents of the Millennium the Revivalists turned to Samuel—whose imagination, which had known so little exercise in the past, became, with this encouragement, perfervid and productive. The reported visions of others were of interest mainly to the seer's immediate circle. Samuel's visions, by contrast, were widely accepted as the truest, most authentic eyewitness accounts of the normally unseen reality for which the Revivalists yearned. In effect, Samuel did their religious imagining for them.[8] His reports are therefore of analytic interest not only for the glimpses they give into this man's imaginal idioverse, but for their status as canons of religious imagination in the Revivalist community at this time. Before turning to this testimony, however, a few additional facts are in order concerning Samuel's family background, since aspects of it will enter into my interpretation of his visionary experiences.

In his prime Samuel's father, Kweando, had been a prominent figure in political and ritual affairs, if only by virtue of being the only male of his generation in the patriline. When Kweando was a child, his mother and only sibling (a younger sister) had been killed in an enemy raid, and his father, Sungweli, did not remarry. Sungweli had no brothers. Of his three younger sisters, two died without issue, while the third married into a distant part of the village and was effectively forgotten by members of Samuel's generation. Accordingly, although Samuel belonged to a populous clan, he was without collateral agnates, and his patriline—which is the most important jural and ritual unit in this society—consisted entirely of his immediate family.

Kweando's public life ended in the early 1960s, when, recently widowed and with old age approaching, he converted to Christianity and assumed the name Noah. By the time of my first fieldwork (1969–72), Noah was becoming enfeebled; and this process noticeably hastened after the death (in 1970) of his tubercular eldest son, Walimini. Noah's other children were, in order of birth following Walimini: a daughter, Iwata'wa, who was married to a powerful man named Kumbwiata; a son, Sali, who was a triple polygynist; and Samuel. When Sali passed away in 1977, soon to be joined by Noah, the mantle of patriline leadership passed to Samuel. Although Walimini and Sali, between them, had sired fourteen children who were still living in 1986, the jural unit over which Samuel newly presided was neither as large nor as jurally effective as one might expect: seven of the offspring were female; two of the sons, in 1986, were still too young to be married, while a third—the eldest of his generation in the family—was an apparently confirmed bachelor; and two of the married sons were permanently employed in other parts of the country. In 1986 the remaining two of Samuel's brothers' sons were young men, newly married and resident in an outlying settlement of the village.

The point to be emphasized is that, upon the deaths of Sali and Noah, Samuel was placed in the unenviable position of suddenly having a large number of jural dependents (widowed brothers' wives and their children) and neither the temperament nor a wider agnatic support group with which to manage it. Furthermore, for reasons mostly having to do with Ribeka's fiery tendencies, relations between Samuel and his affines were recurrently strained and generally unreliable as a source of emotional or material assistance.[9] Such conditions would have taxed the powers of most men, let alone someone who, like Samuel, was accustomed to the nurturance, protection, and direction of others: his father, older brothers, and wife. But Samuel, by force of imagination and circumstance, and with the naive luck usually given to children and lunatics, solved his predicament in such a way as to preserve his dependency needs, at the same time as to shoulder the spiritual burden of the patriline, the village, and beyond. In achieving this Samuel was not unlike other charismatic leaders, elsewhere and of greater fame, whose dependency needs are matched only by the needs of others to depend on them. Consider, then, the products and functions of Samuel's religious imagination.

The Stranger-Guide

Samuel described his religious experiences to me in a series of interviews, the tone of which reflected yet another radical change in his demeanor. Previously, Samuel had behaved in a shy, diffident manner, never offering more than a minimal answer to any question put to him. This time, the minimalism was on my part. In answer to my opener, "Tell me your story," Samuel spoke at great length without interruption or further prompting. His story had a rehearsed quality, as though refined through many retellings, and was delivered with a gravity suggestive of the fact that Samuel was used to being taken very seriously by previous audiences. The story is of interest both for its depiction of the imaginal content of Samuel's present religious consciousness, and for the close, analytically significant coincidences it shows between the rise of these images and specific, traumatic events in his personal life. As disclosed in the following highlights, Samuel's symbolic achievement lies not in the creation of wholly new images—most of those he reports are familiar from sermons and other forms of Christian discourse in the village—but in the way he authenticates these stock elements by narrativizing them in relation to his personal experience and in accord with broader, pre-Christian cultural understandings.

Samuel began by saying that when I knew him before (1969–72), his Christian belief was not strong. He attended church, but without an understanding of spiritual matters and without his surface Christianity affecting his general behavior. His true conversion occurred during the First Revival (ca. 1977). He realized that his previous behavior was leading him to Hell. Fear of this prospect caused him to relinquish all residual attachment to Custom, and to renounce sinful behavior such as lust, adultery, competitiveness, and petty theft.

At the time of the First Revival, it was assumed by the Christians that any deaths among themselves were the result of Heathen retaliation for the Revival's assault on Custom. Sali, Samuel's next-eldest brother, also joined the First Revival and was one of those who died in the Heathen attack.[10] At Sali's funeral Samuel "died"; an evil spirit took him and he lost consciousness; but he fought and defeated it.

A short time later, Samuel was again inhabited by an evil spirit. It took the form of a large lump on the inside surface of his right forearm. He went to Kumbwiata, his elder sister's husband, who was a prominent traditional healer and recent convert to revivalist Christianity, and asked him to lance the lump with a razor. But when Kumbwiata went to cut it, it slid out from under the blade and moved to the other side of the arm. By now everyone realized that this was no ordinary lump. Finally, by sneaking up on it and stabbing at it suddenly and vigorously, Kumbwiata succeeded in releasing its contents. Blood spurted from the wound "as if a water tank had sprung a leak." At the same time the possessing spirit, using Samuel's voice, cried for mercy and begged Kumbwiata to stop, saying that the operation was killing it. The flowing blood turned black as the evil flowed out of Samuel's body. Kumbwiata wanted to bind the wound, but Samuel would not allow it until the bleeding had almost stopped of its own accord. Then Samuel's own spirit left his body.

The spirit traveled a few paces to Bwi'ingili (the large clearing in the center of the village, adjacent to the mission compound) where it beheld a large wooden cross decorated with red and green painted markings. At its base stood a man whom "Samuel" (i.e., his spirit) did not recognize. Off to one side, some distance from the cross, stood another stranger, who beckoned to "Samuel" by crooking his finger. The man was tall, with especially dark skin ("like a Solomon Islander"), straight black hair, and with a solid, well-fed physique. This man told "Samuel" to watch the man standing at the base of the cross. As he did so, the man walked away from the cross and started down a wide road, which "Samuel" had not noticed until then. The road was beautifully landscaped with flowers and trees, and the embankments rose steeply on each side. The road looked very inviting. As "Samuel" watched, the man proceeded down the road without looking back. He did not see, therefore, that the road was continually closing behind him, forming a mountainous wall that joined with the steep embankments. Before long, the road itself ended in a high wall, and the man turned to find himself imprisoned by walls on all sides. Fire arose all around him, and "Samuel" could see the man writhing in pain and could hear his screams. But the man did not die; the fire did not consume him. He simply continued to burn—and burn.

"Samuel" turned to the stranger, who led him over to the cross. When he arrived at the base and had stood there for a moment, the stranger indicated that he should look behind it. There he saw that a small road—not particularly attractive or inviting—led off in the direction of Selembungambel (a nearby hamlet). "Samuel" followed it for a few yards, and then noticed that the road farther on was lined with attractive, iron-roofed houses. "Samuel" turned and found that the stranger had followed him down the road. The latter told "Samuel" that he must always follow the straight road, never deviating from it in the slightest degree.

Samuel illustrated this last point by drawing a straight line on the ground in front of where he sat. Using the stick, he also indicated lines that departed from, or deviated for a time from, the main path. If ever he starts to veer from the proper course, he will hear the stranger's warning voice and feel a warning slap on his arm. Samuel recalled having one Sunday prepared to cut a coconut. As he swung at it, the bush-knife was invisibly yanked out of his hand and flung across the clearing. Ribeka, who was present, was amazed and amused. Some Christians accused him of faking the incident. Samuel claims not to have resented their skepticism, saying he would have reacted the same, in their place, but he insists that it happened in the way described, and he is convinced that his Stranger-Guide had yanked the knife from his hand in order to prevent him from violating the Sabbath.

When I asked him what the road in his vision might have meant, Samuel confidently replied that the first was the road to Hell, the second the road to Heaven. The former—wide and inviting—is the road most people choose to follow. The latter—narrow and mean—is followed by few. Straightness refers to virtue and the careful observance of the Christian code of conduct. Referring to the coconut-cutting incident and to the fact that other Christians apparently do not avoid such activities on the Sabbath, I asked if the Stranger in the vision requires greater discipline of Samuel than of other persons? Eagerly, Samuel answered that, indeed, he had been singled out for unusually harsh disciplines. That is why, he added, his spiritual powers are so much greater than those of anyone else.

I asked if Samuel had any idea as to the identity of the black Stranger. No, Samuel said, he had not looked closely at him, and in any event it was difficult to see his face clearly. We discussed the possibility that he was God, an angel, or a ghost; but Samuel was reluctant to speculate on this matter.

Two general points are in order. First, although I doubt very much that Samuel was wilfully deceiving me, I think it likely that a large element of retrospection figures into this and other experiences that he recounted to me. As mentioned before, the story sounded rehearsed. Over the many retellings that certainly occurred, the narrative would have been refined, perfected, and perhaps embellished. Gaps would have been filled, inconsistencies resolved. The process would have been so subtle that Samuel would have had little trouble maintaining belief, in his own mind, that his account was a faithful description of what he originally saw. Second, Samuel's subjective acceptance of those events, as remembered, together with their fantastical quality, engenders a close experiential resemblance between visions of this sort and sleeping dreams. Thus, it is understandable that Samuel, perceiving these visionary happenings in the light of his cultural understandings concerning dream phenomena (Tuzin 1975), would interpret them as quite literal events. For him, they are what they are—not ciphers standing for some other meaning that must be interpreted. The roads to Heaven and Hell *actually* lead from Bwi'ingili, where a wooden cross actually stands. All elements are real and extant; it is just that they are invisible to normal perception. In this respect, also, the local ontology of visions is identical to that of sleeping dreams, namely, as experiences of the spirit as it wanders loose from the body. Under questioning, Samuel did readily interpret the roads' destinations as being Heaven and Hell, respectively. But this realization was actually a form of secondary elaboration; it did not enter into the vision, per se, suggesting that the latter was formed of images belonging to a memory domain that did not yet include refined elements of Christian theology. Under the psychologically primitive conditions of the vision, the one road leads to literal entrapment and nonconsuming fire; to Samuel in the normal state of wakefulness, this is what Hell is. Images of pretty flowers, trees, and iron-roofed houses are likewise indicative of Heaven.

It would be an easy mistake to dismiss Samuel's vision as a Christian cliché. The wooden cross, roads leading either to bliss or perdition, the nonconsuming fire, the presentation of choice and temptation—these details are undoubtedly traceable to Christian influences. Furthermore, from a dramaturgical standpoint, the vision suspiciously resembles a sermonizing tactic missionaries (going all the way back to Paul the Apostle) commonly use in communicating Christian concepts to an untutored audience, which is to utilize concrete, locally intelligible images to create a parable with the appropriate moral outcome. And yet, although some elements in Samuel's account are almost certainly adopted from Christian teachings to which he had been exposed, there is at least one that is importantly innovative in respect of the character and aspirations of the Revival: the Stranger-Guide, whose skin was "as black as a Solomon Islander's."

The significance of this detail is potentially two-fold. First, Revivalists say their movement was initially imported from Malaita by visiting native pastors from the mother branch of the South Sea Evangelical Mission (now Church). In view of the meticulous Arapesh concern with priority in ritual matters, the Stranger-Guide of Samuel's vision might well signify the spiritual subordination of Ilahita to its Solomon Islands' preceptors. Second, and perhaps more salient, Samuel's spontaneous mention of the Solomon Islands was made with explicit reference to the Stranger-Guide's skin color. Papua New Guinea mainlanders (including Samuel and many others in Ilahita) who have worked on the plantations of Bougainville, express awe and fascination with the blue-black coloration of many of the inhabitants of that island. In the human realm, it is the epitome of blackness, the quintessential opposite of whiteness. Although most of its members (including Samuel) were initially converted to Christianity by the South Sea Evangelical Mission (now Church), the Revival is strongly antagonistic to that establishment. Both the indigenized Church leadership and its influential European advisors are critical of the Revival's cargo-cult overtones and ecstatic forms of worship. Members of the Revival respond by accusing the official Church of attempting to suppress or deny the workings of the Holy Spirit. That Samuel went out of his way to emphasize the blackness of the Stranger-Guide's skin is thus consistent with, and arguably significant of, the Revival's antiestablishment, antiwhite sentiments.

In summary, Samuel's vision was a blend of traditional ontological understandings concerning dreamlike states, images of local personages and settings, Christian clichés and messages, ideas derived from the immediate political scene, and a dash of cargo cultism. As public reference points, these elements constituted the vision's appeal to the Revivalist community at large. But the vision also fulfilled an important private need in providing Samuel with a spiritual Guide soon after the death of his brother Sali. From my description of his previous character and later family circumstances, it should come as no surprise that Samuel's dependency needs are unusually intense. His devotion to Ribeka is largely intelligible in these terms, but Samuel also requires the protection of a strong, masculine figure. At his middle-aged time of life, most Arapesh men have sons entering adulthood; but Samuel, as mentioned, is childless.[11] Following the death of their eldest brother, Walinimi, in 1970, Sali—a powerful and feared man—had become Samuel's chief protector. His death was a traumatic loss. The vision, however, imaginatively created a Guide—a tall, black man who appeared only once, with a face difficult to see clearly, but whose guiding voice speaks to Samuel to this day.

The Crippling Effects of a Father's Death

Feelings of loss and abandonment were again assuaged with Christian ideas, this time expressed in a vision that Samuel recalled having experienced in about 1978, at the time of his father Noah's death. Interestingly, although Arapesh individuals frequently evince symptoms of neurotic guilt over a parent's death (Tuzin 1975), and although, as we shall see, Samuel's immediate circumstances would have especially favored the appearance of such symptoms, nothing of the sort suggests itself (to me) in Samuel's account of this vision. Indeed, the very absence of predictable guilt in direct association with Noah's death, is a key element in the interpretation of other events soon to be described.

Samuel was cradling Noah when he died. Just as the old man breathed his last, "Samuel" (i.e., his spirit) saw Noah's spirit rise up from the corpse and walk away. "Samuel" stood up and followed "Noah" at a distance of about thirty feet.

At this juncture I asked Samuel why his spirit had followed that of Noah. He replied that he saw his father leaving and automatically wanted to go with him. Was it a matter of curiosity? No, said Samuel, it was a simple, unreflective desire to be with his father and to go where he went. After a few more nondirective attempts to elicit a fuller description of what motivated the spirit, I asked, "Did your reaction resemble that of a child who sees his father head off for the gardens and wants to go with him, for the simple reason that he is leaving?" Samual eagerly agreed that this was exactly the sort of situation he was describing.

Shortly after the two spirits had started off, they came upon an old woman, bent with age and hobbling slowly and unsteadily with the aid of a stick. It was Haukuwa, a woman of the village who had died a few hours earlier. She looked confused and despondent. "What's the matter?" they asked. "I have revealed all my sins but one," she answered, "and now I do not know where to go." Feeling sorry for her, the two spirits left and went on their way.

Farther along, "Samuel" saw "Noah" enter the base of a wooden cross. "Samuel" followed him and found himself entered upon a different world.[12] He saw "Noah" proceeding down a straight, narrow road, until he came to a table set with food and water. Around the table sat eight or nine well-dressed men, some of whom were white-skinned, while others were black-skinned. As "Noah" approached the group, he bowed his head in respectful greeting, and the men returned the bow. "Noah" sat down with them, and as he did he instantly became a young man again, dressed in new European clothes.

As "Samuel" watched from a distance, he suddenly saw his mother (who had died in about 1960, just before Samuel was baptized) come running. Crying, she threw her arms around "Noah's" neck. "Oh, you've all come now! Walimini, Sali and now you. But you've left Falipen behind! What will become of him?" "Do not worry," the other men said dismissively, "he is doing good works in the village." Samuel's mother was calmed by this news, and she left the gathering.

"Samuel" felt very happy at seeing his father admitted to what was obviously a group of important men in the afterlife. As he watched, ranked legions of the dead, all dressed in white, came marching in perfect array to where the men sat. "Samuel" noticed Kwalo (a deceased neighbor), Walimini and Sali in the front rank. This also made him happy. The "army" advanced to the table and, in unison, bowed to those who were seated. The latter returned the salute, and the army marched away.

Then "Samuel" noticed that there was a stream beyond where the men were seated. On the far side was Mwinimbel (deceased, 1970), who was suffering from hunger and thirst. Mwinimbel called to the men at the table, begging them to give him food and water; but they ignored him, saying to each other that Mwinimbel had been a bad man.

Feeling pleased and satisfied by all that he had seen, "Samuel" returned to his body, where it sat, immobile, next to Noah's earthly remains.

To understand the significance of this vision, it must be noted that Noah's demise preceded by only one or two weeks the sudden onset of Samuel's crippledness. This affliction was supposedly Samuel's God-given punishment for disobeying divine instructions and yielding to the temptation of custom. The tradition in question was the men's ambitious cultivation of especially large or especially numerous yams (*Dioscorea alata, D. esculenta*). The displaying and competitive exchanging of yams formed the center of the men's prestige complex (Tuzin 1972), which, along with the Tambaran Cult, had long been a target of the Mission's cultural eradication endeavors. In that year (1978), some weeks before harvest, Samuel was making a routine inspection of his garden, when he was intrigued to notice that one of his yam plantings (*D. esculenta*) had produced a very large offspring. As he excitedly prepared harvest magic to administer the following day, God's voice addressed him, warning that he must not commit this sinful act. Samuel was troubled by this, but the yam was too magnificent to resist. He completed the magical procedures.

Before the harvest could take place, Noah died. It occurred to Samuel that the loss of his father might have been God's punishment for his recent act of disobedience. On the other hand, Samuel reasoned, Noah was very old and could not have lived much longer, anyway. Moreover, if Samuel's interpretation was correct, it meant that the punishment had already occurred—the damage already done—in which case there was no reason not to proceed with harvesting the prize yam. In due course, the tuber was unearthed and brought to Samuel's house in the village.

The following day, Samuel took his eldest brother's son, Nangaha, back to the garden to help him with additional harvesting tasks. Samuel decided to sleep that night in his garden house, and in the late afternoon sent Nangaha home. In the twilight, as he reclined against a house post, he felt a voice start in the pit of his belly, rise up his esophagus, and emerge from his mouth with the urgent warning that he should return home immediately, or else he would not be able to do so. Alarmed, Samuel did as the voice instructed and arrived back home soon after Ribeka had gone to sleep. He went to bed feeling troubled but physically intact, and remembers going outside during the night to urinate. At dawn, though, when he tried to arise at the normal time, his knees would not support him. When he called for stinging nettles and used them on the dead knees, the voice returned, saying, "What do you think you're doing? This is the way it will be from now on. You disobeyed, and this is your punishment." Prayers for mercy were not heeded. A month-long visit to the Wewak Hospital yielded nothing: the physical examinations, X-rays, and blood tests failed to disclose any organic reason for Samuel's complaint.

Nowadays, Samuel is reconciled to his condition, and he no longer bothers to ask God to restore the strength in his legs. God warned him not to use the harvest magic, because, according to Samuel, to do so would result in a giant yam that would be a source of pride and boastfulness. "I sinned by deliberately disobeying God's order. God is our father; and just as we punish our children when they disobey, so does he punish me. He has promised that I will live to old age, but not that I will ever walk again."

In the absence of any detectable organic basis for Samuel's disability, we must consider the possibility that it is a conversion symptom. The striking coincidence between its onset and the death of Samuel's father supports this interpretation, as does the fact that Samuel was—again coincidentally—experiencing objective guilt over the business of the yam magic. Whether he actually imagined God's voice speaking a warning to him, Samuel was aware he was violating Christian prohibitions against the use of gardening magic and against the ambition to produce large yams. He also knew that his misdeed would provoke criticism from the Christians and, according to the prevailing Christian ideology, God's displeasure. Considered in the light of all these factors together, the absence of guilt ideation in the vision coincident with Noah's death is highly significant; for, under the circumstances, it appears strongly to be an instance of active denial. Samuel's vision has it that Noah arrives in the afterlife, smartly dressed, to be lovingly reunited with his wife and received as an honored guest at a mixed-race banquet hosted by none other than God Himself. Noah is joining Heaven's blessed élite. Legions composed of the Christian dead pay him homage, while his old enemy, the old sinner Mwinimbel, hungers and thirsts miserably on the opposite shore.

Samuel's vision projects an eternity of youth, honor, importance, new clothes, food and drink in banquet proportions, marital and sexual felicity, camaraderie with white men, companionship with God, righteous triumph over one's enemies—an inventory of rewards that, by implication, makes life compare poorly with death. And this, I suggest, is precisely the point of Samuel's vision: to convince himself that Noah is better off dead. Although traditional Arapesh notions about the afterlife were vague and inconsistent, they did agree on one point: that death is a grim, unhappy, and even frightful condition. The paradaisical condition promised by Christianity may be an appealing alternative; but, if taken too far, as it presently is in Ilahita, this consolation becomes an impediment to the successful working-through of the mourning response.[13] Samuel's affliction demonstrates the gross, psychodynamic inadequacy of his visionary handling of Noah's death. Instead of being causally connected in Samuel's interpretation, the death and the affliction were made into separate Christian object lessons for the edification of the religious community. In the case of the affliction, however, this could not be done without stretching credibility; for even the most doctrinaire village Christian would concede that permanent paralysis of the knees is a punishment out of all proportion to using gardening magic to harvest a large yam, however special this sinner was in the eyes of God. And yet Samuel was driven to this interpretation because it was the most readily available means for disguising to consciousness the traumatic guilt which, *ex hypothesi*, he felt over the death of his father—a guilt that was denied and therefore exacerbated in the vision.

The evidence that Samuel actually experienced guilt over the death of his father is necessarily circumstantial. To begin with, such emotions are extremely common among the Arapesh, and a good deal of mortuary practice and ideation is intelligible as a culturally constituted means for resolving the self-punishing thoughts aroused at the death of a close family member—prototypically, a parent (Tuzin 1975). As a Revival enthusiast, Samuel eschewed those traditional ideas and procedures, thus depriving himself of any therapeutic value they might have availed him at the time of Noah's death. Furthermore, as noted earlier, Noah's old-age infirmities were already well advanced when last I saw him, in 1972. In the remaining six years of his life, his feebleness steadily progressed to the point where he was almost totally helpless. Although Samuel's memory of that period did not dwell on this aspect of Noah's final years, he did mention that the old man's continuance had been a burden to his family—especially Samuel and Ribeka, to whose household he belonged—and that his expiration had been more an occasion for self-interested relief, than for grief (cf. note 13). All of this does not prove, of course, that Samuel had wished his father dead, or that the event of his death prompted primary guilt feelings; but on both ethnographic and general grounds, it would be difficult to infer otherwise.

As to why Samuel's psyche converted unconscious guilt feelings into a state of being crippled, we need only to refer to his previously discussed dependency needs and untoward, burdensome rise to the head of his patriclan, not to mention his unusual aversion to physical work. Overnight, Samuel's disability restored him to the dependent condition of a child; freed him from many of the material responsibilities that he had recently acquired; and, by virtue of its divine source, greatly enhanced his budding claim to having God's special attention. Without any hint of malingering, one must admit that the secondary rewards attendant on Samuel's affliction were very impressive, indeed, and were perfectly suited to his requirements.

Practical Prophecy

The visions thus far described came upon Samuel spontaneously, under emotionally trying circumstances. They are "charter" experiences in at least two senses. First, as acute resonators of immediate emotional needs and circumstances, they are important anchor points for Samuel's own belief in his God-given, visionary power. Second, as major reference points in the community's present Christian understandings, they set forth narrativized images of the triumvirate of all rationalized ethical systems that are cast in religious terms: proper religious conduct, divine rewards, and divine punishments. Just as charter myths and charter dreams create a fund of charisma from which subsequent operations draw authority, so these charter visions principally authorize Samuel's continuing prophetic and divinatory activities.

When a need for mystical services arises, Samuel induces a vision through prayer. Once, for example, the teenage daughter of a neighbor came to him, hoping he could tell her the whereabouts of a lost key. Samuel prayed and in the ensuing vision correctly saw the key lying under the thatch at the side of the girl's house. A more important application of Samuel's gift, one that draws petitioners from many miles away, is the treatment of illness. Looking at a patient and holding his or her wrist are sufficient for Samuel to make his diagnosis. If simple sickness is the problem, prayer and medicine (Western or traditional) are employed. If the illness is caused by possession by an evil spirit, Samuel drives it out with an aggressive, exorcistic prayer delivered loudly in the name of Jesus. Once, for example, while Samuel was spending a month in the Wewak Hospital having his legs tested, the doctors brought to him a man in an agitated state of lunacy. Samuel induced a vision in which he saw a rat-sized pig lurking in the man's midsection. The pig squealed, using Samuel's voice. Samuel prayed and ordered the pig, which was an evil spirit in disguise, to leave the man's body, which it did. Samuel's spirit chased the pig all the way back to the man's place in the Wosera, a distance of about one hundred miles. There the pig paused, thinking it was safe. But Samuel drove it farther on, deep into the forest, far away from where it could do additional harm. Samuel's spirit returned to his body, and he "awoke" to find that the man had fully recovered his sanity. The man was very grateful to Samuel and shook his hand warmly. News of Samuel's powers spread quickly through the hospital, and for the remainder of his stay he was called upon to treat and advise many of the other patients.

Aside from the fact they were induced by Christian prayer, Samuel's spiritual approaches to finding the key and curing the man's overt madness were not dissimilar from traditional shamanistic divinatory and healing procedures, which sometimes involved possession by ancestral spirits.[14] In my final examples, this general form is importantly combined with specifically Christian contents, thereby, as in the charter visions, communicating exemplary images and homiletic messages to the entire audience of believers.

Kwapisi, a woman of about Samuel's age and the wife of the local pastor, had apparently died, and Samuel was besought to resurrect her. He joined the crowd gathered in the house where she lay, told the Heathens to leave, fastened the door, and prayed. During the prayer a vision came to him in which he saw that "Kwapisi" was already seated in a chair in God's house. "Samuel" rapped on the door and called for her to come with him. God told her to go, but she said she would rather stay where she was. God insisted, saying, "They are calling to you." "Kwapisi" obeyed and returned to her body, intending to reenter it through a hole (about three inches in diameter) in its side. But while her spirit had been gone a membrane had grown across the hole, blocking the way. A man's hand—"Samuel" could not see whose—held a knife and cut the obstruction. Kwapisi's spirit started to crawl headfirst through the hole; but with its legs still outside, it became stuck. In the name of Jesus, "Samuel" prayed with renewed vigor, and the spirit managed to complete its reentry.

On another occasion Samuel lost consciousness and his spirit found itself in a room, wherein were seated God and a number of persons whom "Samuel" did not recognize. In a book that lay open on a table in the room, "Samuel" saw written the number of Balemama, an older man of Samuel's clan. God was about to erase the number, because Balemama had recently removed cement and cordyline markers from a land boundary that was under dispute. God told "Samuel" that thereafter he (Samuel) would be the one to decide whether prophecies were true or false. God was giving him the power to judge. "Samuel" returned to his sleeping body and, upon awakening, told Balemama that he would have to answer for his act after he died.

Joining our discussion at this point, Ribeka explained that Christian Revivalists enjoy two categories of "blessing." Those who are literate enough to read the Bible and understand its teachings are blessed with the ability to preach and explicate the religious messages, and to lead in the singing of hymns. She included herself in this category. Those who cannot read and who are not tainted by a history of Tambaran involvement are blessed with the gift of prophecy. Samuel, she said proudly, is the only person who possesses both kinds of blessing. In addition to his special power to discriminate between the true and false prophecy of others, Samuel is able to recover the disembodied souls of persons at or near death, identify thieves, find lost objects, and predict the outcome of events. These powers have been demonstrated many times over the last ten years—and each time it happens, the people's faith in Samuel and in the religious cause he champions, grows stronger.

Conclusion

I have dealt here with only those details of Samuel's character, imagination, and personal history which, in my view, afford a consistent picture of how this man, in these times, came to occupy a position of spiritual preeminence in the large Christian community of Ilahita and its social environs. The full story of religious imagination in this village, even as it is centered on this man, would require an examination of Samuel's many other visions and related experiences; a comparison of these with the large corpus of visions and prophecies claimed by others; and a more complete account of the complex circumstances that converted Ilahita from being the regional center of the Tambaran, to being the regional center of the Christian Revival. Such a treatment would quickly expose the strand of cargo-cult ideation and practice running through the entire fabric of religious imagination in Ilahita—a thread as strong as it is difficult to follow, the end of which, interestingly, is held by a woman who is the daughter of Samuel's long-dead brother, Walimini. But stories, even those of an ethnographic type, can sometimes tell too much; and in telling this one I chose for the sake of analytic clarity to risk the omissions.

As Margaret Mead stated in the passage quoted near the beginning of this chapter, the fit between a leader and his times often assumes a miraculous quality. Congenial to the anthropological perspective, with its emphasis on collective phenomena, is the idea that the individual is entirely a creature of his or her cultural circumstances. But the "fit" of which Mead spoke runs both ways. In some situations one is reminded of the star soccer player, whose control of the ball is so masterful that it appears to follow him, rather than the reverse. The career of Samuel's religious imagination had this quality, insofar as the visions he created from an amalgam of inner and outer ideas were purveyed to a public that was eager to accommodate itself to them. Such an effect is certainly most noticeable under conditions of religious change, during times when society is open to considering new imaginal possibilities. But even after a new equilibrium is attained, we may be sure that it will not be perfect, and that religious culture will continue to draw nourishment and validity from its sources in the religious imagination.

NOTES

Acknowledgments. The information on which this study is based was gathered in thirty-two months' ethnographic fieldwork in Ilahita village during the periods 1969–72 and 1985–86. For major funding, I am grateful to the Research School of Pacific Studies, Australian National University, and to the U.S. National Science Foundation. For a supplemental grant-in-aid, I am grateful to the Wenner-Gren Foundation for Anthropological Research. I am also indebted to the following individuals for their criticisms of an earlier version of this paper: Douglas Hayward, Gilbert H. Herdt, Michele Stephen, Daniel Fessler, and Fitz John Poole.

1. This concept, known as "methodological individualism" (Popper 1950, 1957; Agassiz 1960; Runciman 1970), is discussed in more general terms in Tuzin (1976:xxv–xxx).
2. For a masterful examination of the great Turkish leader, Mustafa Kemal Atatürk, in these terms, see Volkan (1981; cf. Volkan and Itzkowitz 1984).
3. More likely, perhaps, the shift in pronunciation comes from a greater familiarity with the written version of the name. I am grateful to David K. Jordan for this suggestion.
4. A woman receives only a clan name, given to her by her father's sister, who, in contrast with male naming practices, continues to use it.

5. Interestingly, a similar notion informs naming practices in Spain and throughout Spanish-speaking Latin America, whereby the law requires that a child's given name be taken from the religious calendar. In the French version, which is somewhat more secular, the Napoleonic Code protects French children from being given frivolous *or non-French* names by the following legal procedure: "Les noms en usage dans les différents calendriers et ceux des personnages connus dans l'histoire ancienne pourront seuls être reçus comme prénoms dans les registres de l'état civil destinés à constater la naissance des enfants, et il est interdit aux officiers publics d'en admettre aucun autre dans leurs actes (L. 11 germinal an XI, 1er avril 1803, art. 1er)."

6. In fairness to Samial, it should be noted that the break in genealogical knowledge seems to have occurred in the preceding generation by virtue of the relatively early death of his father's father and father's mother. In Ilahita, such knowledge rigidly passes from parent to child. Thus, when Ego loses his parents while he (Ego) is still a child, he is unlikely ever to learn of his ancestry, for it is not in anyone else's interests to tell him.

7. See Tuzin (1982:331–332) for a description of this incident.

8. George Devereux's (1980:25) concept of the "deputy lunatic of the group" is useful in understanding the psychosocial processes surrounding the development and applications of Samuel's religious imagination.

9. During the mid-1970s, for example, a series of squabbles caused Ribeka's classificatory brother—the village councillor mentioned earlier—to remove himself and his family to another part of the village. Kumbwiata, on the other hand, had always lived in a different part of the village.

10. This would have been a compelling interpretation: Sali was very prominent in Tambaran affairs, and thus his conversion would have seemed to the "heathens" to have been an especially painful and damaging betrayal.

11. To be exact, Samuel and Ribeka have (as of 1986) two adopted children: a son (b. 1970) given to them by Ribeka's classificatory

brother—the village councillor mentioned early in this chapter—and a daughter (b. 1981), who, as a toddler, had been found abandoned by Ribeka during a revivalist visit she had made to a village nearby. Whereas Samuel is passive toward the children and tolerantly shares his dependency with them, both are doted on and spoiled by Ribeka—to the point where the daughter insists on being carried everywhere, and the son is unruly and enjoys playing off his adopted and natural parents against each other. In any case, at the time of Sali's death Samuel's adopted son would have been only about eight years old.

12. The idea that a tree or post may mark the passage between this and other worlds has traditional precedents. Thus, the *ha'awin* banana plant is viewed as the "door of the dead" (Tuzin 1977:212), and Tambaran spirits are conceived of as passing between their world and ours via the effigy posts of the spirit house (Tuzin 1980:168).

13. Revivalist Christians proscribe funeral tears and virtually all elements of traditional mortuary ceremonialism, on the grounds that such displays of grief sinfully deny the bliss and blessedness the baptized deceased now enjoys. This suppression of the mourning response only serves to intensify and prolong psychological problems of adaptation to the loss of a loved one. In one case that I recall vividly, I went to offer my condolences to an unusually talented and educated forty-year-old man who, one hour before, had found his ancient mother expired in her bed. The death was unexpected, for the old lady was in apparently excellent health and had been her usual jovial self when I had exchanged greetings with her the preceding evening. To my surprise, my friend seemed pleased and exhilarated over his mother's death. Not only was she in Heaven, he crowed, her death would spare him the continued nuisance of having to care for her. After he had calmed down, I asked him to tell me things he remembered about his mother. He described a woman who had been ever loving and caring towards him. When he recalled how, every week during the years he attended Bible school ten miles away, his mother would carry a back-breaking load of yams to him, his

eyes welled with tears. But only for an instant: quickly recovering his chilling ebullience, he again reminded me (and himself) that her death was a good thing for both of them.

14. As part of the religious hysteria that appeared to grip the village during the period of my 1985–86 fieldwork, there was a very great frequency of seemingly psychotic episodes, usually involving sexual (in the case of women) or violent (in the case of men) expressions. These attacks responded well to spiritual ministrations, and thus they provided Samuel and the other Revivalist "healers" with numerous opportunities to demonstrate their God-given powers.

POSTSCRIPT

After this chapter was in proof, I discovered that Young (1988) has described and interpreted a situation in terms nearly identical to those of one of the key episodes presented here. Keyayala is a Kalauna man, who, like Samuel, became mysteriously crippled after the death of his powerful father. Young writes (1988:126),

> As Michael Jackson . . . has shown, an inability to walk is a common if not natural symbol for prevented or delayed succession: Keyayala's excessive filial piety and prolonged post-mortem identification with his powerful father are aptly expressed in the physical imagery of his useless legs. It is quite possible, therefore, that his affliction was psychosomatic and self-induced. Unable fully to succeed his father, Keyayala wanted to regress to the "good times" of his father's protection and provisioning, and much of his behavior can be interpreted as an unconscious desire to annul if not reverse time.

CONCLUSION

Constructing Sacred Worlds and Autonomous Imagining in New Guinea

Michele Stephen

DESPITE the seemingly insurmountable problems in investigating subjective experience cross-culturally—problems so expertly reviewed by Gilbert Herdt in the opening chapter—we will continue to attempt cross-cultural interpretation and comparison. The alternative is to admit not only that anthropology itself is impossible (Spiro 1984), but that communication between members of different cultures is impossible. We will continue to try to understand what is in another person's mind, even though we can never hope to have complete knowledge of this, for the alternative is to abandon any attempt at human understanding. We can only, to turn Evans-Pritchard's (1937) observation concerning the Azande back on ourselves, reason within the framework of concepts available to us. If we are not to abandon all attempts to understand the experience of individuals in other cultures and to trace what is common to human psychological processes in general, then we must be prepared to continually revise our interpretive models as new data becomes available, and in accordance with developments within other disciplines. The contributors to this book have grappled with these problems in their own individual ways to translate subjective experience across formidable cultural divides. The success of their attempts is for others to judge. In this final chapter I will not try to summarize their arguments or classify all the rich variations of religious imagination they depict. Each author must speak for himself or herself.

Instead, I wish to confine the discussion to certain themes and ideas that the concept of autonomous imagination outlined in Part One crystallizes for me. I propose that dreams, waking visions, and many altered states of consciousness—mental events having the appearance of being sensory perceptions of an external, phenomenological world—arise from a subliminal stream of imagery thought. This stream of imagery thought also intrudes upon, and is interwoven into, ordinary waking thought; it is presumed to constitute part of the normal information-processing procedures of the brain. Under specific conditions, such as sensory deprivation and REM sleep, where cortical arousal is high and sensory input low, this stream of imagery may enter consciousness in the form of dreams or waking visions (West 1975; Hartmann 1975; Cartwright 1978; Singer 1976, 1977). The actual process of imaginative construction always remains outside consciousness; but its products, the dream or vision or similar

212 Michele Stephen

experience, may emerge into conscious awareness. I refer to the process of construction as autonomous imagination, and to its products as autonomous imagining.

Autonomous imagining takes many forms, which may be spontaneous, as in dreaming and unsolicited visions, or which may be brought under a certain degree of conscious control, as in hypnosis or controlled spirit mediumship. As a mode of thought, autonomous imagining is characterized by several features clearly distinguishing it from imagination as employed in ordinary waking consciousness (cf. Price-Williams 1987). Not only is the imagery of autonomous imagining experienced as an external, independent reality, but it displays a much greater freedom and richness of imaginative inventiveness, and a different access to memory. Significantly, autonomous imagining is highly responsive to external suggestion and direction, and cultural context. Furthermore, it exerts a special influence over mental and bodily processes outside conscious awareness and volitional control. This unique imaginative mode plays an important role in the construction of sacred realities, not only in Melanesia and other tribal cultures, but in world religious experience.

The contributions to this volume alone would be sufficient to reveal—if it were not already apparent (Stephen 1979)—the importance of dreams, visions, spirit possession, mediumship, and other altered states of consciousness in New Guinea religious experience. Because I propose that religious experience cross-culturally is grounded in the psychological reality of a special imaginative process operating outside ordinary awareness, my view may appear to come very close to the psychoanalytic position that religion is but the product of unconscious fantasy. And this view might be expected to apply with particular force to New Guinea, where the products of unconscious fantasy evidently play so large a part in constructing sacred realities.

Freudian theory maintains that religion is merely illusion, based on unconscious dependency needs, disguised in the symbolic forms of religious belief and ritual (Freud 1927). For Freud, the interests of culture and the hidden desires of the unconscious, represented in the private experience of the individual, are antithetical and necessarily opposed. Gilbert Herdt has shown here—with considerable theoretical daring and novelty—that in fact the two must be seen as inextricably woven together, culture emerging from the deepest emotional needs of the individual person to bridge the gap between self and Other. My view of religion, in consonance with Herdt's arguments, is that religious rituals and symbols are not attempts to disguise, but rather to identify and bring into consciousness, subliminal fantasy—or imagination. Thus, religion can be seen as a means of using and directing to cultural and group ends autonomous imagination and imagining. I wish to use this perspective to reflect upon several important aspects of New Guinea religious experience explored in this volume.

Spirit Mediumship

Bruce Knauft's chapter on Gebusi spirit mediumship provides an unusually fine-grained ethnographic illustration of the distinctive imaginative mode of thought I identify as autonomous imagining. The songs of the spirit medium, which are composed and performed during the night-long séance and serve as the vehicle of the spirit world communications, are evidently the products of a creative, imaginative capacity operating outside conscious awareness and yet responsive to cultural logic and guidance.

These songs contain vital information concerning the community and result in social action by it. They are believed to be the communications of the spirits possessing the medium. Knauft carefully examines the construction of the medium's pronouncement, as woven into the aesthetic form of the spirit song, and comes to the conclusion that conscious manipulation on the part of the medium is not involved. The medium is not consciously aware of having produced the songs or their pronouncements. It is as if there were a special kind of logic operating; as if mediums have developed a subliminal mode of imaginative consciousness that encodes on a meta-level appropriate cultural criteria for acceptable spiritual and social declaration.

The spirit medium seems to be employing a special mode of imagining very similar to that found in the Western context of hypnotic age regression and "reincarnation" experiences (Hilgard 1977; Bowers 1976; Sheehan and McConkey 1982). The medium is complying with external instructions—the cultural expectations surrounding the possessing spirit's performance—and combining material stored in memory concerning social relationships and behavior (but possibly not available in waking consciousness) with imaginative narrative—to create a performance that comes not from his conscious contriving, but from some invisible source—identified as the spirit world. The imaginative feat involved is not inconsiderable, Knauft points out. The medium must invent a hundred or more new songs during the séance, each complying with elaborate aesthetic and cultural conventions. Yet at the end of the night, he emerges "refreshed and ready for a day of full activity," unlike the weary audience who must catch up on their lost sleep.

Does the medium's capacity to produce elaborate imagery in a dissociated state indicate that he is psychotic? Knauft considers that psychodynamic factors are less significant in the performance than the medium's sensitivity to cultural demands, pointing out that the medium's vocation is unmarked by phenomena such as traumatic illness, hysteria, or unsolicited possession.

Yet against this, we should note that the key themes of the séance—sexuality and aggression—even though they are culturally elaborated themes among the Gebusi, are nevertheless ones we might expect to arise from unconscious motivations, or at least to be closely bound up with them. But this is certainly no reason for insisting on the primacy of psychodynamic factors here, rather they seem melded with cultural concerns. Perhaps we can regard the Gebusi medium (and others like him) as a gifted individual, along the lines of the creative artist who can bring into consciousness a subliminal mode of imagery thought and guide it to meet cultural ends?

Certainly he uses this ability on behalf of the group. It is evident the medium plays a crucial role in engaging and guiding the imaginative processes of the audience. The themes of the songs—arising from the autonomous imagery produced by the medium—play on strong emotions. They move, by association, between two apparently opposed extremes: from sexual arousal to sexual longing and frustration, to loneliness and loss of loved ones in death, to death and violence in hunting wild pigs, and then to death in hunting down the cause of loneliness and loss—the sorcerer/witch.[1] Thus, the emotions of the audience are aroused by aesthetic, imaginative means.

It is this fusing of the emotions of the audience with the medium's pronouncement that gives conviction to the latter; the spirit judgment appeals to the emotions of the participants and is emotionally satisfying to them. But there is more than this. The medium's imagery seems to bring about a resolution of conflicts between external, cultural demands that social relationships within the group remain harmonious and subjective emotional pressures for revenge. In the movement of the séance from sexual joking to revenge, the emotional needs for revenge experienced individually by participants are evoked and collectively shaped, then channeled and used in the interests of the group to form the basis of collective community action.

In the aesthetic excitement of such powerful emotions, the psychophysiological processes of the participants may be influenced, as Knauft suggests, activating linkages on a somatic level to heighten the conscious emotional response. This reflects the way in which other processes outside consciousness can be influenced by imagery, and the reciprocal flow between culture and these other levels of individual functioning via autonomous imagination.

We who value rational, conscious thought processes (even if we don't always act upon them!) are likely to feel uneasy about this reliance on a medium's dissociated, hallucinatory state to provide the basis of an important public decision. The Gebusi, presumably, see themselves as relying upon a more powerful Other, much as William James observed that Christian religious experience involves the surrendering of the self to a more powerful other.

Since the matter usually being pronounced upon in the spirit séance is the identification of those responsible for witchcraft/sorcery attacks, what is in fact involved is the identification of negative feelings hidden from conscious awareness. Thus, the subliminal imagery of the medium may provide a most appropriate means of identifying these trends. As we shall now see, witchcraft and sorcery beliefs can be understood as the means of bringing into consciousness subliminal negative fantasies.

Witchcraft and Sorcery

Eytan Bercovich points out in his chapter on Nalumin witchcraft that the classic psychoanalytic view of witchcraft maintains that such beliefs arise out of projected unconscious hostility, thus shielding consciousness from the anxiety caused by ambivalence in close relationships. Yet he shows in his very sensitive analysis of subjective experience that witch beliefs do not really operate as a defense mechanism against ego anxiety for the Nalumin—rather, such beliefs serve to make the individual more aware *consciously* of the possibility of hidden hostility in others and in himself.

The Nalumin witchcraft ideology makes explicit what people everywhere would like to deny—that bitter, destructive urges lie beneath the surface of close relationships. As outside observers versed in theories of unconscious aggression, even we are shocked to find that people believe kin, neighbors, and friends are guilty of horrendous crimes against them, at a hidden level. Perhaps what shocks us is that these beliefs do not disguise the ambivalence in close relationships but rather state it as an existential fact of the human condition, making it a focus of moral and public concern. In Western culture we do repress our negative feelings to those close to us; thus it is particularly offensive—indeed almost incomprehensible—to us that these ambivalences are exposed publicly in sorcery and witchcraft beliefs.

This public recognition of ambivalence makes the Nalumin keenly aware of the consequences of their actions toward others. Each needs to demonstrate that he or she is not a witch, yet inevitably his or her actions will provoke others. As Bercovitch (this volume) puts it, "Everyone must struggle against being identified as a witch." The ideology of witchcraft does not provide the satisfaction of shielding the self from the knowledge of its own destructive impulses, since it serves to focus the individual's attention on the consequences of his or her own negative actions toward others.

The image of the witch might be seen as a projection of unconscious fantasy in the sense that it represents a "throwing before" consciousness of inchoate feelings originating outside ordinary awareness. In focusing public attention on the negative aspects of close relationships, witch beliefs render this an aspect of existence that cannot be ignored or totally repressed, but must be dealt with at a conscious level. This is not to say that this negative element is, or can be, treated in a purely rational way; we are, after all, talking of very powerful emotions. Rather, these negative feelings are dealt with on an imaginative level, worked through in the symbolic imagery of the witch.

Kakar (1983) observes that in traditional Indian healing techniques the symptom tends to be dealt with in the symbolic idiom in which it is expressed. The possessing spirit is exorcised and the patient recovers; instead of attempting, as in psychoanalysis, to translate the unconscious fantasy into rational terms and thus dispel it. It seems to me that we find in witch beliefs a similar pattern.

Imagination, both conscious and outside conscious awareness, works through the negative emotional aspects of human relationships via the symbolic image of the witch.[2] Uncovering the identity of the witch—achieved through involved processes of identification and differentiation—becomes the means of dealing on a *conscious* imaginative level with the consequences of these destructive emotions. This does not rid the community of such feelings, indeed it may exacerbate them, but it does give some definable form to otherwise inchoate and unmanageable passions.[3]

The Witch and Accountability of the Self

The tendency to regard witchcraft and sorcery in Melanesia as a single phenomenon has obscured the wide variety and striking differences in the roles played in Papua New Guinea societies by persons believed to possess mystical powers to harm others (Stephen 1987c). Within this great diversity, I have identified two opposite ends of a spectrum. At one end we find individuals believed to have hidden powers to harm others, who are blamed for death and illness in the community and, on this account, are socially despised and vulnerable to public accusation, exile, or execution. At the opposite end are individuals believed to control mystical means to kill others, who are believed to use their powers on behalf of the community and, on this account, are socially powerful and rewarded for their services. Guided by the labels many ethnographers have used, I have referred to the socially despised and condemned as "witch" and the socially powerful as "sorcerer." Countless variations and permutations ranging between these two extremes are to be found in Melanesia.

Nalumim ideology and social practice, when placed on a continuum ranging from the despised witch to the socially powerful and rewarded sorcerer, closely approaches the negative pole of these two extremes; and in my view represent a classic Melanesian variant of witch beliefs (so do the Gebusi, even though Knauft refers to "sorcery"). The witch is an insider who secretly devours neighbors and kin; and whose monstrous deeds can be stopped only by being publicly identified and executed (though this may be difficult to carry out in practice). Bercovitch's data suggest a further clarification of the distinctions I have tried to draw between the role of witch and sorcerer: the different accountability for self involved.

The nefarious acts of the witch, as Bercovitch reveals, are carried out in the unseen world, through the action of the witch's soul, and it is the soul of the victim that the witch attacks and destroys. Likewise, as I describe in the case of the Mekeo sorcerer (Stephen 1987b), it is the soul of the sorcerer that attacks the soul of the victim. But an important difference exists. Whereas the sorcerer consciously directs the action of the soul to achieve particular ends, the witch does not, but is rather merely the vehicle of the destructive urges of the soul. This is indicated in the common belief in Melanesia, as elsewhere, that the witch is possessed by some evil supernatural entity, and is either consciously unaware of being a witch, or incapable of directing or reversing the destructive effects of the witchcraft (Reay 1987; Riebe 1987). In any event, the witch has no conscious choice but to do evil.

Even witches who can control their powers to the extent of directing them at particular victims (Riebe 1987) cannot reverse their destructive influence and heal the victim, as can the sorcerer. The witch, on the surface an ordinary member of the community, is compelled to perform aggressive and destructive acts by a part of the self outside conscious awareness. Because the witch's actions are determined by unseen forces, not by conscious, human choice, the only way to deal with a witch is to destroy the entity controlling its human host. (Often this requires nothing less than the death of the witch.)

Beliefs in witchcraft and sorcery reveal the powerful negative and destructive influence autonomous imagination may exert, an aspect so formidably chronicled by Freud. The psychoanalytic position asserts that contents of the unconscious represent repressed material originally found in the conscious, it recognizes only the negative influence of this material. The argument put forward here is that a subliminal stream of imagining deals with all incoming experience, though separately and in a different way from conscious thought; it thus must deal with both negative and positive emotions. Since pain, loss, and suffering are so much a part of human existence, autonomous imagining must be occupied with such themes. Indeed, the negative content and influence on consciousness of autonomous imagining makes it at least as important a cultural concern as does its positive influence. This seems especially clear in New Guinea cultures, where so much concern centers upon the dangerous mystical powers exerted by human and supernatural agents (Stephen 1987a)—on the destructive powers of the sacred Other.

Beliefs in witchcraft, in the terms presented here, provide a cultural means of identifying, bringing into awareness, and dealing with imagination operating outside consciousness but exerting a powerful negative influence on it. The cultural symbol of witchcraft provides a collective means of directing and guiding the autonomous imagining of the individual—of providing shared cultural themes for private imaginative elaboration, both in and outside consciousness.

The Shaman

The shaman's powers are characteristically used for healing, and sometimes for more destructive purposes, as Gilbert Herdt's chapter on Sambia shamanism reveals. Shamanic rituals in New Guinea (Herdt 1977; Stephen 1979), as elsewhere (Eliade 1964), involve the inducing of an altered state of consciousness—a dream or waking vision—wherein the shaman's soul goes out in search of the patient's soul in order to retrieve it.

In Part One, I discussed the extensive evidence from Western psychology and clinical practice indicating the powerful therapeutic influence of imagery and imagination (reviewed in Sarbin and Slagle 1979; Singer and Pope 1978b; Schultz 1978). In Western techniques, such as hypnotism and the various guided imagery therapies, the patient is usually encouraged to experience an altered state of consciousness (told to relax, for example), while guided by the suggestions and instructions of the therapist. A contrast, which I think has so far gone unnoticed, is that in shamanism and other traditional healing techniques, it is the healer, not the patient, who induces an altered state in himself, wherein he experiences the healing imagery. This imagery may be acted out in a dramatic performance for the patient and the group, or simply narrated to the patient. Thus, the healing imagery is presented to the consciousness of the patient, but emerges from the altered state of the healer.

The traditional healer attempts to engage his own subliminal stream of imagery to provide a healing symbol. That is to say, he uses his special capacity to bring this imagery into consciousness and use it to a particular end. He employs autonomous imagining so as to connect the external situation of the patient with some imaginatively persuasive imagery or narrative of healing restoration. We saw an example of this in the case of the Mekeo patient whose soul was divined as being trapped in the box of powerful magical relics.

Since the ordinary person is not able to easily bring autonomous imagining into consciousness—witness the few patients with whom hypnosis can be used successfully (Bowers 1976:79–84)—the shaman attempts to perform this service for him, providing imagery that will engage, stimulate, and guide in a positive direction the patient's conscious and subliminal imagining (cf. Lévi-Strauss 1972).

Anthropologists have long insisted that shamanism should not be explained in terms of Western psychopathology, yet the close linkage documented in the ethnographic literature of the shaman's vocation with illness, trauma, and psychic conflict seems hard to overlook (For a review of the literature, see Peters and Price-Williams 1980). What alternate explanation can we offer? Can we perhaps simply regard him as a gifted individual who has access to a special imaginative capacity that he uses on his own behalf, as well as that of the community?

Where the shaman's task is primarily that of healing, it may be that experience of one's own is a most effective way of learning to use autonomous imagining to create healing imagery. Indeed, it appears that the shaman often cures his own ills by learning to bring under a degree of conscious control the action of autonomous imagining (cf. Ellenberger 1970 and the "creative malady"). Psychic conflict may provide a trigger to bring autonomous imagery into consciousness (I will return to this point later). But once the illness is mastered and the conflict resolved, the shaman's visions become a controlled ability he uses on the behalf of others. Moreover, not all shamans come to their vocation through illness, as Herdt (1977) shows here for the Sambia; nor do Mekeo dream diviners and sorcerer/magicians.

Healing imagery may be constructed from imaginative processes, much as we know literary and artistic creations are constructed in such a manner.

The Shaman's Familiar

In focusing on the Sambia shaman's familiar, Gilbert Herdt provides a novel perspective on the shaman's own inner experience. Herdt's sensitive analysis reveals that the shamanic familiar cannot be regarded as a disguise or defense mechanism; rather, it is a subtle representation of certain self-alien aspects of the shaman's inner experience, serving not to hide them from consciousness, but to bring them into the shaman's conscious awareness. This is very similar to Bercovitch's arguments concerning Nalumin witchcraft, with the difference that in the case of witchcraft, only negative feelings and emotions are involved, whereas in the case of the Sambia shaman, both positive and negative aspects of a more powerful Other are at work.

The Sambia familiar seems located somewhere between the soul, *koongu* (which is accepted as part of the self, yet a strangely alien part whose actions and desires may be hidden from conscious thought), and the totally independent spirit world. There is self (*koontu*, conscious thought) and dream self (*koongu*, soul), and allied to this dual self, but distinct from it, is a more powerful entity—the familiar—which guides and assists the dream self in its contacts with the spirit world. This familiar is more powerful than, and more truly part of, the spirit world than the dream self, though it attaches to the dream self in a specially intimate relationship. Ranged along an axis of increasing self-alien inner experience, from what are clearly my own thoughts and desires, to those that seem quite external to self, the Sambia shaman's familiar perhaps provides the point at which, for Sambia, inner experience becomes a world beyond the self, yet still linked to it.

As a more powerful entity than the dream self and capable of aiding and guiding it in the spirit world, the familiar is valued and courted by the shaman, and the special relationship he builds up with it often begins in childhood.

Herdt's description of childhood shamanic experiences is particularly striking in terms of cross-cultural comparisons. The Sambia familiar often emerges as a childhood playmate of the same age, who then develops with the shaman. It has been observed in the psychological literature on Western adults possessing a capacity for vivid imagery experiences, including hypnosis, that they often reported having elaborate childhood experiences of imaginary playmates (Hilgard 1965; J. Hilgard, 1979). But whereas a Western child is taught to outgrow such fantasies, the Sambia child with similar experiences is taught and encouraged to develop his or her capacity into maturity. The relationship with the childhood playmate is fostered until it becomes a powerful helper and guide to the spirit realm.

Sambia evidently regard shamanism as involving a special ability to engage with the powerful images of the spirit realm, and the appearance of the imaginary playmate is one of the first signs that an individual possesses such talent. This sign is encouraged and developed. It is not going too far, I think, to suggest that the familiar is a representation of a unique talent which, like artistic inspiration, is felt to emanate from some powerful Other. The Sambia shaman experiences and represents this talent as his "familiar"—his "daimon," or demon, which, according to the *Concise Oxford Dictionary*, has the meaning in Greek mythology of "attendant or indwelling spirit." And consider the word *genius*, which is usually taken to mean extraordinary intellectual or artistic ability: its first meaning, derived from its Latin origin, is listed as "tutelary spirit of person or place"! These etymologies reveal, as Gilbert Herdt shows in his discussion of the Greek term *psyche*, how the views of the ancient classical world, still underlying our own meanings, may help to illuminate Melanesian concepts of the sacred Other. The shaman's familiar, his daemon or genius, represents aspects of what we would understand as his inner self, but which he experiences as the presence of a more powerful Other.

In contrast to the Nalumin symbol of the witch, which brings into consciousness the individual's buried aggressions and negative feelings toward others, the Sambia familiar brings to consciousness an awareness of greater potentialities within the individual. In Jungian terms the familiar would thus reflect an aspect of the archetype of the Self (Jung 1976).

The narrative of Saku's dream provides an example of a more negative nature, in which the familiar acts to harm someone else, in the shaman's defense. Nevertheless, it reveals that the dream brings to the shaman greater self-awareness. When Saku first had the dream, he was made aware of a desire to hurt his wife, which he may or may not have realized before having the dream. What he did not seem to be aware of at this stage were his aggressive feelings toward his old stepmother. But when he learned she was ill, and that he and his familiars were identified as the cause, then he accepted and recognized that his old aggression was involved. There seemed to be a clear emotional link between recent experience—in which a woman, his wife, belittled him for his physical inadequacies—and more distant childhood experience—in which his step-mother had belittled and maltreated him for much the same reasons. Also in the dream, it is his father and his wife who attacked him, as in the past it was his father and his stepmother who used to ill-treat him. He is perhaps surprised that these old feelings are still so powerful and dangerous, but the identification of his familiar as the culprit revealed to him just how strong these emotions remain—and the need to deal with them at a conscious level by performing a curing ritual for the old woman. Thus, the whole incident is a kind of revelation to him, and an opportunity to bring into consciousness feelings that if not repressed, were at least screened from his awareness.

An important point is raised here about the shaman's responsibility for the actions of the familiar; it relates to points already made concerning the difference between the accountability of the self in the case of the witch and the sorcerer. In common with the sorcerer, and unlike the witch, the Sambia shaman is held responsible for controlling the action of his familiar, and he possesses the capacity to reverse any aggressive action through healing.

Also revealed is a crucial difference between the accountability of the spirit medium and the shaman. In the case of the Gebusi, the medium is considered to have no responsibility whatsoever for the spirit pronouncements. His role is simply to provide a contact with the spirit world by his soul vacating its body so that the spirit woman may use it to communicate directly with the living. As Knauft explains, the medium is not even considered to be present at the séance. The Sambia shaman, however, leaves his body, and through the medium of his own dream self, in the company of his familiar, acts directly upon the spirit world—as does the Mekeo sorcerer. Thus, not only a different accountability is involved, but also a very different relationship to the spirit realm on the part of the human intermediary. Only when we have additional fine-grained descriptions, such as those provided by Knauft and Herdt, will we be able to fully understand the significance of these variations.

The Innovative Prophet

Donald Tuzin's remarkable portrait of Samuel, the Ilahita prophet, reveals the importance of the products of autonomous imagination in situations of religious change. Samuel provides a classic example of the religious prophet who is overtaken by his own autonomous imagery and then gains control of it, using it to create new religious symbols by which to engage the imagination of others.

Samuel is the leader of a Christian ecstatic movement in a community that has only recently rejected the pagan past. His visions and revelations provide the basis of spiritual authority and judgment for the group. In common with the shaman and many innovative prophets (as indicated in the now extensive literature on Melanesian cargo cults), Samuel's vocation stems from an illness suggesting intense psychic conflict. Tuzin carefully examines the role of psychodynamic factors, demonstrating the way in which Samuel's own inner needs and conflicts, related particularly to the deaths of his brothers and father, play a crucial role in the construction of his visions.

Tuzin (this volume) stresses that Samuel possesses the ability to extract from these inner conflicts public symbols that speak to the group. He rejects the notion that Samuel can be regarded as insane, despite the bizarreness of many of his visionary experiences. Nevertheless, he sees Samuel's paralysis as a conversion symptom that primarily serves to disguise from consciousness "the traumatic guilt which, *ex hypothesi*, he felt over the death of his father." Although the paralysis is a remarkable somatization of an internal state, it does much more than shield Samuel's ego from unconscious guilt, and it reveals as much as it conceals.

Samuel is a man physically and temperamentally unsuited to achieving success in the context of traditional Ilahita culture, and he lives in the shadow of successful and powerful brothers. Even so, he does not find it easy to discard the old system in favor of Christianity. His paralysis, he believes, is God's punishment for not resisting the temptation to compete in the traditional context of yam growing and competitive masculinity. His longing for recognition, his ambition to succeed—and presumably win the father's approval—are revealed by his inability to pass up the chance for the prestige his flourishing yam crop might confer on him. Though he knows he lacks the abilities to succeed in the old system, he is unable, consciously, to make a clean break with it. A new Father has called him, but he is unable to give Him complete allegiance.

Then the very day after harvesting the prize yam, Samuel awakes—paralyzed. His decision has now been made for him: he can no longer even try to compete in the traditional context, indeed he can barely survive in it. Moreover, he has been physically and visibly singled out by God's punishment—his own flesh has become a symbol of His power.

The paralysis serves as a symbol connecting Samuel's inner desire to be free of the traditional system to the external fact of a physical disability: *should not compete* is translated into *cannot compete*, thus reconciling the conflict between his two worlds. The father's death triggers emotional responses and patterns grounded in childhood experience and far removed from conscious awareness. Through the combinatory processes of autonomous imagination, these childhood patterns are melded with recent, more conscious, adult experience related to Samuel's moral crisis concerning fear of God's punishment, the difficulty of rejecting traditional values (and fear of the father's punishment), and his desire to realize his potential as a leader and inspirer of men. All these are fused in a dramatic sign that forever cuts him off from the old way and commits him irrevocably to the new. The paralysis becomes both a personal and a public symbol expressing Samuel's changed status as one of the spiritually elect and his utter commitment to the new dispensation. Others do not need to suffer the same fate in order to convert; they have Samuel as their martyr, his patience and forbearance in face of this martyrdom arouses their wonder, admiration, and imagination.

In Samuel's case imaginative processes operating outside conscious awareness have constructed a powerful new synthesis out of personal conflicts, emotions, and strivings. The symbols have transcended their origins (Obeyesekere 1981:192) and have produced a new vision of self—a masterful personality, one whose spiritual authority is recognized by the community as a whole.

In examining the content of Samuel's visions, Tuzin observes the amalgam of inner and outer ideas to be found there. Unconscious motivations and cultural influences, both traditional and Christian, shape these experiences of the sacred Other. Though Tuzin places much stronger emphasis on psychodynamic factors than does Knauft in the case of the Gebusi medium, both seem to be describing very similar imaginative processes. Tuzin, however, implies that conscious rehearsing and retelling of Samuel's experiences have contributed significantly to their present form. Although I think he is correct in drawing attention to the subtle yet pervasive processes of conscious revision, often in response to audience participation (Burridge's [1960] study of the Tangu "myth dream" provides a revealing analysis of this), the combination of elements he describes in Samuel's visions is exactly what we would expect to emerge from autonomous imagining as, for instance, was clearly illustrated in the case of the Gebusi medium and the hypnotic states discussed earlier.

This fusing of inner and outer events is precisely the task of autonomous imagination. It is a process whereby inner states and external events are woven into a third realm—a world imagined, yet one that appears to exist as independently of self as the external, cultural world. It is this capacity that seems to provide the innovative prophet with his vision of a new sacred order. As Samuel's case reveals, he is attempting to deal with the conflict of old and new. He is likely to be alienated from the old system, either consciously or at a deeper level. His autonomous imagining will seek to create some harmony out of the external cultural influence and his inner needs and desires; and the more acute his own inner conflicts, the greater will be this necessity. As an individual who has the special ability to bring his subliminal stream of imagery thought into consciousness, he is able to envision what is taking place there and to communicate to others the new "world as imagined" that he finds there. His bringing into consciousness of this recombination of external, cultural "realities" and internal needs then provides the basis for a new, shared religious symbolism.

We have seen that healing symbols can arise from autonomous imagining and communicate to levels of mind and body outside conscious, volitional control. Religious symbols also seem to follow the same pattern, arising from the autonomous imagery of the prophet and then engaging the imagination of others at a conscious, and presumably also a subliminal, level. As Tuzin observes, "Samuel did their religious imagining for them."

Autonomous imagining provides the vehicle not only for imagination originating outside conscious awareness to shape cultural symbols, but also for cultural symbols to engage and shape deep motivation in individuals. But as yet, the ways in which cultural symbols may influence unconscious processes have hardly been seriously considered, by anthropology or psychology. Nor can we explain why the prophet's imagery communicates to others, any more than we can easily explain why a work of art communicates to others; indeed, perhaps it is even more difficult since with a work of art there are at least technical considerations to take into account in judging it.

Autonomous Imagination and Cultural Innovation

In many respects the role of the prophet is similar to that of the spirit mediums and the shamans described here. For example, the Gebusi medium, the Sambia and Nalumin shamans, the Mekeo dream diviner, and Samuel all employ altered states of consciousness to communicate with the spirit world, and use their powers to very similar ends such as divination, finding lost objects, and healing. But whereas mediums and shamans work within an established symbolic system,[4] the prophet achieves a radical break with the past, revealing a new sacred order of things.

The role of dreams, visions, possession, and ecstasy in New Guinea cargo cults has long been documented, though usually in negative terms implying cultural disintegration and despair—"cargo cult hysteria," the "Vailala Madness" (Worsley 1970). Some time ago (Stephen 1977) I suggested that such phenomena might be better understood as analogous to shamanic ecstasy, wherein direct communication with sacred powers was sought to obtain a new dispensation and a new moral order. I later (Stephen 1979) followed this with the argument that such experiences were an established part of traditional New Guinea religious experience and needed little adaptation to be drawn upon in the crisis created by colonial intrusion and conquest. Given the nature of autonomous imagining as discussed in this volume, it is surely obvious why such experiences should provide a continuing source of cultural creativity and innovation. This creativity, I should emphasize, stems not merely from the indigenous epistemology and cultural valuation of dreams, visions, and other states as sources of divine revelation—something long revealed in Lawrence's (1964) classic study of Melanesian world view and cargoism—but also from the actuality of autonomous imagination as an intrinsic psychological process.

A Special Talent

I was impressed, as I read these case studies, by the sense that shaman, medium, and prophet are individuals who possess a special talent they employ creatively to group ends. Although I consider that autonomous imagination is an intrinsic psychological process existing in all human beings, the ability to gain control over this capacity and use it consciously is a skill not available to all. Rather, as we observe in the case studies, a special talent is indicated, one that enables some individuals to connect with their own subliminal stream of imagery thought and use it to form imagery that communicates to others.

The process seems similar to that of artistic creation. It is one that takes place both inside and outside conscious awareness. (The role of imagery thought produced by unconscious and preconscious processes in artistic and scientific creativity is a theme that has had a long history, ever since Freud [1908]; see Koestler 1964; Rothenberg 1979; Bowers 1984; Bowers and Bowers 1979.) Healing imagery, spirit world pronouncements, and images of a new moral order seem to arise from the autonomous imagining of the creative individual. The construction of this imagery takes place outside consciousness; it then emerges into awareness, where it may undergo conscious reshaping (as in the case of Samuel's visions). Shaman or prophet then communicates the imagery to the community—presents it to the conscious thought and awareness of patient or audience, thus stimulating group imagination on conscious and, presumably, unconscious levels.

It is well established in Western psychology that imagery and imagination can in fact influence mental and even physical processes outside conscious awareness and control (Sarbin and Slagle 1979; Bowers 1976; Singer and Pope 1978b). We can, therefore, be fairly certain that the imagery of the shaman and prophet does communicate to, and influence, the audience at levels deeper than purely conscious ones. What we do not understand are the psychological and neurophysiological processes behind it. But one thing seems clearly indicated: the involvement of strong emotion and feeling. We are not dealing here with images or symbols that communicate precise, unambiguous cognitive information, but with the arousal and direction of strong emotion. This is most clearly illustrated in Bruce Knauft's analysis of the Gebusi séance and in the conversion experience of the prophet Samuel, the dream of the Sambia shaman, Saku, and in Nalumin witchcraft beliefs. The communication involved in the shaman and medium's imagery seems to take place primarily via emotion and feeling.

Gender and Autonomous Imagining

My argument that shamans, mediums, and prophets possess a particular talent for autonomous imagining also raises certain issues related to the gender of such persons. Herdt notes (Part Two, this volume) the prominence of Sambia female shamans in a culture dominated by a strongly masculine ethos, familiar in many New Guinea cultures, where women in most contexts are seen as inferior to men. Despite certain disadvantages under which female shamans must operate, some Sambia women become great shamans. A quick review of the literature would soon reveal the prominence of women as mediums and sha- mans in many New Guinea societies (Stephen 1979; Wagner 1972), nor are women prophets lacking in Melanesia (Stephen 1977; Lawrence 1964; Burridge 1960; Trompf 1977; Worsley 1970). A similar prominence of females in such roles is found cross-culturally (Lewis 1971; Bourguignon 1973).

The association of "ecstatic religions" (Lewis 1971) with peripheral groups in society has made the connection between women and roles involving ecstatic performance appear to be a function of women's peripheral and disadvantaged role in male-dominated societies. Thus, possession, shamanic ecstasy, medium- ship, and the like are seen as protests or socially sanctioned outlets for feminine discontent. This association joins the argument that new religious movements, characterized by ecstatic experiences, begin as protests against some existing or intrusive power, for example, New Guinea cargo cults as protests against colo- nial exploitation (Worsley 1970).

Yet here among the male-dominated Sambia, we find women assuming positions that amount to the central spiritual authorities recognized by the cul- ture. My intention is merely to draw attention to the fact of women's promi- nence in such roles in New Guinea, and to suggest that perhaps a talent for autonomous imagining is so valued in New Guinea cultures that individuals possessing it may achieve prominence despite their sex. It is only when we rec- ognize the existence of this capacity that such an argument makes sense.

The Concept of the Soul

The concept of the soul connects the phenomena discussed so far. It is the soul of the shaman that journeys into the spirit world and retrieves the soul of the patient, thus curing him. It is the soul of the prophet Samuel that experi- ences the dreams and visions that bring him knowledge of the sacred realm. It is through the soul's leaving the Gebusi medium's body, that a spirit woman is able to possess his body and speak through it. And in witchcraft (Stephen 1987c), as in sorcery, it is the soul of the witch that attacks the soul of the vic- tim. Among the Mekeo, magic in general operates through the action of the soul of the magician on the soul or image of the subject.

All persons, through the medium of their soul, exist partly in the hidden, incorporeal realm of sacred powers. And it is through the actions of his or her soul that the person gains knowledge of and access to these powers, both cre- ative and destructive. Gaining control over the soul enables the shaman, the ma- gician, the prophet, the diviner to gain direct knowledge of the hidden world, through dreams and visions, and to act upon the souls of others in the hidden world, either destructively, as in sorcery or constructively as in healing.

The Soul and Defining the Sacred Other

In discussing the concept of "waking dreams," Price-Williams (1987) has recently raised the question of how sacred worlds revealed in dreams and other altered states of consciousness are emically distinguished from ordinary, waking experience. The concept of the soul may provide an important clue here. In my chapter on the Mekeo concept of the soul, I observe that for Mekeo the special nature of the events of the dream world are very clearly marked off from events in waking experience by representing the events of the dream as the actions of the soul. Likewise, the appearance in waking experience of an autonomous image lacking bodily substance—for example, a reflection or shadow, or a ghost—is also clearly demarcated by referring to such an image by the same term that is used for the soul—lalauga. Gilbert Herdt notes a similar distinction among the Sambia. A brief perusal of Frazer's (1913) often devalued but still classic study, *The Golden Bough,* will soon reveal how widespread such distinctions are cross-culturally. The point remains to be established by careful comparative research, but my guess is that the concept of the soul, world-wide, serves to discriminate between the "realities" of what our culture categorizes as inner and outer experience. It thus represents an important epistemological distinction between different realms of experience.

Soul, Self, and the Unconscious

It is pointed out in the case of the Gebusi, the Ilahita, the Nalumin, the Sambia, and the Mekeo that even ordinary people are believed to have some access and knowledge of the spirit world in their dreams, but this knowledge is hazy and incomplete compared with the insight of the medium or prophet. All people, however, are subject to the influence of the events experienced by their soul in the hidden world, even though most of them are not aware of what is transpiring there. It is because these hidden events are believed to exert such an important influence on the ordinary conscious experience of everyone that the insight of the medium and the shaman is so vital to the community.

The preceding chapters have revealed several striking parallels between Western psychological concepts of an unconscious mind and Melanesian religious notions of an invisible realm of creative and destructive forces that powerfully influences ordinary existence (see also Herdt 1987d).

Bercovitch (this volume) in his study of Nalumin witchcraft observes:

Ultimately, the opposition of the unconscious and conscious is at the center of Freud's theory. Consciousness is achieved only by the initial suppression of most of the contents of the unconscious, but the unconscious nevertheless reenters the area of consciousness by concealing itself in other forms. In a strikingly similar way, the Nalumin place much emphasis on the existence of forces and facts that are hidden to ordinary perception and consciousness but which reenter the visible world with significant effect.

In my chapter on the Mekeo concept of the soul, I drew out the similarities between two Western theories of the unconscious mind, those of Freud and Jung, and the folk notion of the soul. The Mekeo concept of soul is not an artifact of metaphysical speculation; it describes a very concrete awareness of another self existing outside conscious awareness. Despite the very obvious differences to be found, the Mekeo concept and Western theories of the unconscious are different kinds of descriptions of the same empirical phenomena—the effects on consciousness of imagination operating outside conscious awareness. In the case of the folk concept, however, the means of identifying, describing, and attempting to deal with this imaginative process is couched in the same metaphoric mode as that in which it is manifested. Gilbert Herdt's discussion of the Sambia soul and of the Ancient Greek notion of *psyche* reveals the importance of the concept in the defining of self in relation to others, but also in representing self to self. In a similar way, I have emphasized Mekeo ideas of the soul as conceptualizations of certain alien aspects of self. These chapters reveal, I think, the impossibility of understanding New Guinea concepts of self and person without attention to the notion of soul.

Perhaps due to the excessive interest in animism in late nineteenth-century and early twentieth-century anthropology, the soul is a concept given little attention today. Herdt notes that where the term is used, it seems generally assumed that its meaning needs little translation across cultures, and that it is at least analogous to the Christian theological notion of a metaphysical entity surviving death (though see Basso 1987). Freudian interpretations (La Barre 1972) maintain that beliefs in the soul represent unconscious inability to accept the painful reality of death.

The ethnographic evidence of the previous chapters, drawn from several very different New Guinea cultures, clearly reveals that the Melanesian concept of the soul relates not primarily to hopes or concern with survival after death, but to the influence on conscious experience of emotions, desires, and forces—positive and negative—belonging to another self hidden from ordinary awareness. As such, it more closely resembles the Freudian unconscious than a supernatural entity, even though the Freudian viewpoint would contest this. The notion of the soul identifies powerful forces outside, but influencing, conscious awareness, and provides the conceptual basis for the cultural means of dealing with them. Witchcraft, sorcery, shamanic healing, magic, and divination can all be seen not as symbolic disguises of unconscious desires but as culturally developed techniques to deal with these forces outside consciousness and put them to conscious use. They are the means with which to identify and deal with the effects of autonomous imagination and imagining, and of using this capacity to group ends.

The soul is clearly a concept of central importance, which we can no longer afford to ignore. One might even say that New Guinea religion is in truth a folk psychology, a means of knowing and guiding the psyche or soul, of alleviating suffering and healing, and leading to greater self knowledge and awareness. New Guinea cultures, as revealed in the pages of this book, seem possessed of a very acute awareness that the self of waking conscious thought is but one aspect of the larger totality of one's being.

Certain folk categories have usually been given one of two mutually exclusive interpretations. Either they have been regarded as purely religious beliefs—i.e., cultural constructions having no basis in empirical reality, the concept of soul, for example, or they have been explained as symptoms of psychological conflict, such as witchcraft. They might, however, be better understood as cultural means of identifying and dealing with what psychoanalysis refers to as unconscious fantasy processes and their effects on consciousness. That is to say, the sacred Other—the invisible realm believed to crucially influence mundane existence in New Guinea, and indeed most human, cultures—is culturally constructed, but from the psychological reality of autonomous imagination.

Emotional Coding and Autonomous Imagination

At this point I would like to return to the general theoretical concerns with which we started, taking up an issue raised earlier in this chapter relating to the communication of imagery via emotion and feeling. It is evident that a very broad generality of pattern is to be observed in New Guinea in spirit mediumship, shamanism, the innovative prophet, witchcraft and sorcery, and the soul concept. The ethnographic chapters of this book are grounded in fine-grained cultural description and analysis; their aim is to reveal the cultural particularity and richness of the religious beliefs and rituals they examine. Yet out of this close attention to cultural particularity and nuance of meaning emerges a similarity in pattern that is recognizable not only across Melanesian cultures, but very widely indeed across a broad spectrum of tribal and other cultures. The Gebusi medium, the Sambia shaman, the Nalumin witch, and Samuel, the Ilahita prophet, are, in all their individuality, familiar to us from countless similar figures chronicled in the comparative literature—likewise the soul concept, which, in the New Guinean cultures described here, can be shown to link all these phenomena. Since many readers will be familiar with the comparative literature, the point need not be labored.

Such a broad similarity in pattern indicates the existence of some psychological universals underlying cultural variation. My arguments here, however, have emphasized that the unconscious does not determine culture, nor does culture determine it; but that via autonomous imagination, the deepest emotional needs of the individual contribute to culture, while at the same time are shaped by it. Autonomous imagining, which is sensitive to both external, cultural influence and inner forces acting on the individual, serves to adjust and harmonize these inner and outer worlds. The implication is that, as a psychological process, it has this function. I wish to add some final—and highly conjectural—points in support of this view.

The information-processing model of hallucinatory experiences outlined earlier proposes that the stream of subliminal imagery is related in some non-specified way to the brain's information-processing procedures—imagery presumably being coded differently from other types of information (see Singer and Pope 1978b:8–10). My hunch is that its function is related to the coding of information according to emotional significance. This would involve coding incoming information in relation to existing emotional configurations and modifying existing configurations to include new information.

It is evident that in the enormously complex linkages of associations in the human brain, emotions play a highly prominent role. Unfortunately, emotion has as yet received very little attention from experimental psychology (Taylor 1979), and the layman is left with little more than common sense as a guide. It is evident that we associate things not just because of similarities of structure, nature, function, or any other rationally determined property, but also according to similarities in the emotions invoked in us by things—even despite their utter disparity in every other respect. For example, word association tests indicate the intense links between stored information and emotions (Dixon 1971, 1981). Emotions are linked to words, to images, to smells; it is this linkage that gives poetry its evocative quality. All art presumably rests in some large measure on the linkage of emotions with specific images, events, and symbols. All stored information must be linked in some way to emotion, and there must be functional reasons for this. I am referring not only to basic instinctual drives but to all the complex emotions that our culture teaches us to discriminate. Furthermore, emotions are clearly linked to somatic processes (Nemiah 1984; Dixon 1981; Sarbin and Slagle 1979); it is now well established that strong emotions immediately produce somatic effects.

We can assume that there must exist a process of information storage and sorting in the mind involving not only associational linkage between separate units of information, but the linking of all information with emotional responses (cf. Dixon 1981:121–131). Emotions may be, in functional terms, an alternative to rationality as a way of knowing, deciding, what is good or bad for the organism (D'Andrade 1984). In human beings the cultural elaboration of emotions is such that highly intricate patterns of linkage must be involved. Autonomous imagination may thus be the first level of mental processes linking incoming data to existing emotional coding, and revising existing emotional configurations in accordance with new experience and information. (Along

Janet's line of argument, there must be some agency composing the emotional and cognitive configuration which is the self [Perry and Laurence 1984:9ff]).

These processes would help to explain the flow of associations in dreams. The dream may represent an attempt to relate new information and experience to emotionally laden past experience stored in memory—perhaps material that is too difficult to accommodate quickly and easily.[5] (Many of the information-processing theories of dreams seem to come close to this argument; for example, Cohen 1979:126–134; Cartwright 1978:74–81; Fishbein 1981; Evans 1983) There is unlikely to be any neat, mechanical matching of emotionally significant material—squares with squares and rectangles with rectangles—but rather some extremely subtle process of combination, comparison, and selection will be required. Because animals also possess emotions, though less differentiated ones, this line of reasoning could take into account the probability that animals dream (Cohen 1979; Jones 1976), since the animal brain also needs to relate incoming data to emotional responses. Dreaming may be an important part of the mammalian brain's procedures for linking sensory data in associational chains with emotional responses. This would correlate with the large amount of time spent in REM sleep by the neonate, and with the theory that the limbic area of the brain—associated with the emotions—is activated in REM sleep (Cohen 1979; Jones 1976).

In the case of the human individual, the creation of emotional responses clearly involves a lengthy developmental sequence. What emotional configurations eventually emerge in the adult person will depend on individual experience, cultural learning, and the inherent structures of the human mind (the basic emotional and instinctual responses, whatever these may be). Freud provides a mapping of some of the basic stages of emotional development that all human beings, because of the nature of human biology and growth, must pass through. The various stages of psychosexual development that Freud (1938a) poses—oral, anal, phallic, and genital—are arguably stages that children universally must pass through on the way to sexual maturity. Each stage is to be achieved and then superseded through the exploring and elaborating of incoming sensory data in relation to its affectual loading.

In the course of constructing each stage of psychosexual development through subconscious imaginative elaboration, there is always the possibility that the process will go astray; a particular stage of development may become difficult to leave because it has become the focus of engrossing fantasy, and thus the individual may become fixated at a particular stage. The course of progress will also be affected by the cultural influence on the child and the symbolic guidelines the culture provides for its fantasy life (cf. Bettelheim 1978). Psychoanalysis may be correct in asserting that all our emotional life stems from these psychosexual roots and the pleasure and pain that they bring. But it is evident that the emotional life of the adult is very complex and changing. The feelings and emotions of any individual must be organized on the basis of infinitely intricate schemata to which culture has contributed a large part, since it is evident from the findings of cultural anthropology (Shweder and Levine 1984), as discussed in Part One by Gilbert Herdt, that our emotions are shaped by our culture, as are the overt expressions of them.

These multiple emotional schemata must somehow be built from and differentiated from the basic emotional responses of the infant. The process continues into adulthood, though some individuals, due to their life experience, may continue to develop new patterns in ways not necessary for others. Presumably, the basic patterns are laid down in childhood, and later development will be modification rather than radical reorganization. Yet it would seem that parenthood, the realizing or failure to realize life ambitions, loneliness, old age, and fear of approaching death would represent important stages for new formations. Erikson (1965) and others have investigated adult development. Jung and his followers have, in fact, been far more concerned with adult than infant and childhood experience. Jung (1978), for example, has shown the importance of religious symbols, and images arising spontaneously in dreams and visions, in reconciling the outer, physical reality of the inevitability of death with the individual's inner, emotional difficulty in accepting an end to self.

Anthropological studies have paid comparatively little attention to these later developmental sequences, but their significance is beginning to come to the attention of Melanesianists. Donald Tuzin has recently suggested to me that male initiation ritual needs to be examined from the point of view of the initiators, the adult men, and the psychological significance of the ritual for them. Even more recently, very similar arguments concerning the role of initiation in dealing with father's jealousy of son have been raised by Hans Brocke (Hamburg University, personal communication).

In the imaginative elaboration of adult emotional schemata, things may go wrong, just as in childhood development. Parenthood, for example, must involve the development of new emotional patterns, and it would be very naive to assume that only instinctual responses are involved. In suggesting that autonomous imagination plays an important role in the process, serving to harmonize outer events and inner feelings, I am not implying that such accommodation is automatic, or always successful. Each stage will involve the development of new needs and desires, which may create inner conflict; one must envision a new or different self at each stage, from vigorous young adulthood through old age. Evidently, some individuals fail to develop the emotional configurations their culture expects of adults. People who undergo unusual or traumatic life experiences may display novel emotional configurations, since their experience disrupts existing patterns of response (Wallace 1972 puts forward a similar argument about cultures as a whole). But they may also be destroyed by them. It is perhaps not surprising that the vocations of the shaman and the religious prophet may often grow out of mastering some "creative illness" (Ellenberger

1970) or personal crisis, whereas the less resilient person, unable to achieve a new emotional and psychic integration, becomes, and remains, sick.

In the case of certain creative individuals who are able to bring their own personal reintegrative symbols—constructed by autonomous imagination—into consciousness, and then give them some concrete form in a religious revelation, a healing symbol, or even a work of art, these private images may become the basis of shared cultural symbols (as Obeyeskere 1981 has revealed in his studies of Sri Lankan prophets) helping others to reintegrate their inner and outer worlds. But how do these private imaginings succeed in communicating to others? I raised this question earlier when I suggested that the imagery of the shaman, the medium, and the prophet seem to communicate to others primarily via emotion and feeling. We can now take this position a little further. If my hunch about emotional coding of information is correct, then we can understand more precisely how this imagery might be connected by a logic of emotion and feeling, a logic of feeling meaningful to other members of the same culture. It is the genius of the artist and the prophet that they can employ autonomous imagining to construct fantasies with emotional relevance to other members of their culture, and in some cases much more widely than this.

I propose that all experience and information stored in memory is linked not only by cognitive pathways of association, but by emotional linkages as well, connecting otherwise unrelated information. Information provided by culture, personal experience, and even information not available to conscious awareness, is linked via emotional significance. A specific image may thus serve to activate such a chain of associations, moving through each of these levels, and produce an emotional response in the individual that may be inexplicable even to him or her. This emotional linkage seems strikingly illustrated in the case of the prophet Samuel and the symbol of his paralysis, which had so many different components of emotional significance, including childhood and adult experience. As a personal symbol, Samuel's paralysis fused a whole range of prior experiences and transformed them into a new, positive emotional and spiritual orientation. The Gebusi séance provides another clear illustration of what I mean. In the séance the audience's emotions are aroused and directed by playing upon certain imagery themes produced by the medium in his songs. Here a number of apparently unrelated contexts of experience—ribald sexual joking leading to serious pronouncement and community revenge—are linked through feelings of frustration and loss. Knauft's analysis reveals the cultural differences involved in structuring such emotional chains, the specific cultural experience (for example, marriage patterns) that underlies the associations. As outsiders, we can recognize the 'logic' of the linking emotions only when the cultural experience giving rise to them is outlined for us. In situations where the contexts of cultural experience were less dissimilar, the emotional connections might be more clear.

By this line of reasoning, cultural symbols, in the sense used here, might be regarded as objectifications of emotional complexes (chains of emotionally linked associations), which need to be read not so much for the cognitive information that they carry (contrast Leach 1976), as for the feelings they evoke in the members of a particular culture. Gilbert Herdt's discussion of Abelam art in Chapter 1 speaks to this issue.

Finally, if subconscious imaginative processes do in fact help to create our emotional schemata and responses, it becomes understandable that intervening in their operation—as in therapy or traditional healing—by providing guides to change their direction or content, can bring about emotional and motivational, and even somatic, change in the individual.

Conclusion

Although it would be comfortable to sit back and let psychological experts provide the psychological theories we need to deal with cross-cultural phenomena, a valuable contribution of cultural anthropology has been to demonstrate the extent to which human experience at every level is shaped by culture. The concept of self, the nature of emotions, the modes of consciousness, the definitions of psychopathology—all have been shown to vary widely across cultures. Only by understanding what is culturally particular can we discover what is universal in the operation of the human mind, thus anthropological studies of psychological phenomena remain essential.

In challenging here certain aspects of psychoanalytic theory, I do not seek to dismiss or totally reject it. My position is that Freud's concepts should be used as a set of brilliant insights into the role of imagination outside consciousness from which we still have a great deal to learn. In common with the other contributors to this volume, I reject any rigid imposition of this theory on the ethnographic data. Anthropology also has much to learn from the insights of Jung and others who have explored more positive aspects of the imaginal realm (cf. Tedlock 1987b; Basso 1987), but we need to avoid doctrinaire commitment to a particular theory. A theme implicitly and explicitly taken up in this volume is the need to reassess existing theories of mind against the cross-cultural data.

Nor is my intention here, in using information-processing models of imagery thought, to reduce religion merely to information processing. Rather, my argument is that autonomous imagination fulfills our need as human beings for a harmony between our external, culturally constructed worlds and our internal worlds of emotion and feeling. Indeed, the one is inevitably shaped by the other as each individual develops from infancy to maturity.

Religion and other cultural symbols provide the means of guiding this process in particular directions. The responsiveness of autonomous imagining to external guidance seems to indicate its need for such guidance, or perhaps can be seen as a necessity for the existence of culture, since without it our inner realities would be ever impervious to cultural influence. Our basic need as human beings for stimulation and guidance of this capacity is perhaps also reflected in the ready acceptance of exotic cults and religions in Western culture today. As Jung (1978) and others have pointed out, a humanistic, rationalist morality appeals to reason and consciousness, but not to the imagination; thus in the West, with the decline of traditional religion, it must turn elsewhere for sustenance.

Geertz (1973:112) observes that in religious symbols and ritual, "the world as lived and the world as imagined . . . turn out to be the same world." The sacred "world as imagined" arises from the autonomous imagination of creative individuals. Its imaginative products, having been brought into conscious awareness, are then fashioned—through sharing and discussion with others, and through conscious revision and shaping—into group symbols. In turn, these shared symbols influence and guide the private fantasies, dreams, and autonomous imaginings of us all, so that, imperceptibly, our individually imagined worlds merge into one.

The ethnographic data discussed here and in the various chapters of this book underline the need to recognize and explore the positive and negative influences of imaginative processes outside conscious awareness. In stressing its creative capacity, however, I do not assert that all creativity stems from autonomous imagining; neither do I mean to dismiss the creative function of consciously exercised imagination, nor denigrate the power of rational thought to create and innovate. My argument is that it represents a different sort of creativity, one not available in ordinary consciousness, and one that seems to come from a source outside the self, thus giving it a special experiential quality that is valued in particular contexts—religious, therapeutic, and artistic. The creativity of rational thought is directed at solving problems presented by external, culturally constructed reality. Autonomous imagining is directed primarily at harmonizing inner and outer worlds; it aims for a balance of feeling.

As Herdt argues in Part One, every individual must create his or her own cultural world through the processes of imagination. Evidently, imagination operating both inside and outside conscious awareness is involved in the constructing of self and other—and sacred Other. Here I have stressed the part played by autonomous imagining, going so far as to suggest that it helps to form the individual's basic patterns of emotional response, and therefore his or her very experience of self.

NOTES

Acknowledgments. I am indebted to Gilbert Herdt for his careful reading and thoughtful comments on several drafts of this chapter, and for his many valuable contributions to the ideas developed in it. I am also grateful to Donald Tuzin for his very helpful comments on the final draft. And I thank all the authors of this volume for their insights and data, which informed my arguments and clarified many issues for me.

1. In my view (Stephen 1987c) "witchcraft," not "sorcery," is a more appropriate description of the phenomena involved here, and one more in keeping with the usual anthropological usage and understanding of these terms. The fact that there is no complete agreement on the definition of these terms (by no means an unusual state of affairs in anthropology or any other discipline), does not obviate the fact that *witch* has been used to denote totally negative images of all that is rejected by self and society, whereas the term *sorcerer* has a double aspect to it, implying power and influence along with a capacity to harm. As long as Melanesianists refuse to distinguish between these gradations of meaning, and insist on placing indiscriminately into the same category the diverse phenomena to be found in Melanesia, we will continue to talk at cross purposes with each other and with ethnographers dealing with other culture areas. And we will certainly fail to understand on a comparative basis the significance—social-structural, cultural, and psychological—of the many modalities of supernatural powers to cause harm that are found in Melanesia.

2. In the Melanesian literature, the emphasis has been almost exclusively on the sociological aspects of witchcraft and sorcery (Stephen 1987c).

3. What, one can only wonder, might be the effects of focusing on this negative aspect in consciousness—does this tend to shape the unconscious fantasy of individuals? This is a problem for future studies to take up.

4. The medium and shaman may be responsible for innovation in certain circumstances; see for example, Schieffelin 1977.

5. In dreams recent sensory data, the "day-residue," evokes past experience stored in memory, but possibly not available to conscious recall. The two or more layers of stored experiences are combined with each other (combinations not restricted by the possibilities of external, cultural reality) in an attempt to establish the appropriate relationship between the new material and existing schema. Perhaps, in the process, a means to resolve the emotions carried by the new material will emerge. Alternatively, the new material may be impossible to link to existing schema. Rivers's (1923) theory of trauma dreams, based on his treatment of shell-shocked soldiers during World War I, comes to mind here. Trauma dreams are recurring nightmares involving the reliving in dream of some actual traumatic experience. In such cases the emotions aroused by some recent experience are so intense that they cannot be integrated into existing emotional configurations, and are therefore experienced again and again in an attempt to finally integrate them.

Bibliography

AGASSIZ, JOSEPH. 1960. Methodological Individualism. *British Journal of Sociology* 11(3): 244–270.

ALLEN, MICHAEL R. 1967. *Male Cults and Secret Initiations in Melanesia*. Melbourne: Melbourne University Press.

———. 1984. Homosexuality, Male Power, and Political Organization in North Vanuatu: A Comparative Analysis. *Ritualized Homosexuality in Melanesia* (G. Herdt, ed.), pp. 83–127. Berkeley: University of California Press.

ASERINSKY, E. and N. KLEITMAN. 1953. Regularly Occurring Periods of Eye Motility, and Concomitant Phenomena, During Sleep. *Science* 118:273–274.

AUSTIN, JOHN. 1962. *How to Do Things with Words*. Cambridge: Cambridge University Press.

BAKAN, P. 1978. Two Streams of Consciousness: A Typological Approach. *The Power of Human Imagination: New Methods in Psychotherapy* (J. L. Singer and K. S. Pope, eds.), pp. 159–184. New York and London: Plenum Press.

BALIKI, ASEN. 1963. Shamanistic Behavior among the Netsilik Eskimos. *Southwestern Journal of Anthropology* 19:380–396.

———. 1970. *The Netsilik Eskimo*. Garden City, NY: Natural History Press.

BANTON, MICHAEL, ed. 1966. *Anthropological Approaches to the Study of Religion*. London: Tavistock.

BARBER, T. X. 1979. Suggested ("Hypnotic") Behaviour: The Trance Paradigm Versus an Alternate Paradigm. *Hypnosis: Developments in Research and New Perspectives* (E. Fromm and R. E. Shor, eds.), pp. 217–271. New York: Aldine.

BARBER, T. X., N. P. SPANOS, and J. F. CHAVES. 1974. *Hypnosis, Imagination and Human Potentialities*. New York: Pergamon Press.

BARON, R. A. 1980. Aggression. *Comprehensive Textbook of Psychiatry*, 3d. ed., vol. 1. (H. I. Kaplan, A. M. Freedman, and B. J. Sadock, eds.). Boston: Williams and Wilkins.

BARTH, FREDRIK. 1975. *Ritual and Knowledge among the Baktaman of New Guinea*. New Haven: Yale University Press.

———. 1987. *Cosmologies in the Making: A Generative Approach to Cultural Variation in Inner New Guinea*. Cambridge: Cambridge University Press.

BASSO, E. 1987. The Implications of a Progressive Theory of Dreaming. *Dreaming: Anthropological and Psychological Interpretations* (B. Tedlock, ed.), pp. 86–104. Cambridge: Cambridge University Press.

BATESON, GREGORY. 1936. *Naven*. Cambridge: The University Press.

———. 1958. *Naven: A Study of the Problems Suggested by a Composite Picture of a Culture of a New Guinea Tribe Drawn from Three Points of View*, rev. ed. Palo Alto: Stanford University Press.

———. 1973. *Steps to an Ecology of Mind: Collected Essays in Anthropology, Psychiatry, Evolution and Epistemology*. London: Paladin or Ballantine.

———. 1976. Some Components of Socialization for Trance. *Socialization as Cultural Communication* (Theodore Schwartz, ed.), pp. 51–63. Berkeley: University of California Press.

———. 1978. Towards a Theory of Cultural Coherence: Comment. *Anthropological Quarterly* 51:77–78.

BEATTIE, JOHN and JOHN MIDDLETON, eds. 1969. *Spirit Mediumship and Society in Africa*. New York: Africana.

BECKER, ERNEST. 1973. *The Denial of Death*. New York: Free Press.

BECKER, HOWARD S. 1963. *Outsiders: Studies in the Sociology of Deviance*. New York: Free Press.

BEEK, ALBERT GOSEWIGN VAN. 1987. The Way of All Flesh: Hunting and Ideology of the Bedamini of the Great Papuan Plateau (Papua New Guinea). Ph.D. diss., University of Leiden.

BELLAH, ROBERT N. et al. 1985. *Habits of the Heart: Individualism and Commitment in American Life*. Berkeley: University of California Press.

BENEDICT, RUTH. 1934. *Patterns of Culture*. Boston: Houghton Mifflin.

———. 1946. *The Chrysanthemum and the Sword*. Boston: Houghton Mifflin.

BERNSTEIN, M. 1965. *The Search for Bridey Murphy*. New York: Doubleday.

BETTELHEIM, BRUNO. 1978. *The Uses of Enchantment: The Meaning and Importance of Fairy Tales*. Harmonsworth: Penguin.

———. 1984. *Freud and Man's Soul*. New York: Vintage Books.

BLOCH, MAURICE. 1973. Symbols, Song and Dance, and Features of Articulation. *European Journal of Sociology* 15:55–81.

———. 1986. *From Blessing to Violence: History and Ideology in the Circumcision Ritual of the Merina of Madagascar*. Cambridge: Cambridge University Press.

BOURGUIGNON, ERIKA. 1968. World Distribution and Patterns of Possession States. *Trance and Possession States* (R. Prince, ed.). Montreal: R. M. Bucke Memorial Society.

———. 1972. Dreams and Altered States of Consciousness in Anthropological Research. *Psychological Anthropology* (F.L.K. Hsu, ed.), pp. 403–434. Cambridge, MA: Schenkman.

———, ed. 1973. *Religion, Altered States of Consciousness, and Social Change*. Columbus: Ohio State University Press.

———. 1976. The Effectiveness of Religious Healing Movements: A Review of Recent Literature. *Transcultural Psychiatric Research Review* 13:5–21.

———. 1979. *Psychological Anthropology: An Introduction to Human Nature and Cultural Differences*. New York: Holt, Rinehart and Winston.

BOUTILIER, J. A., D. T. HUGHES, and S. W. TIFFANY, eds. 1978. *Mission, Church, and Sect in Oceania*. Lanham, MD: University of America Press.

BOWERS, K. S. 1976. *Hypnosis for the Seriously Curious*. Monterey, CA: Brooks/Cole.

———. 1984. On Being Unconsciously Influenced and Informed. *The Unconscious Reconsidered* (K. S. Bowers and D. Meichenbaum, eds.), pp. 227–272. New York: John Wiley and Sons.

BOWERS, P. G. and K. S. BOWERS. 1979. Hypnosis and Creativity: A Theoretical and Empirical Rapprochement. *Hypnosis: Developments in Research and New Perspectives* (E. Fromm and R. E. Shor, eds.), pp. 351–379. New York: Aldine.

BOWERS, K. S. and D. MEICHENBAUM, eds. 1984. *The Unconscious Reconsidered*. New York: John Wiley and Sons.

BOWLBY, JOHN. 1969. *Attachment and Loss*, vol. 1: Attachment. New York: Basic Books.

BROWN, MICHAEL F. 1988. Shamanism and Its Discontents. *Medical Anthropology Quarterly* 2:102–120.

BROWN, ROGER and JAMES KULIK. 1982. Flashbulb Memories. *Memory Observed* (Ulric Neisser, ed.), pp. 23–40. New York: W. H. Freeman.

BURRIDGE, KENELM O. L. 1960. *Mambu: A Melanesian Millennium*. London: Methuen.

———. 1969. *Tangu Traditions*. Oxford: Clarendon Press.

CAMPBELL, JOSEPH. 1949. *The Hero with a Thousand Faces*. Cleveland: World.

CANTRELL, EILEEN M. n.d. Gebusi Gender Relations. The University of Michigan.

CARTWRIGHT, R. D. 1969. Dreams as Compared to Other Forms of Fantasy. *Dream Psychology and the New Biology of Dreaming* (M. Kramer, ed.), pp. 361–372. Springfield, IL: Charles C. Thomas.

———. 1978. *A Primer on Sleep and Dreaming*. Massachusetts, CA: Addison-Wesley.

CASTANEDA, C. 1974. *Tales of Power*. New York: Simon and Schuster.

CAUTELA, J. R. and L. McCULLOUGH. 1978. Covert Conditioning: A Learning-Theory Perspective on Imagery. *The Power of Human Imagination: New Methods in Psychotherapy* (J. L. Singer and K. S. Pope, eds.), pp. 227–278. New York and London: Plenum Press.

CLIFFORD, JAMES. 1982. *Person and Myth: Maurice Leenhardt in the Melanesian World*. Berkeley: University of California Press.

COHEN, D. B. 1979. *Sleep and Dreaming: Origins, Nature and Functions*. Oxford: Pergamon Press.

COHLER, BERTRAM. 1982. Personal Narrative and Life Course. *Life Span Development and Behavior* (B. Baltes and O. G. Brim, Jr., eds.), vol. 4, pp. 205–241. New York: Academic Press.

CONCISE OXFORD DICTIONARY, THE. 1982. Oxford: Clarendon Press.

COOPER, L. M. 1979. Hypnotic Amnesia. *Hypnosis: Developments in Research and New Perspectives* (E. Fromm and R. E. Shor, eds.), pp. 305–349. New York: Aldine.

CORBALLIS, M. C. 1983. *Human Laterality*. New York, London: Academic Press.

CRAPAZANO, VINCENT. 1977. Introduction. *Case Studies in Spirit Possession*, pp. 1–35. New York: Wiley.

———. 1980. *Tuhami: Portrait of a Moroccan*. Chicago: University of Chicago Press.

———. 1986. Hermes' Dilemma: The Masking of Subversion in Ethnographic Description. *Writing Culture* (J. Clifford and G. Marcus, eds.), pp. 51–76. Berkeley: University of California Press.

CRICK, F. and G. MITCHISON. 1983. The Function of Dream Sleep. *Nature*, July 14.

D'ANDRADE, R. G. 1984. Cultural Meaning Systems. *Culture Theory: Essays on Mind, Self, and Emotion* (R. A. Shweder and R. A. LeVine, eds.), pp. 88–119. Cambridge: Cambridge University Press.

———. 1986. Three Scientific World Views and the Covering Law Model. *Metatheory in Social Science* (D. W. Fiske and R. A. Shweder, eds.), pp. 19–41. Chicago: University of Chicago Press.

DAVIDSON, J. M. and R. J. DAVIDSON, eds. 1980. *The Psychobiology of Consciousness*. New York and London: Plenum Press.

DAVIDSON, R. J. 1980. Consciousness and Information Processing. *The Psychobiology of Consciousness* (J. M. Davidson and R. J. Davidson, eds.), pp. 11–46. New York and London: Plenum Press.

DESCOLA, PHILIPPE and JEAN-LUC LORY. 1982. Les guérriers de l'invisible: sociologie comparative de l'aggression chamanique en Papouasie Nouvelle-Guinée (Baruya) et en Haute-Amazonie (Achuar). *L'Ethnographie* 87–88:85–109.

DEVEREUX, GEORGE. 1980. Normal and Abnormal. *Basic Problems of Ethnopsychiatry*, pp. 3–71. Chicago: University of Chicago Press.

DIMOND, S. 1972. *The Double Brain*. Edinburgh and London: Churchill and Livingstone.

DIXON, N. F. 1971. *Subliminal Perception: The Nature of a Controversy*. London: McGraw-Hill.

———. 1981. *Preconscious Processing*. Chichester: John Wiley and Sons.

DODDS, E. R. 1951. *The Greeks and the Irrational*. Berkeley: University of California Press.

DOI, TAKEO. 1973. *Anatomy of Dependence*. Tokyo: Kodansha.

———. 1986. *The Anatomy of Self* (M. A. Harbison, trans.). Tokyo: Kodansha.

DUERR, H. 1985. *Dreamtime: Concerning the Boundary between Wilderness and Civilization.* (Felicitas D. Goodman, trans.). New York: Basil Blackwell.

DURKHEIM, EMILE. 1964[1895]. *The Rules of Sociological Method.* New York: Free Press.

––––––. 1965[1915]. *The Elementary Forms of the Religious Life* (J. W. Swain, trans.). New York: Free Press.

DWYER, PETER AND MONICA MINNEGAL. 1988. Supplication of the Crocodile: A Curing Ritual from Papua New Guinea. *Australian Natural History* 22:490–494.

ECO, UMBERTO. 1979. *The Role of the Reader: Explorations in the Semiotics of Texts.* Bloomington: University of Indiana Press.

ELIADE, MIRCEA. 1964[1951]. *Shamanism: Archaic Techniques of Ecstasy* (Willard R. Trask, trans.), Bollengen Series #74. Princeton, NJ: Princeton University Press.

ELLENBERGER, H. F. 1970. *The Discovery of the Unconscious.* New York: Basic Books.

ERIKSON, E. H. 1965. *Childhood and Society.* Harmondworth: Penguin Books.

ERNST, THOMAS M. 1978. Aspects of Meaning of Exchange Items among the Onabasulu of the Great Papuan Plateau. *Trade and Exchange in Oceania and Australia* (J. Specht and J. P. White, eds.). *Mankind* 11:187–197.

––––––. 1984. Onabasulu Local Organization. Ph.D. diss., The University of Michigan.

EVANS, C. 1983. *Landscapes of the Night: How and Why We Dream.* New York: Viking Press.

EVANS, F. J. 1979. Hypnosis and Sleep: Techniques For Exploring Cognitive Activity During Sleep. *Hypnosis: Developments in Research and New Perspectives* (E. Fromm and R. E. Shor, eds.), pp. 139–183. New York: Aldine.

EVANS-PRITCHARD, E. E. 1937. *Witchcraft, Oracles and Magic among the Azande.* Oxford: Clarendon Press.

––––––. 1965. *Theories of Primitive Religion.* Oxford: Oxford University Press.

EVANS-WENTZ, W. Y. 1967. *Tibetan Yoga and Its Secret Doctrines.* New York: Oxford University Press.

FELD, STEVEN. 1982. *Sound and Sentiment: Birds, Weeping, Poetics, and Song in Kaluli Expression.* Philadelphia: University of Pennsylvania Press.

FIELD, M. J. 1969. Spirit Possession in Ghana. *Spirit Mediumship and Society in Africa* (J. Beattie and J. Middleton, eds.), pp. 3–13. New York: Africana.

FIRTH, RAYMOND. 1959. Problems and Assumptions in an Anthropological Study of Religion. *Journal of the Royal Anthropological Institute* 89:129–148.

FISCHER, ROLAND. 1971. A Cartography of the Ecstatic and Meditative States. *Science* 174: 897–904.

FISHBEIN, W., ed. 1981. *Sleep, Dreams and Memory. Advances in Sleep Research*, vol. 6. New York: Spectrum.

FLACELIERE, ROBERT. 1965. *Greek Oracles* (D. Garma, trans.). London: Paul Elek.

FORGE, A. 1966. Art and Environment in the Sepik. *Proc. Royal Anthropological Institute* 1965:23–31.

––––––. 1970. Learning to See in New Guinea. *Socialization: The Approach from Social Anthropology* (P. Mayer, ed.), pp. 269–291. London: Tavistock.

FORTUNE, REO F. 1932. *Sorcerers of Dobu.* London: George Routledge.

––––––. 1935. Manus Religion. *Memoir of the American Philosophical Society.* Philadelphia.

FOUCAULT, MICHEL. 1976. *Mental Illness and Psychology* (Alan Sheridan, trans.). New York: Harper Colophon.

FOULKES, D. W. 1966. *The Psychology of Sleep.* New York: Charles Scribner's Sons.

FOX, ROBIN. 1967. Totem and Taboo Reconsidered. *The Structural Study of Myth and Totemism* (E. Leach, ed.), pp. 161–178. London: Tavistock.

FRAZER, J. G. 1913. *The Golden Bough: A Study in Magic and Religion.* London: Macmillan.

FREEMAN, J. DEREK. 1967. Shaman and Incubus. *Psychoanalytic Study of Society* 4:315–343.

FRENCH, T. AND E. FROMM. 1964. *Dream Interpretation*. New York: Basic Books.

FREUD, SIGMUND. 1908. Creative Writers and Day-Dreaming. *The Standard Edition of the Complete Psychological Works of Sigmund Freud*, vol. 9. London: Hogarth.

——. 1927. The Future of an Illusion. *The Standard Edition of the Complete Psychological Works of Sigmund Freud*, vol. 21. London: Hogarth.

——. 1933. *New Introductory Lectures on Psychoanalysis*. London: E. L. Bernays.

——. 1938a. Three Contributions to the Theory of Sex. *The Basic Writings of Sigmund Freud*. London: Allen and Unwin.

——. 1938b. The Psychopathology of Everyday Life. *The Basic Writings of Sigmund Freud*, pp. 35–150. New York: Modern Library.

——. 1961a[1923]. The Ego and the Id. *Standard Edition of the Complete Psychological Works of Sigmund Freud*, vol. 19, pp. 3–66. London: Hogarth.

——. 1961b[1927]. The Future of an Illusion. *Standard Edition of the Complete Psychological Works of Sigmund Freud*, vol. 21, pp. 3–57. London: Hogarth.

——. 1965[1900]. *The Interpretation of Dreams*. Standard Edition 4–5 (J. Strachey, ed. and trans.). London: Hogarth.

——. 1971. *The Complete Introductory Lectures on Psychoanalysis*. London: Allen and Unwin.

FROMM, E. 1979a. Quo Vadis Hypnosis? Predictions of Future Trends in Hypnosis Research. *Hypnosis: Developments in Research and New Perspectives* (E. Fromm and R. E. Shor, eds.), pp. 687–703. New York: Aldine.

——. 1979b. The Nature of Hypnosis and Other Altered States of Consciousness: An Ego-Psychological Theory. *Hypnosis: Developments in Research and New Perspectives* (E. Fromm and R. E. Shor, eds.), pp. 81–103. New York: Aldine.

FROMM, E. AND R. E. SHOR. 1979a. Underlying Theoretical Issues: An Introduction. *Hypnosis: Developments in Research and New Perspectives* (E. Fromm and R. E. Shor, eds.), pp. 3–13. New York: Aldine.

——, eds. 1979b. *Hypnosis: Developments in Research and New Perspectives*. New York: Aldine.

GADAMER, 1965. *Truth and Method*. New York: Crossroad.

GALIN, D. 1974. Implications for Psychiatry of Left and Right Cerebral Specialization. *Archives of General Psychiatry* 31:572–583.

GEERTZ, CLIFFORD. 1966a. Religion As a Cultural System. *Anthropological Approaches to the Study of Religion* (M. Banton, ed.), pp. 1–46. London: Tavistock.

——. 1966b. *Person, Time and Conduct in Bali: An Essay in Cultural Analysis*. Yale Southeast Asia Program, Cultural Report No. 14. New Haven: Yale University Press.

——. 1968. *Islam Observed*. New Haven: Yale University Press.

——. 1973. *The Interpretation of Cultures*. London: Hutchinson.

——. 1983a. "From the Native's Point of View": On the Nature of Anthropological Understanding. *Local Knowledge*, pp. 55–72. New York: Basic Books.

——. 1983b. *Local Knowledge*. New York: Basic Books.

GELL, ALFRED. 1975. *Metamorphosis of the Cassowaries*. London: Athlone.

GINZBURG, CARLO. 1985. *The Night Battles* (J. and A. Tedeschi, trans.). New York: Penguin.

GLICK, L. 1973. SORCERY AND WITCHCRAFT. *Anthropology in Papua New Guinea* (I. Hogbin, ed.), pp. 182–186. Melbourne: Melbourne University Press.

GLUCKMAN, M., ed. 1962. *Essays in the Ritual of Social Relations*. Manchester: Manchester University Press.

——. 1965. *Politics, Law, and Ritual in Tribal Society*. New York: Mentor Books.

GODELIER, MAURICE. 1972. Le Visible et l'invisible chez les Baruya de Nouvelle-Guinée. *Langues et Techniques* (J. Thomas and L. Bernot, eds.). *Nature et Société* 2:263–269.
———. 1982. Social Hierarchies among the Baruya of New Guinea. *Inequality in New Guinea Highlands Societies* (Andrew J. Strathern, ed.), pp. 3–34. Cambridge: Cambridge University Press.
———. 1986. *The Making of Great Men: Male Domination and Power among the New Guinea Baruya*. Cambridge: Cambridge University Press.
GRANERO, FERNANDO S. 1986. Power, Ideology and the Ritual of Production in Lowland South America. *Man* 21:657–679.
GREENBERG, R. 1970. Dreaming and Memory. *Sleep and Dreaming* (E. Hartmann, ed.), pp. 258–267. Boston: Little Brown.
GREENLEAF, E. 1978. Active Imagining. *The Power of Human Imagination: New Methods in Psychotherapy* (J. L. Singer and K. S. Pope, eds.), pp. 167–196. New York and London: Plenum Press.
GROLNICK, SIMON. 1987. Reflections on Psychoanalytic Subjectivity and Objectivity as Applied to Anthropology. *Ethos* 15:136–143.
HADFIELD, J. 1974. *Dreams and Nightmares*. Harmondsworth: Penguin.
HALIFAX, JOAN. 1979. *Shamanic Voices*. New York: E. P. Dutton.
HALLOWELL, A. I. 1966. The Role of Dreams in Ojibwa Culture. *The Dream in Human Society* (G. E. von Grunebaum and R. Caillois, eds.). Berkeley: University of California Press.
———. 1967. The Self and Its Behavioral Environment. *Culture and Experience*, pp. 75–110. New York: Schocken Books.
HARRISON, SIMON J. n.d. Stealing People's Names: Social Structure, Cosmology and Politics in a Sepik River Village. Ph.D. diss., Australian National University, 1982.
HART, C.W.M. 1963. Contrasts between Prepubertal and Postpubertal Education. *Education and Culture* (G. Spindler, ed.), pp. 400–425. New York: Holt, Rinehart and Winston.
HARTMANN, E., ed. 1970. *Sleep and Dreaming*. Boston: Little Brown.
———. 1975. Dreams and Other Hallucinations: An Approach to the Underlying Mechanism. *Hallucinations: Behaviour, Experience, and Theory* (R. K. Siegel and L. J. West, eds.). New York: John Wiley and Sons.
HAU'OFA, E. 1981. *Mekeo: Inequality and Ambivalence in a Village Society*. Canberra: Australian National University Press.
HAUSER-SCHAEUBLIN, B. 1977. *Franen in Kararau*, vol. 18. Basler Beitraege Zur Ethnologie.
HERDT, G. 1977. The Shaman's "Calling" among the Sambia of New Guinea. *Folie, Possession et Chaumanism en Nouvelle-Guineé* (B. Juillerat, ed.), special volume, *Journal de la Société des Océanistes* 56–57:153–167.
———. 1981. *Guardians of the Flutes: Idioms of Masculinity*. New York: McGraw-Hill.
———, ed. 1982a. *Rituals of Manhood: Male Initiation in New Guinea*. Introduction by R. M. Keesing. Berkeley: University of California Press.
———. 1982b. Fetish and Fantasy in Sambia Initiation. *Rituals of Manhood* (G. Herdt, ed.), pp. 44–98. Berkeley: University of California Press.
———. 1982c. Sambia Nose-bleeding Rites and Male Proximity to Women. *Ethos* 10:189–231.
———, ed. 1984a. *Ritualized Homosexuality in Melanesia*. Berkeley: University of California Press.
———. 1984b. Ritualized Homosexuality in the Male Cults of Melanesia, 1862–1982: An Introduction. *Ritualized Homosexuality in Melanesia* (G. Herdt, ed.), pp. 1–81. Berkeley: University of California Press.
———. 1984c. Semen Transactions in Sambia Culture. *Ritualized Homosexuality in Melanesia* (G. Herdt, ed.), pp. 167–210. Berkeley: University of California Press.

———. 1986. Madness and Sexuality in the New Guinea Highlands. *Social Research* 53: 349–368.

———. 1987a. The Accountability of Sambia Initiates. *Anthropology in the High Valleys: Essays in Honor of K. E. Read* (L. L. Langness and T. E. Hays, eds.), pp. 237–282. Novato, CA: Chandler and Sharp.

———. 1987b. Homosexuality. *The Encyclopedia of Religion*, vol. 6, pp. 445–452 (15 volumes). New York: Macmillan.

———. 1987c. *Sambia: Ritual and Gender in New Guinea*. New York: Holt, Rinehart and Winston.

———. 1987d. Selfhood and Discourse in Sambia Dream Sharing. *Dreaming: Anthropological and Psychological Interpretations* (B. Tedlock, ed.), pp. 52–97. Cambridge: Cambridge University Press.

———. 1987e. Transitional Objects in Sambia Initiation Rites. *Ethos* 15:40–57.

———. 1988. The Ethnographer's Choices. *Choice and Morality* (G. Appell and N. Madan, eds.), pp. 159–192. Stony Brook, NY: SUNY Press.

HERDT, GILBERT and FITZ JOHN P. POOLE. 1982. Sexual Antagonism, Gender and Social Change in Papua New Guinea. Special issue of *Social Analysis* No. 12.

HERDT, GILBERT and ROBERT J. STOLLER. 1985. Sakulambei—A Hermaphrodite's Secret: An Example of Clinical Ethnography. *Psychoanalytic Study of Society* 11:117–158.

———. 1989. *Intimate Communications: Erotics and the Study of Culture*. New York: Columbia University Press.

HIATT, L. R. 1971. Secret Pseudo-procreative Rites among Australian Aborigines. *Anthropology in Oceania: Essays Presented to Ian Hogbin* (L. R. Hiatt and C. Jayawardena, eds.), pp. 77–88. Sydney: Angus and Robertson.

HILGARD, E. R. 1965. *Hypnotic Susceptibility*. New York: Harcourt Brace and World.

———. 1977. *Divided Consciousness: Multiple Controls in Human Thought and Action*. New York: John Wiley and Sons.

HILGARD, J. 1979. Imaginative and Sensory-Affective Involvements in Everyday Life and Hypnosis. *Hypnosis: Developments in Research and New Perspectives* (E. Fromm and R. E. Shor, eds.), pp. 483–517. New York: Aldine.

HOGBIN, I. 1970. *The Island of Menstruating Men: Religion in Wogeo, New Guinea*. Scranton: Chandler.

———, ed. 1973. *Anthropology in Papua New Guinea*. Carlton: Melbourne University Press.

HSU, F.L.K., ed. 1972. *Psychological Anthropology*. Cambridge, MA: Schenkman.

HWEKMARIN, L., J. JAMENAN, D. LEA, A. NINGIGA, and M. WANGU. 1971. Yangaru Cargo Cult 1971. *Journal of Papua New Guinea Society* 5(2):3–27.

IHARA, SAIKAKU. 1972[1928]. *Comrade Loves of the Samurai* (E. P. Mathers, trans.). Rutland, VT: Charles E. Tuttle.

JAFFE, Y., N. MALAMUTH, J. FEINGOLD and S. FESHBACH. 1974. Sexual Arousal and Behavioral Aggression. *Journal of Personality and Social Psychology* 30:759–764.

JAMES, WILLIAM. 1958[1902]. *The Varieties of the Religious Experience*. New York: Mentor.

———. 1980. *Principles of Psychology*. 2 vols. New York: Dover.

———. 1986. The Scope of Psychology. *The Psychology of Consciousness* (R. Ornstein, ed.), pp. 4–10. New York: Penguin.

JARVIE, I. C. 1964. *The Revolution in Anthropology*. Chicago: Henry Regency.

JAUSS, HANS ROBERT. 1982. Towards an Aesthetic of Reception (Timothy Bahti, trans.). Minneapolis: University of Minnesota Press.

JENNESS, DIAMOND. 1922. *The Life of the Copper Eskimo. Report of the Canadian Arctic Expedition 1913–18, Vol. 9, Pt. A.* Ottawa: F. A. Acland.

JONES, BARBARA. 1980. *Consuming Society: Food and Illness among the Faiwol.* Ph.D. diss., University of Virginia.

JONES, R. M. 1976. *The New Psychology of Dreaming.* Harmondsworth: Pelican.

JORALEMON, DONALD. 1984. The Role of Hallucinogenic Drugs and Sensory Stimuli in Peruvian Ritual Healing. *Culture, Medicine, and Psychiatry* 8:399–430.

JUILLERAT, BERNARD, ed. 1977a. "Folie," Possession et Chamanisme en Nouvelle-Guinée. *Journal de la Société des Océanistes,* vol. 33, special issue.

————. 1977b. Introduction. *Journal de la Société des Océanistes* 33:115–122.

JUNG, C. G. 1966. *The Practice of Psychotherapy* (R.F.C. Hull, trans.). Princeton: Princeton University Press.

————. 1976. *The Collected Works of C. G. Jung,* vol. 9. Princeton: Princeton University Press.

————. 1977. *Psychology and the Occult.* Princeton: Princeton University Press.

————. 1978. *Man and His Symbols.* New York: Doubleday.

KAKAR, SUDHIR. 1983. *Shamans, Mystics and Doctors.* Boston: Beacon.

————. 1985. Psychoanalysis and Non-Western Cultures. *Intl. Rev. Psycho-anal.* 12:441–448.

————. 1986. Psychotherapy and Culture: Healing in the Indian Culture. *The Cultural Transition* (M. I. White and S. Pollak, eds.), pp. 9–23. Boston: Routledge and Kegan Paul.

KATZ, RICHARD. 1983. *Boiling Energy: Community Healing among the Kalahari Kung.* Cambridge: Harvard University Press.

KEESING, ROGER M. 1982a. Introduction. *Rituals of Manhood: Male Initiation in Papua New Guinea* (G. Herdt, ed.). Berkeley: University of California Press.

————. 1982b. *Kwaio Religion.* New York: Columbia University Press.

KELLY, RAYMOND C. 1976. Witchcraft and Sexual Relations: An Exploration in the Social and Semantic Implications of the Structure of Belief. *Man and Woman in the New Guinea Highlands* (Paula Brown and Geogeda Buchbinder, eds.), pp. 36–53. American Anthropological Association Special Publication No. 8. Washington, DC: American Anthropological Association.

————. 1977. *Etoro Social Structure: A Study in Structural Contradiction.* Ann Arbor: University of Michigan Press.

————. 1988. Etoro Suidology: A Reassessment of the Pig's Role in the Prehistory and Comparative Ethnology of New Guinea. *The Mountain Papuans* (James F. Weiner, ed.). Ann Arbor: University of Michigan Press.

KENNEDY, JOHN G. 1967. Nubian Zar Ceremonies as Psychotherapy. *Human Organization.* 26(4).

KIEV, A., ed. 1964. *Magic, Faith, and Healing: Studies in Primitive Psychiatry Today.* New York: Free Press.

KLEINMAN, ARTHUR. 1988. *The Illness Narratives.* New York: Basic Books.

KLINE, M. V., ed. 1956. *A Scientific Report on the Search for Bridey Murphy.* New York: Julian Press.

KNAUFT, BRUCE M. 1983. Good Company and Anger: The Culture and Sociology of Sorcery among the Gebusi of the Strickland Plain, Papua New Guinea, 2 vols. Ph.D. diss., The University of Michigan.

————. 1985a. *Good Company and Violence: Sorcery and Social Action in a Lowland New Guinea Society.* Berkeley: University of California Press.

————. 1985b. Ritual Form and Permutation in New Guinea: Implications of Symbolic Process for Socio-Political Evolution. *American Ethnologist* 12:321–340.

————. 1986. Text and Social Practice: Narrative "Longing" and Bisexuality among the Gebusi of New Guinea. *Ethos* 14:252–281.

————. 1987a. Managing Sex and Anger: Tobacco and Kava Use among the Gebusi of Papua New Guinea. *Drugs in Western Pacific Societies: Relations of Substance* (Lamont Lindstrom, ed.), pp. 73–98. A.S.A.O. Monograph No. 11. Lanham, MD: University Press of America.

————. 1987b. Homosexuality in Melanesia: The Need for a Synthesis of Perspectives. *Journal of Psychoanalytic Anthropology* 10:155–191.

————. 1987c. Reconsidering Lethal Violence in Simple Human Societies: Homicide among the Gebusi of New Guinea. *Current Anthropology* 28:457–500.

————. 1989. Bodily Images in Melanesia: Cultural Substances and Natural Metaphors. *Fragments for a History of the Human Body, Part Three* (Michel Feher, Ramona Nadaff, and Nadia Tazi, eds.), pp. 198–279. *Zone* 5:198–279. New York: Urzone.

KOESTLER, A. 1964. *The Act of Creation*. New York: Macmillan.

KOHUT, H. 1971. *The Analysis of the Self*. New York: International University Press.

————. 1979. The Two Analyses of Mr. Z. *Intl. J. Psychoanal.* 60.

KRACKE, WAUD H. 1980. Amazonian Interviews: Dreams of a Bereaved Father. *Annual of Psychoanalysis* 8:249–267.

————. 1987a. Encounter with Other Cultures: Psychological and Epistemological Aspects. *Ethos* 15:58–81.

————. 1987b. Dream, Myth, Thought, and Image: An Amazonian Contribution to the Psychoanalytic Theory of Primary Process. *Dreaming: Anthropological and Psychological Interpretations* (B. Tedlock, ed.), pp. 98–131. Cambridge: Cambridge University Press.

KRACKE, WARD H. and GILBERT HERDT. 1987. *Interpretation in Psychoanalytic Anthropology*. Special Issue of *Ethos*, no. 15.

————. 1987. Introduction. *Interpretation in Psychoanalytic Anthropology*. Special issue of *Ethos* 15:3–7.

KRAMER, M., ed. 1969. *Dream Psychology and the New Biology of Dreaming*. Springfield, IL: Charles C. Thomas.

KRIPPNER, S. and W. HUGHES. 1970. Dreams and Human Potential. *Journal of Humanistic Psychology* 10:1–20.

LA BARRE, W. 1972. *The Ghost Dance: Origins of Religion*. London: George Allen and Unwin.

LA FONTAINE, JEAN S. 1985. *Initiation*. New York: Penguin.

LANDTMAN, GUNNAR. 1927. *The Kiwai Papuans of British New Guinea*. London: Macmillan. [Johnson Reprint Corp., London, 1970]

LANGER, SUSANNE K. 1967. *Mind: An Essay on Human Feeling*, vol. 1. Baltimore: Johns Hopkins University Press.

LANGEVIN, RON, ed. 1985. *Erotic Preference, Gender Identity, and Aggression in Men: New Research Studies*. Hillsdale, NJ: Lawrence Erlbaum Associates.

LANGNESS, L. L. 1974. Ritual Power and Male Domination in the New Guinea Highlands. *Ethos* 2:189–212.

LANGNESS, L. L. and T. GLADWIN. 1972. Oceania. *Psychological Anthropology*, new ed. (F. Hsu, ed.), pp. 167–200. Cambridge, MA: Schenkman.

LANGNESS, L. L. and T. E. HAYS, eds. 1987. *Anthropology in the High Valleys*. Novato, CA: Chandler.

LAWRENCE, P. 1964. *Road Belong Cargo: A Study of the Cargo Movement in the Southern Madang District New Guinea*. Manchester, Carlton: University of Manchester and Melbourne University Presses.

————. 1973. Religion and Magic. *Anthropology in Papua New Guinea* (I. Hogbin, ed.), pp. 201–226. Carlton: Melbourne University Press.

————. 1984. *The Garia*. Carlton: Melbourne University Press.

246 *Bibliography*

LAWRENCE, P. and M. J. MEGGITT, eds. 1965. *Gods, Ghosts and Men in Melanesia.* Melbourne: Oxford University Press.
LAYARD, JOHN W. 1930a. Malekula: Flying Tricksters, Ghosts, Gods and Epileptics. *Journal of the Royal Anthropological Institute* 60:501–524.
———. 1930b. Shamanism: An Analysis Based on Comparison with the Flying Tricksters of Malekula. *Journal of the Royal Anthropological Institute* 60:525–560.
———. 1942. *Stone Men of Malekula.* London: Chatto and Windus.
LEACH, E. R. 1954. *Political Systems of Highland Burma.* Boston: Beacon Press.
———. 1976. *Culture and Communication: The Logic By Which Symbols are Connected.* Cambridge: Cambridge University Press.
LEE, RICHARD B. 1978. Trance Cure of the !Kung Bushmen. *Health and the Human Condition* (Michael H. Logan and Edward E. Hunt, Jr., eds.), pp. 195–202. North Scituate, MA: Duxbury Press.
LEENHARDT, MAURICE. 1979. *Do Kamo* (Basia M. Gulati, trans.). Chicago: University of Chicago Press.
LESSA, WILLIAM A. and EVON Z. VOGT, eds. 1972a. *Reader in Comparative Religion: An Anthropological Approach.* New York: Harper and Row.
———. 1972b. Shamanism. *Reader in Comparative Religion: An Anthropological Approach*, 3d ed. (W. A. Lessa and E. Z. Vogt, eds.). New York: Harper and Row.
LEUNER, H. 1978. Basic Principles and Therapeutic Efficacy of Guided Affective Imagery (GAI). *The Power of Human Imagination: New Methods in Psychotherapy* (J. L. Singer and K. S. Pope, eds.), pp. 125–166. New York and London: Plenum Press.
LÉVI-STRAUSS, CLAUDE. 1962. *La Pensee Sauvage.* Paris: Plon.
———. 1963. *Totemism* (R. Needham, trans.). Boston: Beacon Press.
———. 1966. *The Savage Mind.* Chicago: University of Chicago Press.
———. 1967[1958]. *Structural Anthropology* (C. Jacobson and B. G. Schoepf, trans.). New York: Anchor.
———. 1972. The Sorcerer and His Magic. *Structural Anthropology.* Harmondsworth: Penguin Books.
LEVINE, ROBERT A. 1982. *Culture, Behavior and Personality*, 2d ed. New York: Aldine.
LEVY, ROBERT. 1973. *The Tahitians.* Chicago: University of Chicago Press.
LEWIS, GILBERT. 1980. *Day of Shining Red.* Cambridge: Cambridge University Press.
LEWIS, IOAN M. 1971. *Ecstatic Religion: An Anthropological Study of Spirit Possession and Shamanism.* Harmondsworth: Penguin.
———. 1986. *Religion in Context: Cults and Charisma.* Cambridge: Cambridge University Press.
LINCOLN, JACKSON S. 1935. *The Dream in Primitive Cultures.* Baltimore: Williams and Wilkins.
LLOYD, G.E.R. 1979. *Science, Folklore and Ideology.* New York: Cambridge University Press.
LOCKE, RALPH G. and EDWARD F. KELLY. 1985. A Preliminary Model of the Cross-Cultural Analysis of Altered States of Consciousness. *Ethos* 13:3–55.
LUDWIG, A. M. 1969. Altered States of Consciousness. *Altered States of Consciousness* (C. T. Tart, ed.), pp. 11–24. New York: John Wiley and Sons.
LUTZ, CATHERINE. 1985. Ethnopsychology Compared to What? Explaining Behavior and Consciousness among Ifaluk. *Person, Self and Experience* (G. M. White and J. Kirkpatrick, eds.), pp. 35–79. Berkeley: University of California Press.
MACLEAN, P. D. 1962. New Findings Relevant to the Evolution of Psychosexual Functions of the Brain. *Journal of Nervous and Mental Disease* 135:289–301.
MALINOWSKI, BRONISLAU. 1926. *Crime and Custom in Savage Society.* Totowa, NJ: Littlefield, Adams.

———. 1935. *Coral Gardens and Their Magic*. 2 vols. Bloomington, IN: Indiana University Press.

———. 1948. *Magic, Science and Religion and Other Essays*. Garden City, NY: Anchor Books.

MARX, KARL. 1977. The Fetishism of Commodities and the Secret Thereof. *Symbolic Anthropology: A Reader in the Study of Symbols and Meanings* (J. L. Dolgin et al., eds.), pp. 245–253. New York: Columbia University Press.

MASLACH, C., P. ZIMBARDO, and G. MARSHALL. 1979. Hypnosis as a Means of Studying Cognitive and Behavioural Control. *Hypnosis: Developments in Research and New Perspectives* (E. Fromm and R. E. Shor, eds.), pp. 649–683. New York: Aldine.

MAUROIS, A. 1954. *Lelia: The Life of George Sand* (Gerard Hopkins, trans.). New York: Harper and Row.

MAUSS, M. 1938. Une Categorie de L'esprit Humaine: La Notion de Personne, Celle de "Moi." *JRAI* 68:263–281.

MEAD, MARGARET. 1956. *New Lives for Old: Cultural Transformations—Manus, 1928–1953*. New York: William Morrow.

MEICHENBAUM, D. 1978. Why Does Using Imagery in Psychotherapy Lead to Change? *The Power of Human Imagination: New Methods in Psychotherapy* (J. L. Singer and K. S. Pope, eds.), pp. 381–394. New York and London: Plenum Press.

MEIGS, ANNA S. 1984. *Food, Sex, and Pollution: A New Guinea Religion*. New Brunswick, NJ: Rutgers University Press.

MOERMAN, DANIEL E. 1979. Anthropology of Symbolic Healing. *Current Anthropology* 20: 59–80.

MOSKO, M. S. 1985. *Quadripartite Structures: Categories, Relations and Homologies in Bush Mekeo Culture*. Cambridge: Cambridge University Press.

MUNN, NANCY. 1973. *Walbiri Iconography: Graphic Representation and Cultural Symbolism in a Central Australian Society*. Ithaca, NY: Cornell University Press.

NEMIAH, J. C. 1984. The Unconscious and Psychopathology. *The Unconscious Reconsidered* (K. S. Bowers and D. Meichenbaum, eds.), pp. 49–87. New York: John Wiley and Sons.

NEWMAN, PHILIP L. 1964. Religious Belief and Ritual in a New Guinea Society. *American Anthropology* 2(4):257–272.

———. 1965. *Knowing the Gururumba*. New York: Holt, Rinehart and Winston.

NOLL, RICHARD. 1985. Mental Imagery Cultivation as a Cultural Phenomenon: The Role of Visions in Shamanism. *Current Anthropology* 26:443–461.

OBEYESEKERE, GANANATH. 1981. *Medusa's Hair*. Chicago: University of Chicago Press.

O'BRIEN, D. and S. TIFFANY, eds. 1984. *Rethinking Women's Roles: Perspectives From the Pacific*. Berkeley: University of California Press.

OCHS, ELINOR and B. SCHIEFFELIN. 1984. Language Acquisition and Socialization: Three Developmental Stories and Their Implications. *Culture Theory* (R. Shweder and R. LeVine, eds.), pp. 276–320. New York: Cambridge University Press.

O'FLAHERTY, WENDY D. 1984. *Dreams, Illusion and Other Realities*. Chicago: University of Chicago Press.

O'NELL, CARL W. 1976. *Dreams, Culture, and the Individual*. Novato, CA: Chandler and Sharp.

ONIONS, C. T., ed. 1966. *The Oxford Dictionary and English Etymology*. Oxford: Clarendon Press.

ORNE, M. T. 1965. The Nature of Hypnosis: Artifact and Essence. *The Nature of Hypnosis: Selected Basic Readings* (R. E. Shor and M. T. Orne, eds.), pp. 89–123. New York, Chicago: Holt, Rinehart and Winston.

―――. 1979. On the Simulating Subject as a Quasi-Control Group in Hypnosis Research: What, Why, and How. *Hypnosis: Developments in Research and New Perspectives* (E. Fromm and R. E. Shor, eds.), pp. 519–565. New York: Aldine.

ORNSTEIN, ROBERT. 1986. *The Psychology of Consciousness*, rev. ed. New York: Penguin.

PAIVIO, A. 1971. *Imagery and Verbal Processes*. New York: Holt, Rinehart and Winston.

PATTERSON, MARY. 1974. Sorcery and Witchcraft in Melanesia. *Oceania* 45:132–160, 212–234.

PEARLMAN, C. 1970. The Adaptive Function of Dreaming. *Sleep and Dreaming* (E. Hartmann, ed.). Boston: Little Brown.

PERRY, C. and J. LAURENCE. 1984. Mental Processing Outside of Awareness: The Contributions of Freud and Janet. *The Unconscious Reconsidered* (K. S. Bowers and D. Meichenbaum, eds.), pp. 9–48. New York: John Wiley and Sons.

PETERS, LARRY G. 1988. Borderline Personality and the Possession Syndrome: An Ethno-Psychoanalytic Perspective. *Transcultural Psychiatric Research Review* 25:5–46.

PETERS, LARRY G. and D. PRICE-WILLIAMS. 1980. Towards an Experiential Analysis of Shamanism. *American Ethnologist* 7:397–418.

―――. 1983. A Phenomenological Overview of Trance. *Transcultural Psychiatric Research Review* 20:5–39.

PIERCE, CHARLES S. 1931. *Collected Papers* (Charles Hartshorne and Paul Weiss, eds.). 8 vols. Cambridge: Harvard University Press.

POLANYI, M. 1966. *The Tacit Dimension*. Garden City, New York: Doubleday Anchor Books.

POOLE, FITZ JOHN P. 1981a. *Taman*: Ideological and Sociological Configurations of "Witchcraft" among the Bimin-Kuskusmin. *Sorcery and Social Change in Melanesia* (Marty Zelenietz and Shirley Lindenbaum, eds.). Special issue, *Social Analysis*, no. 8. Adelaide.

―――. 1981b. Transforming "Natural" Woman: Female Ritual Leaders and Gender Ideology among Bimin-Kuskusmin. *Sexual Meanings* (S. B. Ortner and H. Whitehead, eds.), pp. 116–165. Cambridge: Cambridge University Press.

―――. 1982. The Ritual Forging of Identity: Aspects of Person and Self in Bimin-Kuskusmin Male Initiation. *Rituals of Manhood: Male Initiation in Papua New Guinea* (Gilbert Herdt, ed.), pp. 100–154. Berkeley: University of California Press.

―――. 1986. Metaphors and Maps: Towards Comparison in the Anthropology of Religion. *Journal of the American Academy of Religion* 54:411–457.

―――. 1987a. Melanesian Religions: Mythic Themes. *The Encyclopedia of Religion* (M. Eliade et al., eds.), vol. 9, pp. 359–365. New York: Macmillan.

―――. 1987b. Personal Experience and Cultural Representation in Children's "Personal Symbols" among Bimin-Kuskusmin. *Ethos* 15:104–135.

POPPER, KARL. 1950. *The Open Society and Its Enemies*. Princeton: Princeton University Press.

―――. 1957. *The Poverty of Historicism*. London: Routledge and Kegan Paul.

PRIBRAM, K. H. 1980. Mind, Brain, and Consciousness: The Organisation of Competence and Conduct. *The Psychobiology of Consciousness* (J. M. Davidson and R. J. Davidson, eds.), pp. 47–64. New York and London: Plenum Press.

PRICE-WILLIAMS, D. 1975a. Cultural Perspective on Altered States of Consciousness. *Explorations in Cross-Cultural Psychology* (D. R. Price-Williams), pp. 81–94. Los Angeles: University of California Press.

―――. 1975b. *Explorations in Cross-Cultural Psychology*. Los Angeles: University of California Press.

―――. 1987. The Waking Dream in Ethnographic Perspective. *Dreaming: Anthropological and Psychological Interpretations* (B. Tedlock, ed.), pp. 246–262. Cambridge: Cambridge University Press.

PRINCE, RAYMOND, ed. 1982. Shamans and Endorphins. *Ethos* 10(2):409–423.

RANK, OTTO. 1971. *The Double* (H. Tucker, Jr., trans.). New York: New American Library.

RAPPAPORT, ROY A. 1971. Ritual, Sanctity, and Cybernetics. *American Anthropologist* 73:59–76.

———. 1979. *Ecology, Meaning, and Religion.* Richmond, CA: North Atlantic Books.

RASMUSSEN, KNUD. 1932. *Intellectual Culture of the Copper Eskimo* (W. E. Calvert, trans.). Report of the Fifth Thule Expedition 1921–1924, vol. 9. Copenhagen: Gyldendalski Boghandel, Nordisk Forlag.

READ, KENNETH E. 1951. The Gahuku-Gama of the Central Highlands. *South Pacific* 5:154–164.

———. 1952. Nama Cult of the Central Highlands, New Guinea. *Oceania* 23:1–25.

———. 1955. Morality and the Concept of the Person among the Gahuku-Gama. *Oceania* 25:233–282.

———. 1965. *The High Valley.* New York: Scribner.

———. 1986. *Return to the High Valley: Coming Full Circle.* Berkeley: University of California Press.

REAY, MARIE. 1959. *The Kuma.* Carlton: Melbourne University Press.

———. 1977. Ritual Madness Observed: A Discarded Pattern of Fate in Papua New Guinea. *Journal of Pacific History* 12 (parts 1 and 2):55–79.

———. 1987. The Magico-Religious Foundations of New Guinea Highlands Warfare. *Sorcerer and Witch in Melanesia* (M. Stephen, ed.), pp. 83–120. New Brunswick, NJ: Rutgers University Press.

REBER, A. S. 1985. *The Penguin Dictionary of Psychology.* Harmondsworth: Penguin.

REINHARD, JOHAN. 1976. Shamanism and Spirit Possession: The Definition Problem. *Spirit Possession in the Nepal Himalayas* (John Hitchcock and Rex Jones, eds.). New Delhi: Vikas.

RICOEUR, PAUL. 1970. *Freud and Philosophy: An Essay on Interpretation* (D. Savage, trans.). New Haven: Yale University Press.

RIEBE, INGE. 1987. Kalam Witchcraft: A Historical Perspective. *Sorcerer and Witch in Melanesia* (M. Stephen, ed.), pp. 211–245. New Brunswick, NJ: Rutgers University Press.

RIVERS, W.H.R. 1923. *Conflict and Dream.* London: Kegan Paul.

ROBIN, ROBERT W. 1982. Revival Movements in the Southern Highlands Province of Papua New Guinea. *Oceania* 52:320–343.

ROHDE, ERWIN. 1925. *Psyche: The Cult of Souls and Belief in Immortality among The Greeks.* London: Kegan Paul.

ROSALDO, MICHELE. 1980. *Knowledge and Passion.* New York: Cambridge University Press.

ROSCOE, PAUL B. 1987. The Far Side of Hurun: Religious Brokerage in a Melanesian Millennium. Unpublished manuscript.

ROTHENBERG, A. 1979. *The Emerging Goddess: The Creative Process in Art, Science and Other Fields.* Chicago: University of Chicago Press.

RUBEL, PAULA G. and ABRAHAM ROSMAN. 1978. *Your Own Pigs You May Not Eat.* Chicago: University of Chicago Press.

RUNCIMAN, W. G. 1970. *Sociology in Its Place and Other Essays.* Cambridge: Cambridge University Press.

RYCROFT, CHARLES A. 1968. *Imagination and Reality: Psycho-Analytic Essays 1951–1961.* London: Hogarth.

———. 1972. *A Critical Dictionary of Psychoanalysis.* Harmondsworth: Penguin.

———. 1977. Is Freudian Symbolism a Myth? *Symbols and Sentiments* (I. M. Lewis, ed.), pp. 129–140. London: Academic Press.

———. 1979. *The Innocence of Dreams.* New York: Pantheon.

SARBIN, T. R. 1965. Contributions to Role-Taking Theory: I. Hypnotic Behaviour. *The Nature of Hypnosis: Selected Basic Readings* (R. E. Shor and M. T. Orne, eds.), pp. 234–254. New York, Chicago: Holt, Rinehart and Winston.

SARBIN, T. R. and R. W. SLAGLE. 1979. Hypnosis and Psychophysiological Outcomes. *Hypnosis: Developments in Research and New Perspectives* (E. Fromm and R. E. Shor, eds.), pp. 273–303. New York: Aldine.

SCHAFFER, ROY. 1980. Narration in the Psychoanalytic Dialogue. *On Narrative* (M.J.T. Mitchell, ed.), pp. 25–50. Chicago: University of Chicago Press.

SCHIEFFELIN, EDWARD L. 1976. *The Sorrow of the Lonely and the Burning of the Dancers.* New York: St. Martin's Press.

———. 1977. The Unseen Influence: Tranced Mediums as Historical Innovators. *Journal de la Société des Océanistes* 33:169–178.

———. 1981. The End of Traditional Music, Dance, and Body Decoration in Bosavi, Papua New Guinea. *The Plight of Peripheral Peoples in Papua New Guinea*, vol. 1: The Inland Situation. (Robert Gordon, ed.). Peterborough, NH: Transcript Printing.

———. 1982. The Bau'a Ceremonial Hunting Lodge: An Alternative to Initiation. *Rituals of Manhood: Male Initiation in Papua New Guinea* (G. Herdt, ed.), pp. 155–200. Berkeley: University of California Press.

———. 1985. Performance and the Cultural Construction of Reality. *American Ethnologist* 12:707–724.

SCHULTZ, K. D. 1978. Imagery and the Control of Depression. *The Power of Human Imagination: New Methods in Psychotherapy* (J. L. Singer and K. S. Pope, eds.), pp. 281–307. New York and London: Plenum Press.

SCHWARTZ, THEODORE. 1962. *The Palian Movement in the Admiralty Island: 1946–1954.* Anthro. papers no. 49. New York: American Museum of Natural History.

———. 1978. Where is the Culture? Personality as the Distributive Locus of Culture. *The Making of Psychological Anthropology* (George Spindler, ed.), pp. 419–441. Berkeley: University of California Press.

SCHWIMMER, ERIC. 1980. *Power, Silence and Secrecy.* Toronto: Semiotic Circle, Victoria University.

———. 1983. The Taste of Your Own Flesh. *Semiotica* 46:107–129.

———. 1986. Icons of Identity. *Iconicity: Essays on the Nature of Culture* (Paul Bouissa et al., eds.), pp. 359–384. Stauffenburg: Verlag.

SHAW, R. DANIEL. 1975. Samo Social Structure. Ph.D. diss., The University of Papua New Guinea.

———. 1982. Samo Initiation: Its Context and Its Meaning. *Journal of the Polynesian Society* 91:417–434.

SHEEHAN, P. W. 1979. Hypnosis and the Processes of Imagination. *Hypnosis: Developments in Research and New Perspectives* (E. Fromm and R. E. Shor, eds.), pp. 381–411. New York: Aldine.

SHEEHAN, P. W. and K. M. McCONKEY. 1982. *Hypnosis and Experience: The Exploration of Phenomena and Process.* Hillsdale, NJ: Lawrence Erlbaum Associates.

SHEIKH, A. A. 1978. Eidetic Psychotherapy. *The Power of Human Imagination: New Methods in Psychotherapy* (J. L. Singer and K. S. Pope, eds.), pp. 197–224. New York: Plenum Press.

SHOR, R. E. 1965. Hypnosis and the Concept of the Generalized Reality-Orientation. *The Nature of Hypnosis: Selected Basic Readings* (R. E. Shor and M. T. Orne, eds.), pp. 288–305. New York: Holt, Rinehart and Winston.

SHOR, R. E. and M. T. ORNE, eds. 1965. *The Nature of Hypnosis: Selected Basic Readings.* New York: Holt, Rinehart and Winston.

SHWEDER, RICHARD A. 1977. Likeness and Likelihood in Everyday Thought: Magical Thinking in Judgments about Personality. *Current Anthropology* 18:637–658.

———. 1984. Anthropology's Romantic Rebellion against the Enlightenment, Or There's More to Thinking Than Reason and Evidence. *Culture Theory* (R. A. Shweder and R. A. LeVine, eds.), pp. 27–66. New York: Cambridge University Press.

———. 1986. Divergent Rationalities. *Metatheory in Social Science* (D. W. Fiske and R. A. Shweder, eds.), pp. 164–196. Chicago: University of Chicago Press.

SHWEDER, RICHARD A. and E. J. BOURNE. 1984. Does the Concept of the Person Vary Cross-culturally? *Culture Theory* (R. A. Shweder and R. A. LeVine, eds.), pp. 159–199. New York: Cambridge University Press.

SHWEDER, R. A. and R. A. LEVINE, eds. 1984. *Culture Theory: Essays on Mind, Self, and Emotion.* Cambridge: Cambridge University Press.

SIEGEL, R. K. and L. J. WEST, eds. 1975. *Hallucinations: Behaviour, Experience, and Theory.* New York: John Wiley and Sons.

SIMON, BENNETT. 1978. *Mind and Madness in Ancient Greece.* Ithaca: Cornell University Press.

SINGER, J. L. 1974. *Imagery and Daydream Methods in Psychotherapy and Behaviour Modification.* New York: Academic Press.

———. 1976. *Daydreaming and Fantasy.* London: George Allen and Unwin.

———. 1977. Ongoing Thought: The Normative Baseline for Alternate States of Consciousness. *Alternate States of Consciousness* (N. E. Zinberg, ed.), pp. 89–120. New York: Free Press.

SINGER, J. L. and K. S. POPE, eds. 1978a. *The Power of Human Imagination: New Methods in Psychotherapy.* New York: Plenum Press.

———. 1978b. The Use of Imagery and Fantasy Techniques in Psychotherapy. *The Power of Human Imagination: New Methods in Psychotherapy* (J. L. Singer and K. S. Pope, eds.), pp. 3–34. New York: Plenum Press.

———, eds. 1987c. *The Stream of Consciousness: Scientific Investigations into the Flow of Human Experience.* Chichester, NY: John Wiley and Sons.

SINGER, M. 1961. A Survey of Culture and Personality Theory and Research. *Studying Personality Cross-Culturally* (Bert Kaplan, ed.), pp. 9–90. New York: Harper and Row.

SØRUM, ARVE. 1980. In Search of the Lost Soul: Bedamini Spirit Seances and Curing Rites. *Oceania* 50:273–296.

———. 1984. Growth and Decay: Bedamini Notions of Sexuality. *Ritualized Homosexuality in Melanesia* (Gilbert H. Herdt, ed.), pp. 318–336. Berkeley: University of California Press.

SPERBER, DAN. 1975. *Rethinking Symbolism* (Alice L. Morton, trans.). Cambridge: Cambridge University Press.

SPIRO, MELFORD E. 1964. Religion and the Irrational. *Symposium on New Approaches to the Study of Religion* (June Helm, ed.), pp. 102–115. Seattle: American Ethnological Society and University of Washington Press.

———. 1965. Religious Systems as Culturally Constituted Defense Mechanisms. *Context and Meaning in Cultural Anthropology* (M. E. Spiro, ed.), pp. 100–113. New York: Free Press.

———. 1968. *Burmese Supernaturalism.* Englewood Cliffs, NJ: Prentice-Hall.

———. 1982. *Oedipus in the Trobriands.* Chicago: University of Chicago Press.

———. 1984. Some Reflections on Cultural Determinism and Relativism with Special Reference to Emotion and Reason. *Culture Theory: Essays on Mind, Self, and Emotion* (R. A. Shweder and R. A. LeVine, eds.), pp. 323–346. Cambridge: Cambridge University Press.

———. 1986. Cultural Relativism and the Future of Anthropology. *Cultural Anthropology* 1:259–286.

SPRINGER, S. P. and G. DEUTSCH. 1981. *Left Brain, Right Brain*. San Francisco: W. H. Freeman.

STEPHEN, MICHELE. 1974. Continuity and Change in Mekeo Society 1890–1971. Ph.D. diss., Australian National University.

———. 1977. Cargo Cult "Hysteria": Symptom of Despair or Technique of Ecstasy? Research Center for South-West Pacific Studies, Occasional Paper. La Trobe University.

———. 1979. Dreams of Change: The Innovative Role of Altered States of Consciousness in Traditional Melanesian Religion. *Oceania* 50:3–22.

———. 1981. Dreaming is Another Power!: The Social Significance of Dreams among the Mekeo of Papua New Guinea. *Oceania* 53:106–122.

———. 1986. Culture, the Hidden Self and the Autonomous Imagination. Paper presented at the Annual Meetings of the American Anthropological Association. Philadelphia.

———, ed. 1987a. *Sorcerer and Witch in Melanesia*. New Brunswick, NJ: Rutgers University Press.

———. 1987b. Master of Souls: The Mekeo Sorcerer. *Sorcerer and Witch in Melanesia* (M. Stephen, ed.), pp. 41–80. New Brunswick, NJ: Rutgers University Press.

———. 1987c. Contrasting Images of Power. *Sorcerer and Witch in Melanesia* (M. Stephen, ed.), pp. 249–304. New Brunswick, NJ: Rutgers University Press.

STEWART, K. 1969. Dream Theory in Malaya. *Altered States of Consciousness* (C. T. Tart, ed.), pp. 159–167. New York: John Wiley and Sons.

STOLLER, ROBERT J. 1973. *Splitting*. New York: Quadrangle.

———. 1979. *Sexual Excitement: The Dynamics of Erotic Life*. New York: Pantheon.

STRANGE, J. R. 1978. A Search for the Sources of the Stream of Consciousness. *The Power of Human Imagination: New Methods in Psychotherapy* (J. L. Singer and K. S. Pope, eds.), pp. 10–29. New York: Plenum Press.

STRATHERN, ANDREW J. 1979. Men's House, Women's House: The Efficacy of Opposition, Reversal, and Pairing in the Melpa *Amb Kor* Cult. *Journal of the Polynesian Society* 88:37–51.

STRATHERN, MARILYN. 1979. The Self in Self-Decoration. *Oceania* 49:241–257.

———. 1981. Culture in a Netbag. The Manufacture of a Subdiscipline in Anthropology. *Man* 16:665–688.

———. 1988. *The Gender of the Gift*. Berkeley: University of California Press.

TART, C. T., ed. 1969a. *Altered States of Consciousness*. New York: John Wiley and Sons.

———. 1969b. Towards the Experimental Control of Dreaming: A Review of the Literature. *Altered States of Consciousness* (C. T. Tart, ed.), pp. 133–144. New York: John Wiley and Sons.

TAUSSIG, MICHAEL. 1987. *Shamanism, Colonialism, and the Wild Man: A Study in Terror and Healing*. Chicago: University of Chicago Press.

TAYLOR, E. 1978. Asian Interpretations: Transcending the Stream of Consciousness. *The Power of Human Imagination: New Methods in Psychotherapy* (J. L. Singer and K. S. Pope, eds.), pp. 31–54. New York: Plenum Press.

TAYLOR, G. R. 1979. *The Natural History of the Mind*. New York: E. P. Dutton.

TEDLOCK, BARBARA, ed. 1987a. *Dreaming: Anthropological and Psychological Interpretations*. Cambridge: Cambridge University Press.

———. 1987b. Dreaming and Dream Research. *Dreaming: Anthropological and Psychological Interpretations* (B. Tedlock, ed.), pp. 1–51. Cambridge: Cambridge University Press.

TEDLOCK, DENNIS. 1983. *The Spoken Word and the Work of Interpretation*. Philadelphia: University of Pennsylvania Press.

TROMPF, G., ed. 1977. *Prophets of Melanesia: Six Essays*. Port Moresby: Institute of Papua New Guinea Studies.

TURNBULL, COLIN M. 1961. *The Forest People*. Garden City, NY: Natural History Press.

————. 1965a. The Mbuti Pygmies: An Ethnographic Survey. *Anthropological Papers of the American Museum of Natural History* 50:139–282.

————. 1965b. *Wayward Servants: The Two Worlds of the African Pygmies.* Garden City, NY: Natural History Press.

TURNER, VICTOR W. 1957. *Schism and Continuity in an African Society.* Manchester: Manchester University Press.

————. 1967a. *The Forest of Symbols.* Ithaca, NY: Cornell University Press.

————. 1967b. A Ndembu Doctor in Practice. *The Forest of Symbols,* pp. 359–393. Ithaca, NY: Cornell University Press.

————. 1968. Mukanda: The Politics of a Non-political Ritual. *Local-Level Politics* (M. Schwartz et al., ed.). Chicago: Aldine.

————. 1969. *The Ritual Process.* Chicago: Aldine.

————. 1978. Encounter with Freud: The Making of a Comparative Symbologist. *The Making of Psychological Anthropology* (G. Splindler, ed.), pp. 556–583. Berkeley: University of California Press.

TUZIN, DONALD F. 1972. Yam Symbolism in the Sepik: An Interpretative Account. *Southwestern Journal of Anthropology* 28:230–254.

————. 1975. The Breath of a Ghost: Dreams and the Fear of the Dead. *Ethos* 3:555–578.

————. 1976. *The Ilahita Arapesh: Dimensions of Unity.* Berkeley: University of California Press.

————. 1977. Reflections of Being in Arapesh Water Symbolism. *Ethos* 5(2):195–223.

————. 1980. *The Voice of the Tamberan: Truth and Illusion in Ilahita Arapesh Religion.* Berkeley: University of California Press.

————. 1982. Ritual Violence among the Ilahita Arapesh: The Dynamics of Moral and Religious Uncertainty. *Rituals of Manhood: Male Initiation in Papua New Guinea* (G. Herdt, ed.), pp. 312–355. Berkeley: University of California Press.

TYLOR, EDWARD B. 1871. *Primitive Culture: Researches into the Development of Mythology, Philosophy, Religion, Language, Art, and Custom,* 2d ed. 2 vols. London: John Murray.

ULLMAN, M. and N. ZIMMERMAN. 1979. *Working With Dreams.* London: Hutchinson.

VAN BAAL, JAN. 1966. *Dema.* The Hague: Martinus Nijhoff.

————. 1981. *Man's Quest for Partnership.* Assen: Van Gorcum.

VAN GENNEP, ARNOLD. 1960. *The Rites of Passage* (M. K. Vizedom and G. L. Caffee, trans.). Chicago: University of Chicago Press.

VERNANT, JEAN PIERRE. 1983. *Myth and Thought among the Greeks.* Boston: Routledge and Kegan Paul.

VOLKAN, VAMIK D. 1981. "Immortal" Atatürk: Narcissism and Creativity in a Revolutionary Leader. *Psychoanalytic Study of Society* 9:221–255.

VOLKAN, VAMIK D. and NORMAN ITZKOWITZ. 1984. *The Immortal Atatürk: A Psychobiography.* Chicago: University of Chicago Press.

WAGNER, ROY. 1972. *Habu: The Innovation of Meaning in Daribi Religion.* Chicago: University of Chicago Press.

————. 1977. Speaking for Others: Power and Identity as Factors in Daribi Mediumistic Hysteria. *Journal de la Société des Océanistes* 33:145–152.

————. 1978. *Lethal Speech.* Ithaca, NY: Cornell University Press.

WALLACE, ANTHONY F. C. 1966. *Religion: An Anthropological View.* New York: Random House.

————. 1969. *Culture and Personality,* 2d ed. New York: Random House.

————. 1972. Revitalisation Movements. *Reader in Comparative Religion: An Anthropological Approach* (W. A. Lessa and E. Z. Vogt, eds.), pp. 503–512. New York: Harper and Row.

WATKINS, M. 1984. *Waking Dreams.* Dallas, TX: Spring.

WEBER, MAX. 1904. *The Protestant Ethic and the Spirit of Capitalism*. London: Allen and Unwin.

WEINER, ANNETTE B. 1976. *Women of Value, Men of Renown. New Perspectives in Trobriand Exchange*. Austin: University of Texas Press.

WEST, L. J. 1975. A Clinical and Theoretical Overview of Hallucinatory Phenomena. *Hallucinations: Behaviour, Experience, and Theory* (R. K. Siegel and L. J. West, eds.), pp. 287–311. New York: John Wiley and Sons.

WHITE, GEOFFREY M. and J. KIRKPATRICK. 1985. *Persons, Self, and Experience*. Berkeley: University of California Press.

WHITING, J.W.M. 1961. Socialization Process and Personality. *Psychological Anthropology* (F.L.K. Hsu, ed.), pp. 355–380. Homewood, IL: Dorsey Press.

WILBERT, JOHANNES. 1987. *Tobacco and Shamanism in South America*. New Haven, CT: Yale University Press.

WILLIAMS, F. E. 1930. *Orokaiva Society*. London: Oxford University Press.

———. 1940. *Drama of Orokolo*. Oxford: Oxford University Press.

WINKELMAN, MICHAEL. 1986. Trance States: A Theoretical Model and Cross-Cultural Analysis. *Ethos* 14:174–203.

WINNICOTT, D. W. 1973. *Reality, Play and Fantasy*. London: Tavistock.

WINTERS, W. D. 1975. The Continuum of CNS Excitory States and Hallucinosis. *Hallucinations: Behaviour, Experience, and Theory* (R. K. Siegel and L. J. West, eds.), pp. 53–70. New York: John Wiley and Sons.

WOODBURN, JAMES C. 1982. Social Dimensions of Death in Four African Hunting and Gathering Societies. *Death and the Regeneration of Life* (Maurice Bloch and Jonathan Parry, eds.), pp. 187–210. Cambridge: Cambridge University Press.

WORSLEY, PETER. 1970. *The Trumpet Shall Sound*. London: Paladin.

YOUNG, FRANK W. 1965. *Initiation Ceremonies: A Cross-cultural Status Dramatization*. Indianapolis: Bobbs-Merrill.

YOUNG, MICHAEL W. 1983. *Magicians of Manumanua: Living Myth in Kalauna*. Berkeley: University of California Press.

———. 1988. Like Father, Like Son: Filial Ambivalence and the Death of Fathers in Kalauna. *Choice and Morality in Anthropological Perspective: Essays in Honor of Derek Freeman* (G. N. Appell and T. N. Madan, eds.), pp. 113–136. Albany: SUNY Press.

ZELENIETZ, MARTY and SHIRLEY LINDENBAUM, eds. 1981. *Sorcery and Social Change in Melanesia*. Special issue, *Social Analysis*, no. 8. Adelaide.

ZILLMANN, DOLF. 1984. *Connections between Sex and Aggression*. Hillsdale, NJ: Lawrence Erlbaum Associates.

ZINBERG, N. E., ed. 1977a. *Alternate States of Consciousness*. New York: Free Press.

———. 1977b. The Study of Consciousness States: Problems and Progress. *Alternate States of Consciousness* (N. E. Zinberg, ed.), pp. 1–36. New York: Free Press.

Index

Abelam art, 36–37
active imagination, 59
adolescent development, 32–33
age regressions, 57, 213
aggression, sexual longing and, 87–90
amae, 23
Ancient Greeks: psyche concept of, 19–20; ritual meaning among, 38; self-concept among, 15; spiritual and empirical concepts of, 18–19; unity of thought and feeling among, 30–31
anger, in revealing witch's identity, 133–135
animism, 102, 228
Apollonian prototype, 15
Aristotle, 31
artistic creativity, 225. *See also* creativity
Asclepius' sons, myth of, 121*n*
assault sorcery, 73
associations, 233
Attic culture, 19, 31
automatic writing, 53
autonomous imagination, 4; cultural innovation and, 224; definition of, 41; emotional coding and, 229–234; fusing of inner and outer events in, 223–224; hallucinations and, 52–53; imagining and, 54, 61–63; in shaman/spirit medium, 96; special talent for, 224–225; themes of, 211–212; unique imaginative process of, 53–54
autonomous imagining: autonomous imagination and, 54, 61–63; bringing into consciousness, 218, 219; characteristics of, 55–61; cultural symbols and, 223–224; distinctiveness of, 55–57; forms of, 212; gender and, 225–226; influence of on involuntary mental and somatic processes, 60–61; responsiveness of to external influence, 57–60

baptismal name, 190
Bateson, Gregory, 8, 26, 48–49

Bellah, Robert, 6
Benedict, Ruth, 15
Bercovitch, Eytan, 46, 215–217, 227–228
Bettelheim, Bruno, 20
big-manship, absence of, 68
biis, 122; children of, 157*n*; invisibility of actions of, 126; recognition and avoidance of, 127–128; victims of, 124–127. *See also* witchcraft
biis yemin, 125
body: return of soul to, 169; soul and, 168–172
bogay sorcery, 73–74, 81–82
Bowers, K. S., 55
brain laterality studies, 51
Brocke, Hans, 232
Brown, Roger, 115

cargo cult hysteria, 224
cargo cults, 224
Cartwright, R. D., 50
Castaneda, Carlos, 185
Christian community: leaders of, 188; rise of consciousness in, 187–208
Christianity: self-concept and, 23–24; Revial movement of, 189–208, 221
cognitive psychology, 49
collective consciousness, 22, 26, 188. *See also* religious imagination
collective imagination, 22, 147–148
collective understanding, 150–151
community, shaman/spirit medium and, 95–96
Comrade Loves of the Samarai, 23
conflict, avoidance of, 33–34
consciousness: achievement of, 155; altered states of, 47–48, 49, 211; Christian, 187–208; divided, 33; Mekeo definitions of, 160–186; waking, 178–180
Coral Gardens and Their Magic, 8
creative imagery, sources of, 48
creative Other, 44–45. *See also* sacred Other